EDUGORILLA
PUBLICATION

NEET MDS

Medical Entrance Exam

Latest Edition
Practice Kit

10 Tests

02 Topic-Wise Test

08 Mock Test

Based On Real Exam Pattern

✓ Thoroughly Revised and Updated

✓ Sample Papers with Answer Keys

Title	: NEET MDS Medical Entrance Exam
Author Name	: Mr. Rohit Manglik
Published By	: EduGorilla Community Pvt. Ltd.
Publishers Address	: 12/651, First Floor Opp. Arvindo Park, Near Jama Masjid, Indira Nagar, Lucknow, Uttar Pradesh-226016, India

Copyright EduGorilla

ISBN : 978-93-91464-75-2

Second Edition

Disclaimer EduGorilla

Compiled and created by EduGorilla Community Pvt. Ltd

Printed By EduGorilla Community Pvt. Ltd.

ROHIT MANGLIK
CEO, EduGorilla

Dear Applicants,

People say *"Success comes to those who work hard."* But I've seen people working hard for their exams day in and day out for marginal success. While others succeed in their examinations by putting in just half the work. So are they God Gifted? No! I believe that it's because they work *smart* and not just *hard*. Similarly, for your exams, you should strategize your preparation so as to increase the likelihood of success. Well with EduGorilla get ready to increase your *chances of selection* in your exam by *16x*.

EduGorilla helps you in not only working *hard* but also working in a *smart and strategic* manner. With EduGorilla's preparation package, you get a chance to make your exam preparation easy, and a fun learning path towards selection. Finding the right path to your preparations can be difficult if you don't know in which direction to head. Don't worry, we have you covered! EduGorilla will be your guide to success in your journey. With our Preparation Package, you can prepare strategically and beat the exam in just one attempt.

EduGorilla's Preparation Package includes-

- **Test Series**
- **Books**

Our preparation package is handcrafted as per the latest changes, expert opinions, and students' discretion. Thus, enabling you to get through each stage of the selection process for your exam.

Our Books are designed by the teachers and experts of the respective exam with a combined 150+ years of experience; to provide you with easy, efficient, and effective learning. Our books are smart, in the sense that not only do they give you the answers to the questions but also provide similar questions for practice.

EduGorilla's competent Test Series gives you real-time experience and confidence through which you can clear your offline or online exam in just one attempt. We currently host 83,000+ mock tests for 1,440+ competitive and academic exams.

Thus, EduGorilla misses no chance to assist you in your preparation and covers all stages of the exam, so that you don't have to look anywhere else.

We provide complete preparation packages for defense, banking, teaching, and other National & State-Level exams. Hence, it doesn't matter which exam you aspire to because you will reach your success.

ALL THE BEST !
Let EduGorilla be your Guide to Success.

Rohit Manglik,
Founder and CEO, EduGorilla

INTRODUCTION

EduGorilla focuses on guiding students to succeed in their examinations. With that in mind, our book, titled "NEET MDS : Medical Entrance Exam", has been drafted through the collective efforts of our distinguished experts with 150+ years of combined experience. This book consists of questions that are created following the latest changes in the syllabus and exam pattern. We compiled the book on the basis of questions that are most likely to appear in the NEET MDS Entrance Exam. Through EduGorilla's "NEET MDS : Medical Entrance Exam" your chances of success will increase 16x.

EduGorilla does this through our Complete Preparation Package. This package consists of well-conceptualized and structured content in the form of questions that are tailor-made according to your needs and will help you practice for exams in a smart way by pinpointing all the necessary information. It also provides smart answer sheet for your self-evaluation. You can assess your shortcomings and work accordingly on areas that may require more of your attention.

EduGorilla promises to help you succeed in your examination and accomplish your dream goals. We believe in our aspirants and see them at the top of the merit list. And the first step towards the top is to start preparing with us. EduGorilla's "NEET MDS : Medical Entrance Exam" includes the following attributes.

➤ Well-Researched Content

➤ Top-Notch Quality

➤ Smart Answer Sheet

➤ Exam Relevant Questions

Therefore, EduGorilla fortifies your preparation and makes it durable enough to help you stand tall and beat the examination.

NEET MDS Entrance Exam
Scan QR code for Eligibility, Exam Pattern, Syllabus and more.

Book ID: 0800

TABLE OF CONTENTS

Part A

Q.1 Which of the following is the only soft tissue of the tooth and is a loose connective tissue enclosed by the dentine?

A. Enamel

B. Periodontal ligament

C. Pulp

D. Cementum

Q.2 All the following cells produce collagen except

A. Osteoblast   **B.** Chondroblast

C. Fibroblast   **D.** Mast cells

Q.3 Which of the following is located between the dentinal tubules or, more specifically, between the zones of peritubular dentine?

A. Predentin   **B.** Reparative dentin

C. Odontoblast process   **D.** Intratubular dentin

Q.4 The size of the apical foramen of maxillary teeth in an adult is:

A. 0.4 mm   **B.** 0.6 mm   **C.** 0.2 mm   **D.** 0.7 mm

Q.5 Which of the following is/are usually asymptomatic unless it/they impinge(s) on nerves or blood vessels?

A. Fibrosis   **B.** Pulp stones

C. Vascular changes   **D.** Permanent pulp

Q.6 Which of the following occurs at the cervical portion of the tooth at the cementoenamel junction and continues to the apex?

A. Dentine   **B.** Enamel

C. Cementum   **D.** Pulp

Q.7 Which of the following is found to be expressed in periodontal ligament cells, dental follicle cells, cementoblasts, odontoblasts, and ameloblasts?

A. Cbfα1   **B.** EGF   **C.** FGF   **D.** CAP

Q.8 Which of the following possesses important immune-modulatory effects and thus is a lymphokine as much as interferon?

A. Interleukin-1   **B.** Interferon-γ

C. Interferon-α   **D.** Interferon-β

Q.9 Which of the following periodontal ligament fibres are the most numerous and occupy nearly $\frac{2^{rd}}{3}$ of the ligament?

A. Alveolar crest group fibers

B. Horizontal group fibers

C. Oblique group fibers

D. Apical group fibers

Q.10 Which of the following bones have complex shapes, notched or with ridges?

A. Short bones   **B.** Flat bones

C. Irregular bones   **D.** Sesamoid bones

Q.11 Which of the following hormones are present on osteoblasts, osteocytes, and osteoclasts?

A. Parathyroid hormones

B. Vitamin D metabolites

C. Estrogen receptors

D. Glucocorticoids

Q.12 Which of the following contains osteons, each of which has a blood vessel in a Haversian canal?

A. Compact bone

B. Bundle bone

C. Alveolar bone proper

D. Spongy bone

Q.13

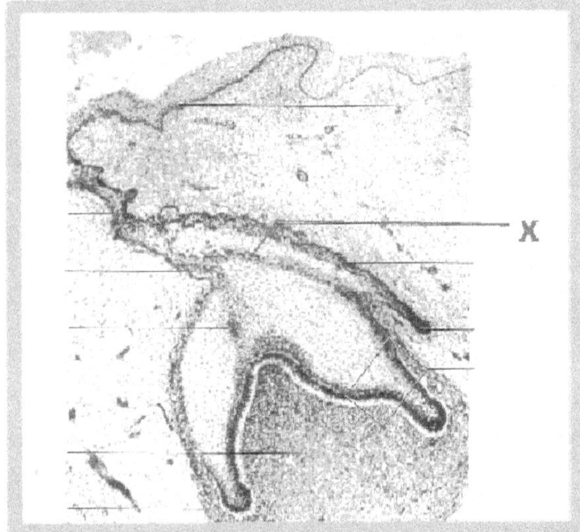

This is the bell stage of tooth development. What does 'X' indicate?

A. Oral epithelium

B. Enamel niche

C. Dental lamina

D. The primordium of permanent tooth

Q.14

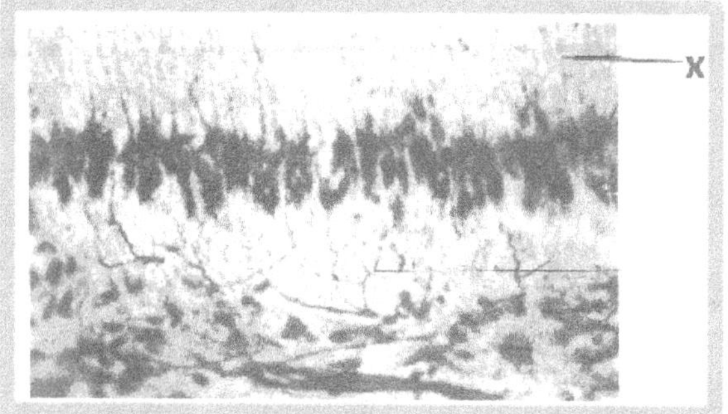

This is the picture of terminal nerve endings located among odontoblasts. Which of the following is indicated through 'X'?

A. Dentine
B. Enamel
C. Pulp pre-dentin border
D. Parietal layer of nerves

Q.15 In which of the following routes is the drug injected as a bolus or infused slowly over hours in one of the superficial veins?

A. Subcutaneous
B. Intramuscular
C. Intravenous
D. Intradermal injection

Q.16 In regards to synthetic reactions, which of the following pathways is important for the activation of many purines and pyrimidine antimetabolites used in cancer chemotherapy?

A. Sulphate conjugation
B. Glycine conjugation
C. Glutathione conjugation
D. Ribonucleoside synthesis

Q.17 Which of the following doses indicates the same dose is appropriate for most patients, individual variations are minor or the drug has a wide safety margin so that a large enough dose can be given to cover them?

A. Standard dose
B. Regulated dose
C. Targeted level dose
D. Titrated dose

Q.18 In regards to the adverse effects of the drugs, which of the following are indirect consequences of a primary action of the drug?

A. Side effects
B. Secondary effects
C. Toxic effects
D. Primary effects

Q.19 Which of the following is used only in the eye as 0.5 – 4% drops?

A. Pilocarpine
B. Muscarine
C. Carbamates
D. Bethanechol

Q.20 In regards to atropine compounds, which of the following drugs is potent and rapidly acting anti-muscarinic lacking central effects?

A. Propantheline
B. Isopropamide
C. Glycopyrrolate
D. Clidinium

Q.21 In regards to adrenergic drugs, which of the following mainly acts indirectly but has some direct action on α and β receptors also?

A. Dopamine
B. Dobutamine
C. Ephedrine
D. Amphetamines

Q.22 In regards to β adrenergic blockers, which of the following is a β₁-selective blocker offering the advantage of less broncho-pulmonary and probably less cardiac, central and metabolic side effects?

A. Timolol
B. Betaxolol
C. Vevobunolol
D. Dipivefrine

Q.23 In regards to 5-HT antagonists, which of the following is the hydrogenation of ergotamine which reduces serotonergic and α– adrenergic agonist actions, but enhances α– receptor blocking property?

A. Ergotamine
B. Dihydro-ergotamine
C. Dihydro-ergotoxine
D. Bromocriptine

Q.24 Which of the following drugs is the first drug to be used in all cases of acute rheumatic fever?

A. Penicillin
B. Aspirin
C. Antipyretic
D. Analgesic

Q.25 In regards to anti-rheumatoid drug immune-suppressants, which of the following drugs is a potent suppressant of cell-mediated immunity?

A. Methotrexate
B. Azathioprine
C. Sulfasalazine
D. Chloroquine

Q.26 Which of the following is neither analgesic nor anti-inflammatory, but it specifically suppresses gouty inflammation?

A. NSAIDs
B. Colchicine
C. Corticosteroids
D. Probenecid

Q.27 In regards to corticosteroids, which of the following topical steroids is available for prophylaxis and treatment of seasonal and perennial rhinitis?

A. Budesonide
B. Fluticasone propionate
C. Flunisolide
D. Circlesonide

Q.28 Which of the following is a dietary fibre from Indian cluster beans which forms a viscous gel on contact with water?

A. Guar Gum
B. Glucomannam
C. Exenatide
D. Sitagliptin

Q.29 Which of the following is a small molecule that is fairly soluble in non-polar solvents?

A. Hydrogen
B. Oxygen
C. Nitrogen
D. Sulphur

Q.30 Which of the following is produced by reddish dinoflagellates that are responsible for the so called red tide?

A. Saxitoxin
B. Neurotoxin
C. Sialotoxin
D. Fibro toxin

Q.31 Which of the following are ligand-gated ion channels or signal transduction proteins?

A. Neurotransmitters receptors

B. Cholecystokinin receptors

C. Glycine receptors

D. Amino acid receptors

Q.32 Which of the following is the response of an axon to its interruption?

A. Wallerian degeneration

B. Axonal transport

C. Synaptic transmission

D. Nerve impulses

Q.33 Which of the following is generally located in a sensory nucleus of the thalamus?

A. First order neuron

B. Second order neuron

C. Third order neuron

D. Fourth order neuron

Q.34

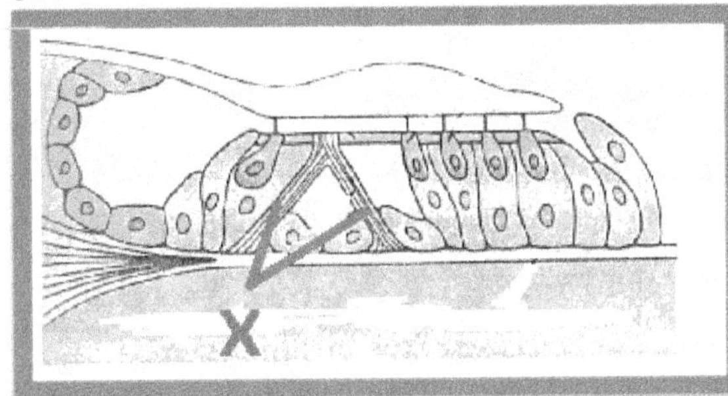

This is the picture of transduction in the organ of Corti. What does 'X' indicate?

A. Basilar membrane

B. Hair cells

C. Reticular lamina

D. Corti's rods

Q.35

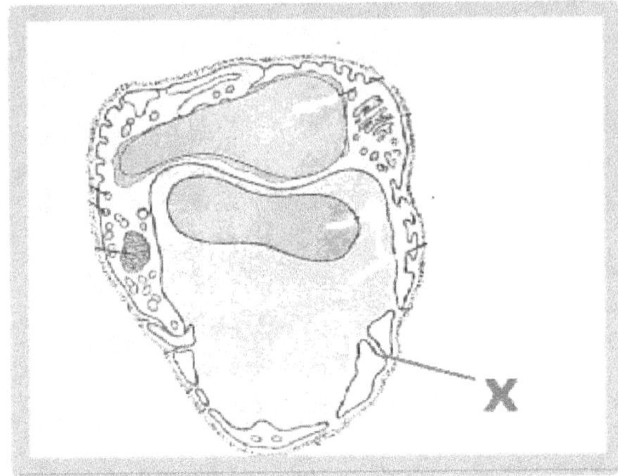

This is the picture showing a composite capillary in cross-section. What does 'X' indicate?

A. Discontinuous endothelium

B. Basement membrane

C. Lumen

D. Tight junction between endothelial cells

Q.36 Defect in renal glucosuria is associated to mutations in:

A. GLUT 1   B. GLUT 2   C. SGLT 1   D. SGLT 2

Q.37 Facilitated transport of glucose that is insulin insensitive (non-dependent) takes place in:

A. Skeletal muscle   B. Liver

C. Adipose tissue   D. Heart

Q.38 Glucose transporter present in the RBC is:

A. GLUT 1   B. GLUT 2   C. GLUT 3   D. GLUT 4

Q.39 Complex polysaccharides are converted to glucose and absorbed with the help of:

A. Na^+K^+ ATPase   B. Sucrose

C. Enterokinase   D. Carboxypeptidase

Q.40 Irreversible step in glycolysis is:

A. Enolase

B. Phosphofructokinase

C. Glyceraldehyde 3 phosphate dehydrogenase

D. Cytokinase

Q.41 In which of the following steps is ATP released?

A. Phosphoenol pyruvate to pyruvate

B. Glyceraldehyde 3 phosphate to 1,3 bisphosphoglycerate

C. Fructose 6 phosphate to fructose 1,6 bisphosphate

D. Glucose to glucose 6 phosphate

Q.42 Which of the following statements is true about glycolysis?

A. Occurs in mitochondria

B. Complete break down of glucose

C. Conversion of glucose to 3C units

D. 3 ATPs being used in anaerobic pathway

Q.43 A number of cartilages form a supportive framework for the _______, which has a hollow central channel.

A. trachea   B. pharynx

C. larynx   D. oesophagus

Q.44 Which of the following contains specialised structures that connect the upper parts of the digestive and respiratory tracts in the head, with oesophagus and trachea, which begin relatively low in the neck and pass into the thorax?

A. Larynx   B. Neck

C. Abdomen   D. Shoulder

Q.45 There is ________ on each side of the superior thoracic aperture at the base of the neck.

A. a brachial plexus   B. an axillary inlet

C. an oesophagus   D. a scapula

Q.46 Except for the mandible, which forms the base of the lower jaw, the bones of the skull are attached to each other by sutures, are immobile, and form the _____.

A. cervix   B. cranium

C. joints   D. ligaments

Q.47 The mastoid part is the most posterior part of the:

A. sphenoid bone **B.** temporal bone
C. occipital bone **D.** hyoid bone

Q.48 During brain development, which of the following becomes the large cerebral hemispheres?

A. Telencephalon **B.** Diencephalon
C. Mesencephalon **D.** Metencephalon

Q.49 Which of the following usually receives cerebral veins from the superior surface of the cerebral hemispheres, diploic and emissary veins, and veins from the falx cerebri?

A. Superior transversal sinus
B. Superior frontal sinus
C. Superior sagittal sinus
D. Superior horizontal sinus

Q.50 Which of the following nerves arises in the midbrain and is the only cranial nerve to exit from the posterior surface of the brainstem?

A. Oculomotor nerve **B.** Trochlear nerve
C. Trigeminal nerve **D.** Optic nerve

Q.51 With regard to upper group of oral muscles, which of the following is more deeply placed and covered by the other two levators and the zygomaticus muscles?

A. Risorius
B. Levator labii superioris
C. Levator labii superioris alaeque nasi
D. Levator anguli oris

Q.52 Which of the following comes from the lacrimal branch of the ophthalmic artery?

A. Mental artery
B. Zygomatico-facial artery
C. Dorsal nasal artery
D. Buccal artery

Q.53 Which of the following is the most superior muscle in the orbit originating from the roof, just anterior to the optic canal on the inferior surface of the lesser wing of the sphenoid?

A. Levator palpebrae superioris
B. Superior orbital fissure
C. Periorbita
D. Superior tarsus

Q.54

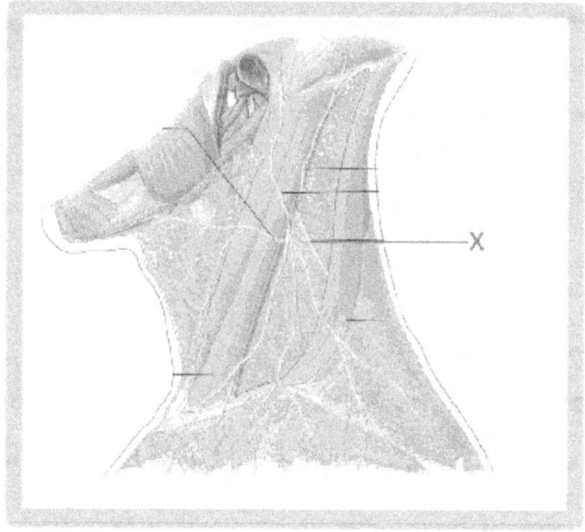

This is the picture of the accessory nerve in the posterior triangle of neck. What does 'X' indicate?

A. Accessory nerve VII
B. Accessory nerve IX
C. Accessory nerve X
D. Accessory nerve XI

Q.55

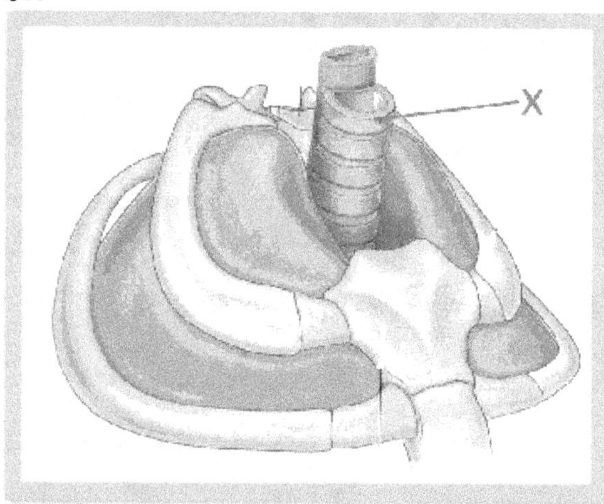

This is the picture of the root of the neck. What does 'X' indicate?

A. TI vertebra **B.** Oesophagus
C. Trachea **D.** Cervical pleura

Q.56

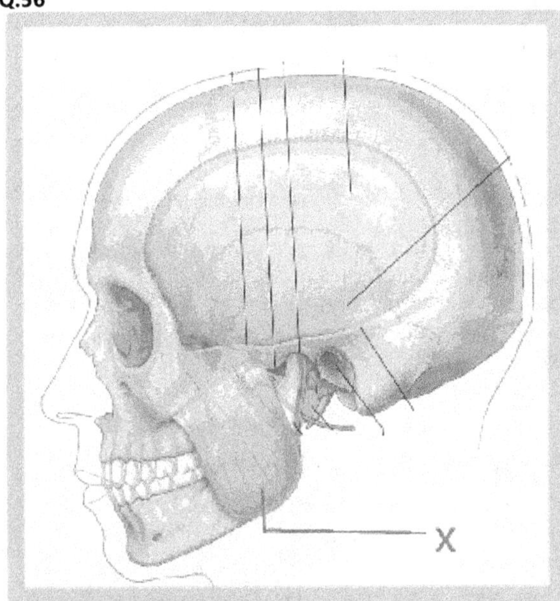

This is the picture of the temporal and infra-temporal fossae. What does 'X' indicate?

A. Ramus mandible **B.** Masseter muscle
C. Infra temporal fossa **D.** Supramastoid crest

Q.57 Which of the following is concerned with whether a proposed action or course of action, in itself and regardless of its consequences, is right or wrong?
A. Virtue ethics
B. Deontological ethics
C. Teleological ethics
D. Clinical ethics

Q.58 Which of the following drugs bind to receptors and block the effects of endogenous ligands, and also stimulate the receptors, causing effects opposite to those of agonists?
A. Agonists **B.** Pure antagonists
C. Partial agonists **D.** Inverse agonists

Q.59 Which of the following mutations cause function of a protein to be reduced or lost?
A. Loss-of-function mutations
B. Gain-of-function mutations
C. Loss-of-cellular-function mutations
D. Gain-of-cellular-function mutations

Q.60 Which of the following syndromes is the most frequently found and best known of these disorders and is caused by an increased dosage of genes on chromosomes?
A. Sjogren's syndrome
B. Down syndrome
C. Velocardiofacial syndrome
D. William's syndrome

Q.61 The complicated proteins are produced in the
A. gall bladder **B.** liver
C. blood cells **D.** endocrine system

Q.62 Which of the following are soluble proteins made up of two heavy and two light chains?
A. Immunoglobulins **B.** Cytokines
C. Lymphoid tissue **D.** Collagen fiber

Q.63 Which of the following syndromes is characterized by accumulation of auto-reactive cells causing lymphadenopathy, splenomegaly and a variety of autoimmune syndromes?
A. Di George syndrome
B. Bare lymphocyte syndrome
C. Autoimmune lympho-proliferative syndrome
D. Autoimmune lymphocyte syndrome

Q.64 Which of the following types of hypersensitivity indicates that the injury is localized to a single tissue or organ?
A. Type I **B.** Type II **C.** Type III **D.** Type IV

Q.65 In regards to transplant rejection, which of the following rejections is mediated by antibody formed dew novo after transplantation?
A. Acute cellular rejection
B. Hyperacute rejection
C. Acute vascular rejection
D. Chronic allograft failure

Q.66 Which of the following nutrients involves the decarboxylation of pyruvate to acetyl-co-enzyme A, which bridges between glycolysis and the tri-carboxylic acid (Krebs cycle)?
A. Riboflavin **B.** Thiamin
C. Niacin **D.** Pyridoxine

Q.67 Which of the following Pellagra diseases is often associated with anorexia, nausea, glossitis, and dysphagia, reflecting the presence of a non-infective inflammation that extends throughout the gastrointestinal tract?
A. Dermatitis **B.** Cholera
C. Diarrhoea **D.** Dementia

Q.68 Which of the following antifungal agents is extremely well absorbed and is used mainly in the treatment of aspergillosis?
A. Itraconazole **B.** Posaconazole
C. Echinocandins **D.** Voriconazole

Q.69 In regards to antiprotozoal agents, which of the following is/are an inhibitor of pyruvate-ferredoxin oxidoreductase-dependent anaerobic energy metabolism in protozoa?
A. Pentavalent antimonials
B. Diloxanide furoate
C. Iodoquinol
D. Nitazoxanide

Q.70 Which of the following disorders is marked by weight loss, arising from food avoidance, often in combination with bingeing, purging, excessive exercise, or the use of diuretics and laxatives?
A. Bulimia nervosa
B. Anorexia nervosa
C. Schizophrenia
D. Somatoform disorder

Q.71 Which of the following diseases is a rare salivary gland tumor and is a small benign lesion that usually occurs in the parotid gland?

A. Oncocytoma

B. Warthin's tumor

C. Myoepithelioma

D. Ductal papilloma

Q.72 Which of the following carcinomas represents 29-34 percent of malignant tumors originating in both major and minor salivary glands?

A. Muco-epidermoid carcinoma

B. Acinic cell carcinoma

C. Sebaceous adenoma

D. Canalicular adenoma

Q.73 Which of the following carcinomas is an uncommon, biphasic low grade epithelial neoplasm composed of variable proportions of ductal and large, clear-staining, differentiated myoepithelial cells?

A. Epithelial-myoepithelial carcinoma

B. Low grade myoepithelial carcinoma

C. Basal cell myoepithelioma

D. Myoepithelial fibroma

Q.74 In which of the following carcinomas do the metastatic lesions contain both the stromal and epithelial elements?

A. Pleomorphic adenoma

B. Carcinosarcoma

C. Malignant myoepithelioma

D. Adenosarcoma

Q.75 Which of the following carcinomas of the salivary gland is a controversial neoplasm that is not included in many classifications of salivary gland tumours?

A. Adenosquamous carcinoma

B. Sebaceous lymphadenocarcinoma

C. Malignant lymphomas

D. Sialadenosis

Q.76 Which of the following tumours appears to be originated from either surface epithelium or remnants of dental lamina?

A. Peripheral ameloblastoma

B. Pituitary ameloblastoma

C. Ameloblastoma

D. Follicular ameloblastoma

Q.77 Which of the following is a squamous cell carcinoma that occurs in the jaw bone?

A. Primary intraosseous carcinoma

B. Ameloblastic carcinoma

C. De novo ameloblastic carcinoma

D. Solid primary intraosseous carcinoma

Q.78 Which of the following is true about mycobacterium other than tuberculosis?

A. Causes disseminated infection

B. Occurs in persons with normal immunity

C. Causes decreased efficacy of BCG due to cross-immunity

D. Person to person transmission

Q.79 Scotochromogens are:

A. Mycobacterium gordonae

B. Mycobacterium marinum

C. Mycobacterium intracellulare

D. Mycobacterium avium

Q.80 Which of the following belongs to photochromogens?

A. M.kansasii

B. M.scorfulosorum

C. M.tuberculosis

D. M.leprae

Q.81 A farmer presents to the emergency department with painful inguinal and history of fever and flu-like symptoms. Clinical examination reveals an ulcer in the leg. Which of the following stain should be used to detect suspected bipolar stained organism?

A. Alberts stain

B. Ziehl nelson stain

C. Wayson's stain

D. McFayden's stain

Q.82 Rapid growing non tuberculous mycobacteria causing lung infection are all, except:

A. M.kansasii

B. M.chenolae

C. M.fortuitum

D. M.abscessus

Q.83 With reference to infection with Escherichia coli, the following are true, except:

A. Enteroagressive E.coli is associated with persistent diarrhea.

B. Enterohemorrhagic E.coli causes haemolytic uraemic syndrome.

C. Enteroinvasive E.coli produces a disease similar to salmonellosis.

D. Enterotoxigenic E.coli is a common cause of traveler's diarrhea.

Q.84 A 20-year old man presented with haemorrhagic colitis. The stool sample grows Escherichia coli in pure culture. The following serotype of E.coli is likely to be the causative agent:

A. O 157:H7

B. O 159:H7

C. O 107:H7

D. O 55:F7

Q.85 Which of the following ulcers has the characteristics such as gravitational ulcer, post phlebitis ulcer?

A. Venous ulcer

B. Trophic ulcer

C. Infective ulcer

D. Diabetic ulcer

Q.86 Which of the following is the spreading inflammation of subcutaneous and fascial planes?

A. Cellulitis

B. Erysipeloid disease

C. Lymphangitis

D. Erysipelas

Q.87 Which of the following is a type of growth anomaly seen in neonates wherein growth from the base of skull protrudes through the mouth?

A. Chordoma

B. Epignathus

C. Ganglion

D. Neurilemmoma

Q.88 Which of the following can be due to water overload or sodium loss?

A. Hyponatremia

B. Hypernatremia

C. Hypokalaemia

D. Hyperkalaemia

Q.89 Which of the following injuries can be haematoma or lacerations?

A. Duodenal injury
B. Pancreatic injury
C. Small bowel injury
D. Blunt trauma

Q.90 Which of the following is a synovial sheath of medial four flexor tendons of hand which extends into the digit of the fifth finger?

A. Radial bursa
B. Ulnar bursa
C. Compound palmar ganglion
D. Apical subungual infection

Q.91 Which of the following is the complication of varicose veins or deep vein thrombosis?

A. Venous ulcer
B. Cirsoid aneurysm
C. Arteriovenous fistula
D. Haemangioma

Q.92 Which of the following occurs in middle-aged and elderly, and is more aggressive than Hodgkin's lymphoma and involves an asymmetrical group of lymph nodes?

A. Non-Hodgkin's lymphoma
B. Hodgkin's lymphoma
C. Lymphoma
D. Lipoma

Q.93 Which of the following carcinomas is a low-grade, locally invasive carcinoma arising from basal layer of skin or muco-cutaneous junction?

A. Basal cell carcinoma
B. Marjolin's ulcer
C. Squamous cell carcinoma
D. Turban tumour

Q.94 Which of the following is the worst type of melanoma?

A. Lentigo maligna melanoma
B. Acral lentiginous melanoma
C. Amelanotic melanoma
D. Desmoplastic melanoma

Q.95 Which of the following is the continuity of the muscle to have its action at the site especially in hand, foot and digits?

A. Tendon
B. Tendon repair
C. Aplasia
D. Fibroma

Q.96

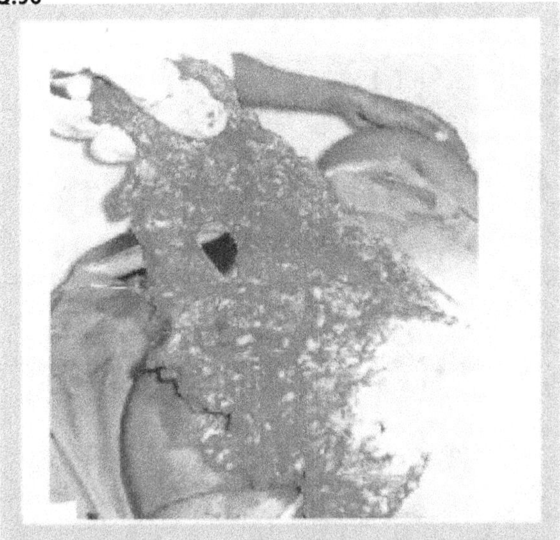

Which of the following injuries/wounds is shown through this picture?

A. Tidy wound
B. Untidy wound
C. Lacerated wound
D. Bruising and contusion

Q.97

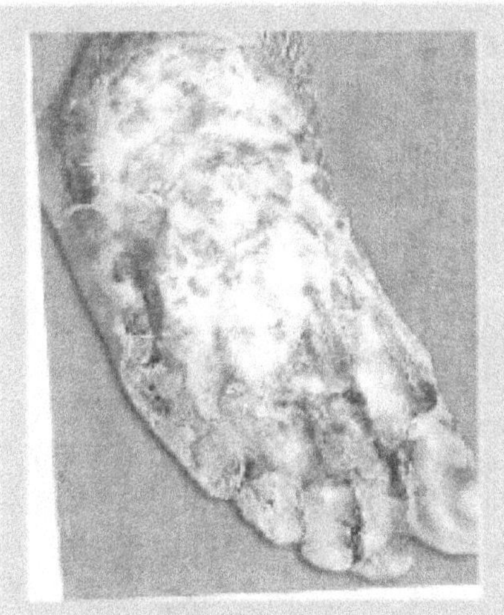

Which of the following injuries/wounds is shown through this picture?

A. Martorell's ulcer
B. Ischaemic ulcer
C. Bairnsdale ulcer
D. Trophic ulcer

Q.98

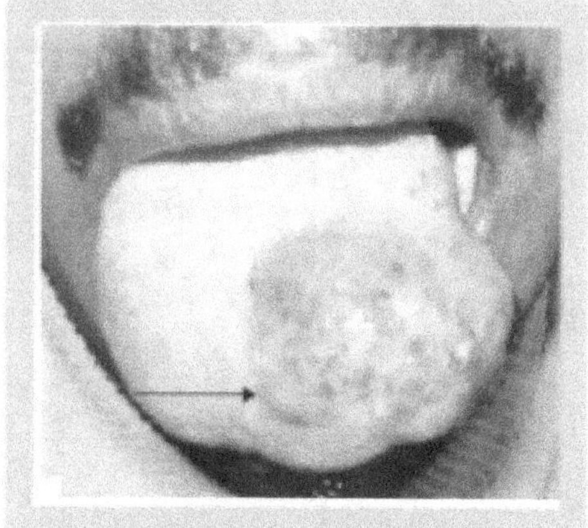

Which of the following diseases is illustrated through this picture?

A. Cavernous haemangioma

B. Cirsoid aneurysm

C. Arterio-venous fistula

D. Haemangioma

Q.99 Which is the most common cause of hypothyroidism

A. Multinodular goitre

B. Lymphoma of thyroid

C. Hashimoto's thyroiditis

D. Reidel's thyroiditis

Q.100 The treatment of anaplastic carcinoma of thyroid is:

A. Total thyroidectomy

B. Palliative radiotherapy

C. Radioactive therapy

D. Tracheostomy

Part B

Q.101 Which of the following is one of the most contagious oral papillary lesions?

A. Fibromatosis gingivae

B. Focal epithelial hyperplasia

C. Retrocuspid papilla

D. Aglossia

Q.102 Which of the following has dominant characteristics, such as a constantly changing pattern of serpiginous white lines surrounding areas of smooth, depapillated mucosa?

A. Hairy tongue

B. Benign migratory glossitis

C. Lingual varice

D. Lingual thyroid nodule

Q.103 Which of the following can produce serious negative effects on the patient's quality of life, affecting dietary habits, nutritional status, speech, taste, tolerance to dental prosthesis and also increase susceptibility to dental caries?

A. Aplasia

B. Xerostomia

C. Atresia

D. Aberrancy

Q.104 Which of the following is a reversible and presumably a controlled, cellular alteration?

A. Dysplasia

B. Apnoea

C. Dementia

D. Delirium

Q.105 Which of the following presents as scaly patches or papules that are pink to red brown in colour, often with central clearing?

A. Cystic basal cell carcinoma

B. Superficial basal cell carcinoma

C. Micro-nodular basal cell carcinoma

D. Pigmented basal cell carcinoma

Q.106 Which of the following lacks evidence of squamous glandular or other types of differentiation?

A. Differentiated carcinoma

B. Undifferentiated carcinoma

C. Adenosquamous carcinoma

D. Basaloid squamous cell carcinoma

Q.107 Which of the following is one of the more biologically unpredictable and deadly of all human neoplasms?

A. Melanoma

B. Nasopharyngeal carcinoma

C. Spindle cell carcinoma

D. Adenoid squamous cell carcinoma

Q.108 Which of the following has features of both fibroblasts and smooth muscle cells?

A. Giant cell fibroma

B. Myo-fibroblast

C. Fibromatose

D. Neuro-fibroma

Q.109 Which of the following is a tortuous mass of small arteries and veins linking a larger artery and a vein?

A. Cirsoid aneurysm

B. varicose aneurysm

C. Aneurysmal varix

D. Intravascular angiomatosis

Q.110 Which of the following is a benign and probably reactive fibroblastic growth extending as a solitary nodule from the superficial fascia into the subcutaneous fat or less frequently into the subjacent muscle?

A. Nodular fasciitis

B. Aggressive fibromatosis

C. Proliferative myositis

D. Atypical fibroxanthoma

Q.111 Which of the following is a multicentric proliferation of vascular and spindle cell components and described as idiopathic multiple pigmented sarcoma of the skin?

A. Kaposi's sarcoma

B. Ewing's sarcoma

C. Chondrosarcoma

D. Osteosarcoma

Q.112 Which of the following consists of single or clustered benign giant cells and tumor cells with clear cytoplasm?

A. Mesenchymal chondrosarcoma

B. Clear cell chondrosarcoma

C. Dedifferentiated chondrosarcoma

D. Secondary chondrosarcoma

Q.113 Which of the following diseases commonly affects the abdominal lymph nodes and spleen?

A. Nodular sclerosis Hodgkin's disease

B. Mixed cellularity Hodgkin's disease

C. Lymphocyte depleted Hodgkin's disease

D. Lymphocyte rich classic Hodgkin's disease

Q.114 Which of the following diseases is characterised by tumours of neuroendocrine origin?

A. Multiple endocrine neoplasia syndrome

B. Neuro-fibroma

C. Traumatic neuroma

D. Alveolar soft part sarcoma

Q.115 For which of the following tumors has it been almost universally agreed that it is not a 'mixed' tumor in the true sense of being teratomatous or derived from more than one primary tissue?

A. Pleomorphic adenoma

B. Myoepithelioma

C. Basal cell adenoma

D. Warthin's tumour

Q.116 Which of the following surfaces is convex in all directions in mandibular canines?

A. Labial surface   **B.** Lingual surface

C. Incisal surface   **D.** Buccal surface

Q.117 Which of the following is a weak anesthetic with a minimum alveolar concentration (MAC) of 105?

A. Nitrous oxide   **B.** Sulfur oxide

C. Nitric oxide   **D.** Nitrogen sulphate

Q.118 Water fluoridation is defined as the controlled adjustment of the concentration of fluoride in a communal water supply so as to achieve a maximum caries reduction and a clinically insignificant level of fluorosis. This was stated by

A. Newbrun   **B.** Gordon Nikiforuk

C. Tewari   **D.** Tendon

Q.119 Which of the following was first recognised by FDA as an effective tooth decay preventive product?

A. Stannous fluoride

B. Sodium chloride

C. Stannous potassium

D. Stannous phosphorus

Q.120 Which of the following is often called white spot lesion?

A. Primary caries   **B.** Incipient caries

C. Occult caries   **D.** Secondary caries

Q.121 Which of the following is a non-fermentable, pleasant tasting, non-cariogenic polyol derived from pentose sugar xylose and is relatively expensive to manufacture?

A. Sorbitol   **B.** Mannitol   **C.** Xylitol   **D.** Isomalt

Q.122 Which of the following has a broad spectrum of antimicrobial activity against Gram-positive bacteria, Gram-negative bacteria, yeast, and Streptococcus mutans?

A. Chlorhexidine   **B.** Triclosan

C. Formaldehyde   **D.** Glutaraldehyde

Q.123 Who stated that when in doubt, assign the lesser score?

A. Russell   **B.** Munich   **C.** Parkin   **D.** John

Q.124 Sea water contains _____ fluoride.

A. 1.2 to 1.4 mg/kg   **B.** 1.3 to 1.5 mg/kg

C. 1.4 to 1.6 mg/kg   **D.** 1.5 to 1 mg/kg

Q.125 Which of the following is a mineralized tissue seeker?

A. Cadmium   **B.** Fluorine

C. Sodium   **D.** Magnesium

Q.126 Which of the following is a clear polyurethane-based product containing 7000 ppm fluoride from difluorosilane?

A. Fluoride varnish   **B.** Duraphat

C. Fluor-protector   **D.** Foam

Q.127 Which of the following mouth rinses is intended to be used by forcefully swishing 10 ml of the liquid around the mouth?

A. Sodium hypochlorite

B. Sodium fluoride

C. Ammonium fluoride

D. Aluminum fluoride

Q.128 Which of the following is a mineral containing varying amount of calcium fluoride?

A. Fluorspar

B. Sodium fluoride

C. Silicofluoride

D. Sodium silicofluoride

Q.129 Which of the following is widely distributed in foodstuffs?

A. Phosphorus   **B.** Calcium

C. Iron   **D.** Iodine

Q.130 Which of the following is freely filtered by the glomeruli and not reabsorbed?

A. Creatinine

B. Urea

C. Bilirubin

D. Lactic dehydrogenase

Q.131 Which of the following is prolonged ischemia or lack of oxygen that causes injury to the heart?

A. Angio-cardiac heart

B. Myocardial infarction

C. Congestive heart failure

D. Hypertension

Q.132 Which of the following occurs as a result of injury to the liver with resultant loss of liver cells and progressive scarring?

A. Cirrhosis

B. Osteoporosis

C. Vitamin D disorder

D. Hyperparathyroidism

Q.133 Which of the following is the force exerted from one occlusal surface to the outer, without any movement?

A. Bruxism

B. Clenching

C. Para-function

D. Masticatory dynamics

Q.134 Bennett movement of the mandible is related to:

A. Condylar rotation

B. Lateral bodily movement of mandible

C. Protrusive movement of the mandible

D. Edge to edge occlusion

Q.135 A removable denture receives additional support and stabilisation from the ______ and from the abutment teeth on the opposite side of the arch.

A. tissues of the residual ridge

B. tissues of the mandibular ridge

C. tissues of the maxillary ridge

D. None of these

Q.136 By crossing the maxillary midline at right angles, the length of the crossing may be ___ and the potential for irritation reduced.

A. minimised   **B.** maximised

C. unchanged   **D.** None of these

Q.137 In the maxillary arch, major connector may cover ____ if its surgical removal is impossible and if it cannot be avoided by altering the design of the major connector.

A. large torus   **B.** small torus

C. Both of the above   **D.** None of the above

Q.138 Hinge axis is located with the help of:

A. Ear rods

B. Maxillomandibular vertical relations

C. Kinematic face bow

D. Orbital pointer

Q.139 Which of the following may be influenced by diameter, longitudinal taper, clasp curvature and metallurgical characteristics of the alloy?

A. Reciprocal element   **B.** Approach arm

C. Terminus   **D.** Flexibility

Q.140 Removable partial dentures are subjected to composite forces arising from three principal

A. Abutments   **B.** Retainers

C. Fulcrums   **D.** Levers

Q.141 Which of the following fulcrums controls the rotational movement of the denture in the sagittal plane?

A. First   **B.** Second

C. Third   **D.** None of these

Q.142

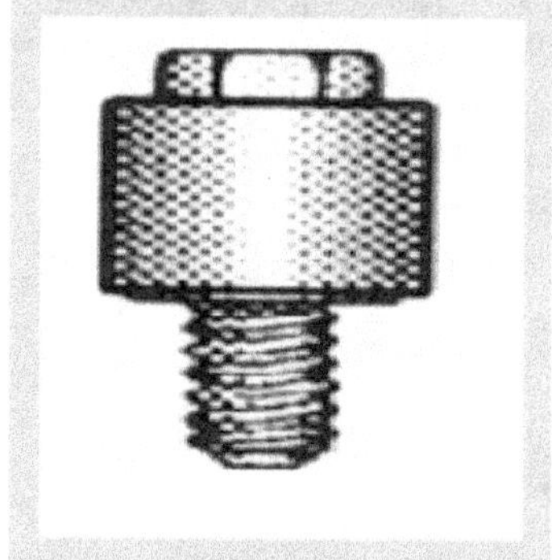

This is the schematic of generic implant components and terminology developed by C. E. Misch and C. M. Misch. Identify the given component.

A. Hygiene screw

B. Abutment for screw, cement and attachment

C. First stage cover screw

D. Implant body or fixture

Q.143

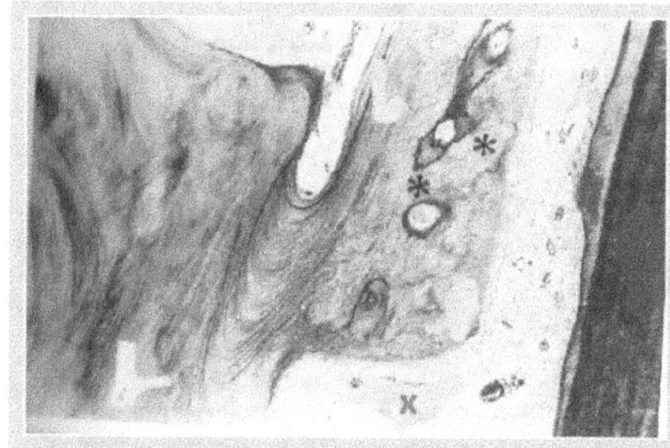

This is a demineralised section of adult human periodontium. What does 'X' indicate?

A. Lamellar bone

B. Marrow space

C. Periodontal ligament

D. Dentin

Q.144 Which of the following is a method for studying the intracranial and extracranial arteries?

A. Arthrography

B. Angiography

C. Sialography

D. Radionuclide imaging

Q.145 Which of the following surgical instruments is more commonly used in abdominal surgeries?

A. C shaped retractor

B. Austin's retractor

C. Cat's paw retractor

D. Langenbeck's retractor

Q.146 In __________, the needle is passed from one edge of the incision to another and again from the latter edge to the first edge and a knot is tied.

A. vertical mattresses suture

B. horizontal mattresses suture

C. anterior mattresses suture

D. posterior mattresses suture

Q.147 Which of the following substances is a gas at temperatures above 108°C, is a highly penetrative, noncorrosive agent with a cidal action against bacteria, spores and viruses?

A. Formaldehyde

B. Ethylene oxide

C. Glutaraldehyde

D. Nitric oxide

Q.148 Which of the following is a DNA virus which causes acute hepatitis?

A. Human T-lymphotropic virus 1

B. Hepatitis B virus

C. Cytomegalovirus

D. Varicella zoster virus

Q.149 Which of the following is a broad spectrum antibiotic?

A. Erythromycin

B. Cephalosporin

C. Penicillin

D. Sulphonamide

Q.150 Which of the following is a sedative, an anxiolytic and an excellent amnestic agent?

A. Benzodiazepin

B. Midazolam

C. Diazepam

D. Flumazeline

Q.151 Which of the following substances is a colourless volatile liquid of mol wt 74, has sp. gr. of 0.719 and a boiling point 35°C?

A. Methane

B. Ethane

C. Halothane

D. Propane

Q.152 Which of the following occurs due to intermittent spasm of the diaphragm?

A. Coughing

B. Hiccup

C. Wheezing

D. Cyanosis

Q.153 Which of the following is advocated in cases of fibrous ankylosis, where the joint space is obliterated with deposition of fibrous bands, but there is not much deformity of the condylar head?

A. Condylectomy

B. Alveolectomy

C. Gingivectomy

D. Gap arthroplasty

Q.154 Which of the following is characterised by pain in the auriculo-temporal nerve distribution?

A. Frey's syndrome

B. Sjogren's syndrome

C. Reinter syndrome

D. Gnarled syndrome

Q.155 Identify the given instrument.

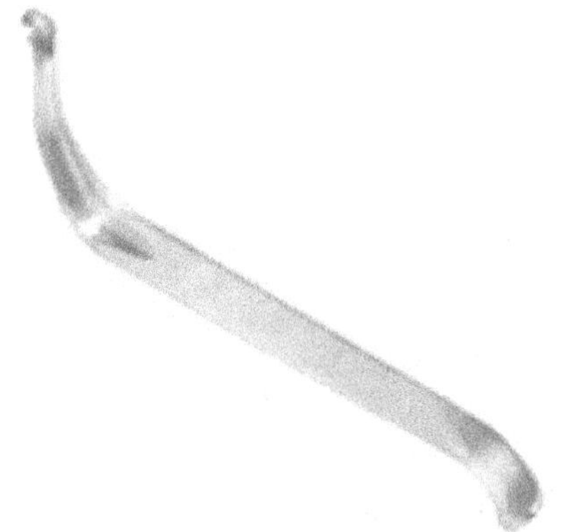

A. Double ended Langen-back's retractor

B. Condyle retractor

C. Cat's paw retractor

D. Tongue depressor

Q.156 Identify the suture given in the picture.

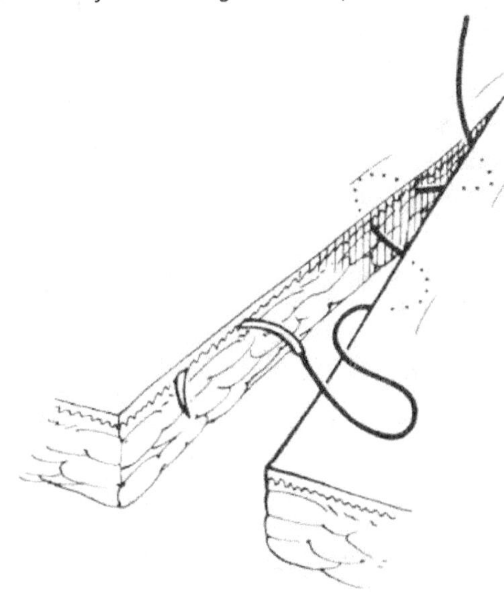

A. Horizontal mattress suture

B. Vertical mattress suture

C. Continuous subcuticular suture

D. Continuous locking suture

Q.157 Death in Ludwig's angina occurs due to:

A. Sepsis

B. Respiratory obstruction

C. Cavernous sinus thrombosis

D. Carotid blow-out

Q.158 Which of the following is a potent immunosuppressive agent used to prevent organ transplant rejection and to treat several diseases of autoimmune origin?

A. Cyclosporine

B. Tacrolimus

C. Nifedipine

D. Cyclosporine A

Q.159 Which of the following can be differentiated because its vesicles are generally more extensive than those in primary herpetic gingiva-stomatitis and on rupture, demonstrate a tendency toward pseudo-membrane formation?

A. Erythema multiforme

B. Stevens Johnson syndrome

C. Bullous lichen planus

D. Desquamative gingivitis

Q.160 Which of the following contains neither cells nor extrinsic or intrinsic fibres, except for a mineralised ground substance?

A. Cellular cementum

B. Acellular afibrillar cementum

C. Acellular extrinsic fibre cementum

D. Acellular cementum

Q.161 Predominant bacteria found in two days old plaque is:

A. Streptococci

B. Bacteroides

C. Spirochaetes

D. Actinomyces

Q.162 Mutations leading to deficiency of which of the following substances result in abnormal bone mineralisation, skeletal anomalies and cementum hypoplasia?

A. Alkaline phosphatase

B. Acid phosphatase

C. Lithium phosphatase

D. Calcium phosphatase

Q.163 Which of the following blood cells may differentiate extensively in the bone marrow and appear in blood as large, granular lymphocytes?

A. T-lymphocytes

B. B-lymphocytes

C. Natural killer cells

D. Neutrophils

Q.164 Which of the following is the most common form of gingivitis?

A. Plaque induced gingivitis

B. Chronic periodontitis

C. Aggressive periodontitis

D. Refractory periodontitis

Q.165 Which of the following cells also function as APCs, expressing both MHC class I and MHC class II?

A. Endothelial cells

B. Osteoblasts

C. Cementoblasts

D. Monocytes

Q.166 Which of the following is inherited and appears to follow an autosomal recessive pattern?

A. Lazy leukocyte syndrome

B. Leukocyte adhesion deficiency

C. Papillon Lefevre syndrome

D. Chediak Higashi syndrome

Q.167 Which of the following is the focal thickening of the arterial intima, the innermost layer lining the vessel lumen and the media, the thick layer under the intima consisting of smooth muscle, collagen and elastic fibres?

A. Atherosclerosis

B. Thrombogenesis

C. Ischemic heart disease

D. Sclerosis

Q.168 Which of the following is a hereditary metabolic disorder that leads to a typical fishy odour of breath, urine, sweat, expired air and other bodily secretions?

A. Trimethylaminuria

B. Phenylketonuria

C. Lipidose

D. Hyperphosphatemia

Q.169 The association of which of the following substances with stannous fluoride resulted in encouraging reductions of morning breath odour, even when oral hygiene is insufficient?

A. Triclosan

B. Amine fluoride

C. Hydrogen peroxide

D. Oxidising lozenges

Q.170

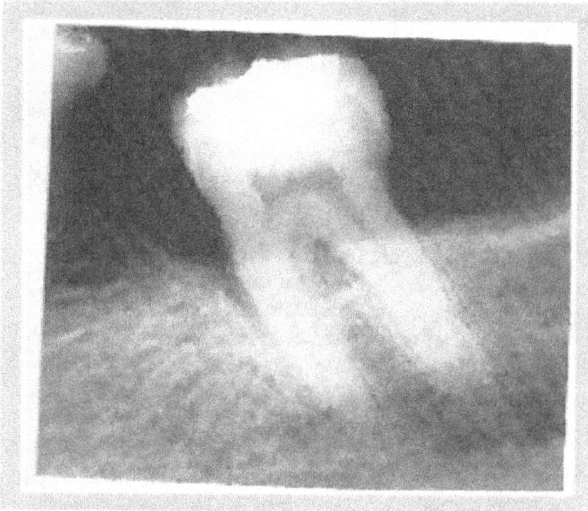

Identify the picture.

A. Atrophic periodontal ligament

B. Bony trabeculae realigned perpendicular to the mesial root of tilted molar

C. Boneless window between adjoining close roots of molars

D. Normal bone contour conforms to the prominence of the roots

Q.171 Supragingival plaque causes:

A. Gingivitis

B. Periodontitis

C. Pericoronitis

D. Aphthous ulcers

Q.172 Which of the following cranial nerves provides sensory fibres to the pharyngeal and facial mucous membrane?

A. Cranial nerve IX

B. Cranial nerve X

C. Cranial nerve XI

D. Cranial nerve XII

Q.173 Which of the following viruses is a ribonucleic acid (RNA) enterovirus?

A. Coxsackievirus

B. Varicella zoster

C. Herpes virus

D. HIV

Q.174 Which of the following results from inhaling dust contaminated with droppings, particularly from infected birds or bats?

A. Histoplasmosis

B. Shingles

C. Erosive lichen planus

D. Chronic bullous disease

Q.175 Which of the following terms is used to describe the presence of thick white lesions with papillary surfaces in the oral cavity?

A. Verrucuous leukoplakia

B. Parulis

C. Chronic multifocal candidiasis

D. Bowen's disease

Q.176 Which of the following diseases presents as multiple yellowish white or white papules?

A. Fordyce's granule

B. Lupus erythematosus

C. Oral lichen planus

D. Erythroplakia

Q.177 Which of the following may occur as either pedunculated or sessile growths on any surface of the oral mucous membrane?

A. Fibrous inflammatory hyperplasia

B. Fibroma epulis

C. Fibroma fissuratum

D. Pulp polyp

Q.178 Which of the following is a rather common exuberant oral epithelial response in which the rete pegs are extended deeply into the underlying connective tissue in an irregular fashion?

A. Pseudo-epitheliomatous hyperplasia

B. Hamartomas

C. Lymphangioma

D. Granular cell tumour

Q.179 Which of the following is a child tumour that resembles ameoblastoma radiologically and histologically and behaves less aggressively than ameloblastoma?

A. Ameloblastic fibroma

B. Ameloblastic chondroma

C. Ameloblastic neuroma

D. Ameloblastic necrosis

Q.180 Which of the following diseases arises from the base of the skull, often extending into the cranial cavity as well as the oral cavity?

A. Teratomas

B. Cherubism

C. Fibroma

D. Chondroma

Q.181 Multiple papules on the lips and gingivae are often present and papillomatosis of the buccal, palatal, faucial and oropharyngeal mucosae often produces a "cobblestone" effect on these mucous membrane in which of the following?

A. Cowden's syndrome

B. Xanthomas

C. Amyloidosis

D. Langerhans cells histiocytosis

Q.182 Which of the following is a white lesion that involves the oral mucosa, cannot be removed by rubbing and cannot be classified as any other lesion following histopathologic examination?

A. Oral hairy leukoplakia

B. Leukoplakia

C. Lichen planus

D. Erythroplakia

Q.183 Which of the following is a para-sympathomimetic agent and has a major effect at the muscarinic cholinergic receptor of salivary gland acinar cells?

A. Pilocarpine

B. Bethanechol

C. Muscarinic

D. Ephinephrine

Q.184 Which of the following diseases is associated with salivary gland dysfunction and bilateral salivary gland enlargement?

A. Chronic alcoholism

B. Anorexia nervosa

C. Induced salivary dysfunction

D. Sialadenitis

Q.185 Which of the following diseases is a form of ductal papilloma and is analogous to the syringocystadenoma papilliferum of the skin?

A. Inverted ductal papilloma

B. Simple ductal papilloma

C. Sialadenoma papilliferum

D. Ductal papilloma

Q.186 Which of the following is also referred to as osteoarthrosis, osteoarthritis and degenerative arthritis and is primarily a disorder of articular cartilage and subchondral bone, with secondary inflammation of the synovial membrane?

A. Degenerative joint disease

B. Rheumatoid arthritis

C. Chondrometaplasia

D. Bruxism

Q.187 Sulphate taste impairment is minimal at levels below

A. 150 mg/litre

B. 250 mg/litre

C. 350 mg/litre

D. 450 mg/litre

Q.188 The health based guideline value of lead is

A. 1.5 mg/litre

B. 0.01 mg/litre

C. 0.001 mg/litre

D. 0.07 mg/litre

Q.189 Which of the following chemical disinfectants reacts with water or stream to produce corrosive fumes of hydrochloric acid?

A. Sodium hypochlorite

B. Chlorine dioxide

C. Ethylene oxide

D. Formaldehyde

Q.190 The deficiency of which of the following nutrients causes angular stomatitis?

A. Thiamine

B. Riboflavin

C. Niacin

D. Ascorbic acid

Q.191 The study which proceeds from cause to effect:

A. Retrospective   **B.** Cohort
C. Case-control   **D.** Descriptive

Q.192 The Constitution of WHO came into force on

A. 7th April 1948
B. 15th September 1981
C. 16th May 1920
D. 1st December 1953

Q.193 Which of the following is highly positively charged, binds to hydroxyapatite and maintains its activity after binding?

A. Lacto-peroxidase   **B.** Lysozyme
C. Lactoferrin   **D.** IgA

Q.194 Which of the following tests estimates the number of S. mutans in mixed paraffin–stimulated saliva when cultured in Mutans Saliva-virus Bacitracin agar?

A. Streptococcus mutans screening test
B. Saliva/tongue blade method
C. Alban test
D. Synder test

Q.195 Which of the following is a phenol derivative which has been recently included in mouth rinses and tooth pastes?

A. Triclosan   **B.** Delmopinol
C. Metallic ion   **D.** Sanguinarine

Q.196 Which of the following tobacco products contains finely powdered air cured and fire cured tobacco leaves?

A. Paan   **B.** Snuff   **C.** Zarda   **D.** Gutka

Q.197 A dentin primer:

A. Etches the dentin
B. Raises the surface-free energy of the dentin
C. Removes the smear layer
D. Bonds the composite

Q.198 Which of the following is one of the most common space controlling appliances used in dental practice?

A. Band and loop space maintainer
B. Crown and loop space maintainer
C. Lingual arch space maintainer
D. Palatal arch

Q.199 Father of Health statistics is:

A. John Snow   **B.** John Graunt
C. Frederick Mc kay   **D.** Pierre Frauchard

Q.200 Sensitivity of a test is its ability to identify:

A. False negative   **B.** True positive
C. True negative   **D.** False positive

Q.201 Which of the following demonstrates the integrated activity of periosteal and capsular matrices in facial growth?

A. Maxillary growth
B. Mandibular growth
C. Alveolar bone growth
D. Frontal bone growth

Q.202 Which of the following is an important element of skeletal growth, functions as a life-long optimisation process for adapting bone mass and architecture to functional needs?

A. Stippling   **B.** Bone remodelling
C. Modelling   **D.** Ledging

Q.203 In _____, crown inclination refers to the labio-lingual or bucco-lingual inclination of the long axis of the crown and not to the inclination of the long axis of the entire tooth?

A. Key I   **B.** Key II   **C.** Key III   **D.** Key IV

Q.204 Which of the following terms indicate teeth or other maxillary structures which are too far forward or too far backward?

A. Attraction and abstraction
B. Anteversion and retroversion
C. Supraversion and infraversion
D. Contraction and distraction

Q.205 Which of the following may be a unilateral or bilateral, partial or complete absence of the clavicle in-conjunction with delayed cranial suture closure, maxillary retrusion and possible mandibular protrusion?

A. Cleidocranial dysplasia
B. Torticollis
C. Cerebral palsy
D. Cerebri palsy

Q.206 In _________, the lower lip is impotent, while the upper lip is quite active as it lengthens and is drawn against the maxillary incisors and alveolar process by the contracting buccinators mechanism.

A. class I malocclusion
B. class II malocclusion
C. class III malocclusion
D. class IV malocclusion

Q.207 Premature extraction of which of the following deciduous teeth will very likely lead to mesial drift of the first permanent molar and blocking of the erupting second premolars?

A. First premolar   **B.** Second molar
C. Third molar   **D.** Second premolar

Q.208 Broad and short type of face is known as:

A. Mesoprosponic   **B.** Euryprosopic
C. Leptoprosopic   **D.** None of the above

Q.209 In _____, bone replaces the resorbed tooth material that leads to ankylosis.

A. surface resorption
B. inflammatory resorption
C. replacement resorption
D. progressive resorption

Q.210 Which of the following is the structural alteration of an object produced by a force per unit area?

A. Stress   **B.** Strain
C. Plastic deformation   **D.** Moment

Q.211 Which of the following is also called as 'ugly duckling stage'?

A. Broadbent's stage
B. Built in pacifier
C. Deglutitional problem
D. Lip biting

Q.212 Which of the following allows genuine intrusive movement of the anterior teeth?

A. V levelling
B. Segmented arch technique
C. Anterior space
D. Cross bite

Q.213 Which of the following is also called Kloehn head gear?

A. Cervical or low pull head gear
B. Combi pull head gear
C. High pull head gear
D. Conjunction head gear

Q.214 Which of the following are those aberrations which extend beyond the teeth and include the maxilla, the mandible tooth or both?

A. Dysgnathic anomalies
B. Dentofacial anomalies
C. Eugnathic anomalies
D. Dental anomalies

Q.215 Which of the following is/are like growth ring(s) and represent(s) the successive apposition of enamel in the form of discrete increments?

A. Hunter schreger bands
B. Incremental straie of Retzius
C. Prismless enamel
D. Enamel tufts

Q.216 Which of the following represents a chronic carious lesion and can become arrested due to a change in the local environment?

A. Chronic caries
B. Arrested caries
C. Incipient caries
D. Acute caries

Q.217 Which of the following materials provide a protective coating to the walls of the prepared cavity?

A. Cavity sealers
B. Cavity liners
C. Cavity bases
D. Cavity fillers

Q.218 Which of the following instruments has a spherical head shape?

A. Round bur
B. Straight fissure bur
C. Tapered fissure bur
D. Inverted cone bur

Q.219 Which of the following removes the water spray from the airotor during cavity preparation procedures at a much slower rate than the high volume evacuator?

A. Rubber dam
B. Cellulose wafer
C. Saliva ejector
D. Cotton Rolls

Q.220 Which of the following is employed primarily on the mesial aspect of maxillary first premolars?

A. Piggyback wedging
B. Double wedging
C. Wedge wedging
D. Light transmitting wedging

Q.221

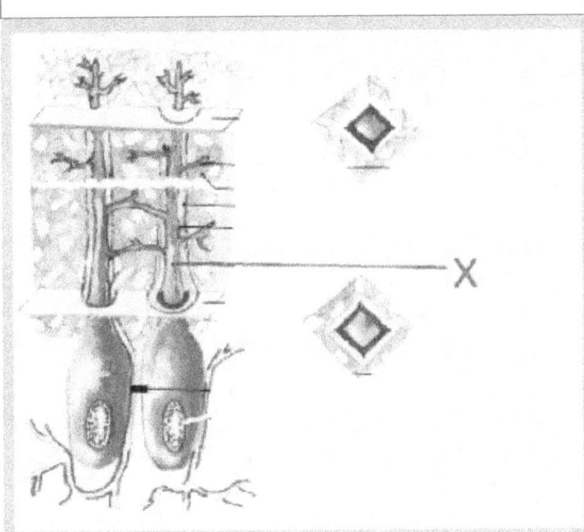

This is the structure of dentin showing odontoblasts and dentinal tubules. Which of the following is indicated by 'X'?

A. Canaliculus
B. Intertubular dentin
C. Odontoblastic process
D. Predentin

Q.222

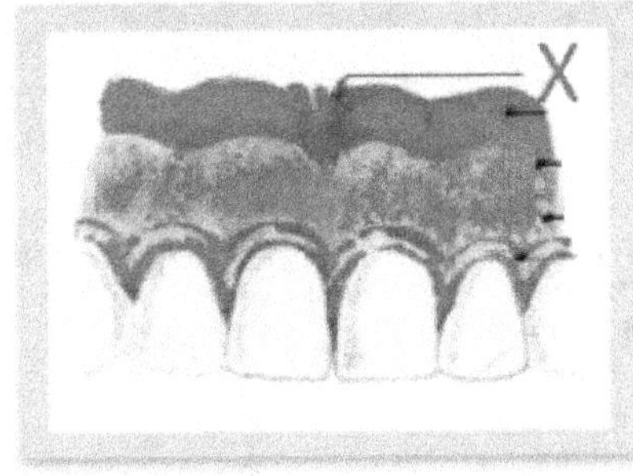

This is the picture of normal gingiva. Which of the following is indicated by 'X'?

A. Frenulum
B. Alveolar mucosa

C. Mucogingival junction

D. Attached gingiva

Q.223 The enamel organ continues to proliferate into the ______ with an uneven rhythmic cell division, producing a convex cap stage of development.

A. mesenchyme   **B.** ecto-mesenchyme

C. endo-mesenchyme   **D.** ameloblast

Q.224 Cementum is deposited in a thin layer at the cementoenamel junctional to form a butt joint:

A. 20%, an overlap joint 70% or a gap between cementum and enamel 10%

B. 30%, an overlap joint 60% or a gap between cementum and enamel 10%

C. 40%, an overlap joint 40% or a gap between cementum and enamel 20%

D. 50%, an overlap joint 40% or a gap between cementum and enamel 10%

Q.225 Gutta Percha (GP) is plasticized (softened) by:

A. Alcohol   **B.** Eugenol

C. Chloroform   **D.** EDTA

Q.226 Which of the following may be partial or total depending on whether part of or the entire pulp is involved?

A. Necrosis of pulp

B. Pulp degeneration

C. Inflammation of the pulp

D. Calcific degeneration

Q.227 Which of the following is a cyst which is a closed cavity or sac internally lined with epithelium, the centre of which is filled with fluid or semisolid material?

A. Radicular cyst   **B.** Condensing osteitis

C. Angular cheilitis   **D.** Necrosis

Q.228

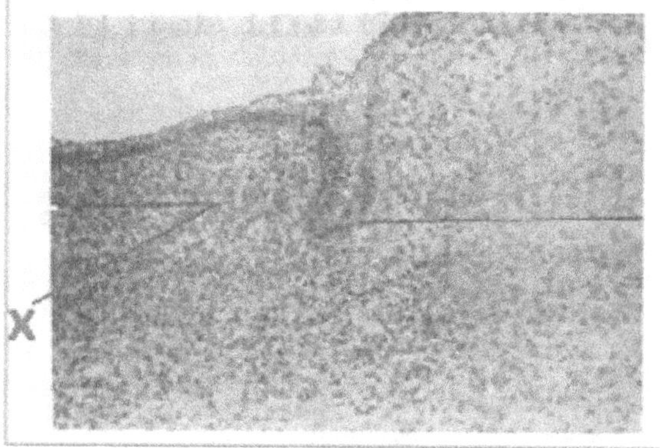

This is the picture of the invagination of the dental lamina from oral epithelium into 'X'. What does 'X' indicate?

A. Endo-mesenchyme   **B.** Ecto-mesenchyme

C. Exo-mesenchyme   **D.** Endochyme

Q.229 When a glass is drawn into a fibre with very smooth surfaces and insignificant internal flaws, what will be its tensile strength?

A. As high as 2800 MPa

B. As low as 2800 MPa

C. As high as 1800 MPa

D. As low as 1800 MPa

Q.230 Which system of alloys has a composition greater than the eutectic?

A. Supraeutectic alloys

B. Hypereutectic alloys

C. Supereutectic alloys

D. Eutectic alloys

Q.231 Which of the following is the stage of polymerisation during which polymer chains cease to grow?

A. Termination   **B.** Setting

C. Resetting   **D.** Stippling

Q.232 Incremental lines of Retzius are seen in:

A. Enamel   **B.** Dentin

C. Cementum   **D.** Pulp

Q.233 Which of the following is the ability of a material to elicit an appropriate biological response to a given application in the body?

A. Biocompatibility   **B.** Biointegration

C. Osseointegration   **D.** Plasticity

Q.234 Which of the following is an aqueous impression used for recording maximum detail?

A. Alginate hydrocolloid

B. Agar hydrocolloid

C. Addition hydrocolloid

D. Colloid

Q.235 Which of the following techniques was originally developed for condensation silicone to minimise the effect of polymerisation shrinkage on the dimensional changes?

A. Putty wash technique

B. Acid etching technique

C. Reline technique

D. Accelerator technique

Q.236 Which of the following is a thermoplastic wax used to make a type of dental impression and dental impression wax?

A. Boxing wax   **B.** Corrective wax

C. Bite wax   **D.** Baseplate wax

Q.237 Which of the following is the process of producing a lustrous surface through the abrading action of fine abrasives bound to a non-abrasive binder medium?

A. Buffing   **B.** Bulk reduction

C. Contouring   **D.** Finishing

Q.238 The first porcelain tooth material was introduced by:

A. DeChemant   **B.** Ash

C. Plateau   **D.** McClean

Q.239 Which of the following is the mineral form of calcite?

A. Arkansas stone   **B.** Chalk

C. Corundum   **D.** Emery

Q.240 Which of the following is a hydrophilic, low-viscosity resin that promotes bonding to a substrate, such as dentin?

A. Primer

B. Resin tag

C. Smear layer

D. Hybrid layer

// Smart Answer Sheet //

Correct — Indicates percentage of students who answered questions correctly.

Skipped — Indicates percentage of students who skipped questions.

Q.	Ans.	Correct / Skipped	Q.	Ans.	Correct / Skipped	Q.	Ans.	Correct / Skipped	Q.	Ans.	Correct / Skipped	Q.	Ans.	Correct / Skipped
1	C	36.67 % / 10.0 %	17	A	28.33 % / 58.34 %	33	C	16.67 % / 58.33 %	49	C	16.67 % / 58.33 %	65	C	8.33 % / 58.34 %
2	D	28.33 % / 56.67 %	18	B	13.33 % / 58.34 %	34	D	20.0 % / 55.0 %	50	B	13.33 % / 58.34 %	66	B	8.33 % / 58.34 %
3	D	21.67 % / 58.33 %	19	A	33.33 % / 58.34 %	35	D	11.67 % / 58.33 %	51	D	6.67 % / 58.33 %	67	D	8.33 % / 58.34 %
4	A	26.67 % / 58.33 %	20	C	8.33 % / 48.34 %	36	D	8.33 % / 58.34 %	52	B	13.33 % / 58.34 %	68	D	8.33 % / 58.34 %
5	B	25.0 % / 58.33 %	21	C	10.0 % / 58.33 %	37	B	16.67 % / 58.33 %	53	A	31.67 % / 58.33 %	69	D	6.67 % / 58.33 %
6	C	31.67 % / 58.33 %	22	B	10.0 % / 56.67 %	38	A	16.67 % / 58.33 %	54	D	23.33 % / 58.34 %	70	B	15.0 % / 58.33 %
7	A	15.0 % / 58.33 %	23	B	15.0 % / 58.33 %	39	B	10.0 % / 58.33 %	55	C	31.67 % / 58.33 %	71	A	10.0 % / 58.33 %
8	B	10.0 % / 58.33 %	24	B	8.33 % / 55.0 %	40	B	20.0 % / 58.33 %	56	B	35.0 % / 58.33 %	72	A	36.67 % / 55.0 %
9	C	30.0 % / 58.33 %	25	B	10.0 % / 58.33 %	41	A	11.67 % / 58.33 %	57	B	8.33 % / 58.34 %	73	A	16.67 % / 58.33 %
10	C	18.33 % / 58.34 %	26	B	16.67 % / 58.33 %	42	C	18.33 % / 56.67 %	58	D	13.33 % / 58.34 %	74	B	3.33 % / 58.34 %
11	C	8.33 % / 58.34 %	27	C	8.33 % / 58.34 %	43	C	8.33 % / 58.34 %	59	A	13.33 % / 58.34 %	75	A	11.67 % / 58.33 %
12	A	18.33 % / 58.34 %	28	A	20.0 % / 56.67 %	44	B	8.33 % / 58.34 %	60	B	26.67 % / 58.33 %	76	A	10.0 % / 58.33 %
13	B	20.0 % / 58.33 %	29	B	10.0 % / 58.33 %	45	B	11.67 % / 58.33 %	61	B	21.67 % / 58.33 %	77	A	11.67 % / 58.33 %
14	A	21.67 % / 58.33 %	30	A	16.67 % / 56.66 %	46	B	35.0 % / 58.33 %	62	A	36.67 % / 58.33 %	78	C	20.0 % / 58.33 %
15	C	28.33 % / 58.34 %	31	A	28.33 % / 58.34 %	47	B	25.0 % / 58.33 %	63	C	23.33 % / 58.34 %	79	A	13.33 % / 58.34 %
16	D	13.33 % / 58.34 %	32	A	25.0 % / 58.33 %	48	A	13.33 % / 58.34 %	64	B	15.0 % / 58.33 %	80	A	16.67 % / 55.0 %

Q.	Ans.	Correct		Q.	Ans.	Correct		Q.	Ans.	Correct		Q.	Ans.	Correct		Q.	Ans.	Correct
		Skipped				Skipped				Skipped				Skipped				Skipped
81	A	15.0 % 58.33 %		97	B	18.33 % 58.34 %		113	B	0 % 100 %		129	A	10.0 % 60.0 %		145	D	20.0 % 60.0 %
82	A	6.67 % 56.66 %		98	A	13.33 % 58.34 %		114	A	30.0 % 60.0 %		130	A	15.0 % 58.33 %		146	B	20.0 % 60.0 %
83	C	16.67 % 58.33 %		99	C	21.67 % 58.33 %		115	A	13.33 % 60.0 %		131	B	30.0 % 61.67 %		147	B	15.0 % 60.0 %
84	A	11.67 % 58.33 %		100	C	13.33 % 58.34 %		116	A	28.33 % 61.67 %		132	A	31.67 % 61.66 %		148	B	25.0 % 61.67 %
85	A	26.67 % 58.33 %		101	B	21.67 % 60.0 %		117	A	26.67 % 60.0 %		133	B	30.0 % 60.0 %		149	A	8.33 % 60.0 %
86	A	28.33 % 58.34 %		102	B	36.67 % 56.66 %		118	B	5.0 % 60.0 %		134	B	33.33 % 55.0 %		150	B	11.67 % 60.0 %
87	B	21.67 % 58.33 %		103	B	35.0 % 61.67 %		119	A	33.33 % 60.0 %		135	A	31.67 % 60.0 %		151	D	0 % 100 %
88	A	26.67 % 58.33 %		104	A	30.0 % 58.33 %		120	B	36.67 % 50.0 %		136	A	18.33 % 61.67 %		152	B	23.33 % 58.34 %
89	A	6.67 % 58.33 %		105	B	0 % 100 %		121	C	28.33 % 60.0 %		137	B	10.0 % 60.0 %		153	A	10.0 % 60.0 %
90	B	16.67 % 58.33 %		106	B	15.0 % 60.0 %		122	A	21.67 % 56.66 %		138	C	15.0 % 60.0 %		154	A	30.0 % 60.0 %
91	A	21.67 % 58.33 %		107	A	26.67 % 61.66 %		123	A	26.67 % 60.0 %		139	D	10.0 % 61.67 %		155	B	8.33 % 61.67 %
92	A	33.33 % 58.34 %		108	B	23.33 % 60.0 %		124	A	15.0 % 55.0 %		140	C	11.67 % 60.0 %		156	C	25.0 % 61.67 %
93	A	33.33 % 58.34 %		109	A	10.0 % 60.0 %		125	B	15.0 % 60.0 %		141	A	8.33 % 60.0 %		157	B	26.67 % 60.0 %
94	C	8.33 % 58.34 %		110	A	20.0 % 60.0 %		126	C	6.67 % 60.0 %		142	B	13.33 % 60.0 %		158	A	15.0 % 60.0 %
95	A	25.0 % 58.33 %		111	A	26.67 % 61.66 %		127	B	23.33 % 60.0 %		143	C	1.67 % 60.0 %		159	A	8.33 % 61.67 %
96	B	18.33 % 58.34 %		112	B	15.0 % 61.67 %		128	A	30.0 % 56.67 %		144	B	23.33 % 58.34 %		160	B	30.0 % 61.67 %

Q.	Ans.	Correct / Skipped	Q.	Ans.	Correct / Skipped	Q.	Ans.	Correct / Skipped	Q.	Ans.	Correct / Skipped	Q.	Ans.	Correct / Skipped
161	A	25.0 % / 60.0 %	177	A	11.67 % / 61.66 %	193	B	5.0 % / 60.0 %	209	C	15.0 % / 60.0 %	225	C	20.0 % / 60.0 %
162	A	33.33 % / 60.0 %	178	A	21.67 % / 60.0 %	194	B	6.67 % / 60.0 %	210	A	28.33 % / 60.0 %	226	A	10.0 % / 60.0 %
163	C	8.33 % / 61.67 %	179	A	16.67 % / 60.0 %	195	A	30.0 % / 60.0 %	211	A	35.0 % / 60.0 %	227	A	31.67 % / 60.0 %
164	A	35.0 % / 61.67 %	180	A	20.0 % / 55.0 %	196	B	21.67 % / 61.66 %	212	B	15.0 % / 56.67 %	228	B	28.33 % / 56.67 %
165	A	6.67 % / 60.0 %	181	A	21.67 % / 60.0 %	197	B	26.67 % / 61.66 %	213	A	5.0 % / 60.0 %	229	A	16.67 % / 61.66 %
166	C	6.67 % / 60.0 %	182	B	28.33 % / 60.0 %	198	A	31.67 % / 60.0 %	214	A	11.67 % / 56.66 %	230	B	6.67 % / 60.0 %
167	A	25.0 % / 61.67 %	183	A	18.33 % / 61.67 %	199	B	10.0 % / 60.0 %	215	B	25.0 % / 60.0 %	231	A	25.0 % / 61.67 %
168	A	8.33 % / 60.0 %	184	D	23.33 % / 60.0 %	200	B	20.0 % / 61.67 %	216	B	28.33 % / 61.67 %	232	A	26.67 % / 60.0 %
169	B	3.33 % / 60.0 %	185	C	10.0 % / 61.67 %	201	B	16.67 % / 61.66 %	217	A	5.0 % / 60.0 %	233	A	33.33 % / 60.0 %
170	B	11.67 % / 60.0 %	186	A	10.0 % / 60.0 %	202	B	28.33 % / 60.0 %	218	A	35.0 % / 56.67 %	234	A	28.33 % / 61.67 %
171	A	33.33 % / 60.0 %	187	B	8.33 % / 60.0 %	203	C	10.0 % / 60.0 %	219	C	21.67 % / 60.0 %	235	A	30.0 % / 61.67 %
172	B	6.67 % / 55.0 %	188	B	10.0 % / 60.0 %	204	B	8.33 % / 60.0 %	220	C	20.0 % / 56.67 %	236	B	10.0 % / 61.67 %
173	A	15.0 % / 60.0 %	189	B	5.0 % / 60.0 %	205	A	33.33 % / 61.67 %	221	C	20.0 % / 60.0 %	237	A	21.67 % / 61.66 %
174	A	25.0 % / 60.0 %	190	B	20.0 % / 60.0 %	206	C	8.33 % / 60.0 %	222	A	26.67 % / 60.0 %	238	A	25.0 % / 60.0 %
175	A	26.67 % / 60.0 %	191	B	13.33 % / 60.0 %	207	B	33.33 % / 60.0 %	223	B	21.67 % / 60.0 %	239	B	21.67 % / 61.66 %
176	A	35.0 % / 60.0 %	192	A	18.33 % / 60.0 %	208	B	26.67 % / 58.33 %	224	B	15.0 % / 58.33 %	240	A	26.67 % / 60.0 %

Performance Analysis

Avg. Score (%)	17.92%
Toppers Score (%)	78.12%
Your Score	

Part A

Q.1 Which of the following diseases is associated with diabetes mellitus, probably as a consequence of polyuria, as well as Parkinson's disease, cystic fibrosis and sarcoidosis?

A. Aplasia   **B.** Xerostomia

C. Atresia   **D.** Aberrancy

Q.2 Which of the following term refers to a duplication of teeth in the normal series and is found at the end of a tooth series?

A. Conical supernumerary

B. Tuberculate supernumerary

C. Supplemental supernumerary

D. Odontoma supernumerary

Q.3 Which of the following term is a poorly understood biologic phenomenon which, in some instances, cannot be clearly differentiated from other process or tissue reaction?

A. Neoplasia   **B.** Aplasia

C. Atresia   **D.** Papilloma

Q.4 Which of the following diseases occurs twice as frequently in men as in women and is less common in darker- skinned individuals?

A. Oral nevi

B. Squamous papilloma

C. Keratoacanthoma

D. Leukoplakia

Q.5 Which of the following diseases is usually of extremely long duration and may or may not necessarily be associated with the use of tobacco?

A. Carcinoma of the buccal mucosa

B. Carcinoma of the gingiva

C. Carcinoma of the floor of the mouth

D. Carcinoma of the tongue

Q.6 Which of the following tumors is indurated and in some instances, appears as an exophtic or fungating growth?

A. Lymphoepithelioma

B. Basaloid squamous cell carcinoma

C. Adenosquamous carcinoma

D. Spindle cell carcinoma

Q.7 Which of the following tumors consists of bundles of interlacing collagenous fibres interspersed with varying numbers of fibroblasts or fibrocytes and small blood vessels?

A. Fibroma   **B.** Chondro-fibroma

C. Fibroblastoma   **D.** Neuro-fibroma

Q.8 True regarding pertussis vaccine is:

A. 95% of vaccinated are protected

B. Erythromycin should be given to contacts

C. Neuroparalytic complication is seen in 1 in 15000

D. Leucocytosis is diagnostic

Q.9 Mechanism of action of pertussis toxin is all except:

A. Act by ADP ribosylation of GI subunit

B. Increase in calcium

C. Act by decreasing GTP

D. Increase in iron

Q.10 In which of the following organisms does the capsule not act as a virulence factor?

A. H. influenza   **B.** S.pneumoniae

C. N. meningitidis   **D.** Bordetella pertussis

Q.11 A 7 month old, partially immunized child presented with cough ending in characteristic whoop. Which of the following is considered the best type of specimen to isolate the organism and confirm the diagnosis?

A. Nasopharyngeal swab

B. Cough plate culture

C. Tracheal – aspirates

D. Sputum

Q.12 Acellular pertussis vaccine contains:

A. Pertactin, flagillary hemagglutinin, cytotoxin, endotoxin

B. Pertactin, flagillary hemagglutinin, fimbriae, endotoxin

C. Pertactin cytotoxin, fimbriae

D. Flagillary hemagglutinin, pertussis toxin, fimbriae

Q.13 All are true statements regarding pertussis, except:

A. Secondary attack rate averages 90% in unimmunized contacts

B. Incubation period is around 14 days

C. Erythromycin is the drug of choice

D. Main source of infection is chronic carriers

Q.14 A veterinary doctor had pyrexia of unknown origin. His blood culture in special laboratory media was positive for gram-negative short bacilli which was oxidase positive. Which of the following is the likely organism grown in culture?

A. Pasturella spp.   **B.** Francisella spp.

C. Bartonella spp.   **D.** Brucella spp.

Q.15 Which of the following substances selectively block dopamine reuptake in brain neurons by dopamine transporters?

A. Amphetamines

B. Hemicholinium

C. Hydrochlorothiazide

D. Fluoxetine

Q.16 Which of the following substances are a large family of cell membrane receptors which are linked to the effector through one or more GTP- activated proteins for response effectuation?

A. Collagen

B. G protein coupled receptors
C. Aminoacids
D. Glutaraldehyde

Q.17 Which of the following drugs refers to drugs which do not act by binding to specific regulatory macromolecules?
A. Non-receptor mediated drug
B. Receptor mediated drug action
C. Combined effects of drugs
D. Opioids mediated drug

Q.18 Which of the following defects is usually seen with indirectly acting drugs, such as ephedrine, tyramine, nicotine?
A. Tachyphylaxis
B. Prophylaxis
C. Anaphylaxis
D. Cumulation

Q.19 Which of the following muscarinic receptors, plays a major role in mediating gastric secretion, relaxation of lower esophageal sphincter on vagal stimulation and in learning, memory, and motor function?
A. M_1
B. M_2
C. M_3
D. M_4

Q.20 Which of the following drugs acts selectively on bronchial muscle without altering volume or consistency of respiratory secretions?
A. Hyoscine butyl bromide
B. Atropine methonitrate
C. Ipratropium bromide
D. Tiotropium bromide

Q.21 Which of the following drugs is a potent mydriatic but its slow and long lasting action is undesirable for refraction testing?
A. ACh
B. Atropine
C. Aspirin
D. Histamine

Q.22 Which of the following antihistaminic drug is largely free of arrhythmogenic potential, but some cases of ventricular arrhythmia in patients with pre-existing long QT interval have been reported?
A. Fexofenadine
B. Loratadine
C. Desloratadine
D. Cetirizine

Q.23 Which of the following drugs is nearly as effective as ergotamine and preferred for parenteral administration because when injected it is less hazardous?
A. Sumatriptan
B. Dihydroergotamine
C. Rizatriptan
D. Bromocriptine

Q.24 Which of the following drugs may be involved in mediating toxin induced increased fluid movement in secretory diarrhoeas?
A. Leukotrienes
B. Prostaglandins
C. Thromboxanes
D. Ergotamine

Q.25 Which of the following drugs blunts diuretic action of furosemide and thiazides and reduces K⁺ conserving action of spironolactone?
A. Atropine
B. ACh
C. Aspirin
D. Ergotamine

Q.26 Which of the following substances is considered to be the most effective agent for arresting the rheumatoid process and preventing involvement of additional points?
A. Silver
B. Gold
C. Auranofin
D. Leflunomide

Q.27 Which of the following substances can potentiate warfarin and theophylline by inhibiting their metabolism?
A. Ergotamine
B. Muscarine
C. Allopurinol
D. Probenecid

Q.28 Which of the following are drugs that act in the CNS to raise the threshold of cough centre or act peripherally in the respiratory tract to reduce tussal impulses or both these actions?
A. Mucolytics
B. Anti-tussive
C. Tussives
D. Nonopioids

Q.29 Fatty acids are transported into the mitochondria following conjugation with carnitine and are sequentially catabolised by a process called α oxidation to produce _____?
A. Pyruvate
B. Acetyl CoA
C. Water
D. CO_2

Q.30 Which of the following cells exhibits features of both the adaptive and innate immune systems. They are morphologically similar to lymphocytes and recognise similar ligands, but they are not antigen specific and cannot generate immunological memory?
A. Mast cells
B. Basophils
C. Natural killer cells
D. Dendritic cells

Q.31 Which of the following diseases is caused by failure of apoptosis of lymphocytes?
A. DiGeorge syndrome
B. Bare lymphocyte syndromes
C. Autoimmune lymphoproliferative syndrome
D. Lymphoedema

Q.32 Which of the following diseases can result in pneumomediastinum, pneumothorax or AGE due to gas passing directly into the pulmonary venous system?
A. Barotrauma
B. Thrombosis
C. Chilblains
D. Hypothermia

Q.33 Which of the following nutrients does the transketolase activity in the hexose monophosphate shunt pathway?
A. Niacin
B. Thiamine
C. Riboflavin
D. Pyridoxine

Q.34 Which of the following substances helps prevent free radicals damage to cells, and monodeiodinase, which converts thyroxine to triiodothyronine?
A. Zinc
B. Selenium
C. Fluoride
D. Calcium

Q.35 Which of the following nutrient deficiency causes keratomalacia?
A. Vitamin A
B. Vitamin B
C. Vitamin C
D. Vitamin D

Q.36 Which of the following drugs causes very little local irritation at injection sites and negligible allergic responses?

A. Ketolides

B. Aminoglycosides

C. Carbapenems

D. Monobactams

Q.37 Which of the following drugs is used orally to treat asymptomatic cyst excreters or in association with another amoebicide to treat extra- intestinal amoebiasis?

A. Diloxanide furoate

B. Iodoquinol

C. Nitazoxanide

D. Paromomycin

Q.38 Which of the following diseases is characterised by neutrophil sequestration in pulmonary capillaries and increased capillary permeability?

A. Acute respiratory distress syndrome

B. Vasodilatation

C. Neurological coma

D. Acute kidney injury

Q.39 Which of the following drug poisonings is associated with metabolic acidosis, hypoprothrombinaemia, hyperglycaemia, hyperpyrexia, renal failure, pulmonary oedema, shock and cerebral oedema?

A. Salicylates

B. Sanguinarine

C. Penicillin

D. Atropine

Q.40 Which of the following drug's misuse produces euphoria, perceptual alterations and conjunctival injection, followed by enhanced appetite, relaxation and occasionally hypertension, tachycardia, slurred speech and ataxia?

A. Cocaine

B. Cannabis

C. Benzodiazepines

D. Metformin

Q.41 Which of the following inhibits a number of tissues esterases, including AchE?

A. Carbamate insecticides

B. Methanol

C. Ethylene glycol

D. Glutaraldehyde

Q.42 Which of the following are perceptions without external stimuli?

A. Hallucinations

B. Elated mood

C. Delusions

D. Depressed mood

Q.43 The following question is regarding the interior view of the base of the skull.

In the anterior half, which of the following is/are a/the centrally placed a cube of bone containing two large air sinuses separated by a septum?

A. Vomer

B. Body of the sphenoid

C. Pterygoid processes

D. Greater wing

Q.44 In the anterior cranial fossa, which of the following part is a sieve-like structure, which allows small olfactory nerve fibres to pass through its foramina from the nasal mucosa to the olfactory bulb?

A. Foramen caecum

B. Cribriform plate

C. Crista galli

D. Orbital part

Q.45 Which of the following is a clear, colourless, cell free fluid that circulates through the subarachnoid space surrounding the brain and spinal cord?

A. Pericardial fluid

B. Cerebrospinal fluid

C. Peritoneal fluid

D. Pituitary gland enzyme

Q.46 Which of the following sinuses are on the clivus, just posterior to the sella turcica of the sphenoid bone?

A. Cavernous sinuses

B. Basilar sinuses

C. Petrosal sinuses

D. Sagittal sinuses

Q.47 In the oculomotor nerve fibres, which of the following are preganglionic parasympathetic fibres that synapse in the ciliary ganglion and ultimately innervate the sphincter pupillae muscle, responsible for pupillary constriction and the ciliary muscles, responsible for accommodation of the lens for near vision?

A. General somatic efferent fibres

B. General visceral efferent fibres

C. Branchial efferent fibres

D. General somatic afferent fibres

Q.48 Which of the following nerves arises from the brainstem between the pons and medulla and passes forward, piercing the dura covering the clivus?

A. Maxillary nerve

B. Mandibular nerve

C. Abducent nerve

D. Facial nerve

Q.49 Which of the following muscles of the face draws the upper lip upward?

A. Mentalis

B. Risorius

C. Zygomaticus major

D. Zygomaticus minor

Q.50 Which of the following facial muscles consists of the transverse and alar parts?

A. Orbicularis oculi

B. Corrugator supercilii

C. Nasalis

D. Buccinator

Q.51 Which of the following nerves exits the skull through the foramen rotundum?

A. Lacrimal nerve

B. Maxillary nerve

C. Mandibular nerve

D. Ophthalmic nerve

Q.52 The frontal belly of occipitofrontalis begins anteriorly where it is attached to the skin of which of the following?

A. Eyes

B. Eyebrows

C. Nose

D. Cheeks

Q.53 Which of the following parts of the paired bony orbits is parallel to each other and each consists of four bones namely the maxilla, lacrimal, ethmoid and sphenoid bones?

A. Roof

B. Medial wall

C. Floor

D. Lateral wall

Q.54

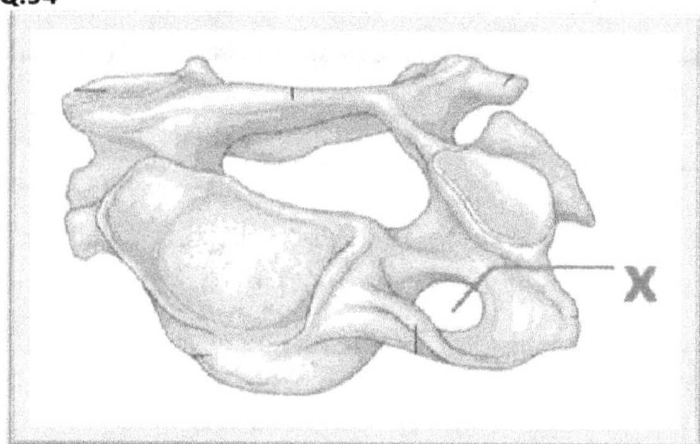

This is the picture of the typical features of the cervical vertebrae. What does 'X' indicate?

A. Spinous process
B. Foramen transversarium
C. Posterior tubercle
D. Anterior tubercle

Q.55

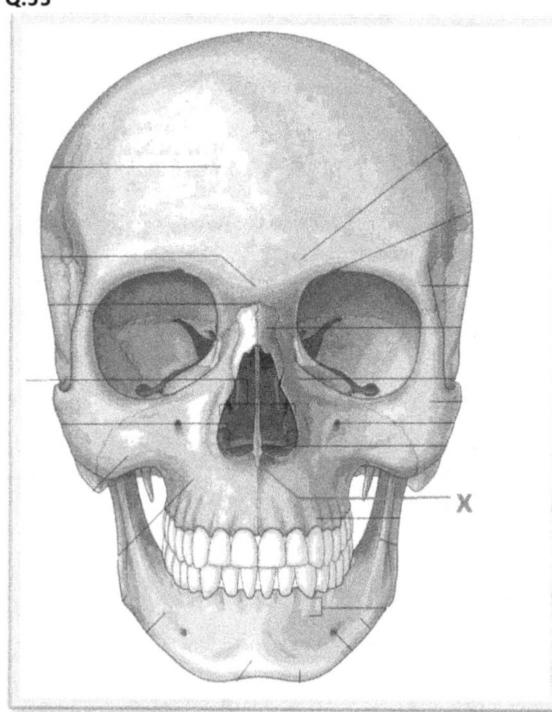

This is the picture of the anterior view of the skull. What does 'X' indicate?

A. Anterior nasal spine   **B.** Alveolar process
C. Oblique   **D.** Line

Q.56

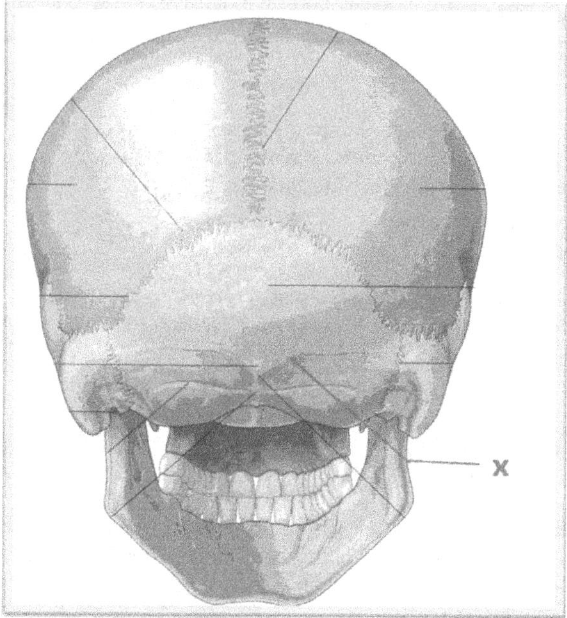

This is the picture of the posterior view of the skull. What does 'X' indicate?

A. Occipitomastoid suture
B. Superior nuchal line
C. Inion
D. Inferior nuchal line

Q.57 Which of the following parts of the tooth is continuous with the periodontal ligament through the apical foramen or through the lateral canals in the root?

A. Pulp   **B.** Dentin
C. Enamel   **D.** Cementum

Q.58 Which of the following cysts may occur at any place along the course of the duct, usually at or near the midline?

A. Branchial cleft cysts
B. Thyroglossal duct cysts
C. Anterior palatine cysts
D. Nasolabial cysts

Q.59 The dentin and pulp develop from the dental:

A. Lamella   **B.** Papilla
C. Follicle   **D.** Vestibular lamella

Q.60 It is suggested that _______ form thixotropic gels in that they can be easily squeezed out by the pressure from the growing crystals.

A. amelogenins   **B.** fibrogenins
C. cementoblasts   **D.** odontoblasts

Q.61 Which of the following dentins, although highly mineralised, is retained after decalcification?

A. Peridentin   **B.** Predentin
C. Intertubular dentin   **D.** Peritubular dentin

Q.62 Which of the following glycoproteins interacts to form cell surface adhesion receptors and is found in pulp to get attached to biologically active molecules like laminin and fibronectin?

A. Hyaluronan

B. Laminin

C. Integrin

D. Fibronectin

Q.63 Which of the following is an important enzyme for vasodilatation and blood pressure regulation?

A. Nitric oxide synthetase

B. Nitrous oxide synthetase

C. Sodium hypochlorite

D. Stannous fluoride

Q.64 Which of the following parts of tooth structure responds to irritation, whether mechanical, thermal, chemical or bacterial, by producing reparative dentin and mineralising any affected dentinal tubules?

A. Dentin

B. Enamel

C. Pulp

D. Cementum

Q.65 Which of the following controls early tooth formation?

A. Dental lamina

B. Dental papilla

C. Dental follicle

D. Vestibular lamina

Q.66 Which of the following growth factors of cementoblast is shown to promote cell proliferation, its migration and angiogenesis?

A. Prostaglandin

B. Fibroblast growth factor

C. Cementum attachment protein

D. Osteopontin

Q.67 Which of the following is a specialised, mineralised, avascular connective tissue covering the anatomical roots of human teeth?

A. Gingiva

B. Cementum

C. Periodontal ligament

D. Dentin

Q.68 Which of the following parts of the tooth is attached to the dentin of the root by cementum and to the bone of the jaws by alveolar bone?

A. Periodontium

B. Gingiva

C. Pulp

D. Alveolar process

Q.69

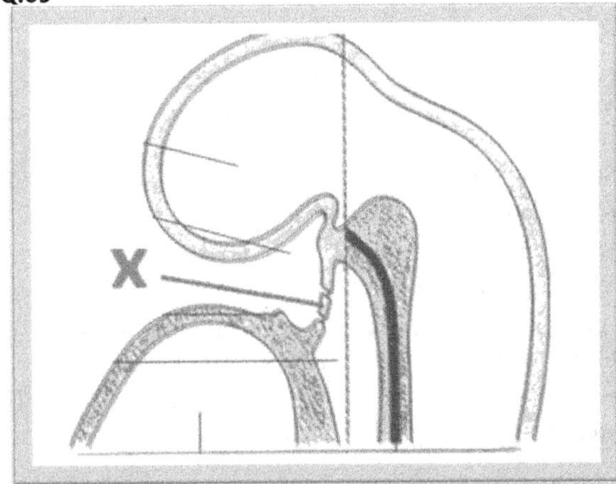

This is the picture of the oropharyngeal development of the human embryo. What does 'X' indicate?

A. Forebrain

B. Oral fossa

C. Buccopharyngeal membrane

D. Foregut

Q.70

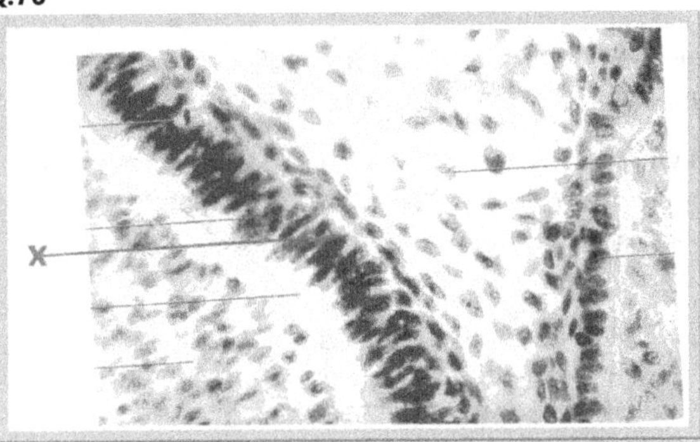

This is the picture of the layers of epithelial enamel organ at high magnification. What does 'X' indicate?

A. Inner enamel epithelium

B. Stratum intermedium

C. Basement membrane

D. Dental papilla

Q.71 Which of the following ulcers erodes into deeper plane like soft tissues, cartilages and bone?

A. Marjolin's ulcer

B. Rodent ulcer

C. Diabetic ulcer

D. Martorells' ulcer

Q.72 Which of the following diseases is a chronic infective acquired condition wherein there is infection of roots of one or both lower incisor teeth forming root abscess?

A. Median mental sinus

B. Cavernous sinus

C. Dural venous sinus

D. Sagittal sinus

Q.73 Which of the following tumors is a variant of aggressive fibromatosis seen in females often associated with Gardner's syndrome?

A. Desmoid tumor

B. Bursae

C. Fibroma

D. Dermoid

Q.74 Which of the following cysts occurs due to herniation of the synovial membrane of the knee joint as a result of chronic arthritis?

A. Semimembranosus bursa

B. Morrant baker's cyst

C. Lymph cyst

D. Lymphangioma

Q.75 Which of the following diseases can occur in diabetes insipidus or chronic renal failure as renal loss of water?

A. Euvolemia

B. Hypovolaemia

C. Hypervolaemia

D. Hypokalaemia

Q.76 Which of the following diseases occurs in critically ill patients after severe trauma, burns, acute pancreatitis, bleeding and sepsis?

A. Multiple organ dysfunction syndrome

B. Sjogren's syndrome

C. Kaposi's syndrome

D. Reinter syndrome

Q.77 Which of the following blood fractions is very useful in DIC and afibrinogenemia?

A. Albumin

B. Plasma

C. Fibrinogen

D. Packed cells

Q.78 Which of the following injuries may be associated with injury to duodenum or portal or superior mesenteric veins?

A. Duodenal injury

B. Pancreatic injury

C. Small bowel injury

D. Colonic injury

Q.79 Which of the following defects refers to localised thickening of palmar aponeurosis and later formation of nodules with severe permanent changes in metacarpophalangeal and proximal interphalangeal joints?

A. Dupuytren's contracture

B. Volkman's ischaemic contracture

C. Syndactyly

D. Callosity

Q.80 Which of the following diseases is persistent, painless cyanosis seen in fingers and often in legs with paraesthesia and chilblains affecting young females?

A. Acrocyanosis

B. Gangrene

C. Livedo reticularis

D. Polyarteritis nodosa

Q.81 Which of the following diseases is common in malaria endemic areas?

A. Burkitt's lymphoma

B. Cutaneous T cell lymphoma

C. Chyluria

D. Chylothorax

Q.82

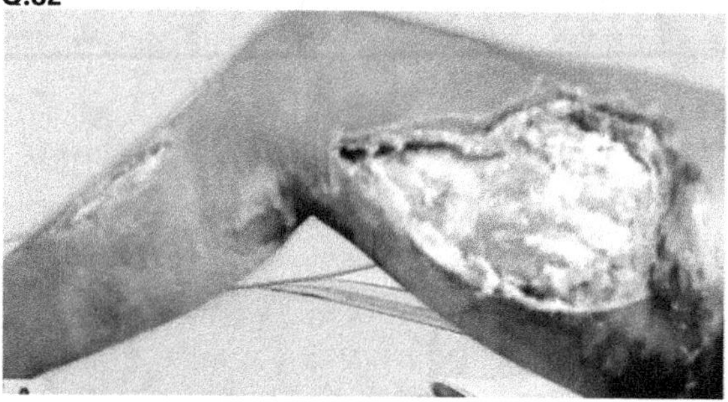

Identify the disease indicated in the picture:

A. Necrotising fasciitis

B. Nosocomial infections

C. Acute pyomyositis

D. Kaposi's sarcoma

Q.83

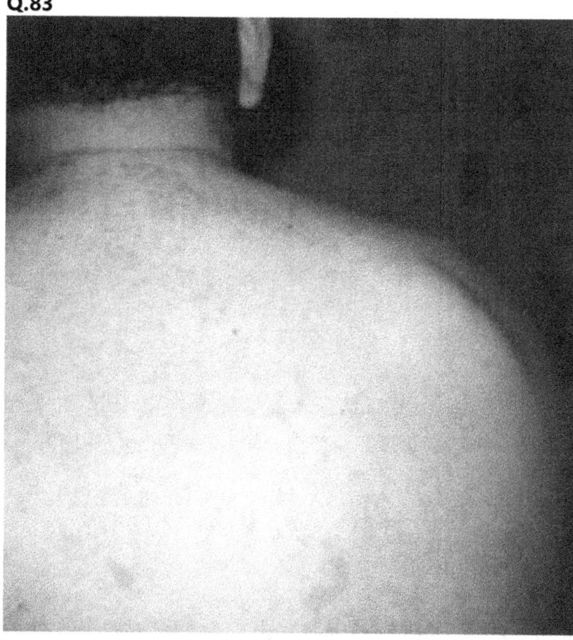

Identify the disease indicated in the picture:

A. Pedunculated lipoma

B. Diffuse lipoma

C. Submuscular lipoma

D. Neurofibroma

Q.84

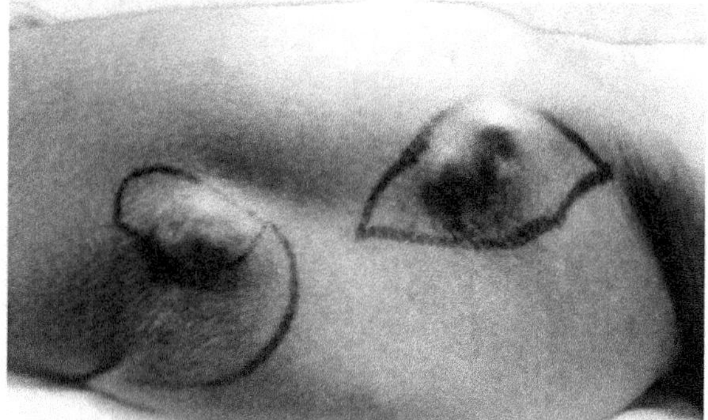

Identify the disease indicated in the picture:

A. Lymph cyst   **B.** Calcinosis cutis
C. Neuroma   **D.** Lymphangioma

Q.85 In jaundice, there is an unconjugated hyperbilirubinemia which is most likely due to:

A. Hepatitis
B. Cirrhosis
C. Obstruction of bile canaliculi
D. Both A and B

Q.86 Bilirubin is conjugated with which of the following?

A. Glycine   **B.** Glutamine
C. Acetyl CoA   **D.** Glucuronic acid

Q.87 Which of the following body secretion is maximum?

A. Salivary   **B.** Gastric   **C.** Sweat   **D.** Lacrimal

Q.88 Histamine stimulates the secretion of :

A. Gastrin by stomach
B. Pancreatic enzymes
C. HCl by stomach
D. Amylase by salivary gland

Q.89 Bile acids are derived from :

A. Bile salts   **B.** Bile pigments
C. A and B   **D.** Cholesterol

Q.90 The most important function of hydrochloric acid in the stomach is :

A. Destruction of bacteria
B. Neutralization of chyme
C. Activation of pepsinogen
D. Stimulation of pancreatic secretion

Q.91 Pancreas produces:

A. Pepsinogen   **B.** Chymotrypsinogen
C. Hydrochloric acid   **D.** All of the above

Q.92 Which of the following is not a polymer of glucose?

A. Glycogen   **B.** Cellulose
C. Amylase   **D.** Insulin

Q.93 An essential for the conversion of glucose to glycogen in liver is :

A. UTP   **B.** GTP
C. Pyruvate kinase   **D.** Guanosine

Q.94 Glycogen synthesis is increased by:

A. Cortisone   **B.** Insulin
C. GH   **D.** Epinephrine

Q.95 Major contribution towards gluconeogenesis is by:

A. Lactate   **B.** Glycerol   **C.** Ketones   **D.** Alanine

Q.96 Gluconeogenesis occurs in the liver and _______.

A. Kidney   **B.** Muscle   **C.** Heart   **D.** Fat

Q.97 The tissue with the highest glycogen content (mg/100gm) is:

A. Liver   **B.** Muscle   **C.** Kidneys   **D.** Testes

Q.98 The first product of glycogenolysis is:

A. Glucose-6-phosphate
B. Glucose1,6 diphosphate
C. Glucose-1-phosphate
D. Fructose-1-phosphate

Q.99 Which of the following substances also inhibit(s) cerebral neurons that are involved in the perception of pain?

A. Opioids   **B.** Non-opioids
C. ACh   **D.** Histamine

Q.100 Which of the following substances influences the environment of neurons of the central nervous system?

A. Cerebrospinal fluid   **B.** Peritoneal fluid
C. Pericardial fluid   **D.** Pituitary enzyme

Part B

Q.101 Which of the following extra-oral examinations includes anterior divergent, posterior divergent and straight?

A. Lateral profile   **B.** Facial divergence
C. Facial form   **D.** TMJ

Q.102 Which of the following growth assessment methods allows the action potential of the muscles of mastication to be correlated with morphological data and normalisation of muscle function in the treatment of malocclusion?

A. Superimposition   **B.** Stereo Pairs image
C. Electromyography   **D.** Vital staining

Q.103 Which of the following terms is the formation of a new response tendency?

A. Acquisition   **B.** Retention
C. Attention   **D.** Modelling

Q.104 Which of the following terms may be associated with over protection or it may be the dominant maternal trait?

A. Over protection   **B.** Over indulgence
C. Over anxiety   **D.** Over identification

Q.105 Which of the following substances has a low blood gas partition coefficient of 0.47, which allows it to remain insoluble in the blood when carried through the body?

A. Nitric oxide   **B.** Nitrous oxide
C. Glutaraldehyde   **D.** Sodium chloride

Q.106 Which of the following drugs is the most widely used oral pre-medicant, which produces dose related anxiolysis and sedation?

A. Muscarine   **B.** Midazolam
C. Diazepam   **D.** Penicillin

Q.107 Which of the following substances does the inhibition of the bacterial enzymes that are necessary for acid formation?

A. Calcium   **B.** Fluoride
C. Potassium   **D.** Chloride

Q.108 Which of the following is defined as a highly specific variable structural entity formed by sequential colonisation of microorganisms on the tooth surface, epithelium and restorations?

A. Calculus **B.** Dental plaque
C. Dental stain **D.** Dental caries

Q.109 Which of the following is the virtual free style of the brushing scene?

A. Charter's method **B.** Scrub brush method
C. Fones method **D.** Roll technique

Q.110 Which of the following is a paste of powdered tobacco, molasses and other ingredients and is primarily used to clean the tooth?

A. Pan masala **B.** Gudakhu
C. Gutka **D.** Zarda

Q.111 Which of the following is a chronic disease that affects the oral mucosa as well as the pharynx and the upper two-third of the oesophagus?

A. Erythroplakia
B. Smoker's palate
C. Oral submucous fibrosis
D. Leukoplakia

Q.112 Which of the following space maintainer appliances is usually indicated to preserve the spaces created by multiple losses of primary molars?

A. Band and loop space maintainer
B. Crown and loop space maintainer
C. Lingual arch space maintainer
D. Palatal arch

Q.113 Which of the following is the gingiva portion between the teeth?

A. Papillary gingiva **B.** Marginal gingiva
C. Attached gingiva **D.** Axial gingiva

Q.114 Which of the following terms is based on the requirement that gingival recession must occur before root surface lesions can begin?

A. Gingival index
B. Root caries index
C. Periodontal index
D. Dental fluorosis index

Q.115 Which of the following defects produces demineralisation of the mineral portion of enamel and dentin, followed by disintegration of their organic component?

A. Dental caries
B. Tooth wear
C. Traumatic injury
D. Developmental defect

Q.116 Which of the following coronal tooth surfaces is away from the anterior midline?

A. Mesial **B.** Distal **C.** Labial **D.** Buccal

Q.117 Which of the following can be invaded by bacteria to form bacterial plaque, which initiates dental caries or periodontal disease?

A. Enamel tuft **B.** Pellicle
C. Cuticle **D.** Enamel lamella

Q.118 Which of the following is the soft, translucent, tenaciously adherent mass accumulating on tooth surfaces?

A. Dental plaque **B.** Dental stain
C. Dental calculus **D.** Dental caries

Q.119 Which of the following is due to elimination of the stagnation area at the approximal surface?

A. Chronic caries **B.** Arrested caries
C. Acute caries **D.** Cavitated caries

Q.120 Which of the following imaging techniques is a non-invasive technique which creates cross sectional images of internal tooth tissues?

A. MRI
B. Computed tomography
C. Optical coherence tomography
D. Ultrasonic imaging

Q.121

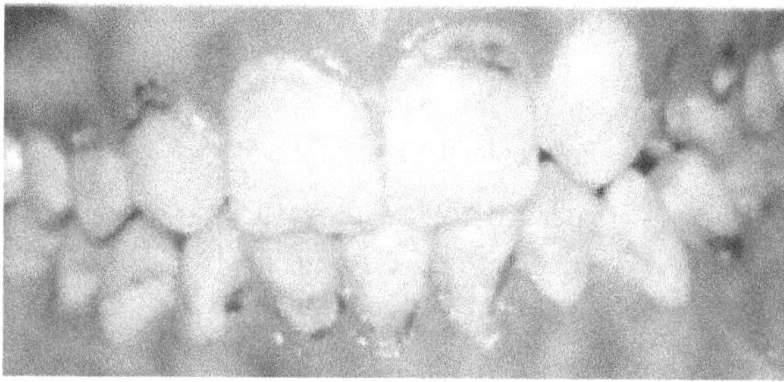

Identify the tooth caries indicated in the picture.

A. Acute caries **B.** Chronic caries
C. Arrested caries **D.** Root surface caries

Q.122

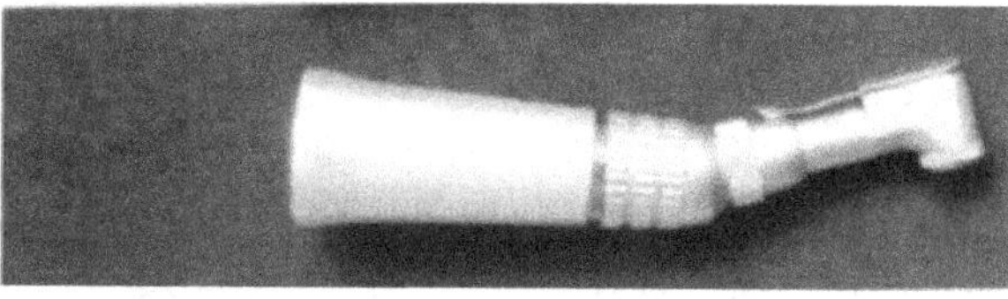

Identify the dental instrument in the picture.

A. Contra angle micromotor handpiece
B. Straight hand piece
C. Friction grip angle hand piece
D. Latch type hand piece

Q.123 Which of the following processes reduces the permeability of dentin and may serve as a pulp protective mechanism?

A. Ankylosis **B.** Sclerosis
C. Autolysis **D.** Dentinogenesis

Q.124 Which of the following cells are involved in the production and maintenance of the reticular fibres found in the cell-free zone?

A. Ameloblasts **B.** Fibroblasts
C. Odontoblasts **D.** Cementoblasts

Q.125 Which of the following cells are found in the bone periphery during periods of bone remodelling?

A. Cementoclasts **B.** Osteoclasts

C. Odontoclasts   **D.** Ameloblasts

Q.126 Which of the following defects may be seen as a chronic, low-grade defensive reaction of the alveolar bone to irritation from the root canal?

A. Granuloma   **B.** Fibroma
C. Neuroma   **D.** Chondroma

Q.127 Which of the following is a method to induce development of the root apex of an immature, pulpless tooth by formation of osteocementum or other bone like tissue?

A. Calcification   **B.** Apexification
C. Pulpotomy   **D.** Osteogenesis

Q.128

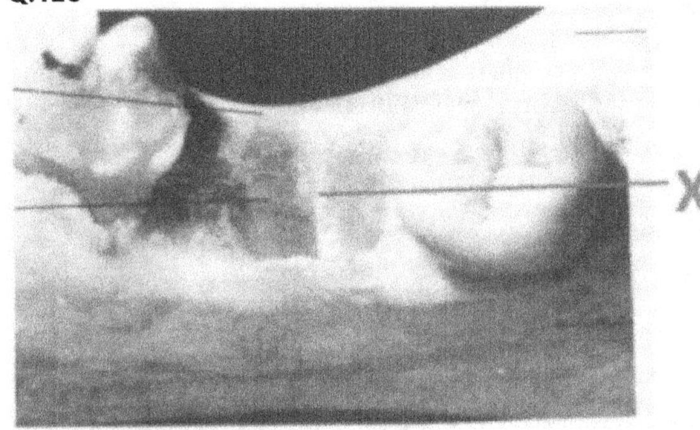

What does 'X' indicate in the image?

A. Vestibular cortical plate
B. Interradicular septum
C. Lingual cortical plate
D. Crest of the alveolar process

Q.129 ECG records the changes in the electrical potential association with ___ of the heart.

A. Relaxation   **B.** Contraction
C. Excitation   **D.** Compression

Q.130 Which of the following substances is an important measure of hepatic function?

A. Chloride
B. Alkaline phosphatase
C. Serum albumin
D. Serum bilirubin

Q.131 Which of the following scans is considered as the 'gold standard'?

A. Ultrasonography
B. Computed tomography scan
C. MRI
D. Digital scan

Q.132 Which of the following diseases is caused by an absolute or relative deficiency of insulin in the body?

A. Diabetes mellitus   **B.** Diabetes insipidus
C. Hepatic disease   **D.** Polyphagia

Q.133 Which of the following is used in conjunction with Rowe's disimpaction forceps to mobilise the maxilla?

A. Hayton William's forceps

B. Walsham's forceps
C. Asche's forceps
D. Gland holding forceps

Q.134 Which of the following is the technique of using extreme rapid cooling to freeze and thereby, destroy tissues?

A. Monopolar diathermy
B. Bipolar diathermy
C. Cryosurgery
D. Angiography

Q.135 Which of the following is used to sterilise items which do not get damaged by high temperatures, such as laboratory glassware, glass syringes and instruments?

A. Hot air oven
B. Glass beads steriliser
C. Ionising radiation
D. Non-ionising radiation

Q.136 Which of the following chemical disinfectants is used with isopropyl alcohol to enhance its efficiency for skin?

A. Chlorhexidine   **B.** Phenolics
C. Glutaraldehyde   **D.** Hypochlorite

Q.137 Which of the following viruses is the causative agent of both chickenpox and shingles, the former is the primary disease and the latter is the secondary disease, caused by the reactivation of the latent virus residing in sensory ganglia?

A. Varicella zoster virus
B. Cytomegalovirus
C. Rubella
D. Hepatitis virus

Q.138 Which of the following acts by inhibiting beta-lactamase enzymes?

A. Clavulanic acid   **B.** Lactic acid
C. Propionic acid   **D.** Hydrochloric acid

Q.139 Which of the following agents inhibits the conversion of folic to folinic acid, which is important for bacterial synthesis of DNA and RNA?

A. Erythromycin   **B.** Sulphadiazine
C. Cotrimoxazole   **D.** Quinolones

Q.140

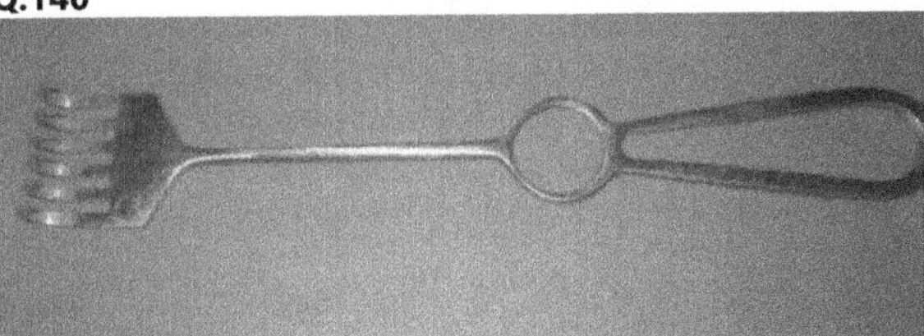

Identify the surgical instrument given in the picture.

A. Double ended Langenback's retractor
B. Condyle retractor
C. Cat's paw retractor
D. Tongue depressor

Q.141

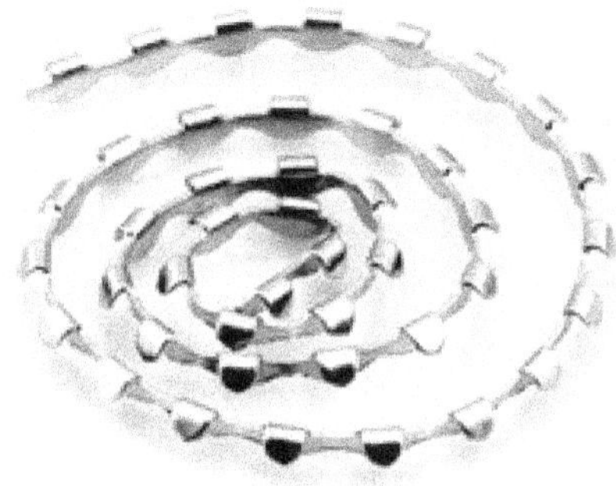

Identify the surgical instrument given in the picture.

A. Bone plates
B. Erich's arch bar
C. Wire spool
D. Nasal rasp

Q.142

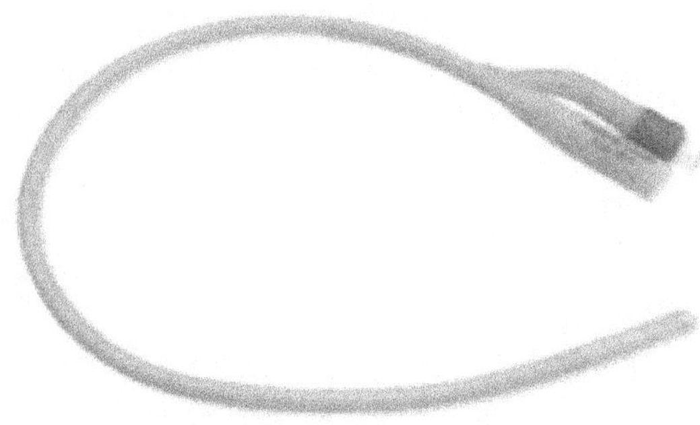

Identify the surgical instrument/tool given in the picture.

A. Infant feeding tube
B. Corrugated rubber drain tube
C. Foley's catheter
D. Ryle's tube

Q.143 Which of the following terms denotes the relation in size between two random quantities?

A. Rate
B. Ratio
C. Proportion
D. Bias

Q.144 Which of the following terms is usually used to designate subgroups of a population that, because of a common ancestral or cultural background, have a generic or environmental milieu, or both, more homogenous than that of the population at large?

A. Ethnic group
B. Bimodality
C. Prevalence
D. Selection group

Q.145 What is the guideline value of zinc in drinking water?

A. 0.001 mg/litre
B. 3 mg/litre
C. 0.5 mg/litre
D. 0.05 mg/litre

Q.146 Which of the following methods allows for the treatment of only limited quantities of waste and is therefore, commonly used only for highly infectious waste, such as microbial cultures or sharps?

A. Inertisation
B. Autoclaving
C. Safe burying
D. Encapsulation

Q.147 Which of the following substances act(s) either as a coenzyme or a catalyst for energy releasing reaction from carbohydrates, lipids and proteins?

A. Vitamins
B. Iron
C. Zinc
D. Amino acids

Q.148 Which of the following substances is water soluble and helps in maintaining the cementing material that holds the body cells together?

A. Vitamin C
B. Iron
C. Calcium
D. Protein

Q.149 Sex identification, which occurs between 3 and 6 years of age, is an important feature of:

A. Oral stage
B. Anal stage
C. Phallic stage
D. Latency stage

Q.150 Which of the following organisations is concerned with human diseases of animal origin, nutrition and rural hygiene?

A. FAO
B. UNICEF
C. CARE
D. WHO

Q.151 Which of the following days is the Anti-AIDS Day?

A. 13th October
B. 1st December
C. 11th December
D. 2nd October

Q.152 Which of the following is a branch of statistics concerned with mathematical facts and data relating to biological events?

A. Epidemiology
B. Biostatistics
C. Social Science
D. Bimodality

Q.153 Which of the following substances is non-cariogenic or even anti-cariogenic?

A. Fructose
B. Sucrose
C. Xylitol
D. Galactose

Q.154 Which of the following can also be naturally acquired when antibodies are being transferred from mother to foetus during pregnancy, to help protect the foetus before and shortly after birth?

A. Acquired immunity
B. Passive immunisation
C. Artificial passive immunisation
D. Active immunisation

Q.155 Which of the following tests measures the milligrams of powdered enamel dissolved in 4 hours by acid formed when the patient's saliva is mixed with glucose and powdered enamel?

A. ORA test
B. Fosdick calcium dissolution test
C. Streptococcus mutans screening test
D. Alban test

Q.156 Which of the following layers consists of glycoproteins, proline-rich proteins, phosphoproteins, histidine rich proteins and enzymes?

A. Pellicle   **B.** Cuticle   **C.** Calculus   **D.** Biofilm

Q.157 Which of the following cells have been identified as tactile preceptors?

A. Mast cells   **B.** Merkel cells
C. Ameloblasts   **D.** Odontoblasts

Q.158 Which of the following substances can accumulate intracellularly when it is not completely degraded by any of the glycolytic pathways?

A. Glycogen   **B.** Glucose
C. Glucagon   **D.** Galactose

Q.159 Which of the following is a product of fibroblasts and cementoblasts and is found in the cervical third of roots in humans, but may extend farther apically?

A. Acellular a fibrillar cementum
B. Acellular extrinsic fibre cementum
C. Cellular mixed stratified cementum
D. Intermediate cementum

Q.160 Which of the following processes occurs in teeth with cemental resorption, which suggests that it may represent a form of abnormal repair?

A. Cementosis   **B.** Ankylosis
C. Autolysis   **D.** Calcification

Q.161 Which of the following is usually seen as an acute lesion that responds well to antimicrobial therapy combined with professional plaque and calculus removal and improved oral hygiene?

A. Necrotizing ulcerative gingivitis
B. Necrotizing ulcerative periodontitis
C. Endodontic periodontal lesion
D. Periodontal endodontic lesion

Q.162 Which of the following diseases is an infectious disease associated with a group of mainly gram-negative bacteria?

A. Gingivitis   **B.** Periodontitis
C. Aplasia   **D.** Atresia

Q.163 Which of the following micro-organisms induces apoptotic cell death?

A. A. actinomycetemcomitans
B. Tannerella forsythia
C. Porphyromonas gingivalis
D. Prevotella intermedia

Q.164 Which of the following processes may be accompanied by alterations in the bacterial content and staining qualities of the plaque?

A. Apoptosis   **B.** Calcification
C. Demineralisation   **D.** Ankylosis

Q.165 Which of the following enzymes possesses enzyme dependent bactericidal activity and enzyme independent bactericidal and fungicidal activity?

A. Lysozyme   **B.** Lactoferrin
C. H_2O_2 **D.** Lactase

Q.166 Which of the following diseases is characterized primarily as involving alternative pathway activation of complement, with C_3 and C_3b cleavage observed in gingival fluids?

A. Acute periodontitis
B. Chronic periodontitis
C. Alveolectomy
D. Gingivitis

Q.167 Which of the following is/are exquisitely sensitive to the LPs produced by specific pathogens?

A. Macrophages   **B.** Microphages
C. Aplasia   **D.** Gingivitis

Q.168 Which of the following substances play a central role in the classic complications of diabetes and may play a significant role in the progression of periodontal disease as well?

A. Accumulated glycation ends
B. G proteins
C. Lysozymes
D. Lactoferrins

Q.169 Which of the following produces generalized demineralization of the skeleton, increased osteoclasts with the proliferation of the connective tissue in the enlarged marrow spaces, and formation of bone cysts and giant cell tumours?

A. Parathyroid hypersecretion
B. Parathyroid hyposecretion
C. Corticosteroid hormoneshyper secretion
D. Lysozymes hypersecretion

Q.170 Which of the following diseases leads to bleeding tendency, which can occur in any tissue but in particular, affects the oral cavity, especially the gingival sulcus?

A. Leukopenia   **B.** Thrombocytopenia
C. Leukemia   **D.** Dysplasia

Q.171 Which of the following diseases is a childhood disease characterized by mild systemic symptoms and a generalized intensely pruritic eruption of maculopapular lesions that rapidly develop into vesicles on an erythematosus base?

A. Small pox   **B.** Chicken pox
C. Herpangina   **D.** Hepatitis

Q.172 Which of the following diseases was classically described as a triad of symptoms including recurring oral ulcers, recurring genital ulcers and eye lesions?

A. Bowen's disease   **B.** Behcet's syndrome
C. Pemphigus   **D.** Dermatoses

Q.173 Which of the following disease's lesion is characteristically large and deep, causing denudation of underlying bone?

A. Mucormycosis   **B.** Blastomycosis
C. Linear IgA disease   **D.** Pemphigoid

Q.174 Which of the following diseases can be attributed to the darker coloration of the mucosa in black persons, rendering the alteration more visible?

A. Leukoedema
B. White sponge nevus
C. Frictional keratosis
D. Linea alba

Q.175 Which of the following diseases is a prototypical example of an immunologically mediated inflammatory condition that causes multi-organ damage?

A. Systemic lupus erythematosus
B. Fordyces granules
C. Hairy tongue
D. Retinoids

Q.176 Which of the following diseases is a clinical term describing an abnormal coating on the dorsal surface of the tongue?

A. Hairy tongue
B. Oral lichen planus
C. Oral submucous fibrosis
D. Lichenoid reactions

Q.177 Which of the following disease's lesions represent multiple microaneurysms owing to a weakening defect in the adventitial coat of venules?

A. Hereditary hemorrhagic telangiectasia
B. Kaposi's sarcoma
C. Angiosarcoma
D. Malignant melanoma

Q.178 Which of the following tumors arising in the carotid and aortic bodies may produce neck masses; they are of a differential cell derivation and are more appropriately referred to as chemodectomas or paragangliomas?

A. Lymphangiomas
B. Glomus tumor
C. Hamartomas
D. Hemangioma

Q.179 Which of the following tumors is an uncommon, slow-growing and aggressive lesion?

A. Central odontogenic fibroma
B. Cementoma
C. Pindborg tumor
D. Compound odontoma

Q.180 Which of the following diseases is the most common malignancy of bone?

A. Osteoma sarcoma
B. Osteogenic sarcoma
C. Osteofibroma
D. Osteoedema

Q.181 Which of the following is the radiographic visualization of the salivary gland following retrograde instillation of soluble contrast material into the duct?

A. Sialography
B. Radiography
C. Angiography
D. Computed tomography

Q.182 Which of the following is a benign self limiting reactive inflammatory disorder of the salivary tissue?

A. Necrotizing sialometaplasia
B. Mucoceles
C. Ranulas
D. Diverticuli

Q.183 Which of the following is an esthetic concern for some patients, and surgery has been performed for cosmetic reasons?

A. Gingival enlargement
B. Benign parotid enlargement
C. Sialadenitis
D. Anorexia nervosa

Q.184

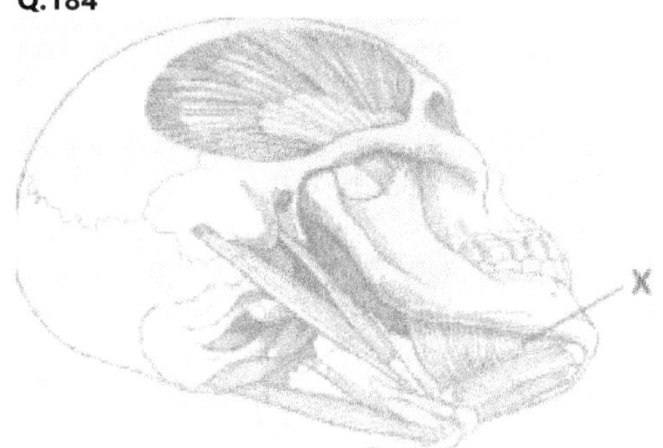

This is the picture of the digastric muscle which is a paired muscle with two bellies. What does 'X' indicate?

A. Temporalis muscle
B. Mylohyoid muscle
C. Digastric muscle
D. Stylohyoid muscle

Q.185

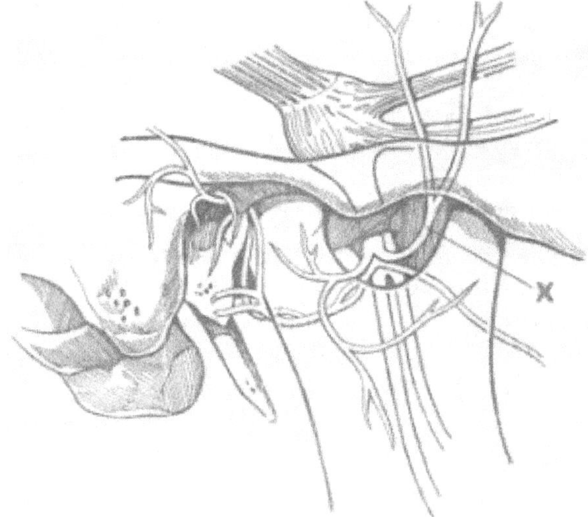

This is the picture of the branches of the auriculotemporal nerve supply sensory innervation of the TMJ. What does 'X' indicate?

A. Trigeminal ganglion
B. Deep temporal ganglion
C. Buccal nerve
D. Lingual nerve

Q.186 Which of the following is a specialised tissue of mesodermal origin?

A. Tooth
B. Bone
C. Nail
D. Hair

Q.187 Which of the following cells are associated with the implantation of the embryo and the formation of the placenta?

A. Trophoblasts
B. Blastocysts
C. Odontoblasts
D. Fibroblasts

Q.188 Which of the following sphenoid bones ossifies endochondrally from a secondary cartilage in the hamular process?

A. Greater wing
B. Lateral pterygoid plate
C. Medial pterygoid plate
D. Anterior part of the body of sphenoid

Q.189 Which of the following forms the boundary between the ramus and the body?

A. Lingual tuberosity
B. Alveolar process
C. Condyle
D. Condyle process

Q.190 Which of the following describes a tooth that has moved around its long axis so that distal aspect is more lingually placed?

A. Disto-lingual rotation
B. Mesio-lingual rotation
C. Transposition
D. Supra occlusion

Q.191 Which of the following is a condition where there is no vertical overlap between upper and lower teeth?

A. Cross bite
B. Deep bite
C. Open bite
D. Over jet

Q.192 Which of the following are the transverse planes that are usually a result of narrowing or widening of the jaws?

A. Skeletal malocclusions
B. Vertical plane malocclusions
C. Sagittal plane malocclusions
D. Interarch malocclusions

Q.193 Which of the following terms is synonymous with Angle's class I malocclusion?

A. Neutrocclusion
B. Distocclusion
C. Mesiocclusion
D. Buccal occlusion

Q.194 Which of the following infections during pregnancy is believed to cause widespread congenital malformations in the child?

A. Maternal congenital syphilis
B. Maternal rubella infection
C. Cleidocranial dysostosis
D. Cerebral palsy

Q.195 Which of the following thyroid defects increases blood calcium?

A. Hypothyroidism
B. Hyperthyroidism
C. Hypoparathyroidism
D. Hyperparathyroidism

Q.196 Which of the following is a concavity that is seen below the lower lip?

A. Mentolabial sulcus
B. Nasal contour
C. Nostril
D. Competent lip

Q.197 Which of the following is the intersection of the lower border of the nose and the outer contour of the upper lip?

A. Subnasale
B. Pronasale
C. Labrale superius
D. Glabella

Q.198

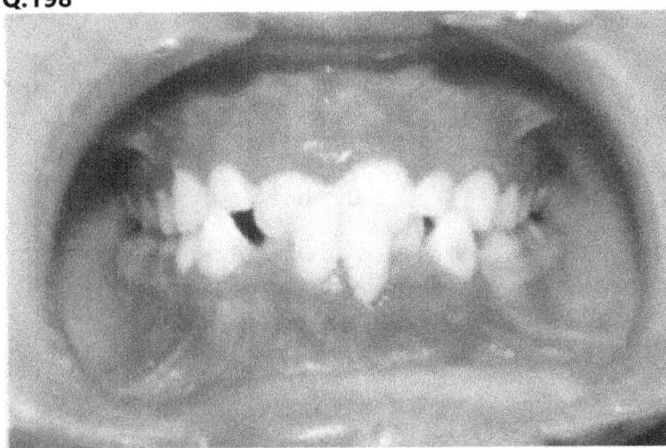

Identify the occlusion in the given picture.

A. Ideal occlusion
B. Balanced occlusion
C. Traumatic occlusion
D. Functional occlusion

Q.199

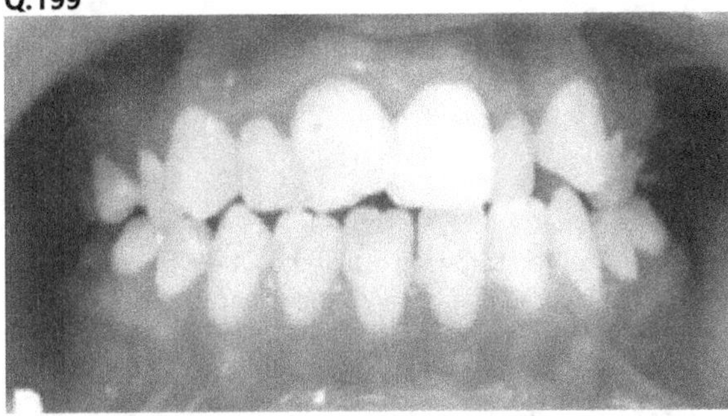

Identify the inclination of the tooth in the given picture.

A. Mesial inclination of the upper right central incisor
B. Mesial inclination of the upper lateral incisor
C. Mesial inclination of the upper left central and lateral incisors
D. Mesial inclination of the upper left central incisor

Q.200 Which of the following diseases is a form of localized scleroderma supported by its concurrence with scleroderma?

A. Hemifacial atrophy
B. Micrognathia
C. Facial hemihypertrophy
D. Macrognathia

Q.201 Which of the following defects is also called foliate tonsil and referring to the vestigial foliate papilla?

A. Lymphoid hamartoma
B. Reactive lymphoid aggregate
C. Lingual thyroid nodule
D. Lingual varices

Q.202 Which of the following cysts is an unusual form of slightly aberrant salivary gland tissue wherein a developmental inclusion of glandular tissue is found within or more commonly, adjacent to the lingual surface of the body of the mandible within a deep and well- circumscribed depressions?

A. Stafne bone cyst   **B.** Talon cusp
C. Median palatal cyst   **D.** Nasopalatine cyst

Q.203 Which of the following defects of the permanent dentition as a whole may be associated with the same local or systemic conditions causing the retardation of deciduous tooth eruption?

A. Delayed eruption   **B.** Multiple eruption
C. Erosion   **D.** Abfraction

Q.204 Which of the following is an exophytic growth made up of numerous, small finger like projections which result in a lesion with a roughened, verrucous or 'cauliflower like' surface?

A. Papilloma   **B.** Acanthoma
C. Oral nevi   **D.** Leukoplakia

Q.205 Which of the following disease's triad of lesions is comparable to the multifocal candidiasis described in western literature?

A. Palatal erythema
B. Papillary atrophy
C. Oral submucous fibrosis
D. Basal cell carcinoma

Q.206 Which of the following diseases is a common lesion of the tongue which has been observed many times to be associated with tongue cancer?

A. Leukoplakia   **B.** Leukoplasis
C. Dysplasia   **D.** Erythroplakia

Q.207 In which of the following diseases, is there a proliferation of surface dysplastic epithelium into the connective tissue as in the typical epidermoid carcinoma?

A. Basaloid squamous cell carcinoma
B. Adenosquamous carcinoma
C. Undifferentiated carcinoma
D. Adenoid squamous cell carcinoma

Q.208 Which of the following diseases is characterized by a poorly delineated, infiltrating cellular proliferation of mature spindle cells arranged in streaming and interlacing fascicles?

A. Giant cell fibroma   **B.** Myofibroma
C. Fibromatosis   **D.** Myeloma

Q.209 Which of the following cysts is similar to and probably related to other reactive non-neoplastic processes, including giant cell reparative granuloma of the jaws, traumatic reactions in periosteum and bone and even florid heterotopic ossification?

A. Aneurysmal bone cyst
B. Giant cell tumor of bone
C. Lipoma
D. Lipoblastoma

Q.210 Which of the following tumors is encapsulated and consists essentially of two basic and characteristic components: a vascular network and a connective tissue stroma?

A. Nasopharyngeal angiofibroma
B. Encephalotrigeminal hemangiomatosis
C. Myxoma
D. Chondroma

Q.211 Which of the following osteoma does not share the markedly limited growth potential of the average osteoid osteoma?

A. Benign osteoblastoma
B. Torus palatinus
C. Osteoid osteoma
D. Chondro-osteoma

Q.212 Which of the following tumors was once considered to be one of the most common of the malignant soft tissue neoplasms?

A. Infantile fibrosarcoma
B. Chondroblastoma
C. Chondroma
D. Nodular fasciitis

Q.213 Which of the following diseases is characterised by a sub-mucosal, cellular aggregation of spindle shaped, fibroblastic cells with relatively pale, oval nuclei; scattered rounded histiocytic cells?

A. Benign Fibrous histiocytoma
B. Synovial sarcoma
C. Liposarcoma
D. Hemangioma

Q.214 Which of the following diseases follows a fulminant course with visceral involvement and minimal skin or mucous membrane involvement?

A. Lymphadenopathic kaposi's sarcoma
B. Hemorrhagic sarcoma
C. Lipoma
D. Lymphoedema

Q.215 Which of the following is a removable partial prosthesis and is completely supported by the implant and the tooth?

A. RP-1   **B.** RP-2   **C.** RP-3   **D.** RP-4

Q.216 Which of the following is the result of both an increased rate and depth of respiration and may be preceded by frequent sighs, such as seen in an anxious patient?

A. Hypersensitivity   **B.** Hyperventilation
C. Hyperthyroidism   **D.** Hypertension

Q.217 When _______ values in the blood are elevated, the complete blood count is evaluated for blood abnormalities.

A. alkaline phosphatase
B. lactic dehydrogenase
C. creatinine
D. bilirubin

Q.218 Which of the following lies in the midline on the palatal aspect of the maxillary central incisors?

A. Incisive foramen   **B.** Apical foramen
C. Maxillary sinus   **D.** Tuberosity

Q.219 Which of the following terms does not represent a contraindication for implants, but does influence treatment planning?
A. Cherubism   **B.** Bruxism
C. Ankylosis   **D.** Autolysis

Q.220 Primordial prevention, a new concept receiving special attention in the prevention of:
A. Chronic disease   **B.** Epidemics
C. Pandemics   **D.** Acute disease

Q.221 Since class III removable partial dentures do not tend to move or rotate in function, there is no need for:
A. Direct retention   **B.** Indirect retention
C. Rocking forces   **D.** Indirect retainers

Q.222 A class II removable partial denture must embody features of:
A. Class III and class I designs
B. Class I and class IV designs
C. Class III and class IV designs
D. Class III, class I, class IV designs

Q.223 Which of the following theories is/are similar to "L–Beam" principle used in building construction?
A. Bending and twisting forces of palatal bar theory
B. Bending and twisting forces of palatal strap theory
C. Bending and twisting forces of horseshoe theory
D. All of the above

Q.224 A patient may complain of excessive palatal coverage due to:
A. Improper positioning of the strap borders
B. Proper positioning of the strap borders
C. Improper positioning of the palatal borders
D. None of the above

Q.225 A clasp assembly must include a rigid component that resists lateral movement of the affected tooth. The component is known as a/an:
A. Encirclement element
B. Support element
C. Stability element
D. Reciprocation element

Q.226 _____ is the characteristic of a clasp assembly that prevents movement of an abutment away from the associated clasp assembly. .
A. Encirclement
B. Support
C. Stability
D. Reciprocation element

Q.227 Which of the following offer(s) less resistance to displacement in the horizontal plane?
A. Rigid clasp   **B.** Flexible clasp
C. Retentive clasp   **D.** All of the above

Q.228 The flexibility of the clasp increases, the vertical and lateral stresses transmitted to the residual ridge are:
A. Decreased   **B.** Increased
C. None of the above   **D.** Either (A) or (B)

Q.229 Which of the following is present in the powder of the acrylic resin?
A. Methyl methacrylate
B. Benzoyl peroxide
C. Hydroquinone
D. D-methyl paratolouidine

Q.230 Cross linking in denture base resin is contributed by__________?
A. Glycol dimethacrylate
B. Benzoyl peroxide
C. N-para toluidine
D. Methyl methacrylate

Q.231 Which of the following inhibitor accelerator system uses light activation composite?
A. Diketone-amine
B. Organic acid-metal oxide
C. Organic acid-peroxide
D. Peroxide-amine

Q.232 Which of the following is an example of a composite material?
A. A filled resin   **B.** Colloidal silica
C. Gold alloy   **D.** Wax

Q.233 Benzoin methyl ether in a polymer indicates that they may be cured in the presence of____________?
A. UV light   **B.** Visible light
C. Infrared light   **D.** Diketone

Q.234 Glycosphingolipid is made up of:
A. Glucose   **B.** Glycerol
C. Thromboxane A2   **D.** Protein

Q.235 Co-efficient of thermal expansion is highest for________.
A. Amalgam   **B.** Silicate cement
C. Gold alloy   **D.** Acrylic resin

Q.236 Which of the following absorbs maximum amount of water?
A. Microfilled resin   **B.** Macrofilled resin
C. Hybrid   **D.** Light cure activated

Q.237 The commonly used laser for curing composite resin is__________.
A. Nd:YAG   **B.** CO_2 **C.** ER:YAG   **D.** Argon

Q.238 The advantage of unfilled methyl methacrylate is that__________?
A. It can be finished smoothly
B. It has a low degree of flow
C. It's non-irritation to pulp
D. It's wear resistant is high

Q.239 Ductility of a material is a measure of it's____________.

A. Grain elongation

B. Anealing

C. Cold working

D. Work hardening

Q.240 Which of the following hardness test is a micro hardness test?

A. Brinnel

B. Knoop

C. Shore-A

D. Rockwell

// Smart Answer Sheet //

Correct — Indicates percentage of students who answered questions correctly.

Skipped — Indicates percentage of students who skipped questions.

Q.	Ans.	Correct	Skipped	Q.	Ans.	Correct	Skipped	Q.	Ans.	Correct	Skipped	Q.	Ans.	Correct	Skipped	Q.	Ans.	Correct	Skipped
1	B	23.26 %	4.65 %	17	A	37.21 %	55.81 %	33	B	16.28 %	55.81 %	49	D	9.3 %	58.14 %	65	B	9.3 %	58.14 %
2	C	34.88 %	55.82 %	18	A	16.28 %	58.14 %	34	B	20.93 %	55.81 %	50	C	23.26 %	58.14 %	66	B	20.93 %	58.14 %
3	A	20.93 %	58.14 %	19	A	9.3 %	58.14 %	35	A	34.88 %	58.14 %	51	B	25.58 %	58.14 %	67	B	34.88 %	58.14 %
4	C	20.93 %	55.81 %	20	C	20.93 %	53.49 %	36	B	13.95 %	58.14 %	52	B	32.56 %	55.81 %	68	A	34.88 %	58.14 %
5	A	11.63 %	58.14 %	21	B	20.93 %	55.81 %	37	B	2.33 %	55.81 %	53	B	23.26 %	55.81 %	69	C	25.58 %	58.14 %
6	A	11.63 %	58.14 %	22	A	13.95 %	55.82 %	38	A	23.26 %	58.14 %	54	B	34.88 %	58.14 %	70	B	9.3 %	58.14 %
7	A	18.6 %	58.14 %	23	B	13.95 %	58.14 %	39	A	23.26 %	58.14 %	55	A	39.53 %	58.14 %	71	B	13.95 %	58.14 %
8	B	11.63 %	58.14 %	24	B	16.28 %	55.81 %	40	B	16.28 %	58.14 %	56	B	34.88 %	58.14 %	72	A	37.21 %	55.81 %
9	A	16.28 %	58.14 %	25	C	4.65 %	58.14 %	41	A	11.63 %	58.14 %	57	A	23.26 %	58.14 %	73	A	13.95 %	55.82 %
10	D	13.95 %	58.14 %	26	B	11.63 %	58.14 %	42	A	32.56 %	55.81 %	58	B	25.58 %	58.14 %	74	B	11.63 %	58.14 %
11	A	18.6 %	58.14 %	27	C	9.3 %	58.14 %	43	B	25.58 %	58.14 %	59	B	30.23 %	58.14 %	75	A	9.3 %	58.14 %
12	D	18.6 %	58.14 %	28	B	30.23 %	55.82 %	44	B	25.58 %	55.82 %	60	A	27.91 %	58.14 %	76	A	39.53 %	58.14 %
13	D	9.3 %	58.14 %	29	B	20.93 %	58.14 %	45	B	34.88 %	58.14 %	61	C	16.28 %	55.81 %	77	C	23.26 %	58.14 %
14	D	16.28 %	55.81 %	30	C	30.23 %	55.82 %	46	B	13.95 %	55.82 %	62	C	20.93 %	58.14 %	78	B	6.98 %	58.14 %
15	A	18.6 %	58.14 %	31	C	18.6 %	58.14 %	47	B	11.63 %	58.14 %	63	A	18.6 %	58.14 %	79	A	13.95 %	58.14 %
16	B	30.23 %	58.14 %	32	A	16.28 %	58.14 %	48	C	23.26 %	58.14 %	64	C	16.28 %	58.14 %	80	A	25.58 %	55.82 %

Q.	Ans.	Correct / Skipped	Q.	Ans.	Correct / Skipped	Q.	Ans.	Correct / Skipped	Q.	Ans.	Correct / Skipped	Q.	Ans.	Correct / Skipped
81	A	18.6 % / 55.82 %	97	A	30.23 % / 58.14 %	113	A	30.23 % / 62.79 %	129	B	13.95 % / 62.79 %	145	B	9.3 % / 62.79 %
82	A	39.53 % / 55.82 %	98	C	11.63 % / 58.14 %	114	B	13.95 % / 62.79 %	130	D	11.63 % / 62.79 %	146	B	6.98 % / 62.79 %
83	B	16.28 % / 58.14 %	99	A	34.88 % / 58.14 %	115	A	32.56 % / 62.79 %	131	B	13.95 % / 62.79 %	147	A	18.6 % / 62.8 %
84	B	16.28 % / 58.14 %	100	A	39.53 % / 58.14 %	116	B	23.26 % / 62.79 %	132	A	25.58 % / 62.79 %	148	A	23.26 % / 62.79 %
85	D	27.91 % / 58.14 %	101	B	23.26 % / 62.79 %	117	B	18.6 % / 62.8 %	133	A	23.26 % / 62.79 %	149	C	18.6 % / 62.8 %
86	D	11.63 % / 58.14 %	102	C	16.28 % / 62.79 %	118	A	34.88 % / 62.79 %	134	C	30.23 % / 62.79 %	150	A	9.3 % / 62.79 %
87	B	20.93 % / 58.14 %	103	A	23.26 % / 62.79 %	119	B	20.93 % / 62.79 %	135	A	18.6 % / 62.8 %	151	B	20.93 % / 62.79 %
88	C	11.63 % / 58.14 %	104	B	18.6 % / 62.8 %	120	C	6.98 % / 58.14 %	136	A	18.6 % / 62.8 %	152	B	32.56 % / 62.79 %
89	D	20.93 % / 58.14 %	105	B	20.93 % / 62.79 %	121	A	6.98 % / 62.79 %	137	A	30.23 % / 62.79 %	153	C	30.23 % / 62.79 %
90	A	11.63 % / 58.14 %	106	B	23.26 % / 62.79 %	122	A	32.56 % / 62.79 %	138	A	30.23 % / 62.79 %	154	C	4.65 % / 62.79 %
91	B	20.93 % / 58.14 %	107	B	20.93 % / 62.79 %	123	B	20.93 % / 62.79 %	139	C	4.65 % / 62.79 %	155	B	13.95 % / 62.79 %
92	D	25.58 % / 58.14 %	108	B	20.93 % / 62.79 %	124	B	18.6 % / 62.8 %	140	C	32.56 % / 62.79 %	156	A	20.93 % / 62.79 %
93	A	16.28 % / 58.14 %	109	B	18.6 % / 62.8 %	125	B	23.26 % / 62.79 %	141	B	20.93 % / 62.79 %	157	B	30.23 % / 62.79 %
94	B	32.56 % / 55.81 %	110	B	20.93 % / 62.79 %	126	A	27.91 % / 62.79 %	142	C	30.23 % / 62.79 %	158	A	20.93 % / 62.79 %
95	A	18.6 % / 58.14 %	111	C	20.93 % / 62.79 %	127	B	27.91 % / 62.79 %	143	B	18.6 % / 62.8 %	159	B	6.98 % / 62.79 %
96	A	23.26 % / 58.14 %	112	C	20.93 % / 62.79 %	128	B	25.58 % / 62.79 %	144	A	27.91 % / 62.79 %	160	B	20.93 % / 62.79 %

Q.	Ans.	Correct / Skipped	Q.	Ans.	Correct / Skipped	Q.	Ans.	Correct / Skipped	Q.	Ans.	Correct / Skipped	Q.	Ans.	Correct / Skipped
161	A	23.26 % / 62.79 %	177	A	16.28 % / 62.79 %	193	A	23.26 % / 62.79 %	209	A	20.93 % / 62.79 %	225	D	6.98 % / 62.79 %
162	B	25.58 % / 62.79 %	178	B	11.63 % / 62.79 %	194	B	13.95 % / 62.79 %	210	A	13.95 % / 62.79 %	226	A	18.6 % / 62.8 %
163	B	6.98 % / 62.79 %	179	A	13.95 % / 62.79 %	195	D	23.26 % / 62.79 %	211	A	9.3 % / 62.79 %	227	B	11.63 % / 62.79 %
164	B	13.95 % / 62.79 %	180	B	20.93 % / 62.79 %	196	A	34.88 % / 62.79 %	212	A	13.95 % / 62.79 %	228	B	9.3 % / 62.79 %
165	A	20.93 % / 62.79 %	181	A	34.88 % / 62.79 %	197	A	25.58 % / 62.79 %	213	A	23.26 % / 62.79 %	229	A	27.91 % / 62.79 %
166	B	13.95 % / 62.79 %	182	A	23.26 % / 62.79 %	198	C	27.91 % / 62.79 %	214	A	23.26 % / 62.79 %	230	A	13.95 % / 62.79 %
167	A	20.93 % / 62.79 %	183	B	4.65 % / 62.79 %	199	A	30.23 % / 62.79 %	215	D	11.63 % / 62.79 %	231	A	23.26 % / 62.79 %
168	A	13.95 % / 62.79 %	184	B	18.6 % / 62.8 %	200	A	20.93 % / 62.79 %	216	B	25.58 % / 62.79 %	232	A	32.56 % / 62.79 %
169	A	20.93 % / 62.79 %	185	B	13.95 % / 62.79 %	201	B	4.65 % / 62.79 %	217	B	6.98 % / 62.79 %	233	A	20.93 % / 62.79 %
170	B	23.26 % / 62.79 %	186	B	16.28 % / 62.79 %	202	A	30.23 % / 62.79 %	218	A	30.23 % / 62.79 %	234	A	9.3 % / 62.79 %
171	B	20.93 % / 62.79 %	187	A	18.6 % / 62.8 %	203	A	32.56 % / 62.79 %	219	B	18.6 % / 62.8 %	235	D	11.63 % / 62.79 %
172	B	23.26 % / 62.79 %	188	C	4.65 % / 62.79 %	204	A	25.58 % / 62.79 %	220	A	16.28 % / 62.79 %	236	A	23.26 % / 62.79 %
173	A	20.93 % / 62.79 %	189	A	16.28 % / 62.79 %	205	A	9.3 % / 62.79 %	221	B	11.63 % / 62.79 %	237	D	16.28 % / 62.79 %
174	A	4.65 % / 62.79 %	190	A	27.91 % / 62.79 %	206	A	20.93 % / 62.79 %	222	A	13.95 % / 62.79 %	238	A	18.6 % / 62.8 %
175	A	34.88 % / 62.79 %	191	C	23.26 % / 62.79 %	207	D	4.65 % / 62.79 %	223	B	4.65 % / 62.79 %	239	A	25.58 % / 62.79 %
176	A	32.56 % / 62.79 %	192	A	11.63 % / 62.79 %	208	C	4.65 % / 62.79 %	224	A	16.28 % / 62.79 %	240	B	23.26 % / 62.79 %

Performance Analysis

Avg. Score (%)	21.98%
Toppers Score (%)	86.46%
Your Score	

Part A

Q.1 Which of the following parts of the jaw forms and supports the sockets of the teeth?

A. Periodontal ligament

B. Alveolar bone

C. Temporo-mandibular joint

D. Maxillary sinus

Q.2 The median strip of _____ extending throughout the length of the embryo induces the neural plate formation within the overlying ectoderm.

A. ectodermal cells

B. endodermal cells

C. mesodermal cells

D. mesenchymal cells

Q.3 Which of the following glands develop as a result of inductive interactions between the ventral forebrain and oral ectoderm and is derived in part from both tissues?

A. Thyroid glands

B. Pituitary glands

C. Thymus glands

D. Nasopharyngeal glands

Q.4 Most of the connective tissue cells underlying the oral ectoderm are of _________ in origin.

A. neural crest

B. neural palate

C. mesenchymal cells

D. endodermal cells

Q.5 At about 7th week, the primary epithelial band divides into an inner process called:

A. Dental lamina

B. Vestibular lamina

C. Primary lamina

D. Dental papilla

Q.6 The junction between inner and outer enamel epithelium is called _____ and it is an area of intense mitotic activity.

A. cranial loop

B. cervical loop

C. dental sac

D. dental papilla

Q.7 In dental papilla, the basement membrane that separates the enamel organ and the dental papilla just prior to dentin formation is called:

A. Membrane preformativa

B. Dental lamina

C. Enamel cord

D. Enamel crest

Q.8 Which of the following genes is a potent inducer of p21, a cyclin dependent kinase inhibitor in the enamel knot?

A. Bmp-4   **B.** SHH   **C.** Fgh-4   **D.** Bmp-2

Q.9 _______ disturbances affect the size or form of the crown of teeth if such effects occur during morpho-differentiation, that is, in utero or in the first year of life.

A. Exocrine

B. Endocrine

C. Parotid

D. Thyroid

Q.10 _______ normally have a clear crystalline appearance, permitting light to pass through them.

A. Enamel rods

B. Enamel sheaths

C. Enamel cords

D. Enamel brochs

Q.11 In Hunter-Schreger Bands, the prisms which are cut longitudinally to produce the dark bands are called___________.

A. diazones

B. parazones

C. patrix

D. matrix

Q.12 Odontoblast processes pass across the dentino-enamel junction into the enamel. Since many are thickened at their end, they have been termed:

A. Enamel spindles

B. Enamel brochs

C. Enamel cords

D. Enamel sheaths

Q.13 Which of the following is the major component of enamel matrix proteins?

A. Ameloblasts

B. Amelogenin

C. Odontoblasts

D. Fibrinogen

Q.14 Which of the following is/are visible only by the electron microscope?

A. Ameloblasts

B. Dentin

C. Collagen fibres

D. Cementum

Q.15 Which of the following is the induction of a developmental abnormality in a fetus by a drug taken during the early stages of pregnancy?

A. Altered pharmacokinetics

B. Teratogenesis

C. Later stages of pregnancy

D. Breastfeeding

Q.16 Which of the following is a membrane-bound compartment found in all cells, with the exception of the erythrocytes and platelets?

A. Mitochondria

B. Nucleus

C. Plasma

D. Golgi bodies

Q.17 Which of the following is a phospholipid bi-layer, with hydrophilic surfaces and a hydrophobic core?

A. Cell membrane

B. Cytoskeleton

C. Endodermis

D. Cell wall

Q.18 Sweat also contains _______, an enzyme that destroys the structural integrity of bacterial cell walls.

A. lysozyme

B. lycine

C. erythromycin

D. leucocyte

Q.19 Which of the following is/are produced by the cells involved in innate and adaptive immune responses and by stromal tissue?

A. Lysozyme

B. Cytokines

C. Mast cells   **D.** Basophils

Q.20 Which of the following is the result of the rapid and complex interplay between the cells and soluble molecules of the innate immune system?

A. Acute inflammation

B. Acute phase proteins

C. Resolution of inflammation

D. Sepsis and septic shock

Q.21 Which of the following stabilise(s) the mast cells membrane, inhibiting release of vasoactive mediators?

A. Corticosteroids

B. Sodium cromoglycate

C. Omalizumab

D. Epinephrine

Q.22 Which vitamin is also known as retinol?

A. Vitamin B   **B.** Vitamin A

C. Vitamin C   **D.** Vitamin D

Q.23 Which of the following is an essential component of many enzymes, including carbonic anhydrase, alcohol dehydrogenase, and alkaline phosphatase?

A. Zinc   **B.** Selenium

C. Fluoride   **D.** Iodine

Q.24 In obstructive jaundice, dietary _____ is not absorbed and it is essential to administer the vitamin in parenteral from before surgery.

A. vitamin A   **B.** vitamin B

C. vitamin C   **D.** vitamin K

Q.25 Which of the following has much better oral absorption than ampicillin?

A. Penicillin   **B.** Amoxicillin

C. Lysozyme   **D.** Ureido-penicillins

Q.26 Which of the following is a cyclic lipopeptide that has bactericidal activity against Gram-positive organisms but no activity against Gram-negatives?

A. Daptomycin   **B.** Fusidic acid

C. Nitrofurantoin   **D.** Linezolid

Q.27

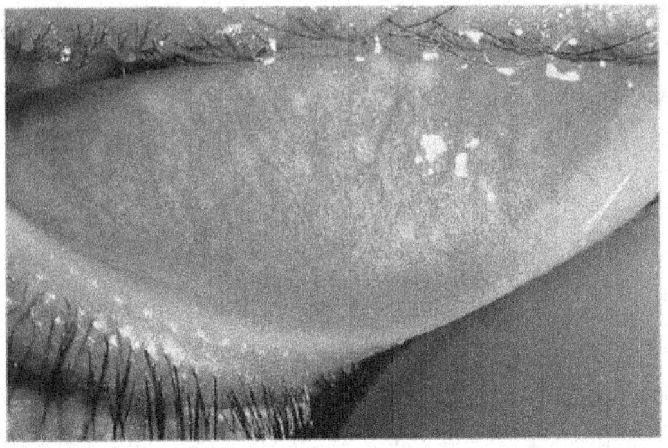

Which of the following diseases is illustrated by this picture?

A. Trachoma

B. Cornea burst

C. Glaucoma

D. Louse-borne relapsing fever

Q.28

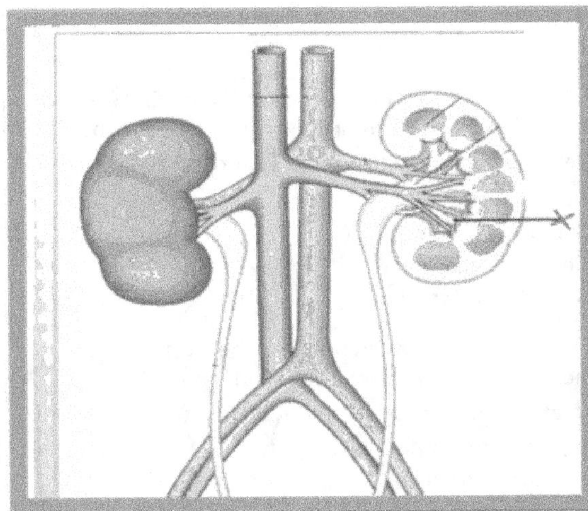

This is the diagram of anatomical relationships of the kidney. What does 'X' indicate?

A. Medulla   **B.** Calyx   **C.** Pelvis   **D.** Cortex

Q.29 Which of the following is the science of drugs?

A. Medicine   **B.** Pharmacology

C. Pediatrics   **D.** Pharmaceutics

Q.30 In which of the following routes of drugs administration, highly lipid-soluble drugs can be applied over the skin for slow and prolonged absorption?

A. Oral   **B.** Sublingual

C. Rectal   **D.** Cutaneous

Q.31 Which of the following is the most important synthetic reaction carried out by a group of UDP-glucuronosyltransferases (UGTs)?

A. Glucuronide conjugation

B. Acetylation

C. Methylation

D. Sulphate conjugation

Q.32 Which of the following excretion passages is/are of minor importance for drug excretion of systemic drugs?

A. Urine   **B.** Faeces

C. Milk   **D.** Saliva and sweat

Q.33 Which of the following is an agent that activates a receptor to produce a sub-maximal effect, but antagonizes the action of a full agonist?

A. Agonist   **B.** Inverse agonist

C. Antagonist   **D.** Partial agonist

Q.34 Many drugs act upon _________ which mediate responses to transmitters, hormones, autacoids and other endogenous signal molecules.

A. physiological receptors

B. drug receptors

C. synthetic receptors

D. biological receptors

Q.35 Which of the following is an inert substance given in the garb of a medicine?

A. Placebo   **B.** CYP isoenzymes

C. DPD   **D.** NAT2

Q.36 Which of the following is observed when single escalating doses are given to small groups of animals that are observed for overt effects and mortality for $1-3$ days?

A. Acute toxicity

B. Sub-acute toxicity

C. Chronic toxicity

D. Special long-term toxicity

Q.37 Which of the following has been the most popular anticholinergic used for peptic ulcer and gastritis?

A. Ipratropium bromide

B. Atropine metho-nitrate

C. Tiotropium bromide

D. Propantheline

Q.38 Which of the following is the drug of abuse and is capable of producing marked psychological, but little or no physical dependence?

A. Ephedrine   **B.** Dobutamine

C. Amphetamine   **D.** Phenylephrine

Q.39 Which of the following α-blockers cyclists spontaneously in the body giving rise to a highly-reactive ethylenimine intermediate which reacts with α-adrenoceptors and other bio-molecules by forming strong covalent bonds?

A. Phenoxy-benzamine   **B.** Phentolamine

C. Terazosin   **D.** Doxazosin

Q.40 Which of the following beta-blockers is preferred for topical use in the eye?

A. Sotalol   **B.** Timolol

C. Pindolol   **D.** Metoprolol

Q.41 Tissues rich in _______ are skin, gastric and intestinal mucosa, lungs, liver, and placenta.

A. atropine   **B.** adrenaline

C. histamines   **D.** eicosanoids

Q.42 To which of the following, the patients of asthma are highly sensitive to?

A. Adrenaline   **B.** Antihistamine

C. Histamine   **D.** Noradrenaline

Q.43 The following are correct about which of the following true neuromas?

(1) It contains only nerve fibres.

(2) Ganglion cells are absent.

(3) It occurs in spinal cord or pia mater.

A. Ganglioneuroma   **B.** Neuroblastoma

C. Myelinic neuroma   **D.** Neurofibroma

Q.44 Which of the following may be due to the renal failure or syndrome of inappropriate ADH secretion (SIADH)?

A. Hypervolemic hyponatraemia

B. Hypovolemic hyponatraemia

C. Normovolemic hyponatraemia

D. Pseudohyponatraemia

Q.45 In which type of shock will there be bradycardia, hypotension, arrhythmias, and decreased cardiac output?

A. Vasovagal shock

B. Neurogenic shock

C. Hypovolaemic shock

D. Cardiogenic shock

Q.46 Which of the following is derived from pooled plasma which contains factors II, IX and X; used in emergency reversal of warfarin therapy in uncontrolled haemorrhage?

A. Fibrinogen

B. Factor VII and IX concentrate

C. Platelet concentrate

D. Prothrombin complex concentrate

Q.47 Which of the following is an anti-pseudomonal and anti-clostridial agent?

A. Silver nitrate

B. Sulfamylon

C. Silver sulfadiazine

D. Sodium hypochlorite

Q.48 Which of the following is/are the most common organ involved in penetrating injuries?

A. Lungs   **B.** Liver   **C.** Heart   **D.** Kidneys

Q.49 Which injury can cause torrential haemorrhage and shock?

A. Liver injury

B. Sphenic injury

C. Renal injury

D. Urinary bladder injury

Q.50 Which of the following Verdan zone systems in the hand begins at the proximal end of the flexor retinaculum and ends at its distal end?

A. Zone I   **B.** Zone II   **C.** Zone III   **D.** Zone IV

Q.51 Which of the following is the bacterial infection of flexor tendon sheaths?

A. Space of parona infection

B. Acute suppurative tenosynovitis

C. Compound palmar ganglion

D. Milker's nodes

Q.52 In which of the following complications of varicose veins, do the patients walk on the tip of toes, like a horse?

A. Deep venous thrombosis

B. Talipes equinovarus

C. Calcification of the wall

D. Marjolin's ulcer

Q.53 Which of the following is a natural anticoagulant, a mucopolysaccharide?

A. Heparin
B. Warfarin
C. Histamine
D. Collagen

Q.54 Epstein–Barr virus may be the etiological agent of which of the following diseases?

A. Cutaneous T cell lymphoma
B. Burkitt lymphoma
C. Chyluria
D. Chylothorax

Q.55

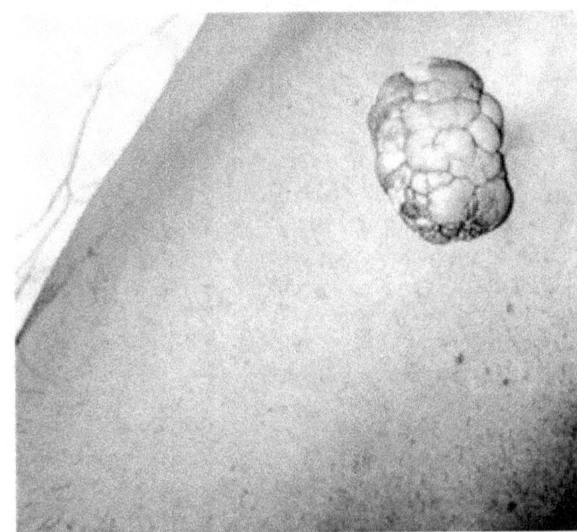

Which of the following diseases is depicted in this picture?

A. Papilloma
B. Fibroma
C. Lymphoma
D. Bursae

Q.56

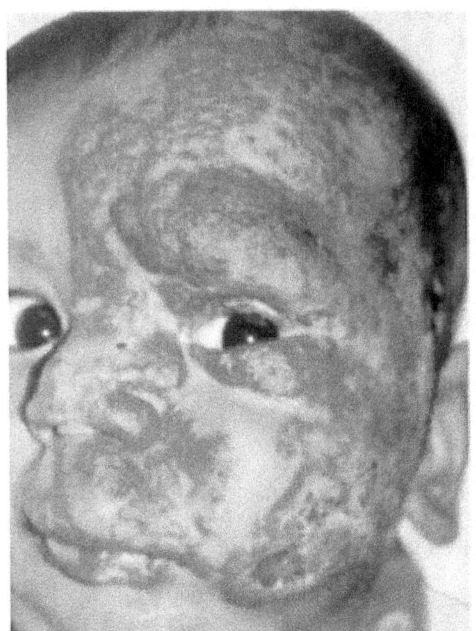

Which of the following diseases is illustrated through this picture of a child?

A. Strawberry haemangioma
B. Salmon patch
C. Port-wine stain
D. Cavernous haemangioma

Q.57 Which of the following is/are a large fibrous glycoprotein that helps cells attach, via cell surface glycoprotein called integrins?

A. Fibronectin
B. Fibroblastic
C. Fibrinogens
D. Connective fibres

Q.58 Molecules can be ejected by the cells through the process of _______.

A. endocytosis
B. exocytosis
C. autolysis
D. catalysis

Q.59 Diffusion is the process whereby atoms or molecules intermingle because of their random thermal motion; it is also called:

A. Brownian motion
B. Kepler motion
C. ionic movement
D. ionic diffusion

Q.60 Which of the following is a specific blocker of the Na^+?

A. Saxitoxin
B. Tetrodotoxin
C. Endotoxin
D. Neurotoxin

Q.61 Which of the following increases the excretion of NaCl and water by the kidney and diminishes the constriction of certain blood vessels?

A. Serine-threonine protein phosphatase
B. Atrial natriuretic peptide
C. Nitric oxide
D. Protein phosphatase

Q.62

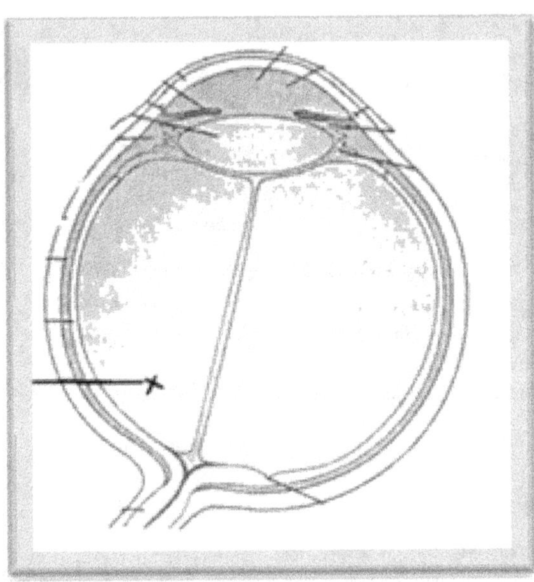

This is the picture of the right eye as viewed from above. What does 'X' indicate?

A. Fovea
B. Optic nerve
C. Vitreous humour
D. Retina

Q.63

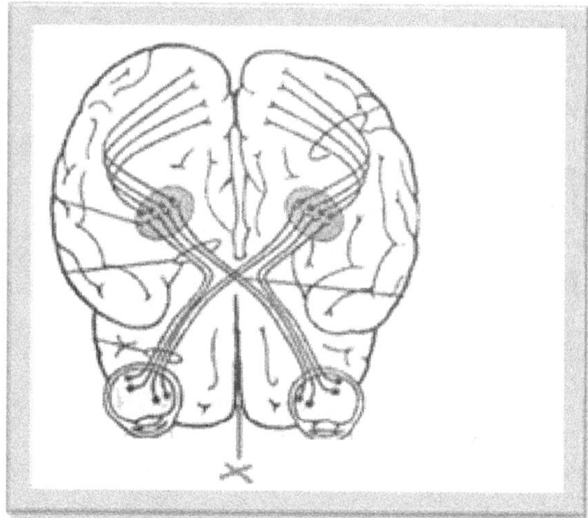

This is the picture of the main visual pathway as viewed from the base of the brain. What does 'X' indicate?

A. Optic radiation
B. Visual cortex
C. Optic chiasm
D. Lateral geniculate nucleus

Q.64 Which of the following is used in the treatment of Isovaleric Acidemia?

A. Arginine
B. Lysine
C. Glycine
D. Methionine

Q.65 The nitrogen atom of aspartate formed from asparagines using enzymes asparaginase is from:

A. Ammonium
B. Glutamate
C. Glutamine
D. Alpha keto-glutarate

Q.66 Amino acid responsible for thioredoxin reductase activation is:

A. Serine
B. Selenocysteine
C. Cysteine
D. Alanine

Q.67 Oxalo-acetate is derived from which amino acids?

A. Glutamine and glutamate
B. Asparagine and aspartate
C. Histidine and arginine
D. Glutamine and proline

Q.68 In one carbon metabolism, serine loses which carbon atom?

A. Alpha
B. Beta
C. Gamma
D. Delta

Q.69 At isoelectric pH, proteins:

A. Have net charge '0'
B. Do migrate
C. Are positively charged
D. Are negatively charged

Q.70 Proteins are linear polymers of amino acids. They fold into compact structures. Sometimes, these folded structures associate to form homo or hetero-dimers. Which one of the following refers to this associated form?

A. Denatured state
B. Molecular aggregation
C. Precipitation
D. Quaternary structure

Q.71 Speckled pattern is seen in:

A. Anti Sm antibody
B. Anti ds DNA antibody
C. Anti histone antibody
D. Anti chromatin antibody

Q.72 Read the following statements regarding HIV vaccine:

Assertion: Vaccine is still in the development phase

Reason: HIV is not attacked by immune system

A. Both assertion and reason are true and reason is the correct explanation for assertion.
B. Both assertion and reason are true but reason is not the correct explanation for assertion.
C. Assertion is true, but reason is false.
D. Reason is true, but assertion is false.

Q.73 The commonest primary immunodeficiency is:

A. Common variable immunodeficiency
B. Isolated IgA immunodeficiency
C. Wiskott-Aldrich syndrome
D. AIDS

Q.74 The percentage of pulmonary emboli, that proceeds to infraction is approximately:

A. $0 - 5\%$
B. $5 - 15\%$
C. $20 - 30\%$
D. $30 - 40\%$

Q.75 Bacteria reproduce mainly by

A. Budding
B. Binary fission
C. Sporing
D. Bacterial components produced by host cells

Q.76 The commonest mass in the middle mediastinum is:

A. lipoma
B. aneurysm
C. lymph node mass
D. congenital cysts

Q.77 The commonest type of emphysema (histologically) is:

A. centri-acinar
B. obstructed
C. irregular
D. pan-acinar

Q.78 A chest physician performs bronchoscopy in the procedure room of the outpatient department. To make the instrument safe for use in the next patient waiting outside, the most appropriate method to disinfect the endoscope is by using:

A. 70% alcohol for 5 min
B. 2% glutaraldehyde for 20 min
C. 2% formaldehyde for 10 min

D. 1% sodium hypochlorite for 15 min

Q.79 Heat labile instruments for use in surgical procedures can be best sterilised by:

A. Absolute alcohol

B. Ultraviolet rays

C. Chlorine releasing compounds

D. Ethylene oxide gas

Q.80 All of the following are true regarding disinfectants, except one. Identify the incorrect statement.

A. Aqueous solutions of glutaraldehyde is sporicidal.

B. Hypochlorites are virucidal.

C. Ethylene oxide is an intermediate disinfectant.

D. Phenol usually requires organic matter to act.

Q.81 Radiation can be used to sterilise all, except:

A. Bone graft

B. Suture

C. Bronchoscope

D. Artificial tissue graft

Q.82 The indicator used in autoclave is:

A. Clostridium tetani

B. Bacillus stereothermophilus

C. Bacillus pumilis

D. Bacillus subtilisavarniger

Q.83 Which of the following is used in digestion and decontamination of sputum in smear preparation?

A. $NaOH$ and N-acetylcysteine combined

B. KOH and N-acetylcysteine combined

C. $NaCl$ and N-acetylcysteine combined

D. KCl and N-acetylcysteine combined

Q.84 Regarding gas gangrene, one of the following is correct. Which one is it?

A. It is due to clostridium botulinum infection.

B. Clostridial species are gram-negative anaerobes forming spores.

C. The clinical features are due to the release of protein endotoxin.

D. Gas is invariably present in the muscle compartments.

Q.85 Which part of the cranial cavity is divided into the anterior, middle, and posterior cranial fossae?

A. Lateral aspect

B. Floor

C. Body

D. Apex

Q.86 Which of the following cranial fossae consists of parts of the sphenoid and temporal bones?

A. Anterior cranial fossa

B. Middle cranial fossa

C. Posterior cranial fossa

D. Floor of cranial fossa

Q.87 Which of the following carries taste from the anterior two-thirds of the tongue and parasympathetic innervation to all salivary glands below the level of the oral fissure?

A. Petrosal nerve

B. Chorda tympani nerve

C. Lingual nerve

D. Mental nerve

Q.88 Which of the following is the major contributor to the lower portion of the lateral wall of the cranium?

A. Sphenoid bone

B. Temporal bone

C. Hyoid bone

D. Occipital bone

Q.89 Which part of the temporal bone is an anterior bony projection from the lower surface of the squamous part of the temporal bone?

A. Tympanic part

B. Petromastoid part

C. Zygomatic process

D. External acoustic opening

Q.90 Which view of the skull shows the frontal bone, parietal bone, and occipital bone?

A. Inferior view

B. Superior view

C. Anterior view

D. Posterior view

Q.91 Which of the following contributes to the formation of the bony nasal septum separating the two choanae?

A. Vomer

B. Sphenoid bone

C. Occipital bone

D. Pterygoid processes

Q.92 Which of the following is the dome-shaped roof that protects the superior aspect of the brain?

A. Calva

B. Sagittal sinus

C. Frontal crest

D. Vomer

Q.93 Which of the following is the thick, tough, outer covering of the brain?

A. Cranial dura mater

B. Arachnoid mater

C. Pia mater

D. Calva

Q.94 Which of the following in brain is hidden from view in the adult brain by the cerebral hemispheres, and consists of the thalamus, hypothalamus and other related structures?

A. Telencephalon

B. Diencephalon

C. Mesencephalon

D. Metencephalon

Q.95 Which of the following internal carotid arteries is formed at the base of the brain by the interconnecting vertebro-basilar and internal carotid systems of vessels?

A. Ophthalmic artery

B. Posterior cerebellar artery

C. Middle cerebral artery

D. Cerebral arterial circle

Q.96 Which of the following sinuses is/are against the lateral aspect of the body of the sphenoid bone on either side of the sellaturcica?

A. Cavernous sinuses

B. Superior sagittal sinus

C. Inferior sagittal and straight sinuses

D. Basilar sinuses

Q.97

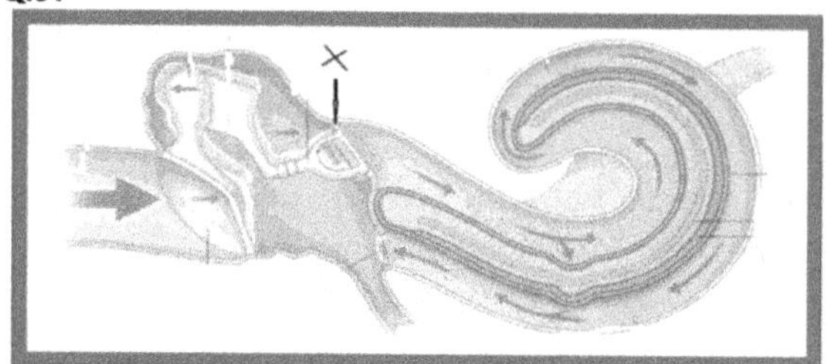

This picture depicts the transmission of sound. What does 'X' indicate?

A. Incus
C. Stapes
B. Oval window
D. Round window

Q.98

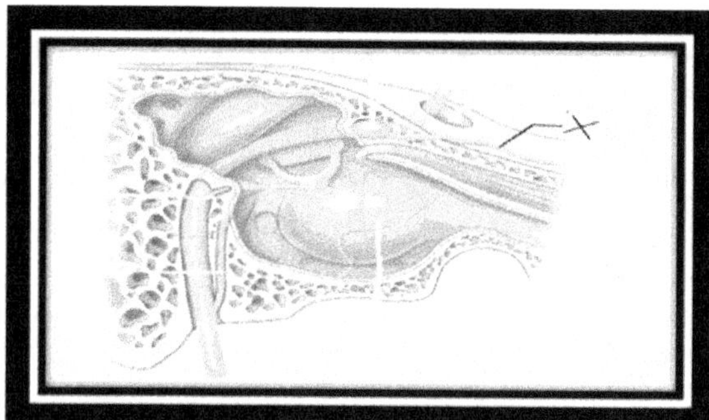

This is the facial nerve in the temporal bone. What does 'X' indicate?

A. Internal acoustic meatus
B. Facial nerve (VII)
C. Greater petrosal
D. Geniculate ganglion

Q.99 Substernal pain is a feature of:

A. Angina
B. Tachycardia
C. Thrombi and emboli
D. Emphysema

Q.100 Secondary hemorrhage appears in:

A. 7-14 days
B. Within 6 hours
C. Due to slipping of ligature
D. Bleeding disorder

Part B

Q.101 During the embryonal period, the depression that forms in the midline of the upper lip is called the ___ and indicates the line of fusion of the medial nasal and maxillary processes.

A. philtrum **B.** cyst **C.** trauma **D.** lesion

Q.102 When is the marked acceleration of mandibular growth observed in fetal life?

A. Seventh to eleventh week
B. Eighth to fourteenth week
C. After first week

D. Sixth to eighth week

Q.103 In bone growth, the proliferating blood vessels from periodontium carry with them undifferentiated ___, which eventually form osteoblasts.

A. endodermal cells **B.** mesenchymal cells
C. ectodermal cells **D.** cementoblasts

Q.104 The cranium grows because of the:

A. Brain grows **B.** Body grows
C. Face grows **D.** Head grows

Q.105 Continued growth of the _____ with the developing dentition increases the height of the mandibular body.

A. maxilla **B.** tongue
C. alveolar bone **D.** gingiva

Q.106 From birth to two years, the _____ is horseshoe shaped and the gum pads extend labially and buccally beyond those in the mandible.

A. maxillary arch **B.** gingiva
C. enamel **D.** dental pulp

Q.107 The time between ______ years of age is critical for developing dentition.

A. seven and eight **B.** eight and nine
C. nine and ten **D.** ten and eleven

Q.108 In labial eruption of incisor, the permanent incisors which replace primary incisors are ____ proclined placing them in a wider arch.

A. lingually **B.** labially **C.** mesially **D.** distally

Q.109 The mandibular long axes tend to diverge following :

A. Maxillary arch
B. Curve of spee
C. Curve of maxillary arch
D. Palatal plate

Q.110 Which of the following laws states that the stresses of tension or pressure on bone stimulate bone formation?

A. Salzmann statement
B. Trajectorial theory of bone formation
C. Laws of transformation of bone
D. Julius wolf statement

Q.111 Which is a mechanically mediated adaptive process for changing a bone's size, shape or position?

A. Bone modelling **B.** Bone remodelling
C. Bone shaping **D.** Moulding

Q.112 Which of the following is the ability of a muscle to shorten its length under innervational impulse?

A. Compressibility **B.** Contractility
C. Contractibility **D.** Compatibility

Q.113 The linear elastic range or extent of elasticity as expressed in ____ is dependent upon the nature of the material involved.

A. Bowman's law **B.** Maxwell's law
C. Hooke's law **D.** Simon law

Q.114 In principles of muscle physiology, the reflex contraction of a healthy muscle which results from a pull on its tendon is called the:

A. Resting length
B. Muscle tonus
C. Stretch or myotatic reflexes
D. Reciprocal innervation and inhibition

Q.115 The probing depth of the clinically normal gingival sulcus in humans is:

A. 1 to 2 mm
B. 1 to 3 mm
C. 3 to 4 mm
D. 2 to 4 mm

Q.116 Which of the following are the most common cells in the periodontal ligament and appear as ovoid or elongated cells oriented along the principal fibres?

A. Osteoblasts
B. Ameloblasts
C. Fibroblasts
D. Cementoblasts

Q.117 What is the shape of the structure of the periodontal ligament?

A. Oval
B. Rectangle
C. Hourglass shape
D. Triangular

Q.118 Which of the following is a poorly defined zone near the cemento-dentinal junction of certain teeth that appears to contain cellular remnants of Hertwig's sheath embedded in calcified ground substance?

A. Cellular mixed stratified cementum
B. Cellular intrinsic cementum
C. Intermediate cementum
D. Acellular extrinsic fibre cementum (AEFC)

Q.119 Which of the following results in the resorption of the root and its gradual replacement by bone tissue?

A. Ankylosis
B. Alveolar process
C. Absorption
D. Resection

Q.120 The bone matrix that is laid down by osteoblasts is non-mineralised _________.

A. osteoid
B. mastoid
C. protrusion
D. projection

Q.121 The human fetus inside the uterus is ______.

A. fertile
B. sterile
C. sensitive
D. insensitive

Q.122 The saliva from light plaque formers ______ the colloidal stability of bacterial suspensions.

A. increased
B. reduced
C. removed
D. unchanged

Q.123 Rapid plaque formers demonstrated higher proportions of gram-negative rods in:

A. 11-day-old plaque
B. 12-day-old plaque
C. 13-day-old plaque
D. 14-day-old plaque

Q.124 Periodontal health is first established in human subjects by cleaning and rigorous oral hygiene measures, followed by abstinence from oral hygiene for:

A. 20 days
B. 21 days
C. 22 days
D. 23 days

Q.125 Which of the following diseases may be accompanied by malodour, pain, and possibly systemic symptoms, including lymphadenopathy, fever and malaise?

A. Necrotizing diseases
B. Bowman's disease
C. Fibroblastic disease
D. Gingivalis

Q.126 Which of the following perio-pathogens is a small, short, straight, or curved rod with rounded ends?

A. Actino-bacillus actino-mycetemcomitans
B. Tannerella forsythia
C. Porphyromonasgingivalis
D. Prevotellaintermedia

Q.127

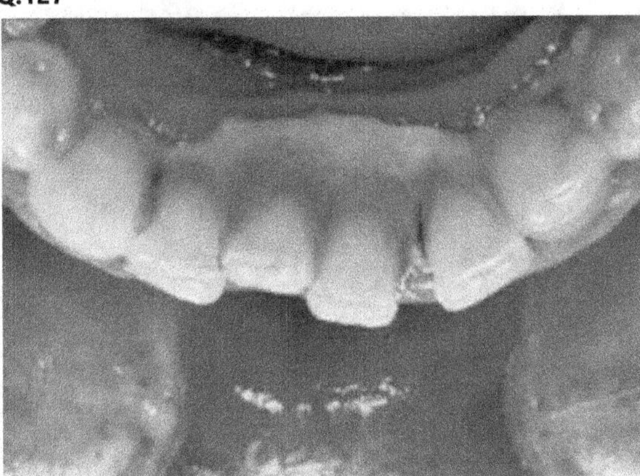

What does this picture represent?

A. Supragingival calculus is depicted on the buccal surfaces of maxillary molars adjacent to orifice for Stenson's duct.
B. Extensive supragingival calculus is present on the lingual surfaces of lower anterior teeth.
C. Substantial reduction in gingival inflammation
D. Dark pigmented deposits of subgingival calculus

Q.128

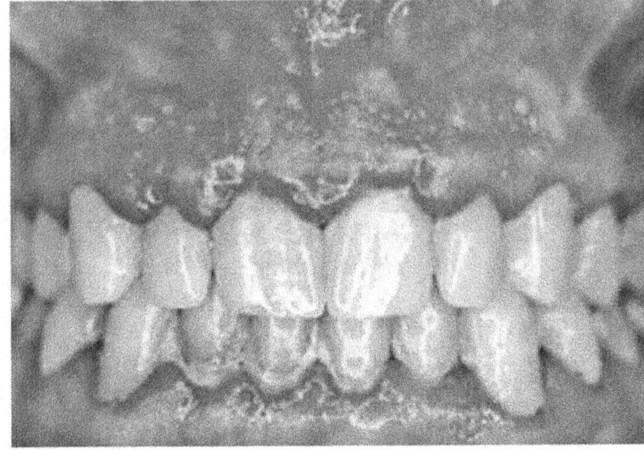

What does this picture indicate?

A. Chronic dental caries
B. Chronic inflammatory gingival enlargement
C. Chronic inflammatory gingival enlargement localised to the anterior region

D. Chronic inflammatory gingival enlargement showing the inflamed connective tissue core and strands of proliferating epithelium

Q.129 Which cranial nerve is called hypoglossal nerve?

A. Cranial nerve XII

B. Cranial nerve XI

C. Cranial nerve X

D. Cranial nerve IX

Q.130 Which of the following has satisfactory topical anaesthetic properties for oral mucosa, in case dyclonine hydrochloride is not available?

A. Diphenhydramine hydrochloride mixed with milk of magnesia

B. Diphenhydramine hydrochloride mixed with milk of caustic soda

C. Diphenhydramine hydrochloride mixed with milk of phosphorous

D. Diphenhydramine hydrochloride mixed with milk of alumina

Q.131 Hand-foot-and-mouth disease is caused by infection with _______ in a majority of cases.

A. Coxsackievirus A5

B. Coxsackievirus A9

C. Coxsackievirus A10

D. Coxsackievirus A16

Q.132 Which of the following are the common causes of the contact oral reactions?

A. Cinnamon

B. Cloves flavour

C. Menthol fresh

D. Artificial essence

Q.133 Which of the following is an intense red band involving the marginal gingiva that does not resolve with standard oral hygiene procedures?

A. AIDS

B. LGE

C. NUG

D. NUP

Q.134 Widely accepted theory of dental caries is

A. Proteolytic theory

B. Proteolytic chelation theory

C. Acidogenic theory

D. Autoimmune theory

Q.135 Which is a chronic autoimmune subepithelial disease that primarily affects the mucous membranes of patients over the age of 50 years?

A. Pemphigus vulgaris

B. Mucous membrane pemphigoid

C. Pemphigus vegetans

D. Bullous pemphigoid

Q.136 Which of the following organisms can grow either in yeast or mycelial form?

A. Blastomycosis

B. Mucormycosis

C. Histoplasmosis

D. Linear IGA disease

Q.137 Which of the following is a common source of burns of the oral cavity?

A. Silver nitrate

B. Acetylsalicylic acid

C. Hydrogen peroxide

D. Sodium hypochlorite

Q.138 Which of the following is a premalignant epithelial lesion that is directly related to long-term sun exposure?

A. Actinic keratosis

B. Induced keratosis

C. Nicotine stomatitis

D. Sanguinaria induced leukoplakia

Q.139 Which of the following is the most common disease associated with oral hairy leukoplakia?

A. RAS Disease

B. HIV infection

C. Candidiasis

D. Denture stomatitis

Q.140 Salivary ___ affects the adherence of Candida to buccal epithelial cells.

A. IgM

B. IgG

C. IgA

D. IgD

Q.141 Which of the following diseases is classified as reticular, atrophic or erosive and bullous?

A. Erythroplakia

B. Bowen's disease

C. Oral lichen planus

D. Lichenoid reaction

Q.142 Which of the following is/are useful, usually in conjunction with topical corticosteroids as adjunctive therapy for OLP?

A. Predispose tablets

B. Clobetasol

C. Retinoids

D. Fluocinonide

Q.143 Which of the following is a slowly progressive chronic fibrotic disease of the oral cavity and oropharynx, characterized by fibroelastic change and inflammation of the mucosa?

A. Hairy tongue

B. Oral submucous fibrosis

C. Miscellaneous lesions

D. Fordyce's granules

Q.144 Which of the following theories states that the organic component of the enamel is first broken down by proteolytic enzymes opening up pathways for bacteria to attack the enamel by other processes such as by acid or chelation?

A. Chemico-parasitic theory

B. Proteolytic theory

C. Chelation theory

D. Bio-parasitic theory

Q.145 In tooth wear, which of the following is the loss of dental hard tissues due to a chemical process not involving bacteria?

A. Attrition

B. Abrasion

C. Erosion

D. Abfraction

Q.146 Most of the hand cutting instruments are made up of

A. Chromium cobalt

B. Carbon steel

C. Tungsten carbide

D. Stainless steel

Q.147 Which of the following dental caries is also called as the reversible caries?

A. Primary caries

B. Secondary caries

C. Incipient caries

D. Cavitated caries

Q.148 In tooth preparation, which of the following refers to the mechanical alteration of a defective, injured or diseased tooth

to best receive a restorative material which will re-establish the normal form, function and aesthetics of the tooth?

A. Cavity preparation

B. Simple cavity preparation

C. Compound cavity preparation

D. Complex cavity preparation

Q.149 The enamel consists of inorganic matter in the form of ______ with a small amount of water and organic matter.

A. hydroxylapatite

B. hydroxyapatite

C. carboxy-apatite

D. hydrochloro-apatite

Q.150 Which of the following dentins is the more mineralised dentin which forms the tubular wall?

A. Peri-tubular dentin

B. Intertubular dentin

C. Predentin

D. Primary dentin

Q.151 Which test is used to evaluate the integrity of the attachment apparatus surrounding the tooth?

A. Palpation

B. Mobility depressibility testing

C. Percussion

D. Test cavity

Q.152 The angle former is a special type of:

A. Chisel

B. Excavator

C. Hatchet

D. Rotatory instrument

Q.153 In odontoblastic processes, which nerves for sensory perception are also found in the pulpal end of the periodontoblastic space of the dentinal tubules?

A. Myelinated nerves

B. Unmyelinated nerves

C. Fibrinogens

D. Myelinated sheath

Q.154 What is the demarcation zone between the secondary and the reparative dentin called?

A. Endometrial line

B. Dead tracts

C. Calico-traumatic line

D. Middle zone

Q.155 If the odontoblasts is injured beyond repair, the degenerated odontoblasts will leave empty tubules, called ______ that allow bacteria and noxious products to enter the pulp.

A. dead cells

B. dead tracts

C. dead tubules

D. degenerated tubules

Q.156

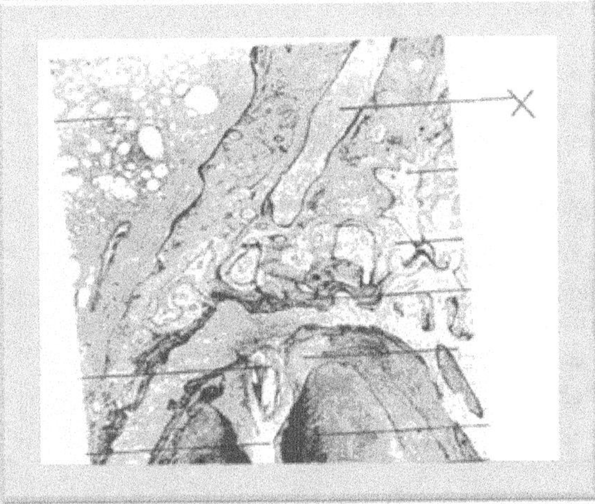

This is the diagram of high magnification of the apical area. What does 'X' indicate?

A. Medullary space

B. Nutrient canal

C. Trabecula

D. Alveolar bone

Q.157

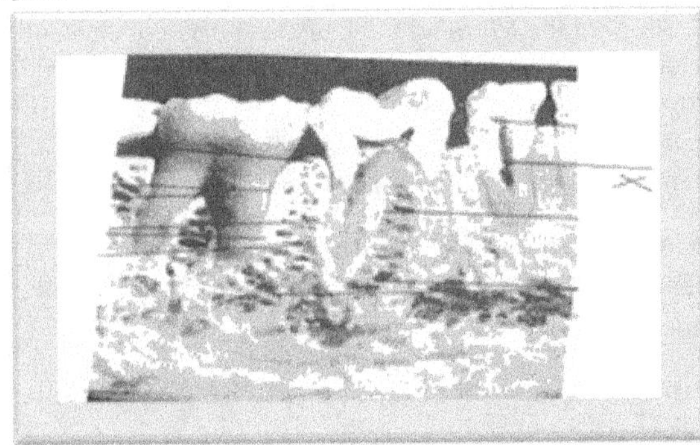

This is the diagram of the sagittal view of the alveolar process. What does 'X' indicate?

A. Pulp chamber

B. Root canal

C. Trabecula

D. Cortical bone

Q.158 In maxillary first primary molar, buccal surface is ____ in all directions.

A. concave   B. convex   C. bipolar   D. oval

Q.159 In prenatal growth, which of the following periods is from fertilization to implantation?

A. Germinal stage

B. Embryonal period

C. Fetal period

D. Postnatal growth

Q.160 When a bone consists of several contagious skeletal units, what are these units termed as?

A. Micro-skeletal units

B. Macro-skeletal units

C. Gigantic skeletal units

D. Congential units

Q.161 Apex of the pedodontic triangle is formed by:

A. Mother

B. Child

C. Dentist

D. None of the above

Q.162 Which of the following occurs in closed primary dentition with the flush terminal plane when erupting first molars cannot shift mesially until the exchange of C, D, and E with 3, 4, and 5?

A. Secondary spacing
B. Inter-canine width increase
C. Late mesial shift
D. Late distal shift

Q.163 In Lampshire's classification of behaviour, which of the following patients passively resists treatment using techniques that have been successful in other situations like at home?

A. Fearful
B. Stubborn/Defiant
C. Outwardly apprehensive
D. Tense cooperative

Q.164 Regarding concepts of sedation and anesthesia, which of the following is a drug-induced depression of consciousness during which patients cannot be easily aroused but respond purposefully following repeated or painful stimulation?

A. Minimal sedation
B. Moderate sedation
C. Deep sedation
D. General anesthesia

Q.165 Which of the following has been tested as possible anti-caries agent by virtue of its enzyme inhibiting activity in the carbohydrate degradation cycle?

A. Vitamin K
B. Vitamin A
C. Vitamin B
D. Vitamin C

Q.166 Pedodontic triangle is formed by:

A. Mischer
B. McDonald
C. Finn
D. Wright

Q.167 Dental caries were reduced by 50% by using which of the following?

A. Sheep Milk extracts
B. Egg yolk
C. Murine monoclonal antibodies
D. Bovine milk

Q.168 Anxiety is:

A. Fear of unknown
B. Fear of stranger
C. Fear of pain
D. Fear to object

Q.169 According to which of the following theory, periodontal disease results from the elaboration of noxious products by the entire plaque flora?

A. Non - Specific plaque hypothesis
B. Specific plaque hypothesis
C. Ecological plaque hypothesis
D. Environmental plaque hypothesis

Q.170 Which of the following is a type of interdental cleaning aid indicated to remove plaque from interproximal tooth surfaces?

A. Charter's method
B. Dental floss
C. Scrub brush method
D. Leonards method

Q.171 Which of the following exhibits both anti-plaque and antibacterial properties?

A. Delmopinol
B. Chlorhexidine-gluconate
C. Sanguinarine
D. Metallic ions

Q.172 Which of the following is the final factor that can impede wound healing?

A. Foreign material
B. Necrotic tissue
C. Ischemia
D. Stress

Q.173 Which No. forceps are easier to use than the No. 150 for upper incisors?

A. No. 1
B. No. 10
C. No. 15
D. No. 151

Q.174 Which disease is a common reason for tooth removal?

A. Pulpal necrosis
B. Periodontal disease
C. Malposed teeth
D. Cracked teeth

Q.175 Which of the following terms includes impacted teeth and teeth that are in the process of erupting?

A. Cracked tooth
B. Erupted tooth
C. Unerupted tooth
D. Malposed tooth

Q.176 The most commonly used classification system with respect to treatment planning uses a determination of the angulation of the long axis of the impacted ______ with respect to the long axis of the adjacent second molar.

A. second molar
B. first molar
C. third molar
D. third premolar

Q.177 The supernumerary tooth in the midline of the maxilla is called:

A. Cracked tooth
B. Impacted tooth
C. Erupted tooth
D. Mesiodens

Q.178 Edema means:

A. Inflammation
B. Swelling
C. Tooth disorders
D. Ulcers

Q.179 The blood in the submucosal or subcutaneous tissues is known as:

A. Trismus
B. Edema
C. Ecchymosis
D. Chemosis

Q.180 Which of the following soft tissue injuries usually results from the rotating shank of the bur rubbing on the soft tissue or on a metal retractor in contact with soft tissue?

A. Tear of a mucosal flap
B. Puncture wound
C. Stretch or abrasion
D. Root fracture

Q.181 Which of the following is delayed healing but is not associated with an infection?

A. Dry socket
B. Wound dehiscence
C. Root fracture
D. Ulcer

Q.182 Which of the following acts is also known as the Kennedy-Kassebaum Act?

A. HIPAA Privacy and Security

B. Title VI, Limited English Proficiency

C. Americans with Disabilities Act

D. EMTALA

Q.183 In evaluation of supporting soft tissue, which aspect of the mandible should be inspected to determine the level of attachment of the mylohyoid muscle in relation to the crest of the mandibular ridge and the attachment of the genioglossus muscle in the anterior mandible?

A. Anterior aspect

B. Posterior aspect

C. Lingual aspect

D. Labial aspect

Q.184

Which forceps are depicted in this given picture?

A. No. 151 forceps

B. No. 1 forceps

C. No. 17 forceps

D. No. 87 forceps

Q.185

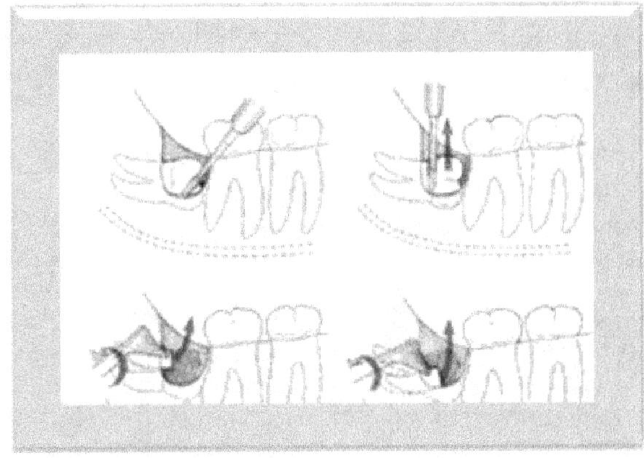

Which of the following angles of removal of impaction is illustrated in the given diagram?

A. Mesio-angular impaction

B. Horizontal impaction

C. Vertical impaction

D. Disto-angular impaction

Q.186 Deficiency of which nutrient during pregnancy may result in a higher risk of having a baby with certain congenital anomalies, including cleft lip and/or cleft palate?

A. Folic acid

B. Vitamin A

C. Iron

D. Vitamin E

Q.187 Which of the following developmental disturbances of the jaws, frequently occurs due to a deficiency in the premaxillary area?

A. Macrognathia of the maxilla

B. Micrognathia of the maxilla

C. Facial hemiatrophy

D. Facial hemihypertrophy

Q.188 Which of the following diseases is an autosomal dominantly inherited disorder characterised by intestinal hamartomatous polyps in association with mucocutaneous melanocytic macules?

A. Cheilitis granulomatosa

B. Peutz-Jegher's syndrome

C. Gnarled syndrome

D. Fordyce's granules

Q.189 Which of the following is a psoriasiform mucositis of the dorsum of the tongue?

A. Benign migratory glossitis

B. Hairy tongue

C. Median rhomboid glossitis

D. Lingual varix

Q.190 Which of the following is a hereditary autosomal dominant syndrome?

A. Aplasia

B. LADD

C. Xerostomia

D. Gnarled syndrome

Q.191 Zyban, a newly introduced drug to aid smoking cessation, can cause ______.

A. aplasia

B. xerostomia

C. sialadenitis

D. atresia

Q.192 Which teeth are prevented from erupting by some physical barrier in the eruption path?

A. Cracked teeth

B. Impacted teeth

C. Supernumerary teeth

D. Submerged teeth

Q.193 Which of the following cysts is a development cyst, non-neoplastic in nature?

A. Nasopalatine duct cyst

B. Median palatal cyst

C. Globulomaxillary cyst

D. Median mandibular cyst

Q.194 Which of the following is the second most common type of oral nevi found in the oral cavity?

A. Junctional nevi

B. Compound nevi

C. Intradermal nevi

D. Common blue nevi

Q.195 Which of the following diseases is a special form of intraepithelial carcinoma occurring with some frequency on the skin?

A. Leukoedema

B. Bowen's disease

C. Multifocal candidiasis

D. Oral lichen planus

Q.196 Which of the following develops most frequently on the exposed surfaces of the skin, the face and the scalp in middle-aged or elderly persons?

A. Epidermoid carcinoma

B. Metastatic carcinoma

C. Basal cell carcinoma

D. Carcinoma of the lip

Q.197 Which of the following consists of the congenital hamartomatous malformations that may affect the eye, the skin, and the central nervous system at different times, characterised by the combination of a venous angioma of the leptomeninges over the cerebral cortex with ipsilateral angiomatous lesions of the face?

A. Sturge-Weber syndrome

B. Nasopharyngeal angiofibroma

C. Lymphangioma

D. Myxoma

Q.198 Which of the following sarcomas occurs most commonly in the long bones of the extremities near metaphyseal growth plates?

A. Chondrosarcoma

B. Ewing's sarcoma

C. Osteosarcoma

D. Kaposi sarcoma

Q.199

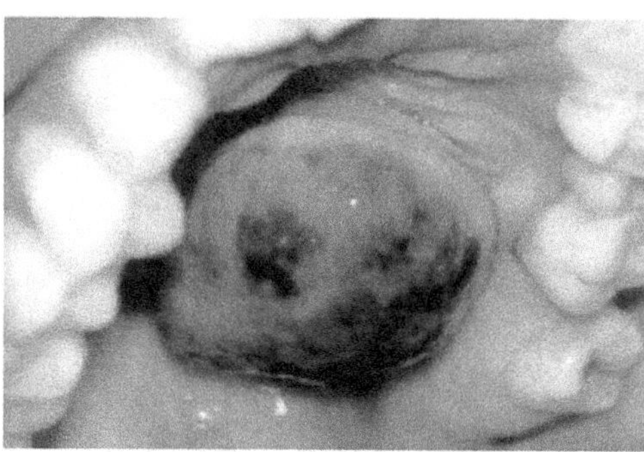

Which of the following carcinomas is illustrated by the above-given picture?

A. Acinic cell carcinoma

B. Mucoepidermoid carcinoma

C. Adenoid cystic carcinoma

D. Cystadenoma

Q.200

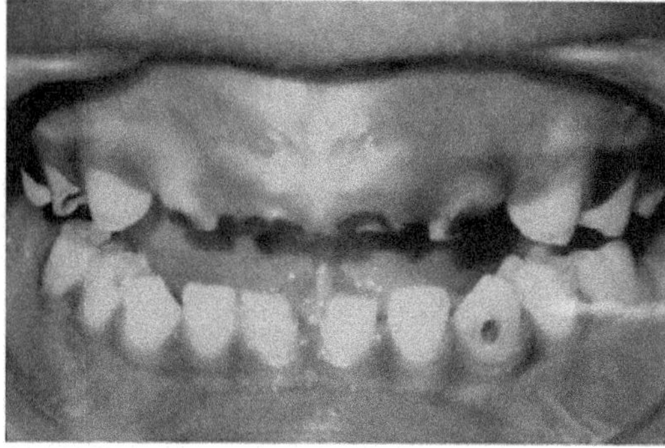

Which of the following caries is illustrated by this picture?

A. Adolescent caries

B. Nursing bottle caries

C. Smooth surface caries

D. Radiation caries

Q.201 Matrix and patrix are the two

A. Retentive assemblies of intra coronal retainer

B. Extra coronal fingers of metal

C. Resultant assembly of extra-coronal retainer

D. Subdivisions of clasps

Q.202 Tooth supported removable partial denture receives support from

A. Natural teeth

B. Artificial teeth

C. Implants

D. Dentures

Q.203 Which of the following may lead to tooth mobility or loss of tooth?

A. Rigidity

B. Infections

C. Allied forces

D. Improper dentures

Q.204 The concentration of forces upon small segments of the residual ridges may cause

A. Compression of the soft tissues

B. Flexibility of the hard and soft tissues

C. Resorption of the hard and soft tissues

D. None of these

Q.205 A supra-bulge direct retainer is frequently referred to as a/an

A. Akers clasp

B. Under cut

C. Roach clasp

D. None of these

Q.206 The two basic categories of direct retainers will be designated as

A. supra-bulge direct retainers

B. infra-bulge direct retainers

C. matrix and patrix

D. Both 1 and 2

Q.207 Experiments by Synge and Dyment in the loading are tolerated over non axial forces by a ratio of

A. 17.5 to 1

B. 17.5 to 0.1

C. 0.175 to 0.1

D. 0.1175 to 1

Q.208 Like a conventional fixed partial denture, ___ removable partial denture is entirely tooth supported.

A. Class II

B. Class IV

C. Class III

D. Class I

Q.209 Who stated, "The first five minutes spent with a patient represent the most important period of dentist-patient interaction"?

A. Dr. Carl Boucher

B. Dr. M. M. Devan

C. Dr. M. M. House

D. None of these

Q.210 Who stated, "We should meet the mind of the patient before we meet the mouth of the patient"?

A. Dr. Carl Boucher

B. Dr. M. M.House

C. Dr. M. M. Devan

D. None of these

Q.211 Most face-bow procedures are based upon _______ points.

A. articular
B. true hinge axis
C. arbitrary axis
D. centric relation

Q.212 The selection of ______ points is dependent upon the type of face-bow and articulator being used.

A. articular
B. true hinge axis
C. arbitrary hinge axis
D. centric relation

Q.213

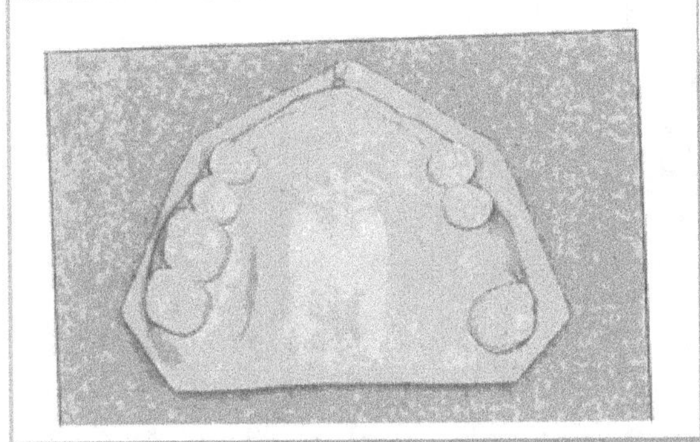

Which of the following Kennedy class arch modifications is depicted by this picture?

A. Kennedy class I
B. Kennedy class II
C. Kennedy class III
D. Kennedy class IV

Q.214

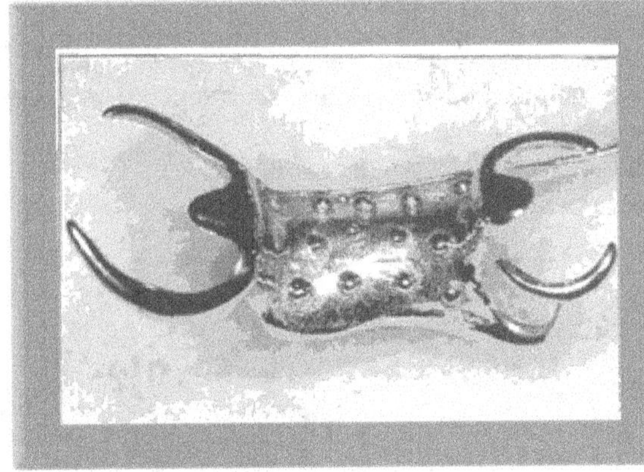

What is represented by this picture?

A. Mesh construction
B. Bead retention
C. Open retention
D. Closed retention

Q.215 What of the following is the second goal of the UN Millennium Development Goals?

A. Eradicate extreme poverty and hunger
B. Achieve universal primary education
C. Promote gender equality and empower women
D. Reduce child mortality

Q.216 Which of the following represents the killing power of a disease?

A. Age specific death rate
B. Case fatality rate
C. Proportional mortality rate
D. Crude death rate

Q.217 In which of the following, has the outcome (e.g., Disease) not yet occurred at the time the investigation begins?

A. Prospective cohort studies
B. Retrospective cohort studies
C. Selection of study studies
D. Combination of Retrospective and Prospective cohort studies

Q.218 Which of the following is a type of preventive trial in which the investigator intervenes to interrupt the usual sequence in the development of disease for those individuals who have risk factor for developing the disease?

A. Clinical trial
B. Preventive trial
C. Risk factor trial
D. Cessation experiment

Q.219 Which of the following is/are the part of rain water that runs off to form streams and rivers which flow ultimately into the sea?

A. Groundwater
B. Shallow water
C. Surface water
D. Ponds and lakes

Q.220 An acceptable pH for drinking water is between:

A. 7 and 8
B. 5.5 and 8.5
C. 6.5 and 8.5
D. 8.5 and 9

Q.221 Which of the following is an example of faecal group of coliform group?

A. E. Coli
B. Klebsiella
C. Plasmodium
D. Paramecium

Q.222 Which of the following chemical disinfectants is active against both bacteria and parasite eggs, and should be used as 2% aqueous solution with acetate buffer?

A. Formaldehyde
B. Ethylene oxide
C. Glutaraldehyde
D. Sodium hypochlorite

Q.223 Vitamin A prophylaxis is an example of:

A. Health promotion
B. Disability limitation
C. Specific protection
D. Primordial prevention

Q.224 Which of the following is required for brain development and function, regulation of body temperature and muscle activity?

A. Iron
B. Protein
C. Calcium
D. Vitamins

Q.225 Which of the following is negatively associated with the risk of oral cancer?

A. Vitamin A
B. Vitamin B
C. Vitamin C
D. Vitamin D

Q.226 The saliva may be slightly acidic as it is secreted at unstimulated flow rates, but it may reach a pH of _______ at high flow rates.

A. 6.8   **B.** 7.6   **C.** 8.8   **D.** 9.8

Q.227 Which of the following is the predominant immunoglobulin present in saliva?

A. IgA   **B.** IgM   **C.** IgG   **D.** IgD

Q.228 Cariogenic plaques contain higher levels of _______ than non-cariogenic plaques.

A. S. cocci   **B.** S. mutans
C. S. mycin   **D.** S. pyogenes

Q.229 Which of the following is caused by a load that tends to stretch or elongate a body?

A. Compressive stress   **B.** Tensile stress
C. Flexural stress   **D.** Shear stress

Q.230 Which of the following is defined as the flexural strain that occurs when the material is stressed to its proportional limit?

A. Flexibility
B. Minimum flexibility
C. Maximum flexibility
D. Elasticity

Q.231 Yield strength often is a property that represents the stress value at which a small amount _______ of plastic strain has occurred.

A. 0.1% to 0.2%   **B.** 0.2% to 0.3%
C. 0.3% to 0.4%   **D.** 0.4% to 0.5%

Q.232 The moving object possesses a known amount of:

A. Potential energy
B. Kinetic energy
C. Rotational energy
D. Translational energy

Q.233 The largest alloy of amalgam alloy is:

A. Silver   **B.** Tin   **C.** Zinc   **D.** Copper

Q.234 Which of the following represents a cast alloy microstructure in which all of the grains have similar dimensions?

A. Grain
B. Dendritic microstructure
C. Equiaxed grain microstructure
D. Microstructure

Q.235 Which of the following phases contains two or more elements, at least one of which is a metal, that are intimately combined at the atomic level?

A. Solid solution   **B.** Alloy system
C. Non-metallic phase   **D.** Peritectic alloys

Q.236 Which of the following represents the polymer material that becomes permanently hard when heated above the temperature at which it begins to polymerise and that does not soften again on reheating to the same temperature?

A. Thermoplastic polymer
B. Thermosetting polymer
C. Thermodynamic polymer
D. Elastomers

Q.237 Resins are composed of very:

A. Small molecules   **B.** Large molecules
C. Small components   **D.** Large components

Q.238 Which polymer has identical monomer units that occur in relatively long sequences along with the main polymer?

A. Random copolymer
B. Block polymer
C. Graft or branched copolymer
D. Monomer

Q.239

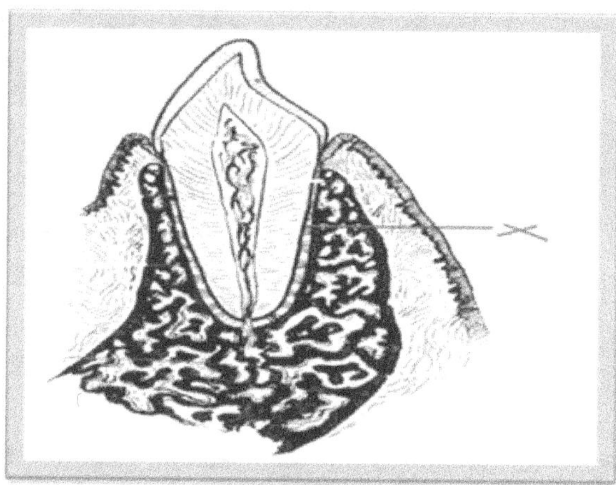

This is the diagram of the cross-sectional view of the natural anterior tooth and supporting tissues. What does 'X' indicate in the diagram?

A. Dentin   **B.** Cementum
C. Alveolar bone   **D.** Gingiva

Q.240

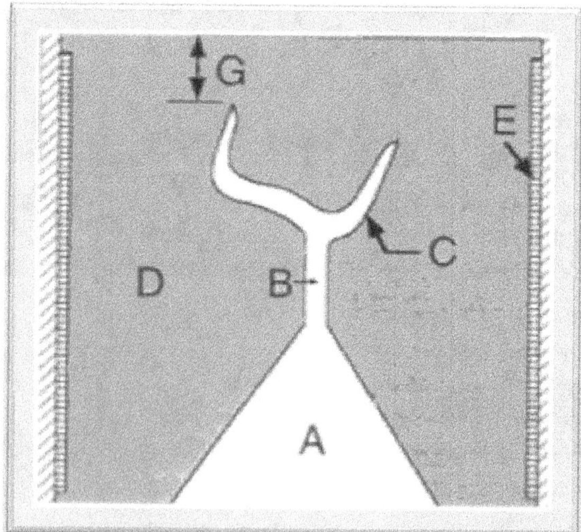

This is the diagrammatic representation of the dental casting mold. What does "C" represent in the diagram?

A. Crucible former

B. Cavity formed by wax pattern after burnout

C. Casting ring

D. Sprue

// Smart Answer Sheet //

Correct — Indicates percentage of students who answered questions correctly.

Skipped — Indicates percentage of students who skipped questions.

Q.	Ans.	Correct / Skipped
1	B	81.25 % / 14.92 %
2	C	22.33 % / 76.76 %
3	B	52.84 % / 45.65 %
4	A	62.55 % / 37.09 %
5	B	40.2 % / 55.13 %
6	B	87.15 % / 11.89 %
7	A	50.09 % / 36.08 %
8	A	22.36 % / 77.03 %
9	B	86.15 % / 13.27 %
10	A	54.54 % / 32.01 %
11	A	62.55 % / 36.5 %
12	A	64.16 % / 33.34 %
13	B	87.24 % / 12.46 %
14	C	55.58 % / 30.47 %
15	B	11.75 % / 82.17 %
16	B	87.16 % / 10.83 %
17	A	77.55 % / 17.15 %
18	A	84.63 % / 12.27 %
19	B	24.47 % / 71.29 %
20	A	46.09 % / 34.08 %
21	B	12.69 % / 83.97 %
22	B	78.78 % / 18.69 %
23	A	44.15 % / 41.74 %
24	D	29.06 % / 68.02 %
25	B	42.74 % / 38.3 %
26	A	25.15 % / 74.67 %
27	A	78.77 % / 12.9 %
28	B	40.44 % / 41.17 %
29	B	77.65 % / 12.29 %
30	D	76.26 % / 16.33 %
31	A	24.2 % / 71.01 %
32	D	80.39 % / 15.52 %
33	D	67.13 % / 31.53 %
34	A	32.44 % / 67.48 %
35	A	58.08 % / 38.88 %
36	A	20.44 % / 67.1 %
37	D	56.72 % / 36.08 %
38	C	81.93 % / 11.8 %
39	A	54.48 % / 44.59 %
40	B	84.32 % / 15.19 %
41	C	15.86 % / 80.6 %
42	C	57.59 % / 37.8 %
43	C	31.92 % / 67.08 %
44	C	60.79 % / 37.17 %
45	B	32.45 % / 67.18 %
46	D	77.9 % / 11.09 %
47	B	29.52 % / 68.47 %
48	B	47.64 % / 36.22 %
49	B	83.99 % / 10.22 %
50	D	78.87 % / 18.56 %
51	B	53.31 % / 39.58 %
52	B	21.93 % / 77.27 %
53	A	78.15 % / 16.05 %
54	B	21.32 % / 70.92 %
55	A	76.04 % / 22.47 %
56	A	68.34 % / 30.56 %
57	A	86.57 % / 10.23 %
58	B	83.88 % / 11.84 %
59	A	55.37 % / 41.43 %
60	B	14.95 % / 71.84 %
61	B	41.55 % / 32.64 %
62	C	85.88 % / 12.0 %
63	B	14.49 % / 75.58 %
64	C	40.03 % / 37.68 %
65	C	30.1 % / 67.64 %
66	B	52.24 % / 42.22 %
67	B	78.32 % / 17.2 %
68	B	76.82 % / 19.42 %
69	A	79.08 % / 19.7 %
70	D	69.21 % / 30.33 %
71	A	30.33 % / 69.0 %
72	C	17.22 % / 77.71 %
73	B	42.85 % / 55.97 %
74	B	81.09 % / 14.65 %
75	B	81.82 % / 16.88 %
76	C	47.32 % / 49.09 %
77	A	43.99 % / 38.76 %
78	B	60.69 % / 32.07 %
79	D	87.22 % / 10.1 %
80	A	42.04 % / 42.67 %

Q.	Ans.	Correct	Skipped
81	C	77.9 %	17.47 %
82	B	41.85 %	41.13 %
83	A	16.86 %	69.71 %
84	D	47.29 %	43.63 %
85	B	25.62 %	68.02 %
86	B	80.73 %	12.65 %
87	B	15.0 %	77.11 %
88	B	81.04 %	14.97 %
89	C	47.57 %	41.84 %
90	B	83.97 %	10.68 %
91	A	54.9 %	33.21 %
92	A	81.4 %	18.45 %
93	A	61.41 %	31.24 %
94	B	25.45 %	67.28 %
95	D	65.6 %	31.83 %
96	A	29.38 %	67.8 %

Q.	Ans.	Correct	Skipped
97	B	50.71 %	42.44 %
98	C	87.18 %	12.03 %
99	A	53.78 %	42.05 %
100	A	14.24 %	82.18 %
101	A	86.15 %	13.01 %
102	B	68.07 %	30.76 %
103	B	11.66 %	69.88 %
104	A	87.81 %	11.63 %
105	C	47.31 %	30.87 %
106	A	13.28 %	82.46 %
107	A	40.54 %	52.36 %
108	B	58.88 %	38.05 %
109	B	25.7 %	70.11 %
110	D	11.03 %	88.46 %
111	A	56.47 %	32.21 %
112	B	88.99 %	10.9 %

Q.	Ans.	Correct	Skipped
113	C	14.77 %	77.15 %
114	C	43.12 %	42.6 %
115	B	88.72 %	10.75 %
116	C	32.62 %	67.2 %
117	C	78.59 %	14.27 %
118	C	12.25 %	67.38 %
119	A	56.11 %	40.54 %
120	A	89.61 %	10.06 %
121	B	46.78 %	51.87 %
122	B	89.54 %	10.1 %
123	D	86.85 %	10.14 %
124	B	83.97 %	11.53 %
125	A	12.8 %	67.42 %
126	A	30.5 %	68.89 %
127	B	76.31 %	20.8 %
128	B	42.97 %	35.64 %

Q.	Ans.	Correct	Skipped
129	A	82.68 %	14.03 %
130	A	13.95 %	84.9 %
131	D	80.65 %	10.69 %
132	A	49.61 %	49.14 %
133	B	28.72 %	68.98 %
134	C	47.37 %	46.07 %
135	B	17.65 %	70.03 %
136	A	83.55 %	13.01 %
137	B	50.3 %	46.14 %
138	A	85.54 %	12.59 %
139	B	14.77 %	67.29 %
140	C	85.98 %	13.79 %
141	C	40.83 %	56.21 %
142	C	24.14 %	70.93 %
143	B	56.81 %	38.55 %
144	B	21.84 %	76.82 %

Q.	Ans.	Correct	Skipped
145	C	87.24 %	10.37 %
146	B	76.61 %	19.47 %
147	C	83.24 %	11.44 %
148	A	21.91 %	76.57 %
149	B	28.27 %	67.46 %
150	A	29.9 %	69.61 %
151	B	21.46 %	77.01 %
152	B	83.09 %	10.79 %
153	B	12.08 %	69.0 %
154	C	10.98 %	72.05 %
155	B	18.36 %	80.69 %
156	B	25.9 %	68.15 %
157	B	77.18 %	19.33 %
158	B	50.55 %	34.54 %
159	A	77.71 %	18.73 %
160	A	80.99 %	11.59 %

Q.	Ans.	Correct / Skipped
161	B	88.57 % / 10.78 %
162	C	26.16 % / 67.67 %
163	B	44.62 % / 51.07 %
164	C	76.77 % / 18.11 %
165	A	64.95 % / 32.4 %
166	D	31.67 % / 68.29 %
167	B	60.26 % / 39.45 %
168	A	51.7 % / 41.14 %
169	A	10.66 % / 68.42 %
170	B	82.74 % / 16.78 %
171	B	87.07 % / 11.04 %
172	D	77.19 % / 14.29 %
173	A	15.58 % / 76.0 %
174	B	69.16 % / 30.55 %
175	C	87.69 % / 11.85 %
176	C	29.63 % / 67.22 %

Q.	Ans.	Correct / Skipped
177	D	67.44 % / 31.26 %
178	B	14.77 % / 68.6 %
179	C	26.4 % / 71.49 %
180	C	32.67 % / 67.06 %
181	A	55.21 % / 37.67 %
182	A	23.12 % / 71.28 %
183	C	15.07 % / 78.08 %
184	A	67.75 % / 30.26 %
185	B	20.35 % / 72.8 %
186	A	83.45 % / 12.52 %
187	B	68.35 % / 30.99 %
188	B	12.44 % / 73.2 %
189	A	77.2 % / 20.62 %
190	B	61.87 % / 32.72 %
191	B	86.08 % / 10.72 %
192	B	56.18 % / 31.28 %

Q.	Ans.	Correct / Skipped
193	A	31.26 % / 67.21 %
194	D	88.48 % / 10.75 %
195	B	52.74 % / 47.02 %
196	C	25.51 % / 69.38 %
197	A	17.26 % / 68.75 %
198	C	66.25 % / 33.13 %
199	A	22.31 % / 68.36 %
200	B	68.34 % / 31.13 %
201	A	77.44 % / 12.1 %
202	A	79.98 % / 12.85 %
203	B	61.74 % / 38.25 %
204	C	12.9 % / 85.21 %
205	A	55.83 % / 37.7 %
206	D	85.26 % / 11.04 %
207	A	44.08 % / 46.52 %
208	C	29.07 % / 67.01 %

Q.	Ans.	Correct / Skipped
209	A	86.77 % / 12.08 %
210	B	57.28 % / 30.82 %
211	C	64.52 % / 34.05 %
212	C	10.37 % / 75.62 %
213	C	28.59 % / 69.38 %
214	B	63.15 % / 33.14 %
215	B	88.67 % / 11.21 %
216	B	11.52 % / 73.86 %
217	A	83.9 % / 14.63 %
218	C	45.71 % / 52.61 %
219	C	77.71 % / 19.84 %
220	C	22.95 % / 72.09 %
221	A	47.54 % / 38.16 %
222	C	16.98 % / 72.86 %
223	C	87.55 % / 10.97 %
224	A	57.17 % / 37.53 %

Q.	Ans.	Correct / Skipped
225	C	78.43 % / 21.47 %
226	B	42.05 % / 33.73 %
227	A	54.13 % / 36.49 %
228	B	27.49 % / 71.85 %
229	B	49.51 % / 36.32 %
230	C	78.65 % / 18.88 %
231	A	14.31 % / 84.88 %
232	B	59.28 % / 35.97 %
233	A	77.37 % / 14.97 %
234	C	27.36 % / 70.44 %
235	A	63.25 % / 31.08 %
236	B	21.69 % / 69.21 %
237	B	84.73 % / 13.3 %
238	B	58.95 % / 32.29 %
239	B	11.22 % / 73.31 %
240	B	47.01 % / 41.83 %

Performance Analysis

Avg. Score (%)	50.83%
Toppers Score (%)	55.94%
Your Score	

Part A

Q.1 Enzyme that protects the brain from free radical injury is:

A. Myelo-peroxidase

B. Superoxide dismutase

C. MAO

D. Hydroxylase

Q.2 Both hyperplasia and hypertrophy are found in:

A. Pregnancy uterus

B. Cardiac muscle in cardiomegaly

C. Skeletal muscle in athlete

D. Breast development in puberty

Q.3 Coagulative necrosis is seen in:

A. TB and gangrene

B. Sarcoidosis

C. Crypto-coccal infection

D. Jaundice

Q.4 Ladder pattern of DNA electrophoresis in apoptosis is caused by the action of:

A. endonuclease

B. transglutaminase

C. DNAase

D. caspase

Q.5 Annexin V is a marker of:

A. Apoptosis

B. Necrosis

C. Atherosclerosis

D. Inflammation

Q.6 In apoptosis, Apaf-1 is activated by release of which of the following substances from the mitochondria?

A. Bcl-2   **B.** Bax   **C.** Bcl-XL   **D.** Bim

Q.7 Which of the following is true about metastatic calcification?

A. Serum Ca level is normal.

B. It occurs in dead dying tissue.

C. It occurs in damaged heart valves.

D. Calcification starts in mitochondria.

Q.8 Which of the following statements is false regarding gram-positive cocci?

A. Staph saprophyticus causes UTI in females.

B. Micrococci are oxidase positive.

C. Pneumococci are encapsulated.

D. Most enterococci are sensitive to penicillin.

Q.9 A patient of RHD developed infective endocarditis after dental extraction. The most likely organism who caused this was:

A. Streptococcus viridans

B. Streptococcus pneumoneae

C. Streptococcus pyogenes

D. S. aureus

Q.10 Streptococcus causing dental caries is:

A. Streptococci equisimilis

B. Streptococci mutans

C. Streptococci pneumoniae

D. Streptococci bovis

Q.11 In a case of neonatal meningitis, etiologic bacteria were found to have properties of -hemolysis, bacitracin resistance and CAMP positive. Which of the following is the most likely causative agent?

A. Streptococcus pyogenes

B. Streptococcus agalactiae

C. Streptococcus pneumoniae

D. Streptococcus faecalis

Q.12 Eight months after prosthetic valve replacement, most common organism causing infective endocarditis is:

A. Staph. epidermidis   **B.** Strep. viridans

C. Staph. aureus   **D.** Hacek

Q.13 Which of the following components of St. pyogenes has cross reactivity with synovium of humans?

A. Capsular hyaluronic acid

B. Cell proteins

C. Group A carbohydrate antigens

D. Peptidoglycan

Q.14 A boy is suffering from skin ulcer. His culture revealed beta hemolysis. School physician said that similar hemolysis was seen in an organism from sore throat. What is the similarity between the both?

A. Protein is same for both

B. C carbohydrate antigen is different

C. C carbohydrate antigen is the same

D. Strain causing both is the same

Q.15 Ritonavir does not inhibit the metabolism of which of the following drugs?

A. Amiodarone   **B.** Phenobarbitone

C. Cisapride   **D.** Atazanavir

Q.16 Alkaline diuresis is done for treatment of poisoning due to which of the following?

A. Morphine   **B.** Amphetamine

C. Phenobarbitone   **D.** Atropine

Q.17 The mitochondrial enzyme involved in the metabolism of clopidogrel and proton pump inhibitors is;

A. CYP2A   **B.** CYP2B

C. CYP3A4   **D.** CYP2C20

Q.18 Which of the following is incorrectly matched regarding drug elimination?

A. Calcium channel blockers : CYP3A4

B. Carve-dilol : CYP2D6

C. Digoxin : P-glycoprotein

D. Sim-vastatin : Glucuronide conjugation.

Q.19 Which of the following is a prodrug?

A. Enalapril

B. Clonidine

C. Salmeterol

D. Acetazolamide

Q.20 Which of the following drugs is an inhibitor of Cytochrome P450 enzymes?

A. Ketoconazole

B. Rifampicin

C. Phenytoin

D. Phenobarbitone

Q.21 In metabolism of xenobiotics, which of the following reactions does not occur in phase I?

A. Oxidation

B. Reduction

C. Conjugation

D. Hydrolysis

Q.22 Which of the following statements is incorrect?

A. Acidic drugs bind to albumin in plasma.

B. Basic drugs bind to alpha-1 acid glycoprotein in plasma.

C. Drugs having higher affinity for a plasma protein can displace the other drug from the same protein.

D. Sex steroid hormones do not bind to any protein in plasma.

Q.23 Alkalinisation of urine is required for decreasing the poisoning due to which of the following?

A. Barbiturates

B. Amphetamine

C. Alcohol

D. Morphine

Q.24 Which of the following does not result in detoxification of drugs?

A. NADPH cytochrome P450 reductase

B. Cytochrome P450

C. Cytochrome oxidase

D. Mono-oxygenase

Q.25 Which of the following antiplatelet drugs is a prodrug?

A. Clopidogrel

B. Tirofiban

C. Aspirin

D. Dipyridamole

Q.26 A highly ionised drug:

A. is excreted mainly by the kidney

B. can cross the placental barrier easily

C. is well absorbed from the intestine

D. accumulates in the cellular lipids

Q.27 The extent to which ionization of a drug takes place is dependent upon pKa of the drug and the pH of the solution in which the drug is dissolved. Which of the following statements is incorrect?

A. pKa of a drug is the pH at which the drug is 50% ionised.

B. Small changes of pH near the pka of a weak acidic drug will not affect its degree of ionisation.

C. Knowledge of pka of a drug is useful in predicting its behaviour in various body fluids.

D. Phenobarbitone with pKa of 7.2 is largely unionised at acid pH and will be about 40% non-ionised in plasma.

Q.28 Which of the following statements regarding bioavailability of a drug is **false**?

A. It is a fraction of administered drug that reaches the systemic circulation in an unchanged form.

B. Bioavailability can be compared in the area under curve after oral and intravenous administration.

C. Drug given by the oral route will have an absolute bioavailability of 100%

D. Bioavailability can be determined from plasma concentration or urinary excretion data.

Q.29

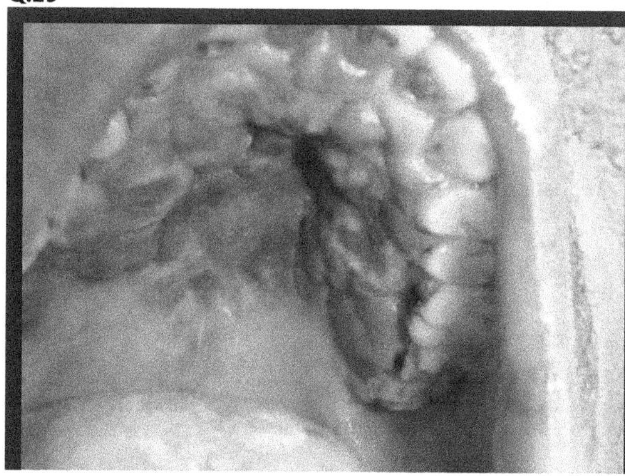

Which of the following diseases is depicted through this picture?

A. Oral Kaposi's sarcoma

B. Toxoplasma Gondii

C. Candidiasis

D. Histoplasmosis

Q.30 Most serious complication of measles:

A. Kopliks spot

B. Parotitis

C. Meningoencephalitis

D. Nephritis

Q.31 Which of the following is defined as the percentage of the test population affected by the index condition and test positive for it?

A. Specificity

B. Sensitivity

C. Very sensitive test

D. Very specific test

Q.32 Which of the following is defined as the percentage of the test population who are healthy and test negative?

A. Specificity

B. Sensitivity

C. Very sensitive test

D. Very specific test

Q.33 Which of the following tests detect most diseases but may generate abnormal findings in healthy people?

A. Specificity test

B. Sensitivity test

C. Very sensitive test

D. Very specific test

Q.34 Which of the following tests may miss significant pathology but is likely to establish the diagnosis, beyond doubt, when the result is positive?

A. Specificity test

B. Sensitivity test

C. Very sensitive test

D. Very specific test

Q.35 Which of the following is concerned both with the standards of conduct and competence expected of members of the medical profession and with the study of ethical problems raised by the practice of medicine?

A. Situation ethics
B. Medical ethics
C. Teleological ethics
D. Research ethics

Q.36 Which of the following is concerned with the character of the persons involved and with their actions?

A. Virtue ethics
B. Medical ethics
C. Teleological ethics
D. Research ethics

Q.37 Which of the following is concerned with whether the condition of a proposed action or course of action, in itself and regardless of its consequence is right or wrong?

A. Virtue ethics
B. Medical ethics
C. Teleological ethics
D. Deontological ethics

Q.38 Which of the following is concerned with the consequence of a proposed action or course of action?

A. Virtue ethics
B. Medical ethics
C. Teleological ethics
D. Deontological ethics

Q.39 Which of the following recognizes and emphasizes the need to consider carefully the context or situation in which a course of action is chosen?

A. Situation ethics
B. Medical ethics
C. Teleological ethics
D. Deontological ethics

Q.40 An abattoir worker developed pustule which later progressed to necrotic ulcer. Which of the following stains is useful demonstration of organism from smear made from pustule?

A. Polychromic methylene blue
B. Calcofluor white
C. Geimsa
D. Modified Kinyon stain

Q.41 Which of the following deals with the relationship between clinicians and individual patients?

A. Clinical ethics
B. Public health ethics
C. Research ethics
D. Deontological ethics

Q.42 Which of the following deals with health issues of groups of people in the community?

A. Clinical ethics
B. Public health ethics
C. Research ethics
D. Deontological ethics

Q.43 Which of the following is also known as histology?

A. Anatomy
B. Gross anatomy

C. Macroscopic anatomy
D. Microscopic anatomy

Q.44 What are the three major groups of planes pass through the body in the anatomical position?

A. Coronal / Sagittal/ Transverse planes
B. Sagittal planes/ Frontal Plane/ Vertical Plane
C. Transverse/ horizontal / axial planes
D. Frontal /vertical / Palatal planes

Q.45 Which planes pass through the center of a body and divide the body into equal left and right halves?

A. Sagittal planes
B. Median sagittal planes
C. Coronal planes
D. Axial planes

Q.46 Which of the following consists of the posterior aspect of a human body?

A. Back
B. Lumbar region
C. Thoracic curvature
D. Cervical region

Q.47 Polyvinyl siloxane or vinyl polysiloxane impression materials are

A. Condensation silicones
B. Addition silicones
C. Polysulphides
D. Silicates

Q.48 Which of the following is an irregularly-shaped cylinder like cavity in the human body?

A. Abdomen
B. Stomach
C. Lower limb
D. Thorax

Q.49 Which of the following is the most important function of thorax?

A. Acts as a machinery of the diaphragm
B. Breathing
C. Protection of the vital organs
D. Protection of the posterior aspects of the diaphragm

Q.50 Which of the following extends from the inferior margin of thorax to the superior margin of pelvis and lower limb?

A. Abdomen
B. Stomach
C. Diaphragm
D. Mediastinum

Q.51 What does the chamber enclosed by the abdomen wall contain?

A. Peritoneal cavity
B. Inferior thoracic aperture
C. Pelvic inlet
D. Diaphragm

Q.52 Pelvic cavity is _____.

A. Cylindrical-shaped
B. Bowl-shaped
C. Oval-shaped
D. Rhomboid-shaped

Q.53 The bladder expands superiorly into the:

A. Abdomen
B. Pelvic cavity
C. Uterus
D. Urethra

Q.54

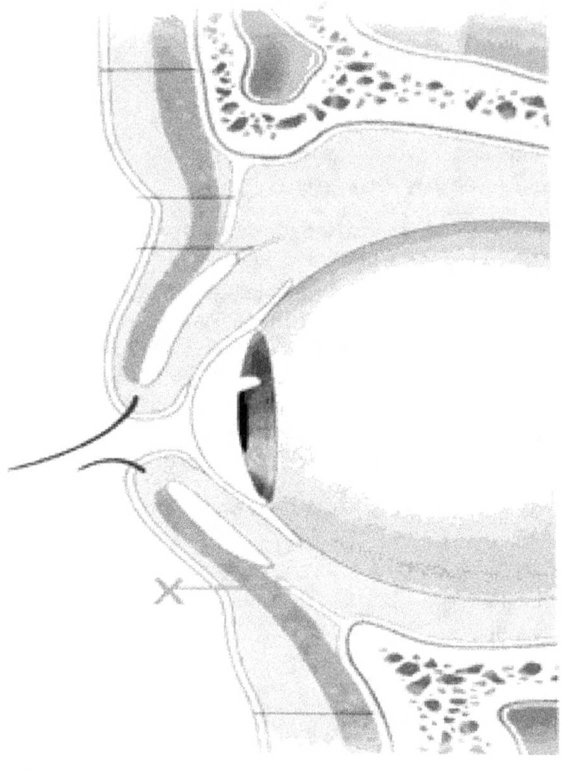

What does 'X' indicate in this picture of eye?

A. Orbital septum   **B.** Periosteum
C. Tendon of levator   **D.** Iris

Q.55

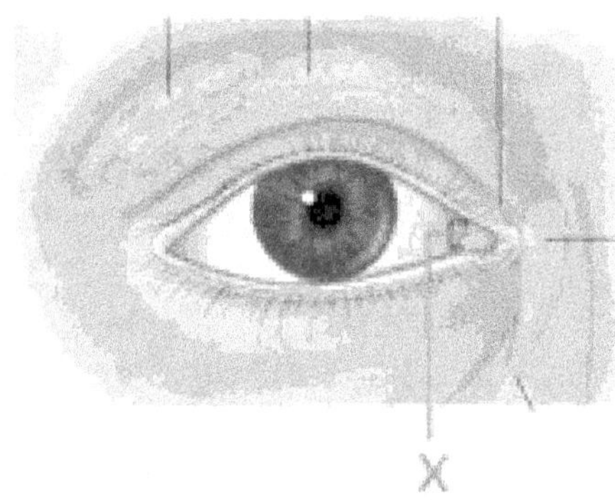

What does 'X' indicate in this picture of eye?

A. Iris   **B.** Puncta
C. Lacrimal sac   **D.** Lacrimal gland

Q.56

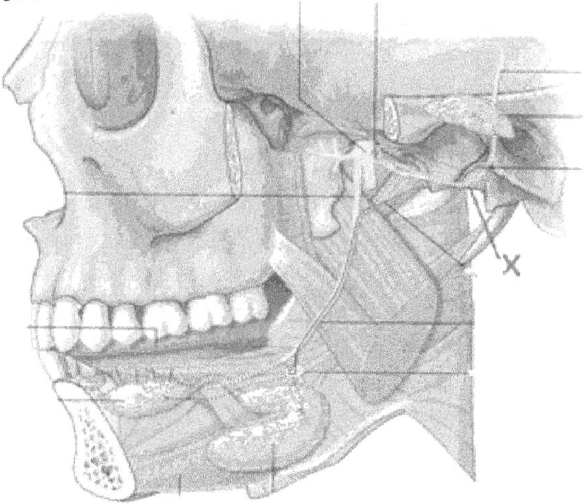

What does 'X' indicate in the above picture?

A. Petro-tympanic fissure
B. Auriculo-temporal nerve
C. Submandibular ganglion
D. Lingual nerve

Q.57 What is the living content of the cell called?

A. Protoplasm   **B.** Endoplasm
C. Cytoplasm   **D.** Nucleus

Q.58 What is the total thickness of the cell membrane?

A. 7 to 9 nm   **B.** 7 to 10 nm
C. 10 to 12 nm   **D.** 4 to 6 nm

Q.59 The process of ingestion of solid particulate matter is called:

A. phagocytosis   **B.** absorption
C. exocytosis   **D.** pinocytosis

Q.60 Which of the following is inherited through maternal line?

A. Cytoplasm   **B.** Nucleus
C. Mitochondria   **D.** Golgi complex

Q.61 An aggregation of similar types of cells is defined as:

A. organ system   **B.** tissues
C. membranes   **D.** None of the above

Q.62 Epithelium acts as a barrier in:

A. skin and urinary bladder
B. kidneys
C. heart
D. abdomen

Q.63 Which of the following contains type IV collagen?

A. Mitochondria   **B.** Basal lamina
C. Reticular lamina   **D.** Zonula occludens

Q.64 Which glyco-protein surrounds the elastic fibers?

A. Fibrillin   **B.** Laminin   **C.** Collagen   **D.** Elastin

Q.65 Which of the following surrounds the endothelial cells of capillaries and venules?

A. Fat cells   **B.** Myo-fibroblast
C. Pericytes   **D.** Pigment cells

Q.66 Which of the following play an important role in defense of the body against microorganism?

A. Lymphocytes   **B.** Monocytes
C. Eosinophils   **D.** Erythrocytes

Q.67 Which of the following stores the nutritional calories?

A. Adipose tissue
B. Loose connective tissue
C. Dense connective tissue
D. Reticular connective tissue

Q.68

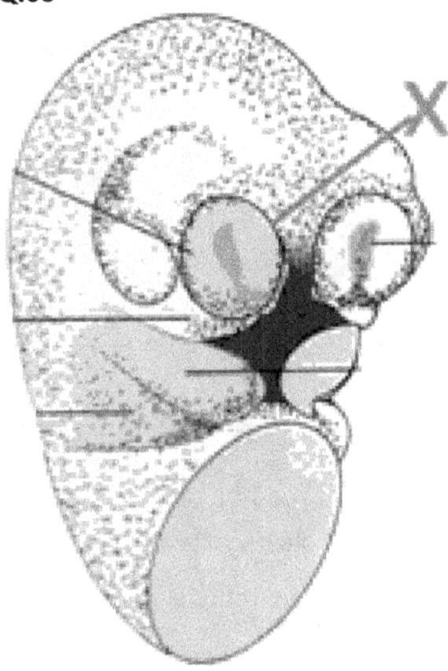

What does 'X' in this schematic diagram of development facial prominences represent?

A. Medial nasal prominence
B. Nasal pit
C. Mandibular prominence
D. Hyoid prominence

Q.69

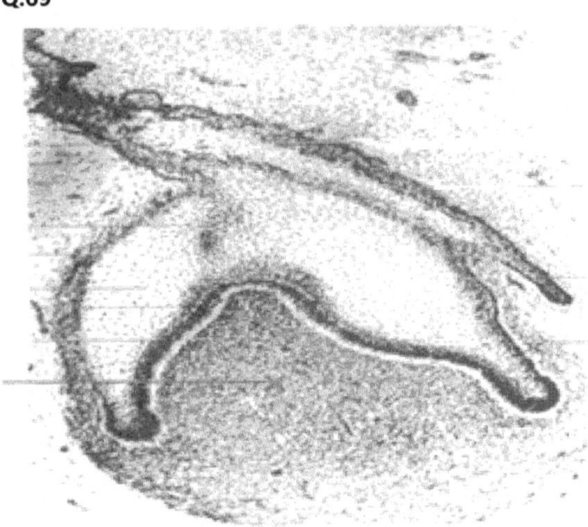

This is the picture of tooth germ of the human embryo. What does 'X' indicate here?

A. Dental lamina   **B.** Dental papilla
C. Enamel niche   **D.** Enamel cord

Q.70 Which of the following is found in the intervertebral discs?

A. Elastic cartilage
B. Hyaline cartilage
C. Fibrocartilage
D. Elastic connective tissue

Q.71

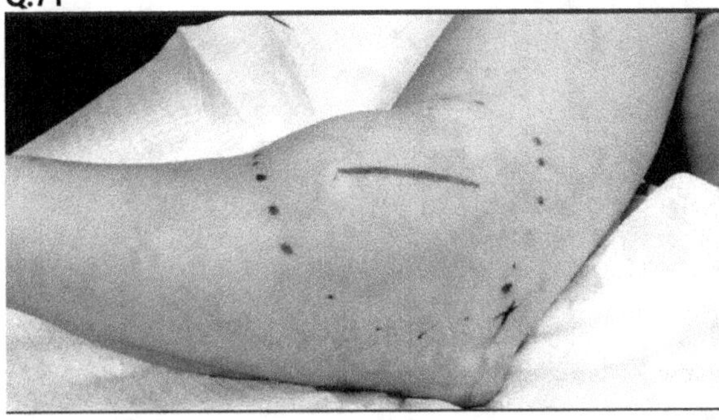

Which of the following tumors is depicted through this picture?

A. Lipoma   **B.** Sebaceous cyst
C. Lymphoma   **D.** Dermoids

Q.72 Which of the following is depicted through this picture?

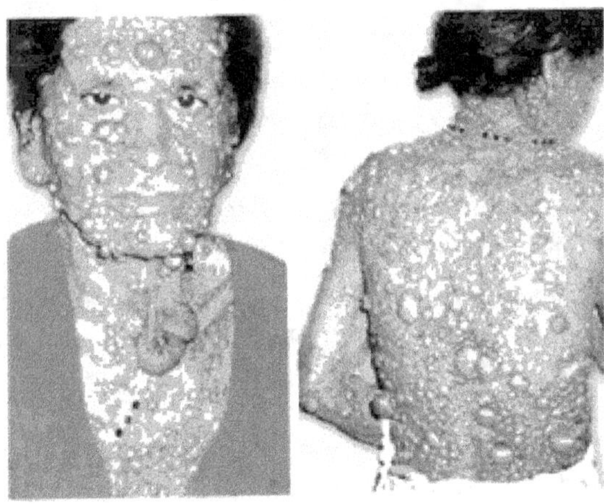

A. Multiple neuro-fibroma
B. Neuroma
C. Fibroma
D. Lymph cyst

Q.73

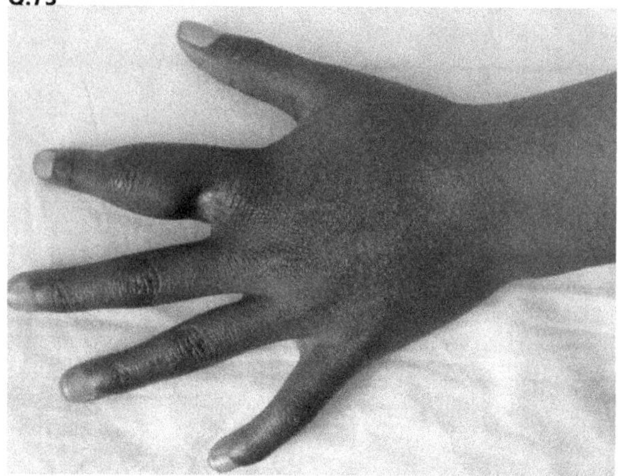

Which of the following diseases is depicted through this picture?

A. Heberden's disease | **B.** Spina ventosa
C. Callosity | **D.** Corn

Q.74 Which of the following is a collection of fluid in a sac lined by epithelium or endothelium?

A. Lipoma | **B.** Cyst
C. Tumour | **D.** Papilloma

Q.75 Following infection can be transmitted by blood transfusion:

A. HIV | **B.** Malaria
C. Hepatitis B | **D.** All of the above

Q.76 Hemorrhage occurring due to raised blood pressure is:

A. Reactionary | **B.** Secondary
C. Both of the above | **D.** None of the above

Q.77 What is the quantity of saliva secreted per day?

A. $1400\ ml$ | **B.** $1200\ ml$ | **C.** $1500\ ml$ | **D.** $700\ ml$

Q.78 In which of the following glands do multiple stones occur with chronic inflammation of the gland (sialadenitis)?

A. Parotid gland
B. Submandibular salivary gland
C. Minor salivary gland
D. Ectopic salivary gland

Q.79 Which of the following is an enlargement of the salivary gland due to fatty infiltration?

A. Sialectasis | **B.** Sialosis
C. Sialadenitis | **D.** Sialagogue

Q.80 Which of the following is an autoimmune disease causing progressive destruction of salivary gland and lacrimal glands?

A. Salivary neoplasm | **B.** Sjogren's syndrome
C. Parotid fistula | **D.** Mikulicz disease

Q.81 Shock which is associated with acquired adrenal insufficiency

A. Cardiogenic | **B.** Septic
C. Neurogenic | **D.** Hypovolemic

Q.82 Which of the following is the most common salivary gland tumour in adults?

A. Salivary neoplasm
B. Pleomorphic adenoma
C. Adenolymphoma
D. Mikulicz disease

Q.83 Which of the following consists of adenoids above, lingual tonsils below and two palatine tonsils laterally (one on each side)?

A. Waldeyer's lymphatic ring (inner)
B. Outer Waldeyer's ring
C. Thoracic outlet syndrome
D. Cervical RIB

Q.84 Which of the following is commonly a congenital lesion?

A. Branchial fistula | **B.** Pharyngeal pouch
C. Laryngocele | **D.** Branchial cyst

Q.85 Which of the following is used in the construction of dental prosthesis but does not become a part of the structure?

A. Direct restorative material
B. Auxiliary dental substance
C. Preventive dental material
D. Restorative dental

Q.86 Which of the following is bonded to another material by means of an adhesive?

A. Cohesive Strength | **B.** Adherend
C. Adhesive bonding | **D.** Cohesion bonding

Q.87 Which of the following are formed from the mutual attraction of positive and negative charges?

A. Covalent bonds | **B.** Ionic bonds
C. Hydrogen bonds | **D.** Metallic bonds

Q.88 which of the following bone is not pneumatic?

A. Mandible | **B.** Frontal
C. Mastoid | **D.** Ethmoid

Q.89 Which of the following represents the resistance of a fluid to flow?

A. Thixotropic | **B.** Viscosity
C. Value | **D.** Tarnish

Q.90 Which of the following qualities of material controls the time rate of a temperature change as heat passes through the material?

A. Thermal conductivity
B. Thermal diffusivity
C. Thermal expansion
D. Thermal resistivity

Q.91 Which of the following represents the relative stiffness of a material ratio of elastic stress to elastic strain?

A. Elastic modulus | **B.** Elastic strain
C. Flexural stress | **D.** Flexural toughness

Q.92 If a body is placed under a load that tends to compress or shorten it, then the internal resistance to such a load is called which of the following?

A. Tensile stress

B. Compressive stress

C. Shear stress

D. Flexural stress

Q.93 Which of the following may be defined as the energy required to fracture a material under an impact force?

A. Fatigue strength

B. Impact strength

C. Flexure strength

D. Tensile strength

Q.94 Which of the following shows a crystalline substance with metallic properties?

A. Non-metal

B. Metal

C. Alloy

D. Compound

Q.95 Danger layer of scalp is:

A. Periosteum

B. Connective tissue

C. Loose areolar tissue

D. Aponeurosis

Q.96 Which of the following requires that the cast alloy is held at a temperature near its solidus to achieve the maximum amount of diffusion without melting?

A. Homogenization

B. Coring

C. Dendrite formation in alloys

D. Interpretation

Q.97 Which of the following indicate(s) that resin should be tasteless, odourless, non-toxic and non-irritating?

A. Biological compatibility

B. Manipulation

C. Physical properties of dental resins

D. Aesthetic properties

Q.98 Acrylic resins are derived from which of the following?

A. Methylene

B. Ethylene

C. Propylene

D. Phenol

Q.99

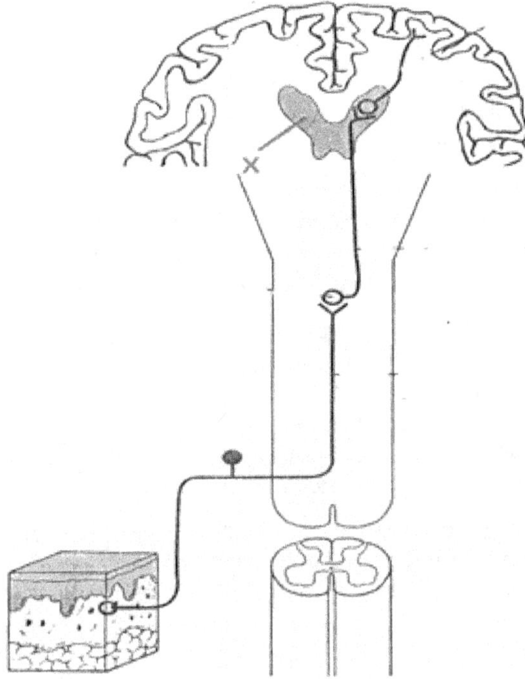

This is the diagram of general arrangement of sensory pathways showing first, second and third order neurons. What does 'X' indicate?

A. Cerebrum

B. Cerebelli

C. Thalamus

D. Cerebral cortex

Q.100 Which of the following divide(s) the cell into components?

A. Cell wall

B. Membranes

C. Cytoskeleton

D. All of the above

Part B

Q.101 Which of the following is an age-defined speciality that provides both primary and comprehensive preventive and therapeutic oral health care?

A. Operative dentistry

B. Pediatric dentistry

C. Public health dentistry

D. Prosthodontics

Q.102 Which of the following examinations represents problems related to jaws, bones and teeth?

A. Intra-oral examination

B. Extra-oral examination

C. General examination

D. Biographical examination

Q.103 What does the preparatory phase represent?

A. Preventive measures like oral health education and oral prophylaxis

B. Step by step planning of all the restorative procedures

C. Instructions given for the maintenance after the dental procedures

D. Medical specialist or family physician

Q.104 Which of the following dentinal layers is more mineralized?
A. Peritubular dentin
B. Inter tubular dentin
C. Dentinal tubules
D. Circum pulpal dentin

Q.105 At what age is the enamel formation for permanent teeth completed?
A. 12 years   **B.** 15 years   **C.** 8 years   **D.** 10 years

Q.106 How does the crown as a whole represent in maxillary second primary molar?
A. Mandibular permanent first molar
B. Maxillary permanent first molar
C. Maxillary permanent third molar
D. Maxillary permanent second molar

Q.107 Which of the following in mandibular second molars has a trunk that bifurcates at a short distance from buccal and lingual borders to form a mesial and a distal branch?
A. Pulp cavity
B. Occlusal surface
C. Root
D. Distal surface

Q.108 The ratio of the number of new cases of a specific disease during a given time period to the population at risk and the whole multiplied by 1000 refers to which of the following term's formula?
A. Attack rate
B. Prevalence
C. Incidence
D. Relationship between prevalence and incidence

Q.109 What does the prevalence rate depend on?
A. Duration of the disease and attack rate
B. Incidence and duration of the disease
C. Duration of the disease and mortality
D. Mortality and birth

Q.110 An example of a disease exhibiting ______ is dental caries.
A. age
B. gender and secular trends
C. bimodality
D. cyclic trends

Q.111 Which of the following is a measure of the association between risk factor and outcome?
A. Estimation of risk
B. Odds ratio
C. Exposure rates
D. Selection bias

Q.112 Which term is defined as the group of people who share a common characteristic or experience within a defined time period?
A. Cohort
B. Bias
C. Analysis and interpretation
D. Follow-up

Q.113 The water bodies such as shallow wells, deep wells, springs are being the sources for which of the following categories of water?
A. Surface water
B. Groundwater
C. Sea water
D. Ponds and lakes

Q.114 What is the guideline value for the true colour units of the drinking water?
A. Up to 14 units
B. Up to 15 units
C. Up to 11 units
D. Up to 12 units

Q.115

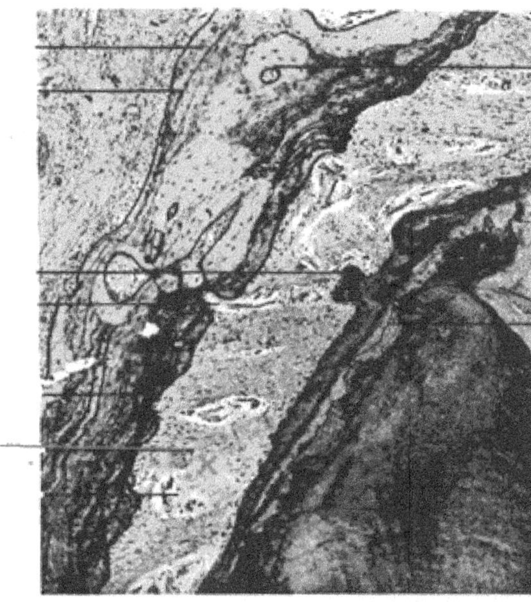

This is the diagram of dental pulp and periradicular tissues. What does 'X' indicate?
A. Interstitial spaces
B. Periodontal ligament
C. Alveolar bone
D. Dentin

Q.116 Which scope of Operative Dentistry includes the maintenance of the vitality of the dental pulp?
A. Material science
B. Pulp physiology and pathology
C. Occlusion
D. Preventive care

Q.117 What is the total number of teeth in human?
A. 32   **B.** 16   **C.** 52   **D.** 20

Q.118 Which of the following is known as Universal System?
A. Federation Dentaire International (FDI) System
B. American Dental Association (ADA) System
C. Zsigmondy Palmer System
D. None of these

Q.119 Which of the following refers to the terminology or set of technical terms that is employed in a particular branch of science?
A. Operative Dentistry

B. Nomenclature
C. Public Health Dentistry
D. Endodontics

Q.120 The coronal portion of each tooth is a:
A. Hollow casing that encloses the pulp
B. Cavity
C. Pulp chamber
D. Dentine

Q.121 Which is the hardest substance in the human body?
A. Tooth enamel
B. Dentine
C. Pulp
D. Cementum

Q.122 The first group of pulpal painful response is associated with:
A. A delta nerve fibres
B. B delta nerve fibres
C. C delta nerve fibres
D. D delta nerve fibres

Q.123 What is/are the periodontal test(s) used in conjunction with percussion?
A. Visual and tactile inspection
B. Palpation, mobility, and depressibility
C. Radiography
D. Electric pulp test

Q.124 Which of the following is/are used to treat acute reversible pulpitis?
A. Pulpectomy
B. Palliative procedures
C. Radiographic examination
D. Anaesthetic test

Q.125 Which of the following is used to seal the tooth in mild cases of an acute alveolar abscess?
A. Antibiotic
B. Antiseptic
C. Astringent
D. Acrylic resin

Q.126 When does the dental pulpal have its genesis about the sixth week of uterine life?
A. During initiation of tooth development
B. During root development
C. During development of caries
D. During development of pulp

Q.127

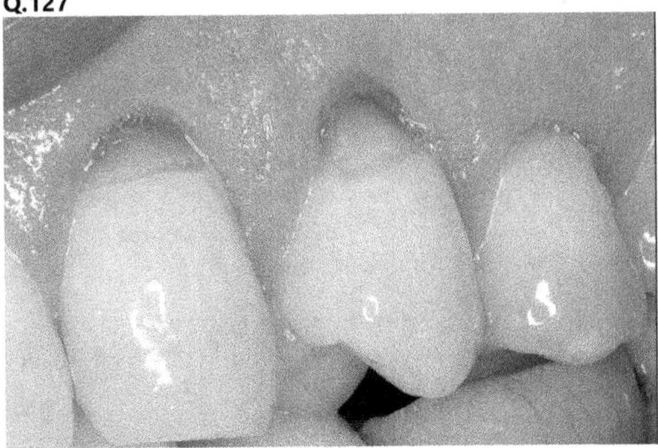

What does this picture indicate?

A. Attrition of mandibular anteriors
B. Cervical abrasion of maxillary anteriors
C. Erosion of maxillary lateral incisor
D. Abfraction of maxillary anteriors

Q.128 Which of the following parts of the dental pulp is indicated by the letter 'X'?

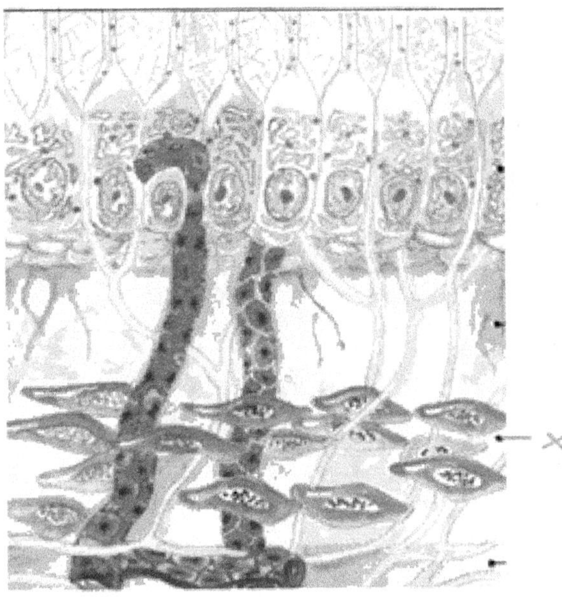

A. Odontoblastic layer
B. Cell free zone
C. Cell rich zone
D. Pulp core

Q.129

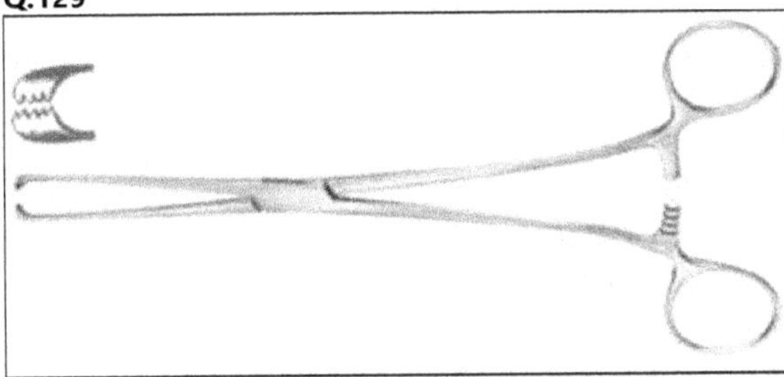

Which of the following surgical tools is/are indicated through this diagram?
A. Allis tissue forceps
B. Rongeurs forceps
C. Weider retractor
D. Minnesota retractor

Q.130

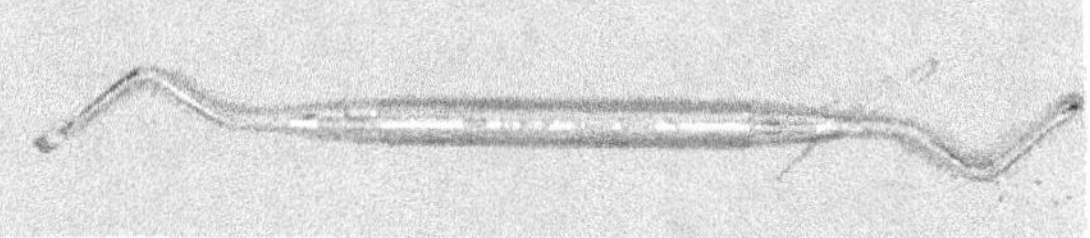

Which of the following surgical tools is indicated through this diagram?
A. Ash curette
B. Periapical curette
C. Excavator
D. Crane pick

Q.131 ______ is important when examining temporomandibular joint function, salivary gland size and function, thyroid gland size, presence or absence of enlarged or tender lymph nodes, and induration of oral soft tissues, as well as for determining pain or the presence of fluctuance in areas of swelling.

A. Palpation
B. Scanning
C. Diagnosis
D. Treatment

Q.132 Physicians commonly use percussion during thoracic and abdominal examinations, and the dentists can use it to test teeth and -

A. trachea
B. paranasal sinuses
C. arches
D. bone ligament

Q.133 The dentist uses ______ primarily for temporomandibular joint evaluation, but it is also used for cardiac, pulmonary, and gastrointestinal system evaluations.

A. anesthetic
B. auscultation
C. palpation
D. treatment

Q.134 The most commonly used medical evaluation physical status classification is:

A. American Society of Anesthesiologists (ASA)
B. United Nation Organisation (UNO)
C. World Health Organisation (WHO)
D. None of these

Q.135 The maxillary sinus drains into the:

A. Sphenoethmoidal sinus
B. Superior meatus
C. Middle meatus
D. Inferior meatus

Q.136 Patients with medical conditions sometimes require modifications of their ______ care when oral surgery is planned.

A. peri-operative
B. buccal
C. prosthesis
D. prosthetics

Q.137 Obstruction of the arterial supply to the ______ is one of the most common health problems the dentists encounter.

A. aorta
B. myocardium
C. tricuspid valves
D. posterior valves

Q.138

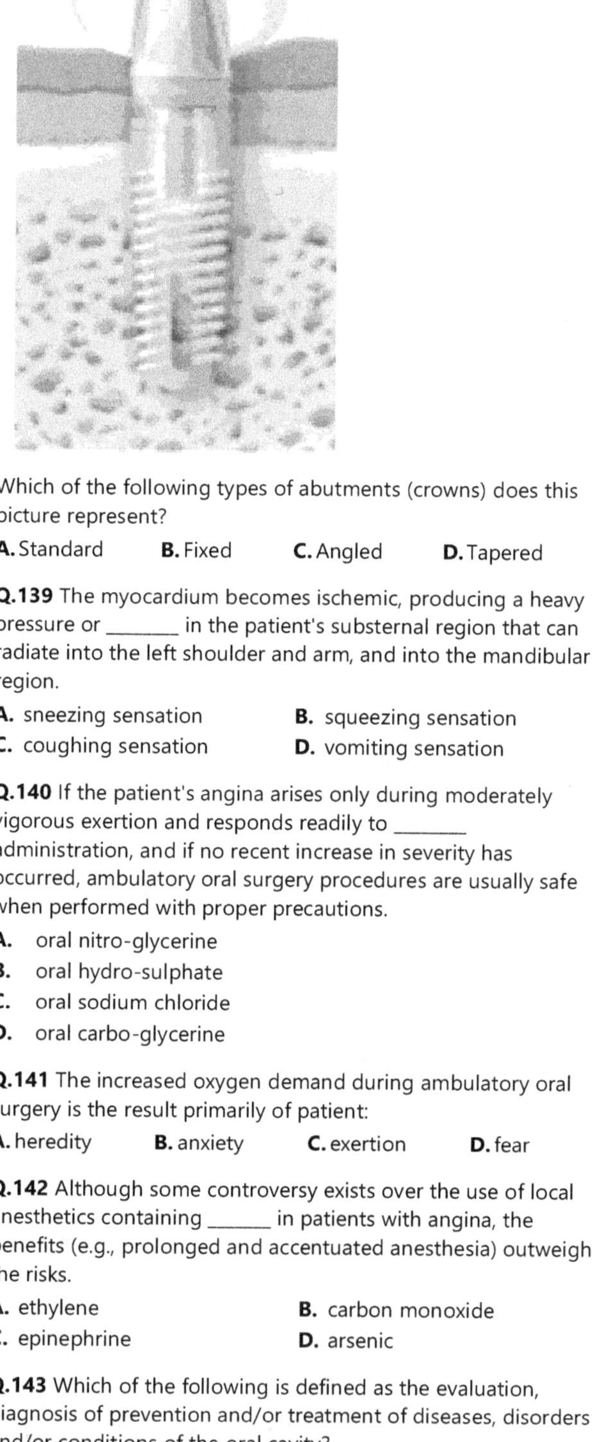

Which of the following types of abutments (crowns) does this picture represent?

A. Standard **B.** Fixed **C.** Angled **D.** Tapered

Q.139 The myocardium becomes ischemic, producing a heavy pressure or ______ in the patient's substernal region that can radiate into the left shoulder and arm, and into the mandibular region.

A. sneezing sensation
B. squeezing sensation
C. coughing sensation
D. vomiting sensation

Q.140 If the patient's angina arises only during moderately vigorous exertion and responds readily to ______ administration, and if no recent increase in severity has occurred, ambulatory oral surgery procedures are usually safe when performed with proper precautions.

A. oral nitro-glycerine
B. oral hydro-sulphate
C. oral sodium chloride
D. oral carbo-glycerine

Q.141 The increased oxygen demand during ambulatory oral surgery is the result primarily of patient:

A. heredity **B.** anxiety **C.** exertion **D.** fear

Q.142 Although some controversy exists over the use of local anesthetics containing ______ in patients with angina, the benefits (e.g., prolonged and accentuated anesthesia) outweigh the risks.

A. ethylene
B. carbon monoxide
C. epinephrine
D. arsenic

Q.143 Which of the following is defined as the evaluation, diagnosis of prevention and/or treatment of diseases, disorders and/or conditions of the oral cavity?

A. Dentistry
B. Histology
C. Pediatric dentistry
D. Prostheses

Q.144 Anthrax is caused by:

A. Bacillus anthracis

B. Streptococcus bacillus

C. Salmonella typhi

D. Plasmodium malariae

Q.145 Which of the following concepts views health as a dynamic equilibrium between man and his environment, and disease as a maladjustment of the human organism to environment?

A. Biomedical concept

B. Ecological concept

C. Psychosocial concept

D. Holistic concept

Q.146 Which of the following is the reservoir for the agents of disease?

A. Environment

B. Nature

C. Ecosystem

D. Man

Q.147 Single-cause idea could not explain:

A. modern diseases of civilisation like coronary heart disease and cancer

B. renal failure

C. depression

D. liver failure

Q.148 Period of pre-pathogenesis refers to:

A. processes in the environment

B. processes in man

C. processes in ecosystem

D. processes in universe

Q.149 Web of causation was coined by:

A. MacMahon and Pugh

B. Pettenkofer

C. Robert Koch

D. Anton van Leeuwenhoek

Q.150 Which of the following committees is known as the health survey and planning committee?

A. Bhore Committee

B. Mudaliar Committee

C. Kartar Committee

D. Srivastava Committee

Q.151 Which of the following aims at bringing preventive care to individuals at special risk?

A. Population strategy

B. Primordial prevention

C. High-risk strategy

D. Health promotion

Q.152 Which of the following is the combined and coordinated use of medical, vocational, social and educational measures for training and retraining the individual to the highest possible level of functional ability?

A. Rehabilitation

B. Disability limitation

C. Primordial prevention

D. Secondary prevention

Q.153 Which of the following represents the frequency of a disease or characteristics expressed per unit size of the population or group in which it is observed?

A. Ratio

B. Rate

C. Proportion

D. Crude death rate

Q.154 Which of the following lipids represent the triglycerides?

A. Simple lipids

B. Compound lipids

C. Derived lipids

D. Saturated Fats

Q.155 Age-specific death rate is the _________ limited to a given age group.

A. birth rate

B. death rate

C. current age

D. adolescence period

Q.156 Proportional mortality rate is defined as the number of deaths due to a particular cause per:

A. 100 total deaths

B. 1000 total deaths

C. 100 or 1000 total deaths

D. 10,000 total deaths

Q.157 What does the abbreviation EBDM stand for?

A. Evidence Based Decision Making

B. Efficient Based Decision Making

C. Effluent Based Decision Making

D. Effervescence Based Decision Making

Q.158 Which of the following changes irregular heartbeat to normal heartbeat?

A. Encainide

B. Epinephrine

C. Amoxicillin

D. None of these

Q.159 Proximity to electromagnetic radiation increases the chances of leukemia in children by:

A. 50%   B. 23%   C. 12%   D. 49%

Q.160

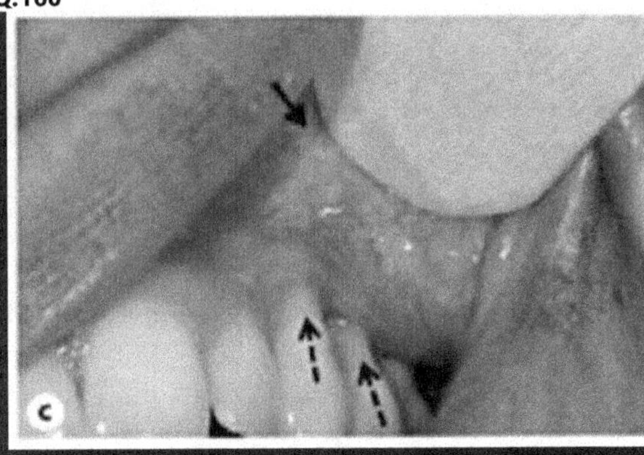

Which of the following diseases is indicated by this diagram?

A. Chemical burn caused by aspirin

B. Overzealous of tooth brush

C. Gingival recession on the maxillary teeth

D. Gingival recession and hyperkeratosis of the vestibular

mucosa

Q.161

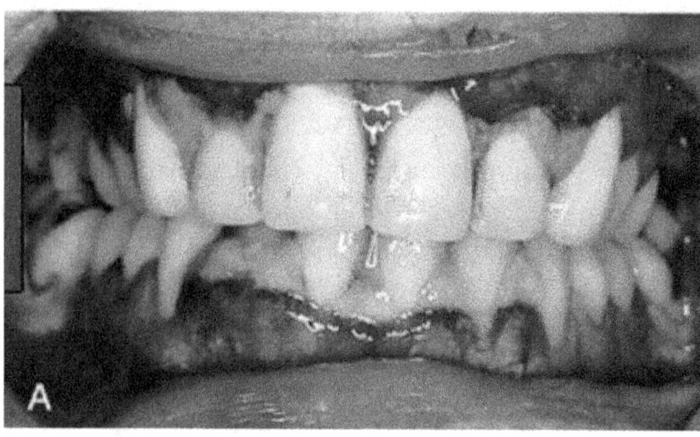

Which of the following is indicated through this picture?

A. Acute myelocytic leukemia
B. Necrosis
C. Agranulocytosis
D. ANUG

Q.162 Which of the following lines the gingival sulcus?

A. Sulcular epithelium
B. Oral epithelium
C. Junctional epithelium
D. Oral mucosa

Q.163 Which of the following form the inner layer of the REE after a tooth erupts?

A. Ameloblasts
B. Endoblasts
C. Cementoblasts
D. Mesenchyme cells

Q.164 Which of the following is/are composed of a complex vascular and highly cellular connective tissue?

A. Gingiva
B. Periodontal ligament
C. Cellular elements
D. Endodontal ligament

Q.165 Which of the following principle fibres of the periodontal ligament extends at right angles to the long axis of the tooth from the cementum to the alveolar bone?

A. Horizontal group
B. Apical group
C. Inter-radicular group
D. Alveolar crest group

Q.166 Best method of communicating with a fearful deaf child is:

A. Speaking loudly
B. Normal conversation
C. Use sign language
D. Speak with prominent lip movement

Q.167 Which is the calcified, avascular mesenchymal tissue that forms the outer covering of the anatomic root?

A. Dentine
B. Pulp
C. Cementum
D. Enamel

Q.168 Which of the following cells produce the organic matrix of bone, and are differentiated from pluripotent follicle cells?

A. Ameloblasts
B. Odontoblasts
C. Osteoblasts
D. Fibroblasts

Q.169 Which accumulation has been suggested to increase with age?

A. Dento-gingival plaque
B. Dental caries
C. Dental plaque
D. Occlusal trauma

Q.170 Which of the following may be factitious as in the case of tooth brush trauma resulting in the gingival ulceration?

A. Traumatic lesions
B. Gingival disease of fungal origin
C. Gingival diseases of viral origin
D. Foreign body reactions

Q.171 What is the normal respiratory rate per minute?

A. 12 to 16 breaths
B. 15 to 25 breaths
C. 10 to 14 breaths
D. 20 to 25 breaths

Q.172 How many types of known herpes viruses are there?

A. 70
B. 100
C. 90
D. 50

Q.173 Which of the following is the generalised primary infection that occurs the first time an individual comes in contact with the virus?

A. Varicella zoster
B. Chicken pox
C. HSV isolation
D. Cytomegalo virus

Q.174 Which of the following is an acute inflammatory disease of the skin and mucous membrane?

A. Erythema multi-forme
B. Human herpes virus
C. Epstein Barr virus
D. Herpes simplex virus

Q.175 Antinuclear antibodies are seen in:

A. SLE
B. systematic sclerosis
C. Morphea
D. All of the above

Q.176 Which of the following is a disorder that is characterised by recurring ulcers?

A. Acute necrotising ulcerative gingivitis
B. Oral ulcers secondary to cancer chemotherapy
C. Contact allergic stomatitis
D. Recurrent aphthous stomatitis

Q.177 Which of the following is a life threatening disease that causes blisters and erosions of the skin and mucous membranes?

A. Pemphigus
B. Pemphigus vulgaris
C. Para-neoplastic pemphigus
D. Pemphigus vegetans

Q.178 Which of the following demonstrates a wide view of the maxilla and mandible as well as surrounding tissues?

A. Panoramic radiography
B. X-rays

C. MRI

D. Tomography

Q.179 In which of the following is an image made of a thin layer of thin tissues that are superficial and deep to the desired region blurred out due to movement of the X-ray tube and film?

A. Conventional tomography

B. Panoramic radiography

C. X-ray

D. MRI

Q.180 Which of the following uses radiofrequency (RF) pulses rather than ionising radiation to produce an image?

A. Conventional tomography

B. Panoramic radiography

C. Ultrasonography

D. Magnetic resonance imaging

Q.181 Which of the following uses the reflection of sound waves to provide information about tissues and their interfaces with other tissue?

A. Conventional tomography

B. Panoramic radiography

C. Ultrasonography

D. Magnetic resonance imaging

Q.182 In which of the following is a substance labelled with a radioactive isotope and injected intravenously?

A. Radionuclide imaging

B. Panoramic radiography

C. Ultrasonography

D. Magnetic resonance imaging

Q.183 In which of the following is a radiopaque contrast medium instilled into the duct of a salivary gland prior to imaging which permits a thorough evaluation of the ductal system of the major glands?

A. Sialography

B. Radionuclide imaging

C. Panoramic radiography

D. Ultrasonography

Q.184 20% of sialoliths are present in the:

A. parotid glands

B. submandibular glands

C. maxillary arch

D. mandibular arch

Q.185 Which of the following provides a good overview of both joints as well as the rest of the maxillofacial complex?

A. Sialography

B. Radionuclide imaging

C. Panoramic radiography

D. Ultrasonography

Q.186 The term 'orthodontics' was coined by:

A. Angle   **B.** Le Foulon   **C.** Kingsley   **D.** Hunter

Q.187 Who is the father of modern dentistry?

A. Pierre Fauchard

B. Edward H Angle

C. Emerson C Angell

D. Le Foulon

Q.188 Which of the following is called as gum pads at the time of birth?

A. Maxillary arch

B. Mandibular arch

C. Alveolar arches

D. Palate

Q.189 Premaxilla is derived from:

A. frontonasal process

B. median process

C. palatine bone

D. maxillary tuberosity

Q.190 At what age is a child expected to have 12 primary teeth and 12 erupted permanent teeth?

A. 4.5 years

B. 6.5 years

C. 8.5 years

D. 11.5 years

Q.191 First evidence of calcification of 3rd molar is seen by the age of:

A. $1\frac{1}{2}$ years   **B.** 4 years   **C.** 6 years   **D.** 10 years

Q.192 Which of the following appreciations is/are important for studying the occlusion?

A. Static

B. Dynamic

C. Both A and B

D. None of these

Q.193 In deep bite cases, the freeway space is:

A. more than normal

B. less than normal

C. Can be either more than or less than normal

D. Cannot be predicted

Q.194 Who introduced the concept of hard tissue paradigm?

A. Kingsley   **B.** Angle   **C.** Case   **D.** Moyers

Q.195 Three-dimensional classification of occlusion was given by:

A. Angle   **B.** Simon   **C.** Deway   **D.** Baume

Q.196 Which of the following facial deformities is extremely stable?

A. Malocclusion

B. Torticlollis

C. Fractured condyle

D. Cleft lip and palate

Q.197 Which of the following conditions is usually present in a class II division 2 malocclusion?

A. Open bite

B. Mesion-occlusion of permanent maxillary first molar

C. Retrusion of maxillary central incisors

D. Retrusion of maxillary lateral incisors

Q.198 Which of the following is not a part of psychic triad?

A. Id

B. Ego

C. Super ego

D. Libido

Q.199 In habitual mouth breathing, respiratory resistance is:

A. more

B. less

C. the same as in structural conditioned mouth breathing

D. None of the above

Q.200 Which of the following is/are a diverse group of deformities in the growth of the head and facial bones?

A. Craniofacial anomalies

B. Congenital deformations

C. Teratogenic agents

D. Micrognathia

Q.201 Which of the following represents the most common benign (non-cancerous) tumour of the skin?

A. Vascular deformation

B. Hemangioma

C. Hemifacial microsomia

D. Deformational plagiocephaly

Q.202 Which of the following is a lethal anomaly characterised by hypoplasia?

A. Agnathia

B. Craniofacial anomaly

C. Micrognathia

D. Macrognathia

Q.203 Which of the following is a rare developmental anomaly characterised by asymmetric overgrowth of one or more body parts?

A. Hemihyperplasia

B. Hemifacial atrophy

C. Atrophy

D. Hyperplasia

Q.204 Which of the following is defined as an abnormal mass of tissue?

A. Neoplasm

B. Papilloma

C. Squamous acanthoma

D. Keratoacanthoma

Q.205 Which of the following is a self-healing carcinoma?

A. Keratoacanthoma

B. Myoepithelioma

C. Basal cell adenoma

D. Leukoplakia

Q.206 Which of the following is a benign neoplasm consisting of cells exhibiting ability to differentiate epithelial and mesenchymal cells?

A. Pleomorphic chondroma

B. Pleomorphic adenoma

C. Polymorphic adenoma

D. Polymorphic chondroma

Q.207 Which of the following represents an uncommon salivary gland tumour?

A. Myoepithelioma

B. Basal cell adenoma

C. Warthin's tumour

D. Oncocytoma

Q.208 Which of the following are derived from epithelium associated with development of the dental apparatus?

A. Odontogenic cysts

B. Dentigerous cysts

C. Eruption cysts

D. Odontogenickerato cysts

Q.209 Which of the following is also known as the sialo-odontogenic cyst?

A. Lateral periodontal cyst

B. Dental lamina cyst

C. Jaw cyst

D. Glandular odontogenic cyst

Q.210 Which of the following is a highly contagious systemic infection occurring predominantly in children?

A. Scarlet fever

B. Diphtheria

C. Tuberculosis

D. Tularemia

Q.211 Which of the following is an acute infection of the nervous system?

A. Tetanus

B. Tularemia

C. Melioidosis

D. Syphilis

Q.212 Which of the following is primarily a venereal disease?

A. AIDS

B. Gonorrhoea

C. Granuloma inguinale

D. Rhinoscleroma

Q.213 Which of the following is caused by Bartonella henselae?

A. Pyogenic granuloma

B. Cat-scratch disease

C. Noma

D. Rhinoscleroma

Q.214 Which of the following diseases occurs in wrestlers?

A. Herpetic whitlow

B. Herpes gladiataram

C. Herpetic eczema

D. Herpetic conjunctivitis

Q.215

Which of the following Kennedy classes of arch modification is illustrated by this picture?

A. Class I   **B.** Class II   **C.** Class III   **D.** Class IV

Q.216

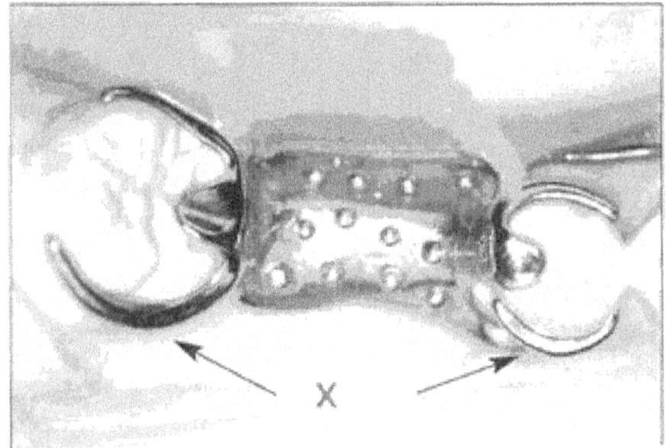

What does 'X' indicate in this retentive clasp assemblies?

A. Reciprocal elements
B. Retentive clasp arms
C. Matrices
D. Patrices

Q.217 Which of the following represents the branch of dental art and science that deals with the replacement of missing teeth and oral tissues to restore and maintain oral form, function, appearance and health?

A. Prosthodontics   **B.** Prosthesis
C. Prosthetics   **D.** Prosthetikos

Q.218 Which of the following are the three major divisions of prosthodontics?

A. Fixed prosthodontics, removable prosthodontics and maxillofacial prosthodontics
B. Fixed prosthodontics, removable prosthodontics and implant prosthodontics
C. Removable complete prosthodontics , removable partial prosthodontics and fixed prosthodontics
D. Complete denture prosthetics, removable prosthetics and fixed prosthetics

Q.219 A dental prosthesis is supported by:

A. abutment
B. dental implants
C. abutment and dental implants
D. prosthesis and prosthetics

Q.220 In removable partial denture prosthodontics, there are two principal types. They are:

A. Extra-coronal retainers and Intra-coronal retainers
B. Direct retainers and Indirect retainers
C. Extra retainers and Intra retainers
D. Retentive clasp and Stable clasp

Q.221 Reciprocal clasp and retentive clasp are the two fingers of metal of:

A. extra coronal retainers
B. intra coronal retainers
C. Both A and B
D. only intra coronal retainers

Q.222 Retention of intra-coronal removable partial dentures is dependent upon exact parallelism of the:

A. retentive assembly   **B.** intrusive assembly
C. extrusive assembly   **D.** stabilised assembly

Q.223 The retentive clasp is located in an undercut area of the clinical crown and resists displacement of the prosthesis______ the underlying hard and soft tissues.

A. away from   **B.** towards
C. on   **D.** in between

Q.224 In extra coronal, the retentive and reciprocal components lie _______ the external surfaces of the abutment.

A. on   **B.** over   **C.** beneath   **D.** away

Q.225 Matrix and patrix are the two:

A. retentive assemblies of intra-coronal retainer
B. extra coronal fingers of metal
C. resultant assembly of extra-coronal retainer
D. subdivisions of clasps

Q.226 Tooth supported removable partial denture receives support from:

A. natural teeth   **B.** artificial teeth
C. implants   **D.** dentures

Q.227 Like their intra-coronal counterparts, extra-coronal attachments derive their retention from closely fitted components termed as _________.

A. Matrices and patrices
B. Extra-coronal attachments
C. Retentive clasp assemblies
D. Semi-precision attachments

Q.228 Which of the surveying tools is used to identify the positions of desired undercuts on a dental cast?
A. Carbon marker
B. Undercut gauges
C. Wax knife
D. Analysing rod

Q.229 Cells have electrical potential difference known as:
A. resting membrane potential
B. passive membrane potential
C. motile membrane potential
D. active membrane potential

Q.230 Which equation is used to determine whether an ion is in equilibrium across a membrane or not?
A. Nernst equation
B. Vander waal's equation
C. Gibbs-Donnan equation
D. Maxwell's equation

Q.231 Which cell may fail to fire an action potential?
A. Slowly polarised
B. Rapidly depolarised
C. Moderately depolarised
D. Depolarised

Q.232 Which of the following is/are responsible for the conduction of action potentials?
A. Step up transformer
B. Local circuit currents
C. Self reinforcement
D. Small electric potential

Q.233 Which gap junctions permit ions to flow from one cell to another?
A. Chemical synapses
B. Electrical synapses
C. Neuromuscular junctions
D. Acetylcholine receptors

Q.234 All of the following are essential amino acids, except:
A. Methionine
B. Lysine
C. Alanine
D. Leucine

Q.235 Which of the following are polar amino acids?
A. Serine and Lysine
B. Tryptophan
C. Tyrosine
D. Valine

Q.236 Which of the following is not included in the basic amino acids?
A. Leucine
B. Arginine
C. Lysine
D. Histidine

Q.237 Guanidinium group is associated with:
A. Tyrosine
B. Arginine
C. Histidine
D. Lysine

Q.238 Which amino acid is produced by adding hydroxyl group to benzene ring chain of phenylalanine?

A. Threonine
B. Histidine
C. Tyrosine
D. Serine

Q.239 Which of the following is a non-aromatic amino acid with a hydroxyl R group?
A. Phenylalanine
B. Lysine
C. Threonine
D. Methionine

Q.240 Which of the following is not an essential amino acid?
A. Tryptophan
B. Threonine
C. Histidine
D. Cysteine

// Smart Answer Sheet //

Correct — Indicates percentage of students who answered questions correctly.

Skipped — Indicates percentage of students who skipped questions.

Q.	Ans.	Correct / Skipped
1	B	86.82 % / 10.9 %
2	A	76.99 % / 12.61 %
3	A	84.46 % / 13.52 %
4	A	83.04 % / 16.89 %
5	A	88.61 % / 10.52 %
6	C	84.42 % / 10.32 %
7	D	54.09 % / 40.0 %
8	D	89.47 % / 10.19 %
9	A	80.94 % / 18.88 %
10	B	86.26 % / 12.09 %
11	B	62.42 % / 35.33 %
12	A	83.77 % / 10.67 %
13	A	85.96 % / 11.92 %
14	C	61.17 % / 30.5 %
15	B	77.89 % / 15.91 %
16	C	87.1 % / 11.87 %
17	C	79.91 % / 15.68 %
18	D	80.74 % / 17.1 %
19	A	85.74 % / 11.72 %
20	A	85.09 % / 10.57 %
21	C	88.83 % / 10.94 %
22	D	81.6 % / 14.21 %
23	A	55.26 % / 41.32 %
24	C	87.5 % / 11.11 %
25	A	84.49 % / 11.35 %
26	A	84.01 % / 11.28 %
27	B	54.5 % / 35.89 %
28	C	87.46 % / 10.63 %
29	A	84.48 % / 14.74 %
30	A	47.93 % / 51.69 %
31	B	81.81 % / 15.7 %
32	A	79.95 % / 14.86 %
33	C	19.28 % / 74.6 %
34	D	44.29 % / 50.37 %
35	B	50.84 % / 40.21 %
36	A	48.82 % / 49.61 %
37	D	67.85 % / 31.03 %
38	C	53.37 % / 34.95 %
39	A	21.58 % / 74.39 %
40	B	83.37 % / 14.12 %
41	A	87.91 % / 11.63 %
42	B	77.48 % / 10.42 %
43	D	83.09 % / 13.94 %
44	A	58.14 % / 30.73 %
45	A	69.86 % / 30.13 %
46	A	89.85 % / 10.08 %
47	B	44.83 % / 45.66 %
48	D	68.1 % / 31.05 %
49	B	40.24 % / 37.08 %
50	A	42.03 % / 36.23 %
51	A	46.45 % / 31.48 %
52	B	88.8 % / 10.78 %
53	A	89.69 % / 10.11 %
54	A	50.37 % / 31.43 %
55	B	46.1 % / 49.39 %
56	B	87.71 % / 10.79 %
57	A	84.57 % / 12.04 %
58	B	85.8 % / 12.88 %
59	A	88.13 % / 11.66 %
60	C	80.35 % / 12.61 %
61	B	78.16 % / 15.62 %
62	A	80.12 % / 16.85 %
63	B	86.3 % / 12.01 %
64	A	88.66 % / 10.17 %
65	C	45.94 % / 32.18 %
66	A	83.83 % / 15.34 %
67	A	84.81 % / 13.32 %
68	A	59.36 % / 32.79 %
69	B	45.15 % / 36.75 %
70	C	81.96 % / 16.72 %
71	A	44.06 % / 39.2 %
72	A	41.99 % / 31.69 %
73	B	87.01 % / 11.07 %
74	B	21.79 % / 72.63 %
75	D	67.7 % / 30.53 %
76	A	61.8 % / 31.52 %
77	C	88.0 % / 10.47 %
78	B	26.03 % / 70.35 %
79	B	30.53 % / 67.34 %
80	B	67.45 % / 30.8 %

Q.	Ans.	Correct / Skipped		Q.	Ans.	Correct / Skipped		Q.	Ans.	Correct / Skipped		Q.	Ans.	Correct / Skipped		Q.	Ans.	Correct / Skipped
81	B	83.47 % / 13.15 %		97	A	83.16 % / 10.88 %		113	B	43.14 % / 38.29 %		129	A	52.27 % / 46.03 %		145	B	47.56 % / 41.19 %
82	B	80.09 % / 12.75 %		98	B	88.54 % / 10.96 %		114	B	85.29 % / 13.22 %		130	B	65.26 % / 33.82 %		146	A	87.27 % / 12.16 %
83	A	57.84 % / 35.57 %		99	C	57.24 % / 40.61 %		115	B	50.81 % / 43.17 %		131	A	12.71 % / 82.92 %		147	A	86.1 % / 11.33 %
84	A	86.84 % / 12.92 %		100	B	79.85 % / 15.35 %		116	B	79.64 % / 13.0 %		132	B	88.38 % / 10.56 %		148	A	84.98 % / 13.75 %
85	B	45.0 % / 52.29 %		101	B	85.09 % / 13.42 %		117	A	87.96 % / 11.71 %		133	B	47.51 % / 35.59 %		149	A	81.21 % / 11.95 %
86	B	80.95 % / 15.09 %		102	A	83.63 % / 15.59 %		118	B	87.43 % / 11.87 %		134	A	86.34 % / 10.68 %		150	B	81.04 % / 15.41 %
87	B	76.67 % / 15.12 %		103	A	79.71 % / 14.21 %		119	B	65.77 % / 30.89 %		135	C	78.12 % / 16.49 %		151	C	86.44 % / 12.04 %
88	A	78.43 % / 15.92 %		104	A	87.66 % / 11.06 %		120	B	77.28 % / 18.52 %		136	A	88.4 % / 11.26 %		152	A	32.05 % / 67.93 %
89	B	77.44 % / 11.15 %		105	C	79.21 % / 12.46 %		121	A	77.64 % / 13.08 %		137	B	81.58 % / 12.23 %		153	B	42.99 % / 47.93 %
90	B	19.54 % / 70.85 %		106	B	88.16 % / 11.08 %		122	A	80.78 % / 16.29 %		138	B	51.42 % / 36.8 %		154	A	40.56 % / 37.93 %
91	A	50.94 % / 39.6 %		107	C	86.59 % / 12.52 %		123	B	54.33 % / 42.98 %		139	B	68.84 % / 30.74 %		155	B	81.43 % / 10.81 %
92	B	60.68 % / 37.86 %		108	C	82.54 % / 17.25 %		124	B	83.93 % / 10.57 %		140	A	14.36 % / 78.51 %		156	C	50.85 % / 45.6 %
93	B	59.27 % / 30.07 %		109	B	84.99 % / 14.28 %		125	B	54.54 % / 40.25 %		141	B	86.05 % / 13.71 %		157	A	77.07 % / 20.15 %
94	C	87.9 % / 10.95 %		110	C	84.16 % / 12.18 %		126	A	86.86 % / 11.34 %		142	C	51.15 % / 43.26 %		158	A	60.21 % / 36.11 %
95	C	80.21 % / 11.05 %		111	B	85.61 % / 11.79 %		127	B	62.81 % / 30.63 %		143	A	52.84 % / 33.61 %		159	D	47.03 % / 49.85 %
96	A	59.33 % / 30.66 %		112	A	53.11 % / 37.22 %		128	C	64.71 % / 32.61 %		144	A	78.37 % / 17.21 %		160	D	51.01 % / 35.34 %

Q.	Ans.	Correct / Skipped		Q.	Ans.	Correct / Skipped		Q.	Ans.	Correct / Skipped		Q.	Ans.	Correct / Skipped		Q.	Ans.	Correct / Skipped
161	A	68.24 % 31.04 %		177	A	11.7 % 87.61 %		193	A	55.76 % 30.75 %		209	D	86.97 % 11.22 %		225	A	54.89 % 32.72 %
162	A	81.1 % 14.51 %		178	A	55.72 % 36.89 %		194	B	85.8 % 10.18 %		210	A	56.53 % 31.87 %		226	A	64.7 % 34.25 %
163	A	65.43 % 33.21 %		179	A	30.8 % 68.2 %		195	B	68.01 % 31.24 %		211	A	83.43 % 11.31 %		227	A	23.93 % 72.94 %
164	B	11.21 % 82.36 %		180	D	12.09 % 71.32 %		196	A	20.72 % 79.2 %		212	B	84.98 % 11.16 %		228	B	30.17 % 68.12 %
165	A	17.69 % 71.42 %		181	C	30.49 % 68.94 %		197	C	17.03 % 73.55 %		213	B	55.88 % 40.64 %		229	A	81.73 % 12.07 %
166	C	58.87 % 39.09 %		182	A	29.52 % 70.21 %		198	D	87.84 % 11.27 %		214	B	50.09 % 40.18 %		230	A	58.28 % 39.7 %
167	C	16.84 % 81.53 %		183	A	20.75 % 71.93 %		199	B	40.52 % 50.78 %		215	B	26.51 % 67.02 %		231	A	84.33 % 10.5 %
168	C	22.21 % 70.95 %		184	A	42.44 % 51.65 %		200	A	22.07 % 70.9 %		216	B	64.42 % 35.57 %		232	B	66.46 % 30.36 %
169	A	40.29 % 55.77 %		185	C	31.29 % 67.02 %		201	B	23.33 % 70.78 %		217	A	24.63 % 72.2 %		233	B	86.31 % 11.63 %
170	A	30.88 % 68.93 %		186	B	80.42 % 16.04 %		202	A	59.88 % 31.34 %		218	A	61.3 % 36.21 %		234	C	80.45 % 17.37 %
171	A	66.09 % 30.1 %		187	A	44.77 % 33.96 %		203	A	21.61 % 75.98 %		219	C	63.6 % 33.09 %		235	A	76.47 % 17.99 %
172	B	23.21 % 69.88 %		188	A	86.47 % 13.37 %		204	A	87.2 % 10.63 %		220	A	61.35 % 30.02 %		236	A	65.51 % 32.83 %
173	B	76.76 % 21.37 %		189	A	66.16 % 33.21 %		205	A	82.74 % 15.78 %		221	A	56.74 % 33.96 %		237	B	88.72 % 10.05 %
174	A	60.5 % 35.35 %		190	C	77.42 % 10.03 %		206	B	29.5 % 67.35 %		222	A	60.3 % 37.71 %		238	C	25.13 % 73.63 %
175	A	10.14 % 84.0 %		191	D	69.73 % 30.17 %		207	A	19.08 % 75.71 %		223	A	43.07 % 55.24 %		239	C	15.27 % 80.5 %
176	D	69.9 % 30.03 %		192	C	67.88 % 31.18 %		208	A	27.31 % 71.57 %		224	A	79.46 % 17.51 %		240	D	57.47 % 31.92 %

Performance Analysis

Avg. Score (%)	52.19%
Toppers Score (%)	65.0%
Your Score	

Part A

Q.1 Which of the following is the one which is released with the death of the bacteria?

A. Exotoxin   **B.** Endotoxin
C. Neurotoxin   **D.** Urotoxin

Q.2 In exotoxins, which of the following is the important toxin which is haemolytic, membrano-lytic and necrotic causing extensive myositis?

A. Lecithinase   **B.** Haemolysin
C. Hyaluronidase   **D.** Proteinase

Q.3 In blood substitutes, which of the following are useful to improve plasma volume?

A. Human albumin   **B.** Dextrans
C. Histamines   **D.** Gelatin

Q.4 In acute suppurative tenosynovitis: Which of the following is the synovial sheath of the flexor tendon of the thumb which extends to the digit?

A. Radial bursa   **B.** Ulnar bursa
C. Hook sign   **D.** Kanavel signs

Q.5 In immunosuppressive agents: Which of the following inhibits cytokines, binding of IL 2 to receptors, blocks macrophage migration and inhibits delayed hypersensitivity reaction?

A. Prednisolone
B. Anti-proliferating agents
C. T cell directed immunosuppressants
D. Co-stimulation blockage agent

Q.6 In zygomatic complex fracture: Which of the following causes a localized depression of the arch which displaces medially and tends to impinge to the coronoid process of the mandible?

A. Fracture of the zygomatic arch
B. Blow-out fracture
C. En-bloc dislocation of zygomatic bone medially
D. Comminuted fracture

Q.7 Which of the following is the thyroid swelling in the posterior third of the tongue, at the foramen caecum, presenting as a rounded swelling?

A. Ectopic thyroid   **B.** Lingual thyroid
C. Thyroglossal cyst   **D.** Aberrant thyroid

Q.8 Which of the following is an autoimmune disease with increased levels of specific antibodies in the blood?

A. Graves diseases   **B.** Toxic adenoma
C. Retrosternal goitre   **D.** Strumaovarii

Q.9 Which of the following is the benign encapsulated tumor occurring commonly in young females of 15-25 years age group?

A. Fibroadenoma   **B.** Phyllodestumor
C. Galactocele   **D.** Anti-bioma

Q.10 In investigations in carcinoma breast: Which of the following techniques is used to show osteolytic secondaries?

A. Chest X-ray
B. X-ray spine
C. Ultrasound abdomen
D. Trucut biopsy

Q.11 The surface area of the peritoneum is _____ equal to the surface area of skin.

A. $2\ m^2$ **B.** $3\ m^2$ **C.** $4\ m^2$ **D.** $5\ m^2$

Q.12 Which of the following is the acquired cyst of the liver after liver injury in blunt abdominal trauma?

A. Polycystic liver disease
B. Neoplastic liver cysts
C. Traumatic liver cysts
D. Hepatic cystadenocarcinoma

Q.13

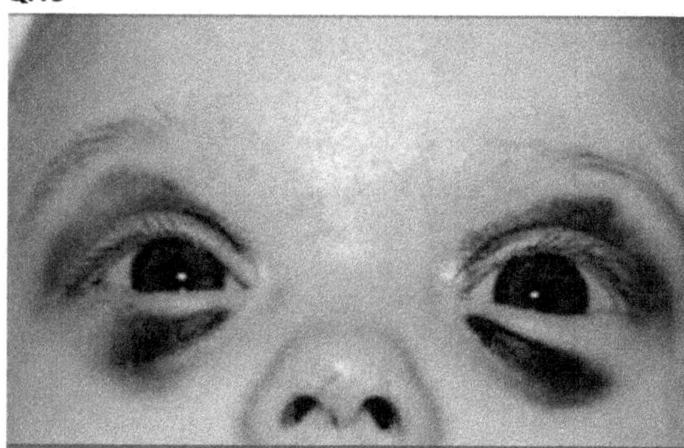

This figure shows the Raccon's eye sign which is infraorbital ecchymosis due to secondaries in the retro-orbital region and it is the typical secondaries in the skull and orbit with primary in the adrenal gland. Which of the following diseases is indicated through this picture?

A. Neuroblastoma
B. Adrenal cortical tumors
C. Pheochromocytoma
D. Parathyroidectomy

Q.14

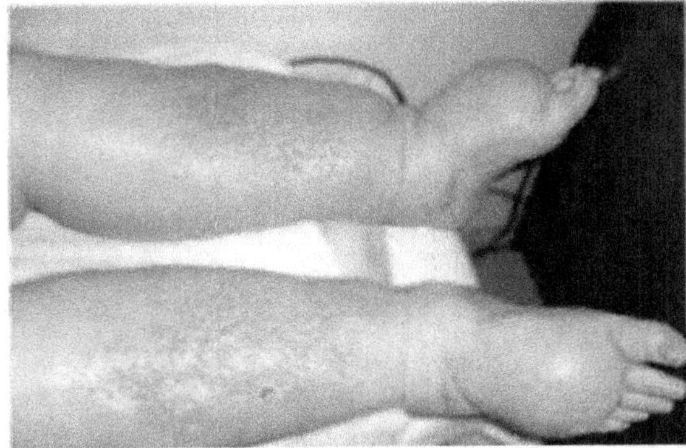

Which of the following diseases is indicated by this picture?

A. Lymphoedema
B. Lymphomas
C. Hodgkin's lymphoma
D. Non-Hodgkin's lymphoma

Q.15 In the systemic route of drug administration, which of the following routes refers to administration by injection and takes the drug directly into the tissue fluid or blood without having to cross the intestinal mucosa?

A. Nasal
B. Parenteral
C. Inhalation
D. Cutaneous

Q.16 Which of the following includes physiological and biochemical effects of drugs and their mechanism of action at organ system subcellular macromolecular levels?

A. Pharmacology
B. Pharmacodynamics
C. Pharmacokinetics
D. Pharmaco-therapeutics

Q.17 Which of the following is the cleavage of drug molecule by taking up a molecule of water?

A. Oxidation
B. Reduction
C. Hydrolysis
D. Cyclization

Q.18 Which of the following have the affinity but no intrinsic affinity?

A. Agonists
B. Competitive antagonists
C. Antagonists
D. Partial agonists

Q.19 In drug dosage, which of the following drug dose indicates that the dose needed to produce maximal therapeutic effect cannot be given because of intolerable adverse effects ?

A. Standard dose
B. Regulated dose
C. Target dose level
D. Titrated dose

Q.20 Which of the following is an opioid antagonist that blocks placebo analgesia?

A. Naloxone
B. Morphine
C. Lidocaine
D. Atropine

Q.21 Local hydrolysis of Ach is less important in _______.

A. CVS
B. ganglia

C. skeletal muscles
D. facial muscles

Q.22 Which of the following is characterised by progressive dementia and is a neurodegenerative disorder primarily affecting cholinergic neurons in the brain?

A. Belladonna poisoning
B. Alzheimer's disease
C. Glaucoma
D. Myasthenia gravis

Q.23 Which of the following relatively M3 selective muscarinic antagonist has preferential action on urinary bladder less likely to cause dryness of mouth and other anticholinergic side effects?

A. Oxybutynin
B. Tolterodine
C. Flavoxate
D. Drotaverine

Q.24 In adrenergic transmission, which of the following is a very efficient mechanism by which NA (Nor-adrenaline) released from the nerve terminal is recaptured?

A. Synthesis of NAs
B. Storage of NAs
C. Release of NAs
D. Uptake of NAs

Q.25 In bronchial asthma, adrenergic drugs, especially _______ are the primary drugs for relief of reversible airway obstruction.

A. β_2 stimulants
B. β_1 stimulants
C. α_1 stimulants
D. α_1 stimulants

Q.26 Which of the following is the non-sedative antihistaminic that is effective in allergic rhinitis and urticaria by single daily dosing, despite a $\frac{t1}{2}$ of $8-10$ hr and no active metabolite?

A. Azelastine
B. Mizolastine
C. Ebastine
D. Levocetirizine

Q.27 Which of the following is the acetylsalicylic acid?

A. Aspirin
B. Histamine
C. Penicillin
D. Analgesic

Q.28 Which of the following is an auto-immune disease in which there is joint inflammation, synovial proliferation, and destruction of articular cartilage?

A. Rheumatoid arthritis
B. Lympho-edema
C. Lymphoma
D. Paralysis

Q.29 Bronchiectasis is most common in which lobe?

A. Right upper lobe
B. Right middle lobe
C. Left upper lobe
D. Left lower lobe

Q.30 An organism used as biofertilizer for raising soybean crop is

A. Nostoc
B. Azotobacter
C. Azospirillum
D. Rhizobium

Q.31 Which of the following conditions are associated with pauci-immune crescentric glomerulonephritis?

A. Henoch-schonlein nephritis
B. Lupus nephritis
C. Microscopic polyangiitis

D. Alport's syndrome

Q.32 A 56-year-old chronic smoker, mass in bronchus resected. What is the possible marker?

A. Cytokeratins
B. Virnentin
C. Epithelial membrane cadherin
D. Leukocyte

Q.33 Lung to lung metastasis is seen in_____.
A. Adenocarcinoma of lung
B. Squamous cell carcinoma
C. Small cell carcinoma
D. Neuroendocrine tumor of lung

Q.34 Which of the following are hypersecretory granules seen in lung cancer?
A. Adeno Ca
B. Small cell Ca
C. Large cell Ca
D. Broncho-alveolar Ca

Q.35 A pleural fibroma is differentiated from mesothelioma by the presence of which of the following in the former?
A. CD14
B. CD24
C. Cytokeratin absence
D. CD34

Q.36 Gastrointestinal enteritis necroticans is caused by which of the following?
A. C. difficile
B. C. perfringens
C. Botulinum
D. C. jejuni

Q.37 Nagler's reaction is done by
A. Cl. Tetani
B. Cl. Botulinum
C. Cl. Perfringens
D. Cl. Septicum

Q.38 Which of the following is the pair of biofertilizers for nitrogen fixation?
A. Azolla and blue-green algae
B. Nostoc and legume
C. Rhizobium and grasses
D. Salmonella and E. coll

Q.39 Which of the following is true about gas gangrene?
A. The underlying skin and muscle are normal.
B. It is caused by tetanospasmin toxin.
C. The muscle rigidity and spasm are characteristic.
D. The most common organism implicated is Clostridium perfringens.

Q.40 Leghaemoglobin occurs in
A. Coralloid root
B. Around bacteroids
C. Around bacteroids
D. Mycorrhiza

Q.41 All of the following are true regarding clostridium tetani, except that
A. It produces heat resistant spores
B. The incubation period is 6-11 days
C. 3 primary doses of vaccine are needed for full protection
D. Man to man transmission is seen

Q.42 Post-transplant lymphoma is?
A. T cell lymphoma
B. B cell lymphoma
C. NK cell lymphoma
D. None

Q.43 Atoms in the solid state combine in a manner that ensures _________.
A. Maximal internal energy
B. Minimal internal energy
C. Stabilised internal energy
D. Equal internal energy

Q.44 Root completion of the mandibular first molar takes place by the age____________?
A. 7-8 years
B. 8-9 years
C. 9-10 years
D. 10 – 11 years

Q.45 Which of the following has been used as an index of the ability of a material to resist abrasion or wear?
A. Hardness
B. Ductility
C. Brittleness
D. Roughness

Q.46 __________, the rods of the human eye are more dominant than the cones, and color perception is lost.
A. At the bright light
B. At low light levels
C. At dark light
D. At dark-less light

Q.47 In the oral environment, which of the following often occurs from the formation of hard and soft deposits on the surface of the restoration?
A. Waxing
B. Tarnish
C. Corrosion
D. Galvanic shock

Q.48 Which teeth in the proximal aspect show a rhomboidal appearance?
A. Maxillary posteriors
B. Mandibular posteriors
C. Maxillary anteriors
D. Mandibular anteriors

Q.49 Which of the following represents a permanent deformation of the material that does not decrease when the force is removed?
A. Elastic strain
B. Plastic strain
C. Strain
D. Non-elastic strain

Q.50 Which of the following materials have a greater stiffness than all other elastomeric impression materials?
A. Polyether impression materials
B. Polymethyl impression materials
C. Poly-propane impression materials
D. Poly-butyl impression materials

Q.51 The shape of the occlusal surface of the permanent maxillary first molar is__________________?
A. Oval
B. Trapezoidal
C. Triangular
D. Rhomboidal

Q.52 The number of point angles in a permanent mandibular first molar is___________?
A. 8
B. 6
C. 4
D. 10

Q.53 Permanent Mandibular central incisor develops from_____________?

A. 3 lobes   **B.** 1 lobes   **C.** 4 lobes   **D.** 5 lobes

Q.54 In the eutectic composition, what are the composition levels of silver and copper in percentage?

A.   72% silver and 28% copper
B.   73% silver and 29% copper
C.   73% silver and 29% copper
D.   75% silver and 31% copper

Q.55 Which is the third group of polymeric materials?

A.   Thermosetting polymer
B.   Thermoplastic polymer
C.   Elastomer
D.   Ionomers

Q.56 Which of the following is a dimensionally accurate reproduction of a part or parts of the oral cavity or extra-oral facial structures produced in a durable hard material?

A. Cast   **B.** Dental implant
C. Arbitrator   **D.** Abutments

Q.57 There are only _____ synovial joints in the head.

A. two   **B.** three   **C.** four   **D.** five

Q.58 Which of the following is/are characterised by small bodies, bifid spinous processes?

A. Cervical vertebrae   **B.** Hyoid bone
C. Sphenoid bone   **D.** Temporal bone

Q.59 At the base of the neck, which of the following is immediately anterior to the esophagus?

A. Pharynx   **B.** Larynx   **C.** Trachea   **D.** Thyroid

Q.60 The forehead consists of the _______, which also forms the superior part of the rim of each orbit.

A. sphenoid bone   **B.** temporal bone
C. frontal bone   **D.** hyoid bone

Q.61 In the lateral portion of the calvaria, in upper regions, the frontal bone articulates with the parietal bone at the

A.   Lambdoid suture
B.   Coronal suture
C.   Squamous suture
D.   Sphenoparietal suture

Q.62 The teeth project from the _____ of the two maxillae.

A.   alveolar arches
B.   pterygoid bone
C.   alveolar bone
D.   periodontal ligament

Q.63 Extending downward from the junction of the body and the greater wings are the

A. Alveolar processes   **B.** Pterygoid processes
C. Pterygoid fossae   **D.** Pterygoid canal

Q.64 The posterior part of the base of the skull consists of the _______ centrally and the temporal bones laterally.

A. sphenoid bone   **B.** hyoid bone

C. occipital bone   **D.** frontal bone

Q.65 The floor in the midline of the middle cranial fossa is elevated and formed by the body of the _______.

A. temporal   **B.** sphenoid   **C.** occipital   **D.** frontal

Q.66 Which of the following is a crescent-shaped structure that projects downward between the two cerebral hemispheres from the dura covering the calva?

A. Dural partitions   **B.** Falxcerebri
C. Tentorium cerebelli   **D.** Falxcerebelli

Q.67 The two vertebral arteries enter the cranial cavity through the foramen magnum and just inferior to the pons fuse to form the

A. Arterial crest   **B.** Subclavian artery
C. Basilar artery   **D.** Ophthalmic artery

Q.68

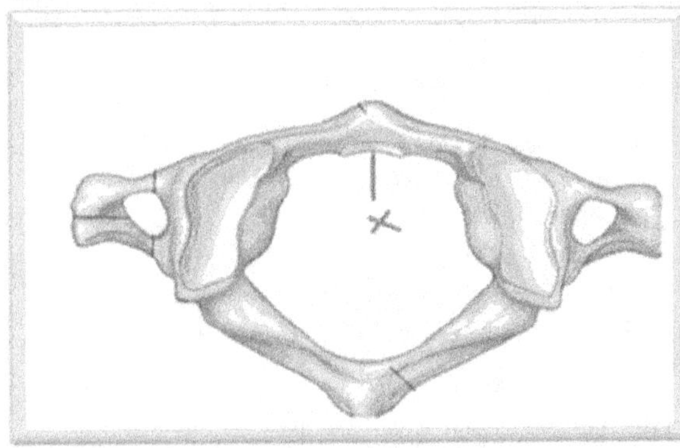

This is the diagram of the atlas vertebra CI (superior view). What does "X" indicate?

A.   Anterior arch
B.   Articular facet for dens
C.   Posterior arch
D.   Lateral mass

Q.69

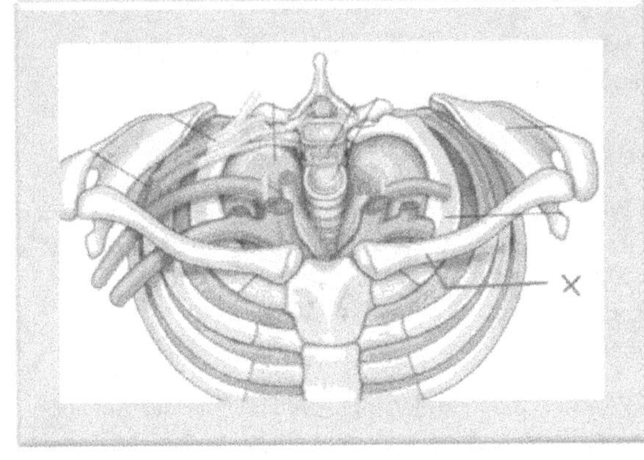

This is the view of the superior thoracic aperture. What does "X" indicate?

A. Rib I   **B.** Clavicle
C. Scapula   **D.** Axillary inlet

Q.70

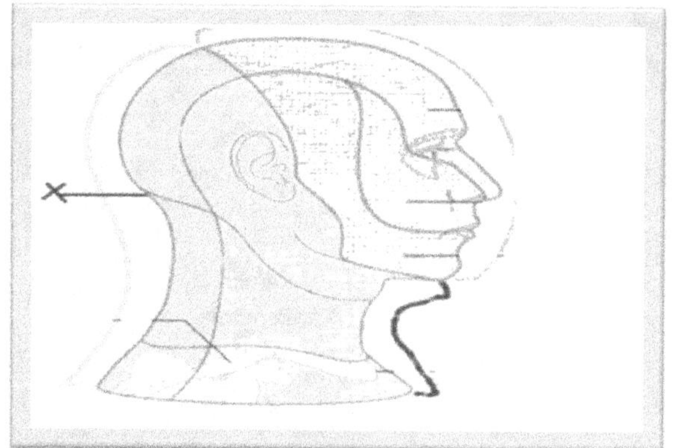

This is the dermatomes of the cervical nerves. What is indicated by the "X"?
A. External occipital protuberance
B. Posterior rami
C. Clavicle
D. Anterior rami

Q.71 Which of the following is an autosomal dominant disorder that presents with early-onset familial colon cancer, particularly affecting the proximal colon?
A. Li – Fraumeni syndrome
B. Hereditary non-polyposis colorectal cancer
C. Familial breast cancer
D. Xerodermapigmentosum

Q.72 Which of the following is a group of acquired and hereditary disorders characterized by the extracellular deposition of insoluble proteins?
A. Amyloidosis
B. Autoantibodies
C. Cryoglobulins
D. Anaphylaxis

Q.73 Which of the following are tender, red, or purplish skin lesions that occur in the cold and wet?
A. Frostbite
B. Chilblains
C. Heat exhaustion
D. Hypothermia

Q.74 Which of the following is required for the synthesis of thyroid hormones?
A. Iron
B. Iodine
C. Magnesium
D. Selenium

Q.75 Which was formerly endemic among poor who subsisted chiefly on maize, which contains niacin, a form of niacin that the body is unable to utilize?
A. Psoriasis
B. Pellagra
C. Biotin
D. Cheilosis

Q.76 Which of the following inhibits mitochondrial function?
A. Praziquantel
B. Atovaquone
C. Thiabendazole
D. Lumefantrine

Q.77 Which of the following can sometimes reverse post synaptic neurotoxic paralysis (- bungaro-toxin-like neurotoxin) but will not usually reverse established pre-synaptic paralysis (- bungaro-toxin-like neurotoxins), so needs to be given before major paralysis has occurred?
A. Antivenom
B. Prophylactic antibiotic
C. Cryoglobulins
D. Anaphylaxis

Q.78 In mood disorders, which is a reversible and selective inhibitor of monoamine oxidase subtype A, which causes minimal potentiation of the pressor response to dietary tyramine?
A. Tricyclic antidepressants
B. Newer antidepressants
C. Moclobemide
D. Monoamine oxidase inhibitors

Q.79 In chronic fatigue syndrome of somatoform disorders, which is characterized by excessive fatigue after minimal physical or mental exertion, poor concentration, dizziness, muscular aches and sleep disturbance?
A. Neurasthenia
B. Hysteria
C. Stomatitis
D. Delirium

Q.80 In neurological para-neoplasmic syndromes, which of the following presents with proximal muscle weakness which improves on exercise and is caused by the development of antibodies to presynaptic calcium channels?
A. Retinopathy
B. Lambert-Eaton syndrome
C. Cerebellar degeneration
D. Peripheral neuropathy

Q.81 Codeine and dihydro-codeine are-
A. non-opioids
B. weak- opioids
C. strong- opioids
D. normal- opioids

Q.82 .... such as codeine linctus, is sometimes effective, particularly for cough at night.
A. Antibiotic
B. Benoxyl
C. Antitussive
D. Paracetamol

Q.83

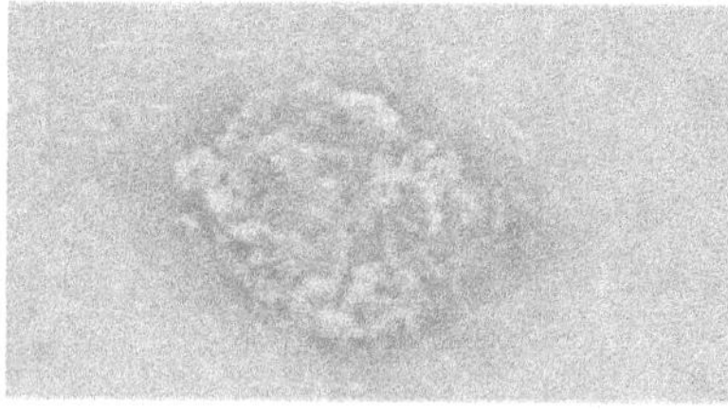

Which of the following primary lesions of skin diseases is indicated in this picture?
A. Papule
B. Petechiae
C. Plaque
D. Pustule

Q.84

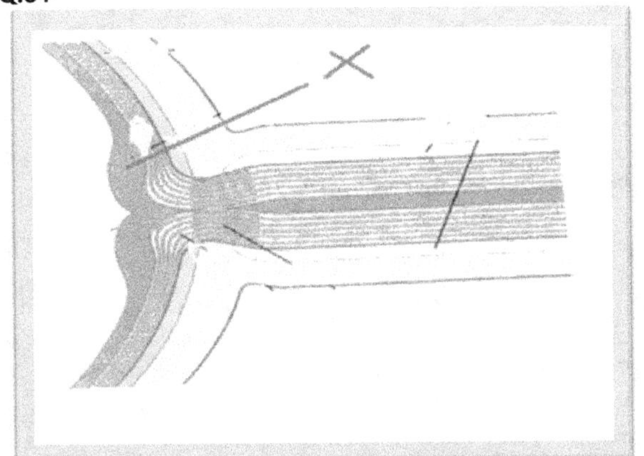

This picture represents the mechanism of optic disc oedema. What does 'X' indicate in the diagram?

A. Choroid
B. Venous dilation
C. Swollen optic disc
D. Swollen axons

Q.85 The maxillary _________ are related to the maxillary sinus in which they have a common nerve supply and their roots are often separated by a thin plate of bone.

A. anterior teeth
B. posterior teeth
C. lingual teeth
D. lateral teeth

Q.86 The tongue forms in the ventral floor of the pharynx after the arrival of the _______ cells.

A. hypoglossal muscle
B. temporalis muscles
C. orbicularis orismuscles
D. master muscles

Q.87 Which of the following cysts may arise from the epithelial rests after the fusion of medial, maxillary and lateral nasal prominences?

A. Nasolabial cysts
B. Globulo-maxillary cysts
C. Anterior palatine cysts
D. Branchial cleft cysts

Q.88 Which of the following condenses to form the dental papilla, which is the formative organ of the dentin and primordium of the pulp?

A. Ecto-mesenchyme
B. Endo-mesenchyme
C. Odontoblasts cells
D. Endoblasts cells

Q.89 Which of the following terms was originally used to describe the narrow, fissure like structures that are seen on almost all surfaces?

A. Cracks
B. Eruption
C. Impaction
D. Enamel brochs

Q.90 At the free border of the enamel organ, the outer and inner enamel epithelial layers are continuous and get reflected into one another as the _________.

A. ameloblasts
B. cervical loop
C. stratum inter-medium

D. enamel brochs

Q.91 Which of the following pass actively through the ruffle ended ameloblasts and passively through the sides of the smoothly ended ameloblasts to the mineralising front?

A. Zinc ions
B. Calcium ions
C. Phosphorous ions
D. Ferric ions

Q.92 In human tooth enamel, the concentration of _______ is 3.2%, which is important as carbonate-rich crystals are preferentially attacked by acids in caries.

A. calcium
B. carbonate
C. phosphorous
D. fluoride

Q.93 The most apparent age change in enamel is _______ or wear of the occlusal surfaces and proximal contact points as a result of mastication.

A. abrasion
B. attrition
C. erosion
D. abfraction

Q.94 Tonofibrils, with an orientation parallel to the surface of the developing enamel, are found in the _________.

A. endoplasm
B. cytoplasm
C. ectoplasm
D. nucleus

Q.95 The projections of the ameloblasts into the enamel matrix have been named as _________.

A. alveolar processes
B. tome's processes
C. cranial process
D. pterygoid process

Q.96 Which of the following indicates the dentin that immediately surrounds the dentinal tubules?

A. Peri-tubular dentin
B. Intertubular dentin
C. Predentin
D. Secondary dentin

Q.97

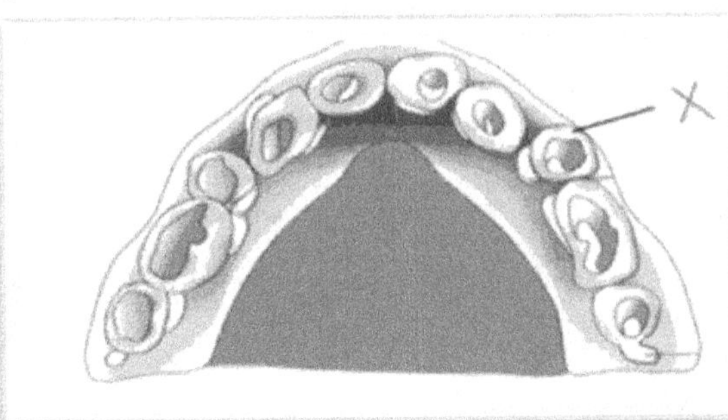

This is the diagrammatic reconstruction of the dental lamina and enamel organs of the mandible. What does "X" indicate?

A. Enamel organs of the deciduous teeth
B. The primordium of permanent tooth
C. The primordium of the first tooth
D. Tooth buds and dental lamina

Q.98

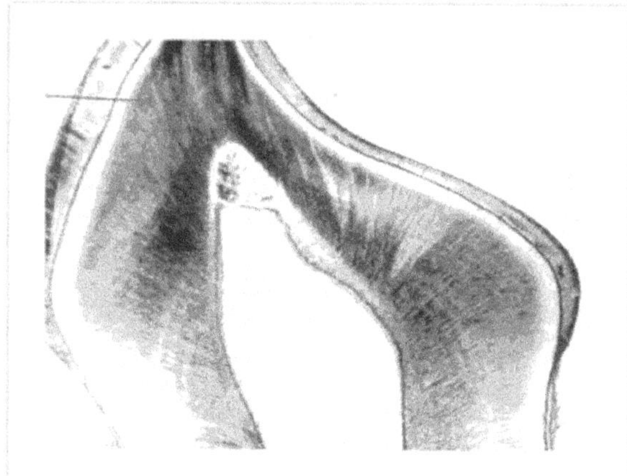

This diagram represents the neonatal line in enamel, the longitudinal ground section of the deciduous canine. What does "X" indicate?

A. Neonatal line in dentin
B. Prenatal enamel
C. Neonatal line in enamel
D. Postnatal enamel

Q.99 Which of the following is the primary fuel for most of the cells of the body?

A. Fat
B. Carbohydrate
C. Glucose
D. Fructose

Q.100 Which of the following is formed from multiple wrappings of the plasma membranes of Schwann cells that wind themselves around the nerve fibre?

A. Fibrin   B. Myelin   C. Auxin   D. Fibroma

Part B

Q.101 In cells and intercellular matrix: The _______ extend processes into canaliculi that radiate from the lacunae.

A. cementoblasts
B. mesenchyme cells
C. osteocytes
D. endocytes

Q.102 When a tooth is shed, its _______ is resorbed.

A. lingual bone
B. alveolar bone
C. periodontal ligament
D. buccal arch

Q.103 Which of the following supplements the venous drainage system?

A. Lymphatics
B. Arteries
C. Ventricles
D. Auricles

Q.104 Which is defined as an inflammatory disease of the supporting tissues of the teeth caused by specific microorganisms or groups of specific microorganisms, resulting in progressive destruction of the periodontal ligament and alveolar bone with pocket formation, recession, or both?

A. Periodontitis
B. Resorption
C. Recession
D. Endodontitis

Q.105 Which is the study of the distribution and determinants of health-related states or events in specified populations and the applications of this study to control health problems?

A. Periodontitis
B. Epidemiology
C. Endodontic
D. Prosthesis

Q.106 Chronic periodontitis generally becomes clinically significant after age _______.

A. 28   B. 29   C. 30   D. 31

Q.107 The inorganic components of plaques are predominantly _______ and phosphorous, with trace amounts of the other minerals, including sodium, potassium, and fluoride.

A. calcium
B. vitamin C
C. zinc
D. manganese

Q.108 Which of the following is one of the rare cocci in periodontitis?

A. P. micros
B. Fuso-bacterium nucleatum
C. Campylobacter rectus
D. Spirochetes

Q.109 Pigmented deposits on the tooth surfaces are called _______.

A. dental plaque
B. dental stains
C. dental caries
D. dental chrome

Q.110 In contours and open contacts: The cusps that tend to wedge food forcibly into interproximal embrasures are known as _______.

A. retentive cusps
B. plunger cusps
C. intra-oral cusps
D. reciprocal cusps

Q.111 Which of the principal fibres of the periodontal ligament extend obliquely from the cementum just beneath the junctional epithelium to the alveolar crest?

A. Transseptal group
B. Alveolar crest group
C. Horizontal group
D. Oblique group

Q.112 The interdependency of the osteoblasts and osteoclasts in remodeling is called _______.

A. coupling   B. grafting   C. splinting   D. stippling

Q.113

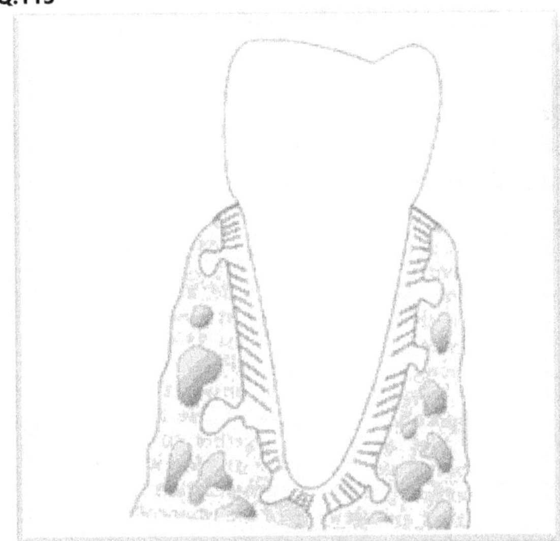

Which of the following is indicated by this diagram?

A. Principal fibre groups
B. Dental plaque
C. Skeletal Fibres
D. Attached gingiva

Q.114

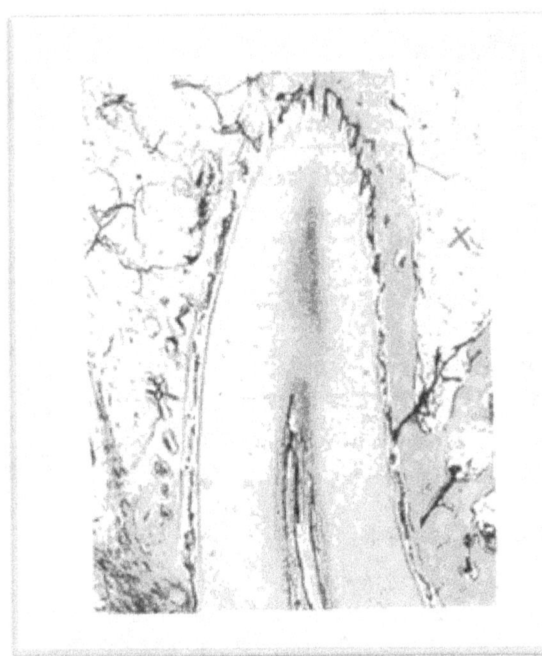

This is the diagram of the vascular supply of monkey periodontium. What is indicated by the 'X'?

A. Longitudinal vessels in the periodontal ligament and alveolar arteries passing through the channels between the bone marrow and periodontal ligament.

B. Longitudinal vessels in the attached gingiva and alveolar arteries passing through the channels between the bone marrow and periodontal ligament.

C. Longitudinal vessels in the periodontal ligament and attached gingiva passing through the channels between the bone marrow and periodontal ligament.

D. Longitudinal vessels in the periodontal ligament and ameloblasts passing through the channels between the bone marrow and periodontal ligament.

Q.115 All the primary teeth are present in a child's mouth by the age of _______.

A. 3 years   **B.** 4 years   **C.** 5 years   **D.** 6 years

Q.116 If the production of _______ starts too early, height will be above normal during childhood, but the final height will be below normal.

A. growth hormone   **B.** sex hormone
C. emergency hormone   **D.** endocrine hormones

Q.117 In mammalian teeth cells: Which of the following cell forms ameloblasts?

A. Stomodeal ectoderm
B. Mesenchyme cells
C. Odontoblasts
D. Endodermal cells

Q.118 Which of the following is the conscious and reality-oriented portion of the mind?

A. Ego   **B.** Superego
C. Id   **D.** Jealous

Q.119 Which of the following observations says that an observant child senses the parental disappointment and has feelings of guilt, mirrored as shyness, retirement and unsureness?

A. Overindulgence   **B.** Overanxiety
C. Over-identification   **D.** Overprotection

Q.120 Which of the following means of increasing the probability of the desired behavior by the withdrawal of or threatening to withdraw a pleasant stimulus?

A. Punishment   **B.** Omission
C. Reinforcement   **D.** Avoidance

Q.121 The presence of food in the stomach reduces the absorption of _______.

A. calcium   **B.** fluoride   **C.** iron   **D.** vitamins

Q.122 Which of the following are the actual observed rates such as the birth and death rates?

A. Crude rates
B. Crude death rates
C. Attack rate
D. Age-specific death rate

Q.123 Which of the following is defined as the ratio of the incidence of disease among exposed persons to the incidence among non-exposed?

A. Odds ratio   **B.** Risk ratio
C. Attack rate ratio   **D.** Mortality ratio

Q.124 Which of the following actions of storage in the purification of water indicates that about 90 percent of the suspended impurities settle down in 24 hours by gravity?

A. Physical action   **B.** Chemical action
C. Biological action   **D.** Nuclear action

Q.125 In household purification of water, high test _________ is a calcium compound that contains 60 to 70 percent available chlorine.
A. sodium hypochlorite
B. hypochlorite
C. lime stone
D. manganese milk

Q.126 Which of the following processes involves mixing waste with cement and other substance before disposal in order to minimize the risk of toxic substances contained in the waste migrating into surface water or groundwater?
A. Incineration   **B.** Encapsulation
C. Inertisation   **D.** Scintillation

Q.127 Which of the following are the complex inorganic nitrogenous compounds composed of carbon, hydrogen, oxygen, nitrogen, and sulfur?
A. Fats lipids   **B.** Proteins
C. Vitamins   **D.** Minerals

Q.128 Which of the following is/are important in the synthesis of proteoglycans, fibronectin, and type 1 pro-collagen, and in epithelial tissue differentiation?
A. Proteins   **B.** Vitamin A
C. Iron   **D.** Calcium

Q.129 Which of the following refers to a defective formation or calcification of enamel due to injury to ameloblasts during enamel formation?
A. Fracture   **B.** Enamel hypoplasia
C. Abfraction   **D.** Erosion

Q.130 Which of the following includes the cavity preparation on the proximal surfaces of anterior teeth without involving the incisal angle?
A. Class I cavity preparation
B. Class II cavity preparation
C. Class III cavity preparation
D. Class IV cavity preparation

Q.131 Which of the following are the small lateral openings along the dentin tubule wall?
A. Pretubular dentin   **B.** Canaliculi
C. Peri-tubular dentin   **D.** Inter-tubular dentin

Q.132 Which of the following is the maximum intercuspation and interdigitation between the upper and lower teeth when the jaws are closed?
A. Non-physiologic occlusion
B. Centric occlusion
C. Centric relation
D. Balanced occlusion

Q.133 Modern diets lack ________, an organic phosphate which can protect against caries.
A. fructose   **B.** phytates   **C.** spirulina   **D.** anzym

Q.134 Whenever _________ is sawed through the contact areas between teeth, and it trays or sheds, then it is a sign of proximal caries.
A. Tooth separation
B. Dental floss
C. Fibre-optic trans-illumination
D. Cervical burnout

Q.135

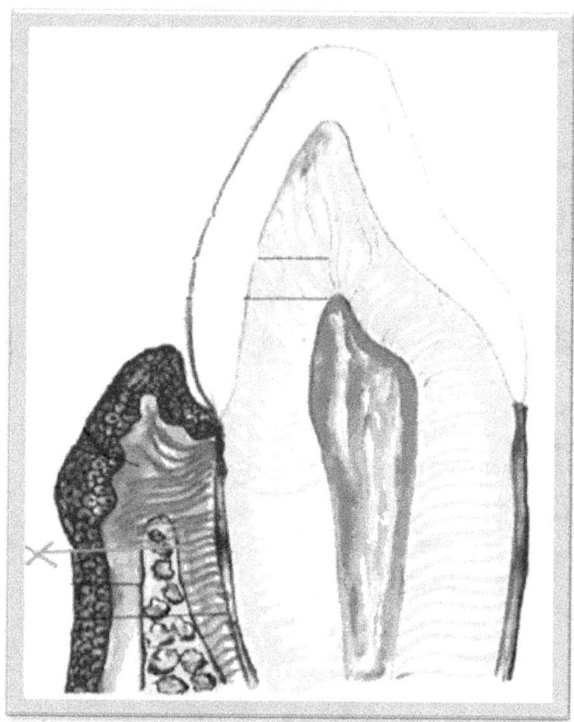

This is the diagram of the supporting tissues of a tooth. What does 'X' indicate?
A. Periodontal ligament
B. Alveolar Bone
C. Cementum
D. Trabecular Bone

Q.136 Which of the following tests is more accurate than some of the tests used to determine the pulp vitality?
A. X-ray radiography
B. Electric pulp testing
C. Mobility de-possibility testing
D. Thermal testing

Q.137 The emergency treatment of acute alveolar abscess differs from that of the acute irreversible pulpitis because
A. The pulp is necrotic, local anaesthesia is not needed routinely
B. The pulp is not necrotic, local anaesthesia is not needed routinely
C. The pulp is necrotic, local anaesthesia is needed routinely
D. The pulp is not necrotic, local anaesthesia is needed routinely

Q.138 ______ analgesics are used to relieve acute, severe pain.

A. narcotic   **B.** non-narcotic
C. local   **D.** opioid

Q.139 The odontoblastic cell bodies form the odontoblastic zone, whereas the odontoblastic processes are located within the _______ matrix and the dentinal tubules, extending into the dentin.

A. peridentin   **B.** predentin
C. tertiary dentin   **D.** osteodentin

Q.140 Which of the following have the function such as elaboration of ground substance and collagen fibres, which constitute the matrix of the pulp?

A. Ameloblasts   **B.** Odontoblasts
C. Fibroblasts   **D.** Cementoblasts

Q.141 Which of the following are the most important cells of the periodontal ligament?

A. Fibroblasts   **B.** Osteoclasts
C. Cementoblasts   **D.** Mast cells

Q.142

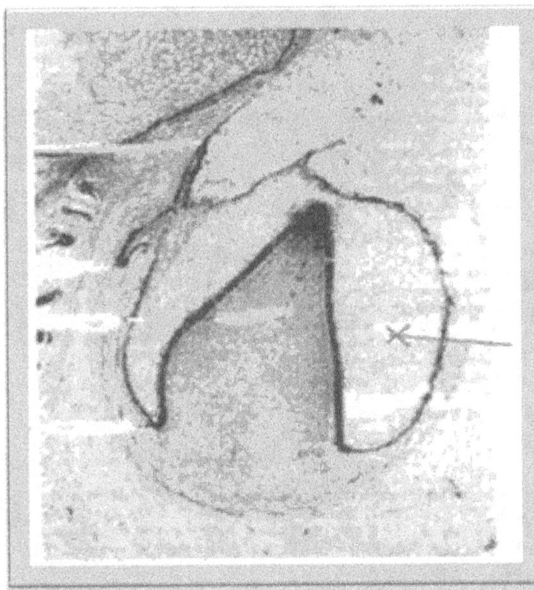

This is the diagram of the bell stage of development of dental pulp and periradicular tissues. What does 'X' indicate?

A. Dental follicle
B. Outer enamel epithelium
C. Stellate reticulum
D. Inner enamel epithelium

Q.143 Which of the following represents the condition in which the sutures in the skull of an infant close too early, causing problems with normal brain and skull growth?

A. Folic acid deficiency
B. Craniosynostosis
C. Hemifacial microsomia
D. Deformational plagiocephaly

Q.144 Which of the following is a chronic swelling of the lip due to granulomatous inflammation?

A. Cheilitis granulomatosa
B. Angular cheilitis
C. Cheilitis glandularis
D. Oral melanotic macule

Q.145 Which of the following is not a disease of the oral mucosa, but rather a developmental anomaly characterized by heterotopic collections of sebaceous glands at various sites in the oral cavity?

A. Fordyce's granules
B. Focal epithelial hyperplasia
C. Retro-cuspid papilla
D. Aglossia and macroglossia syndrome

Q.146 Which of the following is a rare disorder characterised by non-cancerous benign growth that may develop in the lymph node tissue throughout the body?

A. Castleman's disease
B. Lymphoid aggregate
C. Angio-lymphoid hyperplasia
D. Lympho-epithelial cyst

Q.147 In xerostomia: Which of the following is the inflammation of the salivary glands which can cause reduced secretion?

A. Duct calculi   **B.** Sialoadenitis
C. Aplasia   **D.** LADD

Q.148 One of the common forms of localised _____ is that which affects the maxillary lateral incisor, a condition that has been called the peg lateral.

A. Microdontia   **B.** Macrodontia
C. Microsomia   **D.** Macrosomia

Q.149 The gross appearance of _____ varies from a filmy opalescence of the mucosa in the early stages to a more definitive greyish – white cast with coarsely wrinkled surfaces in the later stages.

A. leukoedema
B. leukocytes
C. intraepithelial carcinoma
D. erythroplasia

Q.150 Which of the following has ultraviolet radiation as the most common cause?

A. Basal cell carcinoma
B. Epidermoid carcinoma
C. Oral submucous fibrosis
D. Oral lichen planus like lesion

Q.151 Which of the following is the most common malignant neoplasm of the oral cavity?

A. Basal cell carcinoma
B. Epidermoid carcinoma
C. Oral submucous fibrosis
D. Oral lichen planus like lesion

Q.152 Which of the following is an exceedingly dangerous disease?

A. Antral carcinoma

B. Carcinoma of the palate

C. Carcinoma of the gingiva

D. Verrucous carcinoma

Q.153 Which of the following has an unknown etiology with some dispute as to whether this lesion represents a reactive or neoplasm process?

A. Peripheral giant cell granuloma

B. Central ossifying fibroma of bone

C. Peripheral ossifying fibroma

D. Giant cell fibroma

Q.154 Which of the following is a benign central tumour composed of mature cartilage, is a well-recognised entity in certain areas of the bony skeleton, but is uncommon in the bones of the maxilla or mandible?

A. Myxoma

B. Chondroma

C. Fibroma

D. Osteoma

Q.155 Which of the following is currently defined as the benign neoplasm of striated muscle tissue, consisting usually of polygonal frequently vacuolated glycogen containing cells with a fine granular deeply acidophilic cytoplasm resembling myofibril in the cut section?

A. Angiomyoma

B. Leiomyoma

C. Rhabdomyoma

D. Myoblastoma

Q.156 Which of the following is also known as Newman's tumor?

A. Congenital granular cell lesion

B. Granular cell myoblastoma

C. Rhabdomyoma

D. Angiomyoma

Q.157

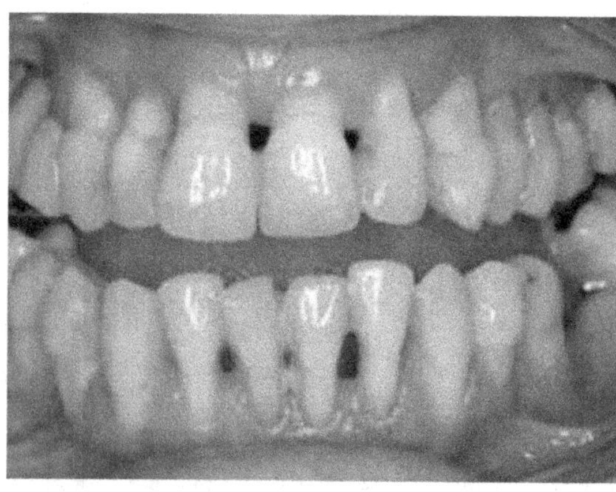

Which of the following disease is depicted by this picture?

A. Chronic periodontitis

B. Aggressive periodontitis

C. Necrotizing ulcerative periodontitis

D. Lateral periodontal abscess

Q.158 Which of the following nerves is tested through its motor supply to the trapezius and sternomastoid muscles?

A. Hypoglossal nerve

B. Accessory nerve

C. Vagus nerve

D. Glossopharyngeal nerve

Q.159 Which of the following drugs indirectly depress the bone marrow and immune response, leading to bacterial, viral, or fungal infections of the oral mucosa?

A. Drugs that cause gingivitis

B. Drugs that cause stomatitis

C. Drugs that cause neural disorder

D. Drugs that cause high fever

Q.160 The connective diseases and abnormal levels of serum iron, folate, vitamin B12 and ferritin causes which of the following diseases?

A. Minor aphthae or major aphthous ulcers

B. Behcet's syndrome

C. Pemphigus

D. Epithelial bullous dermatoses

Q.161 In pemphigus Vulgaris: Death occurs most frequently in elderly persons and in patients requiring high doses of .... who develop infections and bacterial septicemia, most notably from staphylococcus aureus.

A. Corticosteroids

B. Testosterone

C. Oxacillin

D. Penicillin

Q.162 Which of the following predominantly affects non-cornified stratified squamous epithelium?

A. White sponge nevus

B. Dyskeratosiscongenita

C. Traumatic keratosis

D. Leukoedema

Q.163 Which of the following is the prototype of the oral infections caused by candida?

A. Stomatitis

B. Thrush

C. Aphthous

D. Cheilitis

Q.164 Which of the following disease occurs most commonly on the skin, as a result of arsenic ingestion?

A. Erythroplakia

B. Bowen's disease

C. Gnarled syndrome

D. Lichenoid reactions

Q.165 Which of the following is a malignant vascular neoplasms, distinct from Kaposi's sarcoma, are not related to human immunodeficiency virus HIV and can arise anywhere in the body?

A. Kaposi's sarcoma

B. Angio-sarcoma

C. Osteosarcoma

D. Varix

Q.166 Which of the following is a disease that generally presents as a white lesion, with variants showing red and desquamative lesions?

A. Smoker's melanosis

B. Pigmented lichen planus

C. Endocrinopathies pigmentation

D. Oral melanosis

Q.167 Which of the following may pose a mechanical problem in the constriction of dentures?

A. Tori
B. Retention
C. Implants
D. Edentulous space

Q.168 Which of the following is a pedunculated haemorrhagic nodule that occurs most frequently on the gingiva and that has a strong tendency to recur after simple excision?

A. Palatal papillary hyperplasia
B. Pyogenic granuloma
C. Giant cell granuloma
D. Fibrous inflammatory hyper-plasias

Q.169 Which are tumor-like malformations composed of seemingly disorganized masses of endothelium-lined vessels that are filled with blood and connected to the main blood vascular system?

A. Hemangiomas
B. Hamartomas
C. Lymphoid hyperplasia
D. Lymphangioma

Q.170 Which of the following of the bone results from an abnormality in the development of bone-forming mesenchyme?

A. Fibrous dysplasia
B. Dysplasia
C. Necrosis
D. Osteosarcoma

Q.171 Which of the following are the neoplasms that are composed of a mixture of tissues more than one of which exhibits neoplastic proliferation?

A. Teratomas
B. Angioma
C. Apnoea
D. Cherubism

Q.172 Cysts of the _______ were thought to arise from pseudostratified columnar respiratory type epithelium rather than from the oral mucosa.

A. ethmoid air sinus
B. frontal sinus
C. maxillary sinus
D. sphenoid sinus

Q.173 Which of the following is an accumulation of fluid in the interstitial space because of transudation from damaged vessels and lymphatic obstruction by fibrin?

A. Hemostasis
B. Edema
C. Inflammation
D. Vesicles

Q.174 If a three-cornered flap is used, the initial reflection is accomplished with the sharp end of the _______ elevator on the first papilla only.

A. No. 7
B. No. 8
C. No. 9
D. No. 10

Q.175 Which of the following cause pericoronitis?

A. Streptococci
B. Parasites
C. Viruses
D. Fungi

Q.176 Which of the following may result from the multiple injections of local anaesthesia, especially if the injections have penetrated muscles?

A. Oedema
B. Trismus

C. Ecchymosis
D. Inflammation

Q.177 Which of the following is the most commonly used flap for small openings?

A. Buccal flap
B. Lingual flap
C. Oral flap
D. Lateral flap

Q.178 Which of the following can be used to help control a bleeding socket?

A. Plastin
B. Collagen
C. Cellulose
D. Absorbable Gelatin sponge

Q.179 What kind of surgery allows the minimal mechanical and thermal injury to occur?

A. Traumatic
B. Atraumatic
C. Occlusion traumatic
D. Incisal traumatic

Q.180 Which of the following processes with a peristome preserves the contour and integrity of the intact socket?

A. Atraumatic extraction
B. Socket preservation
C. Interim prosthesis design
D. Traumatic extraction

Q.181 Which of the following is a component of the implant system that screws directly into the implant?

A. Interim abutment
B. Abutment
C. Healing screw
D. Implant body

Q.182 Which of the following ensures that two machined surfaces are always in contact?

A. Implant analog
B. Waxing sleeve
C. Prosthesis
D. Impression coping

Q.183 Infection from most maxillary teeth erodes through the

A. facial cortical plate
B. enamel cords
C. buccal cortical plate
D. periodontal ligament

Q.184

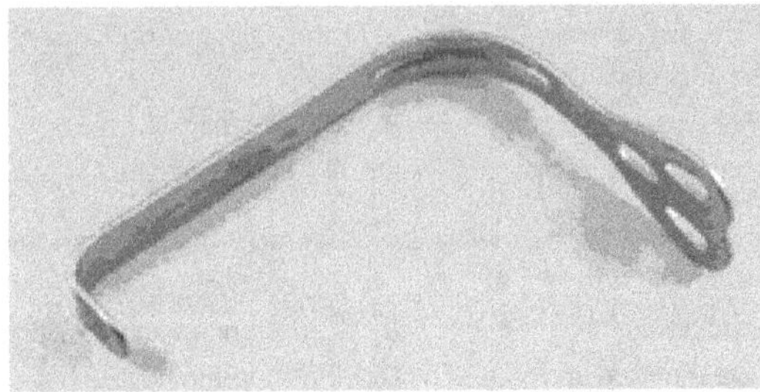

Which of the following is shown in the given picture?

A. Rongeurs
B. Weider retractor
C. Minnesota retractor
D. Austin retractor

Q.185

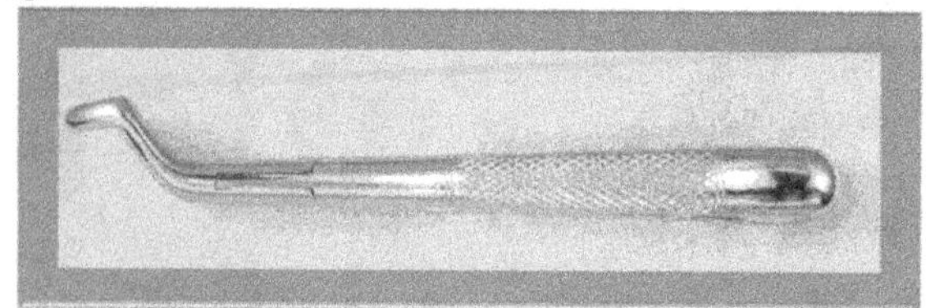

Which of the following is indicated by the superior view of this surgical tool?

A. No. 150 forceps
B. No. 151 forceps
C. No. 210S forceps
D. No. 150S forceps

Q.186

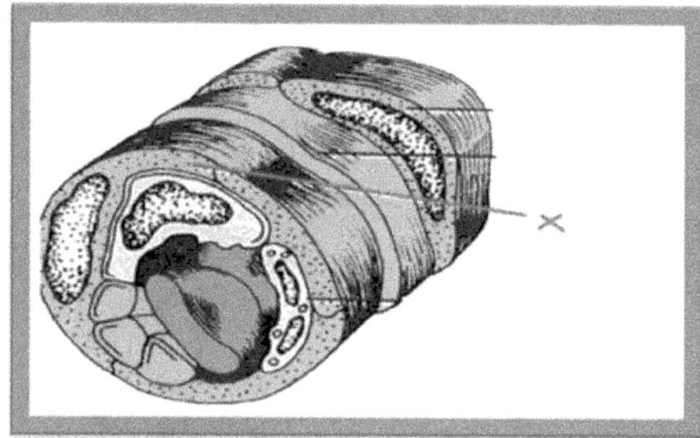

This is the picture of early vascular responses to injury. What does 'X' indicate?

A. Pericyte
B. Basement membrane
C. Endothelial cell
D. Marginatingpolymorpho-nuclear leukocyte

Q.187 Which of the following plays a role in the biosynthesis of corticosteroids?

A. Pyridoxine
B. Pantothenic acid
C. Ascorbic acid
D. Nicotinic acid

Q.188 Which of the following is a free radical scavenger and protects the cell membrane from oxidative damage?

A. Vitamin K
B. Vitamin B
C. Vitamin D
D. Vitamin E

Q.189 The Government of India adopted rapid and inclusive growth as its core theme in the

A. 8th Five-year plan
B. 9th Five-year plan
C. 10th Five-year plan
D. 11th Five-year plan

Q.190 Which of the following is an assembly of all the adults of the village which meets at least twice a year?

A. Gram Sabha
B. Gram Panchayat
C. Nyaya Panchayat
D. Dharma Panchayat

Q.191 Which of the following are a group of extracellular enzymes involved in the synthesis of polymers from sucrose?

A. Glucosyl-transferases
B. Salivary amylases
C. Cellulases
D. laccases

Q.192 The _______ is a thin, saliva-derived layer which forms on the tooth surface immediately on exposure to saliva.

A. pellicle **B.** caries **C.** calculus **D.** stain

Q.193 Which of the following is an odourless, tasteless gas, giving no warning of its presence in most circumstances?

A. Nicotine
B. Tar
C. Carbon monoxide
D. Nitrogen oxides

Q.194 Which of the following is/are capable of adversely affecting the facial appearance of an individual?

A. Malalignment of teeth
B. Malocclusion
C. Occlusion
D. TMJ problems

Q.195 Which of the following is similar to the lingual arch space maintainer?

A. Palatal arch
B. Transpalatal arch
C. Distal shoe space maintainer
D. Band and bar space maintainer

Q.196 Which of the following habits has a profound effect on the dentofacial region?

A. Thumb sucking
B. Tongue thrusting
C. Mouth breathing
D. Teeth biting

Q.197 In dentition status, unexposed roots are coded

A. 6 **B.** 7 **C.** 8 **D.** 9

Q.198 Which of the following indices was designed to assess the plaque control status among naval personnel and to measure any subsequent changes?

A. Glass index
B. Navy plaque index
C. Calculus surface index
D. Calculus surfaces severity

Q.199 Which of the following is a term applied to those dental laboratory technicians who are permitted to fabricate dentures directly for patients without a dentist's prescription?

A. School dental nurse
B. Denturist
C. Physician
D. Dental health educator

Q.200 Cartilage differs from the bone in that it grows by?

A. Appositional growth pattern
B. Interstitial growth pattern
C. Growth of cells in lacunae
D. None of these

Q.201 Specific types of removable partial dentures are-

A. Fixed prosthodontics, removable prosthodontics and maxillofacial prosthodontics
B. Tooth – supported removable partial denture
C. Tooth – tissue supported partial denture
D. Option (B) and (C)

Q.202 The centric relation occurring at varying degrees of the mandibular opening must precede

A. Forward & downward movement of the condyles
B. To & fro movement of the condyles
C. Spindles of the condyles
D. Rotatory movements of the condyles

Q.203 Which of the following is correct?

A. Resorption may result in decreased ridge height and decreased support for the associated denture bases.
B. Resorption gives stability to the dentures bases
C. Resorption un-changes the height of the ridges
D. Rigidity may result in decreased ridge height and decreased support for the associated denture bases.

Q.204 Which is the second fundamental requirement of a major connector?

A. It must not permit impingement upon the free gingival margins of the remaining teeth.
B. Rigidity
C. Promote patient comfort
D. Less flexible

Q.205 An infra-bulge or bar type direct retainer is often called as _______.

A. akers clasp
B. under cut
C. roach clasp
D. None

Q.206 The component of a clasp that provides vertical support for the prosthesis is called a _______.

A. rest
B. rest seat
C. retentive arm
D. suprabulge retainers

Q.207 Compared to a fixed prosthesis, a removable prosthesis does not connect its abutments as _______ to one another.

A. stability
B. support
C. rigidity
D. None

Q.208 DeVan determined that the muco-periosteum of the residual ridge offers the only ______ of the support provided by a periodontal ligament.

A. 0.04%
B. 0.4%
C. 4%
D. 0.39%

Q.209 Kennedy bar is also known as:

A. Double lingual bar
B. Lingual plate
C. Lingual bar
D. Palatal plate

Q.210 Many clinically acceptable prostheses have been discarded because patients were not ______ prepared to receive them.

A. mentally
B. physically
C. socially
D. All

Q.211 Face-bows such as the ______ are placed into the patient's ears, much like a stethoscope.

A. hanau Spring-Bow
B. hanau Wide-Vue articulator
C. Both
D. None

Q.212 The ear-type face-bows record the positions of the _______ auditory openings.

A. External
B. Internal
C. Posterior
D. Anterior

Q.213

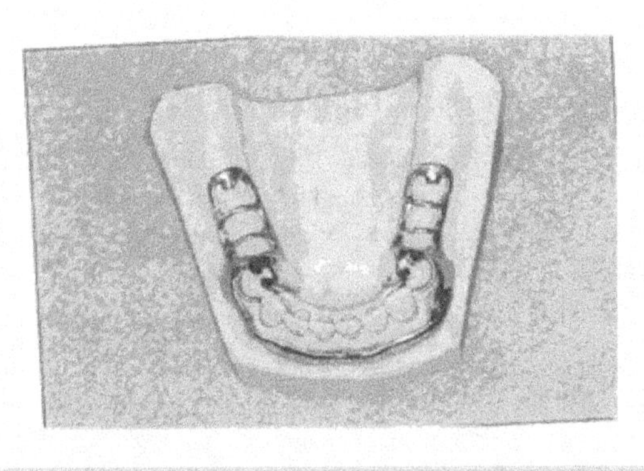

Which of the following major connectors is indicated by this picture?

A. Double lingual bar major connector
B. Labial bar major connector
C. Lingual bar major connector
D. Lingual plate major connector

Q.214

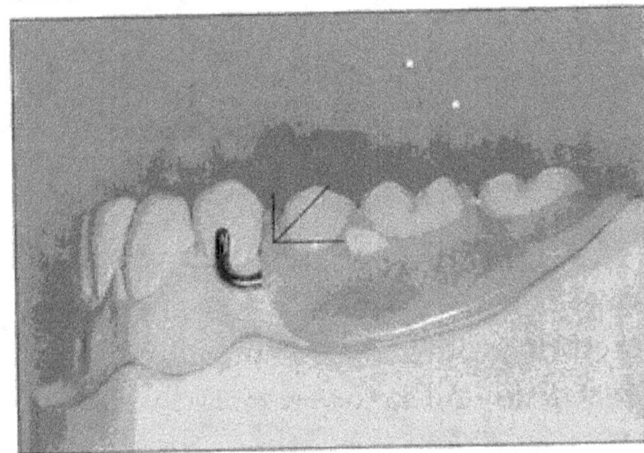

Which of the following Kennedy Class prostheses is indicated by this picture?

A. Kennedy Class I prosthesis
B. Kennedy Class II prosthesis
C. Kennedy Class III prosthesis
D. Kennedy Class IV prosthesis

Q.215 In growth of the mandible, which of the following stops at the point which will later become the mandibular lingual and the remaining part of Meckel's cartilage continues on its own to form the spheno-mandibular ligament and the spinous process of the sphenoid?

A. Ossification
B. Palpation
C. Proliferation
D. Deglutition

Q.216 Weinmann and Sicher have strongly supported their contention that the _______ is the major growth centre of the mandible and is endowed with an intrinsic genetic potential.

A. contour
B. condyle
C. dental implant
D. dental cast

Q.217 One of the strongest forces absorbed by the cranial and facial superstructures is the

A.   Torquing force
B.   Force of occlusion
C.   Force of mastication
D.   Force of impaction

Q.218 Any complete definition of _______ should convey the impression of normality, balanced relations, bilateral symmetrical activity and the state of being unstrained.

A. face-bow
B. centric relation
C. complete dentures
D. prosthesis

Q.219 Which of the following are guided by the working side canines, with disclusion of all the other teeth on both working and non-working sides?

A.   Anterior movements of the mandible
B.   Posterior movements of the mandible
C.   Lateral movements of the mandible
D.   Lingual movements of the mandible

Q.220 The dentist must be fully aware that there is no other joint in the body that is used more than the _______.

A.   gliding joint
B.   hinge joints
C.   saddle joints
D.   temporo-mandibular joints

Q.221 Regarding works by Roth(1981): When the teeth are in centric occlusion, there should be _________ in the buccal segments.

A.   odd bilateral contacts
B.   even bilateral contacts
C.   odd unilateral contacts
D.   even unilateral contacts

Q.222 Which of the following may involve four tissue systems: teeth, bones, muscles, and nerves?

A. Occlusion
B. Malocclusion
C. Centric relation
D. Face-bows

Q.223 Which of the following is a congenital and frequently hereditary defect that may cause a dental malocclusion?

A.   Torticollis
B.   Cleido-cranial dysostosis
C.   Cerebral palsy
D.   Congenital syphilis

Q.224 Which of the following terms implies absence of only a few teeth?

A. Hypodontia
B. Hyperdontia
C. Oligodontia
D. Anodontia

Q.225 The size of teeth is largely determined by _________.

A. growth
B. gender
C. heredity
D. hormones

Q.226 _______ serve not only as organs of mastication but also as space savers for the permanent teeth.

A. maxillary arch
B. mandibular arch
C. deciduous teeth
D. alveolar bone

Q.227 Which of the following cysts can also cause abnormal eruptive paths?

A. Coronal cysts
B. Residual cysts
C. Bilateral cysts
D. Oral cyst

Q.228 If _______ or temporary stopping is used as a temporary filling material before placing the permanent restoration, the approximating teeth may be moved apart by the plunger-like action of the ruberoid mass, even before the permanent restoration is placed.

A. gutta-percha
B. plaster of paris
C. acrylic resin
D. alumina

Q.229 Which of the following is/are the integral membrane protein(s) that span(s) the hydrophobic lipid matrix of the post-junctional membrane?

A.   Collagen
B.   Acetylcholine receptor
C.   Amino acids
D.   Cellulose

Q.230 Which of the following contains the nucleus and nucleolus of the neuron?

A. Cell wall
B. Cell body
C. Cell membrane
D. Cytoplasm

Q.231 Half-life of TGF-beta is:

A. 24 hr
B. 48 hr
C. 10-12 min
D. 3-5 min

Q.232 In sensory pathways, which of the following is generally located in a sensory nucleus of the thalamus?

A.   First order neuron
B.   Second order neuron
C.   Third order neuron
D.   Fourth order neuron

Q.233

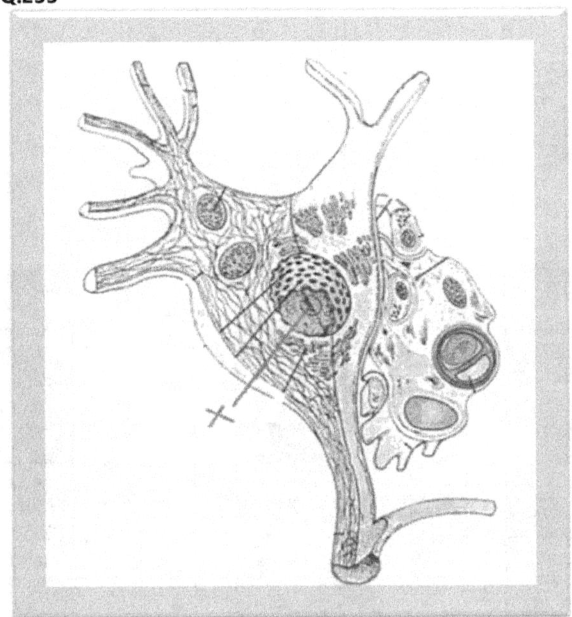

This is the diagram of the organelles of the neurons. What is indicated by the letter 'X'?

A. Nucleus   **B.** Nucleolus

C. Nuclear pore   **D.** Golgi apparatus

Q.234 Polypeptide formation in amino acid is by:

A. Primary structure

B. Secondary structure

C. Tertiary structure

D. Quaternary structure

Q.235 What type of protein is Casein?

A. Lipoprotein   **B.** Phosphoprotein

C. Glycoprotein   **D.** Flavoprotein

Q.236 An alpha helix of a protein is most likely to be disrupted if a missense mutation introduces the following amino acid within the alpha helical structure:

A. Alanine   **B.** Aspartic acid

C. Tyrosine   **D.** Glycine

Q.237 Following SDS PAGE electrophoresis, protein is found to be 100 kDa after treatment with mercaptol-ethanol, it shows two bands of 20 KDa and 30 KDa widely separated. The true statement is:

A. Protein has undergone hydrolysis of S-S linkage

B. It is a dimer of 2 subunits of 20 and 30 KDa

C. It is a tetramer of 2, 20 KDa and 2, 30 KDa

D. Protein breaks down due to non-covalent linkage

Q.238 Protein is purified using ammonium sulphate by:

A. salting out

B. ion-exchange chromatography

C. mass chromatography

D. molecular size exclusion

Q.239 Methods used to study the structure of proteins include all of the following, except:

A. UV spectroscopy

B. NMR spectroscopy

C. X-ray crystallography

D. Edman's technique

Q.240 True about double diffusion technique is:

A. Radial immunofluorescence

B. Invented by Oakley Fulthorpe

C. Ougundi technique

D. Ouchterlony double immune diffusion

// Smart Answer Sheet //

Correct — Indicates percentage of students who answered questions correctly.

Skipped — Indicates percentage of students who skipped questions.

Q.	Ans.	Correct / Skipped
1	B	88.78 % / 11.07 %
2	A	15.61 % / 74.92 %
3	B	45.55 % / 31.69 %
4	A	19.5 % / 78.01 %
5	A	10.41 % / 68.27 %
6	A	30.23 % / 69.74 %
7	B	55.85 % / 35.98 %
8	A	83.0 % / 14.29 %
9	A	49.96 % / 32.65 %
10	B	54.2 % / 40.25 %
11	A	65.24 % / 32.66 %
12	C	55.02 % / 32.25 %
13	A	80.55 % / 12.89 %
14	A	53.25 % / 34.44 %
15	B	21.74 % / 69.06 %
16	B	41.59 % / 43.22 %
17	C	78.1 % / 20.06 %
18	B	56.34 % / 40.79 %
19	D	28.04 % / 68.83 %
20	A	65.03 % / 32.16 %
21	B	77.32 % / 12.99 %
22	B	84.74 % / 12.76 %
23	B	54.78 % / 35.76 %
24	D	24.51 % / 70.83 %
25	A	62.56 % / 37.37 %
26	B	23.99 % / 73.17 %
27	A	87.24 % / 10.2 %
28	A	51.19 % / 30.95 %
29	D	85.17 % / 11.57 %
30	D	15.83 % / 68.09 %
31	C	41.77 % / 31.37 %
32	A	31.57 % / 68.24 %
33	A	81.39 % / 12.9 %
34	B	55.82 % / 39.03 %
35	C	62.67 % / 35.29 %
36	B	42.33 % / 34.04 %
37	C	69.65 % / 30.12 %
38	A	40.41 % / 56.04 %
39	D	57.73 % / 38.97 %
40	C	15.74 % / 81.88 %
41	D	52.75 % / 32.17 %
42	B	50.16 % / 34.55 %
43	B	51.95 % / 38.05 %
44	C	18.81 % / 81.08 %
45	A	42.79 % / 54.62 %
46	B	19.14 % / 74.45 %
47	B	18.37 % / 79.81 %
48	B	19.65 % / 75.39 %
49	B	59.24 % / 35.18 %
50	A	48.72 % / 43.45 %
51	D	60.75 % / 37.91 %
52	C	26.77 % / 67.88 %
53	C	55.26 % / 34.25 %
54	A	54.1 % / 44.45 %
55	C	41.21 % / 33.84 %
56	A	56.67 % / 36.3 %
57	A	62.25 % / 34.35 %
58	A	46.28 % / 43.88 %
59	C	45.4 % / 34.67 %
60	C	60.23 % / 30.32 %
61	B	52.72 % / 39.27 %
62	A	61.94 % / 36.13 %
63	B	43.16 % / 37.83 %
64	C	50.47 % / 49.32 %
65	B	28.14 % / 71.3 %
66	B	23.93 % / 69.64 %
67	C	46.08 % / 30.63 %
68	B	52.29 % / 40.03 %
69	B	45.53 % / 34.32 %
70	A	62.66 % / 30.91 %
71	B	40.39 % / 46.89 %
72	A	26.29 % / 72.53 %
73	B	69.34 % / 30.55 %
74	B	65.82 % / 31.77 %
75	B	55.42 % / 40.67 %
76	B	44.82 % / 36.77 %
77	A	26.8 % / 68.59 %
78	C	50.66 % / 45.22 %
79	A	51.87 % / 32.73 %
80	B	63.59 % / 35.33 %

Q.	Ans.	Correct / Skipped
81	B	26.23 % / 69.58 %
82	C	59.7 % / 30.9 %
83	A	53.23 % / 43.12 %
84	B	40.16 % / 34.58 %
85	B	24.12 % / 69.82 %
86	A	67.93 % / 31.65 %
87	B	40.23 % / 40.81 %
88	A	62.55 % / 34.72 %
89	A	65.29 % / 32.3 %
90	B	13.24 % / 76.64 %
91	B	46.97 % / 52.79 %
92	B	21.18 % / 72.37 %
93	B	68.17 % / 30.0 %
94	B	13.78 % / 83.15 %
95	B	58.01 % / 30.31 %
96	A	45.65 % / 42.31 %

Q.	Ans.	Correct / Skipped
97	A	47.22 % / 31.59 %
98	A	20.59 % / 76.24 %
99	C	64.29 % / 34.96 %
100	B	66.81 % / 32.92 %
101	C	61.67 % / 31.25 %
102	B	46.89 % / 30.88 %
103	A	28.63 % / 68.01 %
104	A	43.57 % / 30.6 %
105	B	43.54 % / 53.6 %
106	C	81.04 % / 18.76 %
107	A	65.79 % / 30.86 %
108	A	41.35 % / 45.84 %
109	B	58.54 % / 30.96 %
110	B	10.49 % / 67.55 %
111	B	60.28 % / 35.65 %
112	A	49.02 % / 42.47 %

Q.	Ans.	Correct / Skipped
113	A	55.15 % / 44.84 %
114	A	58.48 % / 31.3 %
115	A	63.75 % / 32.22 %
116	B	41.11 % / 48.99 %
117	A	63.65 % / 33.85 %
118	A	54.74 % / 43.18 %
119	C	32.81 % / 67.08 %
120	C	62.1 % / 31.64 %
121	B	89.14 % / 10.44 %
122	A	56.96 % / 30.18 %
123	B	21.12 % / 78.76 %
124	A	41.52 % / 58.11 %
125	B	68.98 % / 30.12 %
126	C	28.32 % / 69.59 %
127	B	58.37 % / 31.76 %
128	B	89.32 % / 10.65 %

Q.	Ans.	Correct / Skipped
129	B	48.62 % / 42.38 %
130	C	63.04 % / 33.32 %
131	B	50.84 % / 33.04 %
132	B	43.32 % / 45.24 %
133	B	43.58 % / 30.72 %
134	B	46.19 % / 46.76 %
135	A	18.49 % / 69.76 %
136	B	55.69 % / 33.51 %
137	A	64.2 % / 30.48 %
138	A	86.34 % / 12.87 %
139	B	31.62 % / 67.18 %
140	C	51.89 % / 41.98 %
141	A	40.91 % / 51.63 %
142	C	63.31 % / 32.98 %
143	B	50.78 % / 41.88 %
144	A	53.71 % / 39.32 %

Q.	Ans.	Correct / Skipped
145	A	80.38 % / 15.28 %
146	A	41.68 % / 35.47 %
147	B	82.65 % / 11.33 %
148	A	57.54 % / 35.92 %
149	A	66.24 % / 32.55 %
150	A	84.18 % / 12.79 %
151	B	60.14 % / 31.93 %
152	A	54.29 % / 36.61 %
153	A	22.28 % / 70.79 %
154	B	42.22 % / 44.46 %
155	C	51.44 % / 46.54 %
156	A	84.94 % / 11.06 %
157	A	69.46 % / 30.14 %
158	B	63.74 % / 34.39 %
159	B	68.99 % / 30.14 %
160	A	49.74 % / 49.13 %

Q.	Ans.	Correct / Skipped		Q.	Ans.	Correct / Skipped		Q.	Ans.	Correct / Skipped		Q.	Ans.	Correct / Skipped		Q.	Ans.	Correct / Skipped
161	A	81.77 % / 16.05 %		177	A	89.09 % / 10.6 %		193	C	57.42 % / 41.48 %		209	A	55.93 % / 33.48 %		225	C	46.43 % / 34.36 %
162	A	69.14 % / 30.11 %		178	B	42.22 % / 31.11 %		194	B	11.97 % / 78.99 %		210	A	46.66 % / 46.9 %		226	C	45.2 % / 35.23 %
163	B	81.59 % / 17.87 %		179	B	54.01 % / 44.32 %		195	A	83.29 % / 14.45 %		211	A	21.7 % / 69.74 %		227	A	58.14 % / 40.47 %
164	B	45.41 % / 37.71 %		180	A	42.55 % / 31.76 %		196	C	41.23 % / 45.79 %		212	A	50.62 % / 36.5 %		228	A	65.98 % / 32.57 %
165	B	56.07 % / 40.98 %		181	B	86.79 % / 10.92 %		197	C	63.24 % / 33.2 %		213	B	86.7 % / 10.92 %		229	B	81.55 % / 14.21 %
166	B	65.15 % / 30.19 %		182	B	45.99 % / 49.55 %		198	B	55.25 % / 37.22 %		214	A	23.36 % / 68.67 %		230	B	49.41 % / 33.01 %
167	A	83.82 % / 11.47 %		183	A	27.64 % / 71.09 %		199	B	56.86 % / 31.04 %		215	A	23.6 % / 72.97 %		231	D	41.51 % / 44.73 %
168	B	43.24 % / 30.99 %		184	B	42.39 % / 39.1 %		200	B	41.37 % / 34.38 %		216	B	68.65 % / 30.63 %		232	C	48.84 % / 44.58 %
169	A	61.46 % / 31.27 %		185	C	67.15 % / 32.1 %		201	D	31.55 % / 67.54 %		217	C	52.24 % / 35.41 %		233	B	30.64 % / 68.68 %
170	A	62.16 % / 32.29 %		186	C	47.62 % / 50.32 %		202	A	45.78 % / 45.5 %		218	B	45.13 % / 48.83 %		234	A	48.68 % / 37.01 %
171	A	87.24 % / 11.5 %		187	B	43.05 % / 31.07 %		203	A	78.95 % / 10.31 %		219	C	80.72 % / 11.31 %		235	B	82.35 % / 17.43 %
172	C	47.21 % / 38.93 %		188	D	76.64 % / 15.75 %		204	A	45.58 % / 32.57 %		220	D	66.99 % / 32.27 %		236	D	60.1 % / 30.81 %
173	B	57.66 % / 41.0 %		189	D	80.09 % / 15.46 %		205	C	64.1 % / 33.49 %		221	B	40.42 % / 46.71 %		237	C	50.89 % / 38.61 %
174	C	41.33 % / 50.8 %		190	A	69.9 % / 30.1 %		206	A	64.91 % / 34.89 %		222	B	63.32 % / 33.02 %		238	A	62.65 % / 31.92 %
175	A	81.07 % / 14.37 %		191	A	47.42 % / 44.33 %		207	C	44.56 % / 33.99 %		223	B	61.64 % / 34.95 %		239	D	85.62 % / 10.83 %
176	B	68.98 % / 30.77 %		192	A	44.13 % / 47.35 %		208	B	83.29 % / 10.37 %		224	A	69.43 % / 30.29 %		240	D	67.14 % / 31.36 %

Performance Analysis

Avg. Score (%)	55.0%
Toppers Score (%)	60.0%
Your Score	

Part A

Q.1

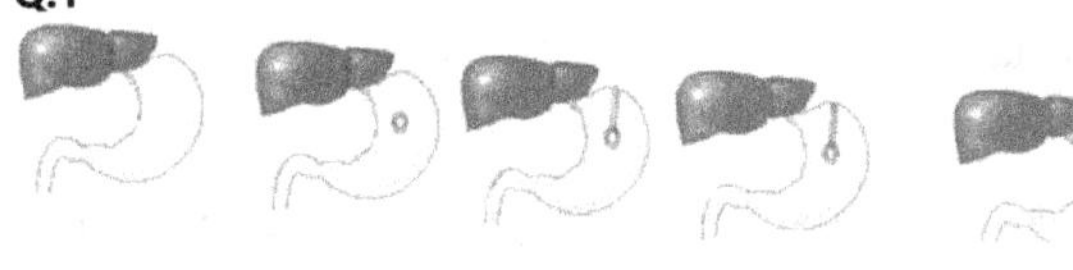

What is represented through these diagrams?

A. Bariatric surgery
B. Vertical banded gastroplasty
C. Laparoscopic RYGB
D. Jejunoileal bypass

Q.2

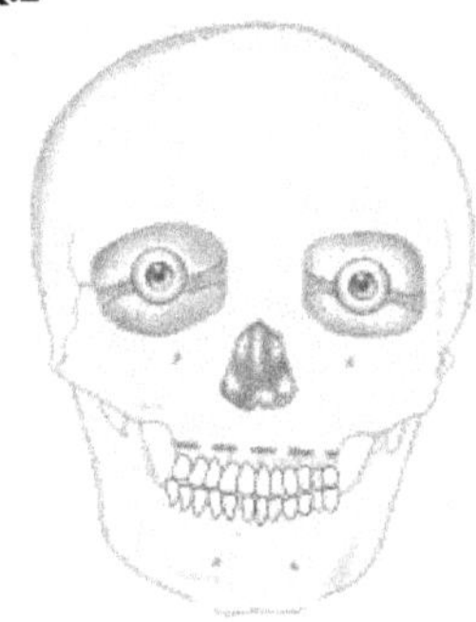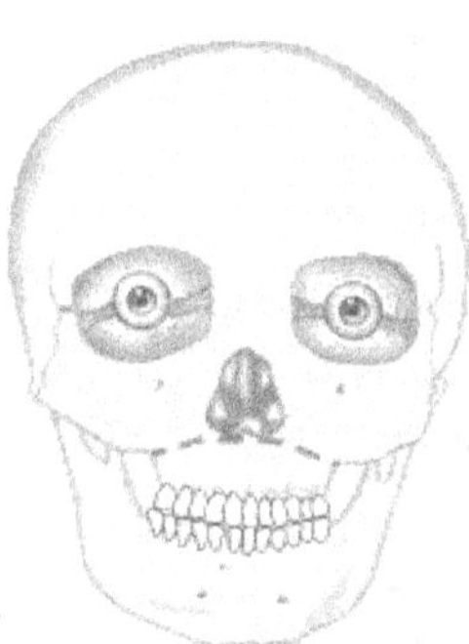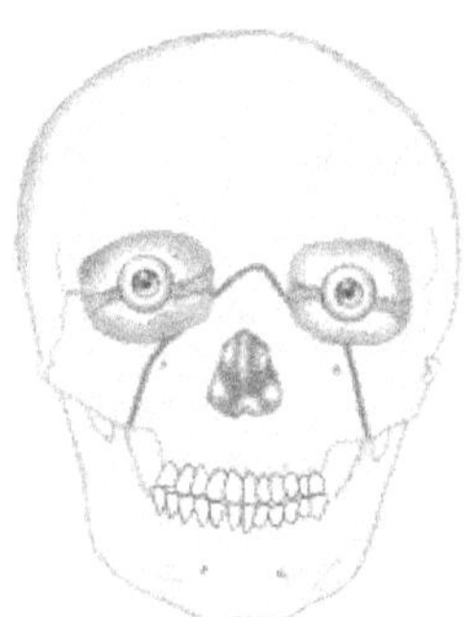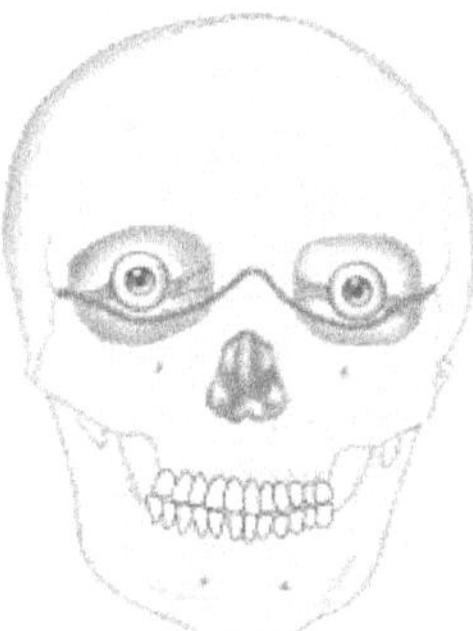

Which of the following is explained through these diagrams?

A. Le Fort classification
B. Rowe and Kelley classification
C. Obwegesor and Dalapont classification
D. Kay and Killey classification

Q.3 How long do partial thickness burns typically take to heal?

A. 3 weeks
B. 2 weeks
C. 2 months
D. 1 week

Q.4 Cause(s) of hypernatremia is/are:

A. renal dysfunction
B. corticosteroids
C. cardiac failure
D. All of the above

Q.5 Shock leads to _________ which activates anaerobic metabolism leading to lactic acidosis.

A. Hypertropia
B. Hypoxia
C. Hypertension
D. Habenula

Q.6 Which of the following causes staining of burnt area?

A. Sulfamylon
B. Silver nitrate
C. Sodium hypochlorite
D. Sodium nitrate

Q.7 Which is the most common organ involved in blunt abdominal trauma?

A. Pancreas
B. Spleen
C. Abdomen
D. Liver

Q.8 Which of the following diseases occurs in subcuticular area under the eponychium?

A. Acute paronychia
B. Chronic paronychia
C. Midpalmar space infection
D. Deep palmar space infection

Q.9 Which of the following is the tissue transfer between two genetically identical individuals?

A. Graft
B. Autograft
C. Isograft
D. Allograft

Q.10 Which bite causes neurotoxicity, muscle spasms, pain, and abdominal cramp and rigidity?

A. Snake bite
B. Spider bite
C. Bee bite
D. Animal bite

Q.11 Dislocation of mandible occurs at:

A. temporomandibular joint
B. atlanto axial joint
C. zygomatico maxillary joint
D. labial joint

Q.12 Which of the following is osteoclastoma causing ulceration and haemorrhage of gum?

A. Granulomatous epulis
B. Giant cell epulis
C. Carcinomatous epulis
D. Fibrosarcomatous epulis

Q.13 Which carcinoma occurs as a superficial proliferative exophytic lesion with minimal deep invasion, often multiple in number?

A. Verrucous carcinoma
B. Carcinoma cheek
C. Gingivobuccal carcinoma
D. Oral and upper aero-digestive cancers

Q.14 Which of the following is a rare, slow growing tumour that occurs almost always in parotid and is composed of cells alike serous acini?

A. Adenoid cystic carcinoma

B. Acinic cell tumour

C. Malignant mixed tumour

D. Adenocarcinoma of salivary glands

Q.15 Which of the following indicates the chemical alteration of the drug in the body?

A. Bioavailability

B. Biotransformation

C. Biolistics

D. Biological alteration

Q.16 Which of the following statement is true about Oxidation.

A. Oxidation occurs when an atom, molecule, or ion loses one or more electrons in a chemical reaction.

B. When oxidation occurs, the oxidation state of the chemical species increases.

C. An older meaning of oxidation was when oxygen was added to a compound.

D. All of the above.

Q.17 Which of the following processes leads to inactivation of the drug in the body fluids by spontaneous molecular rearrangement without the agency of any enzyme?

A. Alkylation

B. Glutathione conjugation

C. Hofmann elimination

D. Acetylation

Q.18 Which of the following principles of drug action means a selective diminution of activity of specialised cells?

A. Stimulation

B. Depression

C. Irritation

D. Replacement

Q.19 Almost all biological reactions are carried out under catalytic influence of:

A. hormones

B. enzymes

C. receptors

D. transformers

Q.20 Which of the following is shortest acting non-benzodiazepine hypnotic?

A. Zaleplon

B. Zolpidem

C. Zopiclone

D. Eszopiclone

Q.21 Which of the following is an autoimmune disorder due to development of antibodies directed to nicotinic receptors (NR) at the muscle endplate?

A. Glaucoma

B. Myasthenia gravis

C. Hashimoto's thyroiditis

D. Rheumatoid arthritis

Q.22 Which of the following is an ultra-short acting ganglion blocker that has been occasionally used to produce controlled hypotension and in hypertensive emergency due to aortic dissection?

A. Varenicline

B. Rimonabant

C. Trimethaphan

D. Mecamylamine

Q.23 Which of the following is a major transmitter in basal ganglia, limbic system, CTZ, anterior pituitary?

A. Nor adrenaline

B. Adrenaline

C. Dopamine

D. Nor dopamine

Q.24 Which of the following raises BP by causing vasoconstriction?

A. Amphetamine

B. Phenylephrine

C. Ephedrine

D. Dobutamine

Q.25 In which of the following mentioned conditions will α blockers be useful?

A. Pheochromocytoma

B. Hypertension

C. Benign prostatic hyperplasia (BPH)

D. Secondary shock

Q.26 Which of the following is an ultra-short acting $\beta 1$ blocker devoid of partial agonistic or membrane-stabilising actions?

A. Bisoprolol

B. Esmolol

C. Celiprolol

D. Acebutolol

Q.27 Histamine is present mostly within storage granules of:

A. stem cells

B. eosinophils

C. neutrophils

D. mast cells

Q.28 Which of the following is a metabolite of hydroxyzine with a marked affinity for peripheral H_1 receptors?

A. Desloratadine

B. Cetirizine

C. Loratadine

D. Fexofenadine

Q.29 In which of the following cytogenic abnormalities, there occurs no change of genetic material?

A. Deletion

B. Insertion

C. Translocation

D. Inversion

Q.30 Loss of hetero-zygosity in references to metastasis means

A. Loss of single-arm of chromosome

B. Loss of mutant allele in mutant gene

C. Loss of normal allele in mutant gene

D. Loss of normal allele in normal gene

Q.31 The chances of having an unaffected baby, when both parents have achondroplasia, are:

A. 10% **B.** 25% **C.** 50% **D.** 100%

Q.32 In Marfan syndrome, aortic aneurysm occurs most commonly in:

A. ascending aorta

B. descending aorta

C. base of aorta

D. arch of aorta

Q.33 Which of the following carcinoma most frequently metastasises to brain?

A. Small cell carcinoma of lung

B. Prostate cancer

C. Rectal carcinoma

D. Endometrial cancer

Q.34 Karyotyping is done with all, except:

A. blood lymphocytes

B. blood monocytes

C. amnions

D. fibroblasts

Q.35 The epithelioid cells and multinucleated giant cells of granulomatous inflammation are derived from:

A. Basophils

B. Eosinophils

C. CD 4+ helper T cells

D. Monocytes

Q.36 Which of the following statements is false about DPT vaccine?

A. Aluminium salt has an adjuvant effect.

B. Whole killed bacteria of bordello pertussis has an adjuvant effect.

C. Presence of a cellular pertussis component increases its immunogenicity.

D. Presence of H. influenza type B component increases its immunogenicity.

Q.37 Positive Schick's test indicates that the person is:

A. immune to diphtheria

B. hypersensitive to diphtheria

C. susceptible to diphtheria

D. carrier of diphtheria

Q.38 Aflatoxins are produced by:

A. Aspergillus niger

B. Aspergillus fumigatus

C. Aspergillus flavus

D. All of the above

Q.39 Tuberculin test denotes:

A. previous or present sensitivity to tubercle proteins

B. that the patient is resistant to TB

C. that the person is susceptible to TB

D. protective immune status of individuals against TB

Q.40 A 30-year-old woman with a bad obstetric history presents with fever. The blood culture from the patient grows gram-positive small to medium Cocco-bacilli that are pleomorphic, occurring in short chains. Direct wet mount from the culture shows tumbling motility. The most likely organism is:

A. Listeria monocytogenes

B. Corynebacterium sp.

C. Enterococcus sp.

D. Erysipelothrix rhusiopathiae

Q.41 A 3-week-old child presented to the paediatrician with meningitis. A presumptive diagnosis of late onset of perinatal infection was made. The CSF culture was positive for gram-positive bacilli. Which of the following characteristics of this bacteria would be helpful in differentiating it from other bacterial agents?

A. Ability to grow on blood agar

B. Ability to produce catalase

C. Fermentative attack on sugars

D. Motility at 25°C

Q.42 Basanti, a 29-year-aged female from Bihar, presents with active TB. She delivers a baby. Which of the following is not suggested in this case?

A. Administer INH to the baby

B. Withhold breast feeding

C. Give ATT to mother for 2 years

D. Ask mother to ensure disposal of sputum

Q.43 Which of the following materials represents a cement, metal or resin–based composite that is placed and formed intraorally to restore teeth or enhance aesthetics?

A. Direct restorative material

B. Indirect restorative material

C. Preventive dental material

D. Temporary restorative material

Q.44 Thermal energy required to convert a solid into a liquid is called

A. heat of vaporisation

B. latent heat of fusion

C. linear coefficient of expansion

D. glass transition temperature

Q.45 What kind of bonds are formed when two valence electrons are shared by the adjacent atoms?

A. Ionic bonds

B. Covalent bonds

C. Metallic bonds

D. Dipole bonds

Q.46 The stress at which a test specimen exhibits a specific amount of plastic strain is called

A. toughness

B. tensile stress

C. yield strength

D. strain rate

Q.47 ....is a measure of the force that can cause an object to rotate about an axis.

A. Pressure   **B.** Stress   **C.** Strain   **D.** Torque

Q.48 Which of the following is defined as a homogeneous, physically distinct and mechanically separable region of a metal microstructure?

A. Membrane

B. Phase

C. Colloidal surface

D. Partition

Q.49 An alloy that contains three chemical elements is called a

A. compound

B. ternary alloy

C. metal

D. composite alloy

Q.50 In which of the following is deformation irreversible and results in a new permanent shape?

A. Elastic

B. Plastic

C. Alloy

D. Visco-elastic

Q.51 Which of the following structural formulae represent a vinyl group?

A. -C = C-   **B.** C = O   **C.** -C-   **D.** C = N

Q.52 Molecular weight of methyl methacrylate is

A. 50 g/mol

B. 58 g/mol

C. 40 g/mol   **D.** 100 g/mol

Q.53 Which of the following is a common component of dental alloys including those used for crowns, fixed partial dentures, removable partial dentures, and some orthodontic appliances?

A. Beryllium   **B.** Mercury

C. Nickel   **D.** Cobalt

Q.54 Which of the following is a component that speeds up the reaction and also refers to the component called catalyst in the reaction of impression materials?

A. Catalytic agent   **B.** Accelerator

C. Base paste   **D.** Colloid

Q.55 Best material for duplicating cast is:

A. Agar-agar   **B.** Alginate

C. Zinc oxide- eugenol   **D.** Plaster of Paris

Q.56 Which of the following are often defined as the fourth state of matter?

A. Alloys   **B.** Colloids   **C.** Resins   **D.** Melt

Q.57 Nuclear medicine involves imaging using _____, which are another type of electromagnetic radiation.

A. UV rays   **B.** Gamma rays

C. X-rays   **D.** IR rays

Q.58 Which of the following is the standard investigation for assessing the urinary tract?

A. Ultrasonography

B. IV Urography

C. MRI

D. Computed radiography

Q.59 The _____ of spinal nerves are segmented in distribution and emerge from the vertebral canal between the pedicles of adjacent vertebrae.

A. 30 pairs   **B.** 28 pairs   **C.** 31 pairs   **D.** 29 pairs

Q.60 Which of the following ligaments supports the head and resists flexion and facilitates returning the head to the anatomic position?

A. Ligamenta flava

B. Ligamentum nuchae

C. Interspinous ligaments

D. Periodontal ligament

Q.61 Which covers the superior, posterior and lateral regions of the head?

A. Face   **B.** Skull   **C.** Scalp   **D.** Head

Q.62 In the neck, muscles of the outer cervical collar

A. move the head and the lower limbs.

B. move the head and the upper limbs.

C. move the shoulders.

D. move the head and the neck.

Q.63 Which of the following directly open(s) into the base of the neck?

A. Superior thoracic aperture

B. Inferior thoracic aperture

C. Upper limbs

D. Posterior thoracic aperture

Q.64 The _________ can be accessed through the nasal cavity by feeding tubes.

A. Lower airway   **B.** Pharynx

C. Larynx   **D.** Digestive tract

Q.65 Mandible consists of the:

A. Body of mandible posteriorly and the ramus of mandible anteriorly

B. Body of mandible anteriorly and the ramus of mandible posteriorly

C. Body of the mandible inferiorly and the ramus of mandible superiorly

D. Body of the mandible superiorly and the ramus of mandible inferiorly

Q.66 The final bony structure visible in a lateral view of the skull is the:

A. maxilla   **B.** mandible

C. alveolar bone   **D.** nasal bone

Q.67

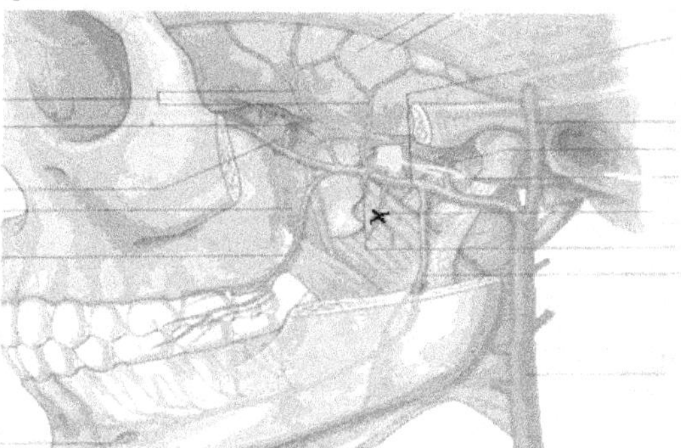

The mark x in the figure indicates:

A. Middle Meningeal Artery

B. Masseteric Artery

C. Pterygoid Artery

D. Superficial Temporal Artery

Q.68

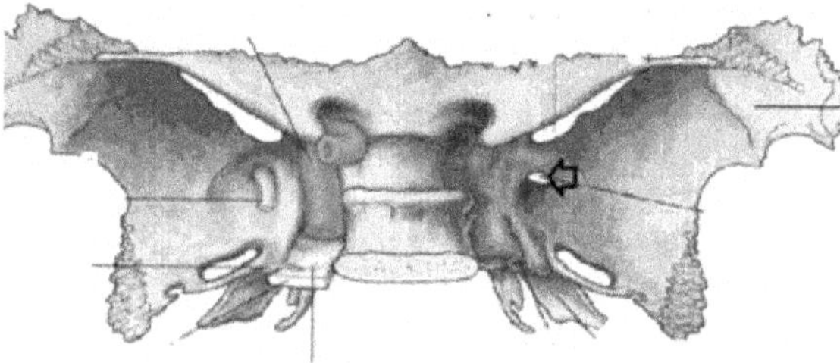

The arrow in the figure indicates:

A. Foramen Ovale

B. Foramen Rotundum

C. Superior Orbital Fissure

D. Inferior Orbital Fissure

Q.69 Which of the following shoulder joints is a synovial ball and socket articulation between the head of the humerus and the glenoid cavity of the scapula?

A. Acromioclavicular joint

B. Glenohumeral joint

C. Sternoclavicular joint

D. Proximal humerus

Q.70 Which of the following shoulder muscles has an extensive origin from the axial skeleton, which includes sites on the skull and the vertebrae from C_1 to T_{12}?

A. Trapezius   **B.** Deltoid

C. Pectoralis muscle   **D.** Levator scapulae

Q.71 Which of the following are the specialised cells from bone marrow stem cells whose major functions are to produce antibodies and interact with T cells?

A. B lymphocytes   **B.** Neutrophils

C. Basophils   **D.** Eosinophils

Q.72

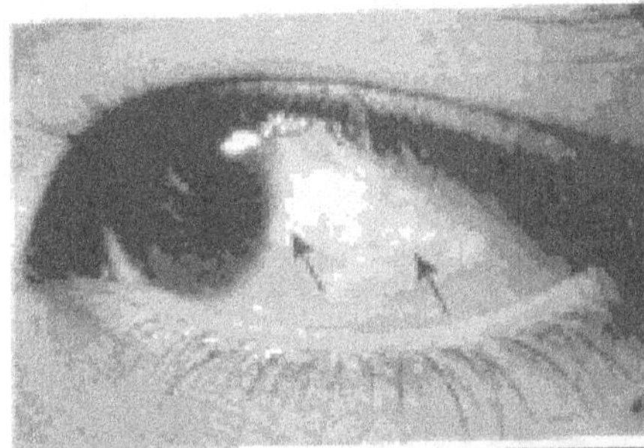

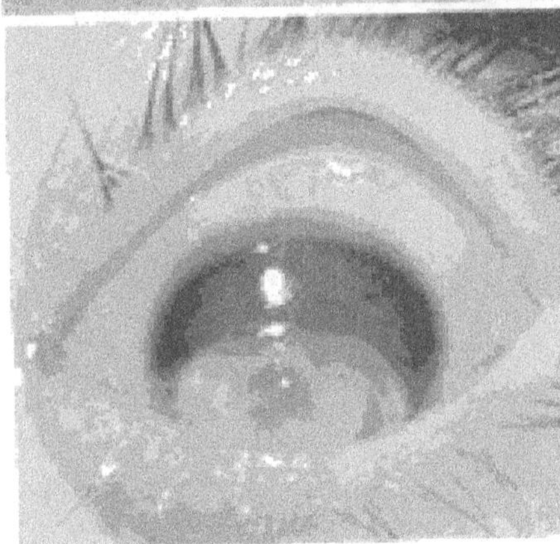

The deficiency of which of the following vitamins causes the above-depicted condition?

A. Vitamin A   **B.** Vitamin B

C. Vitamin C   **D.** Vitamin D

Q.73 Which of the following is the episodic, localised, non-pitting swelling of submucous or subcutaneous tissues?

A. Angioedema

B. Hereditary angioedema

C. Acquired C1 inhibitor deficiency

D. Peanut allergy

Q.74 Which of the following exists when the body's normal thermal regulatory mechanisms are unable to maintain heat in a cold environment and core temperature falls below $35°C$?

A. Hypothermia   **B.** Heat syncope

C. Thermoregulation   **D.** Hypernatraemia

Q.75 Which of the following is defined as the death due to asphyxiation following immersion in a fluid?

A. Drowning

B. Near drowning

C. Deep venous thrombosis

D. Venous thrombosis

Q.76 From 20 different amino acids that make up protein structure, how many are essential amino acids?

A. Eleven   **B.** Nine   **C.** Eight   **D.** Ten

Q.77 Which of the following helps prevent dental caries, since it increase the resistance of the enamel to acid attack?

A. Zinc   **B.** Selenium

C. Fluoride   **D.** Iodine

Q.78 Which of the following are incapable of independent replication, and instead subvert the cellular processes of host cells?

A. Prions   **B.** Viruses   **C.** Bacteria   **D.** Fungi

Q.79 Witch's chin is not associated with:

A. ptosis of mentalis muscle

B. long-term edentulous mandible without denture

C. loss of muscle attachment

D. increased vertical dimensions

Q.80 Which of the following have the broadest antibiotic activity of the beta-lactam antibiotics, and include activity against anaerobes?

A. Monobactams

B. Carbapenems

C. Penicillins

D. Cephalosporins and cephamycins

Q.81 Which of the following antifungal agents are being supplanted by less toxic agents?

A. Echinocandins   **B.** Polyenes

C. Triazoles   **D.** Imidazoles

Q.82 Which of the following are the protective end regions of the chromosomes which shorten with each cell division?

A. Chromatids   **B.** Telomeres

C. Centromeres   **D.** Chromonemata

Q.83 Which of the following determines the work that the ventricle performs under given loading condition?

A. Myocardial contractility

B. Cardiograph

C. Coronary Circulation

D. Pressure-Volume loop

Q.84 The movement of oxygen from the left ventricle to the systemic tissue capillaries is referred to as:

A. oxygen consumption
B. oxygen delivery
C. oxygen circulation
D. oxygen distribution

Q.85

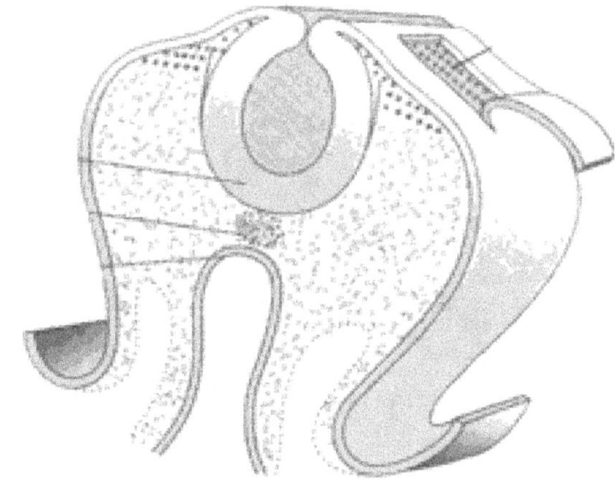

What does this diagram represent?
A. Neural tube formation
B. Developmental of facial nerves
C. Development of human face
D. Development of human secondary palate

Q.86 A vertical extension of the enamel knot is called the:
A. enamel cementum
B. enamel cord
C. enamel septum
D. enamel navel

Q.87 Which stage of tooth development is characterised by the commencement of mineralisation and root formation?
A. Cap stage
B. Bud stage
C. Bell stage
D. Advanced bell stage

Q.88 What percentage of inorganic material is present in enamel?
A. 98%
B. 96%
C. 90%
D. 88%

Q.89 In which stage of the life-cycle of the ameloblast, does the reduced enamel epithelium proliferate and seems to induce atrophy of the connective tissue separating it from the oral epithelium, so that fusion of the two epithelia can occur?
A. Formative stage
B. Desmolytic stage
C. Protective stage
D. Maturative stage

Q.90 Dentin consists of _____ inorganic material.
A. 70%
B. 96%
C. 60%
D. 35%

Q.91 The main body of dentin is composed of:
A. interproximal dentin
B. intertubular dentin
C. intermedial dentin
D. organic material

Q.92 Dentins, which are formed before root completion, are known as:
A. secondary dentins
B. primary dentins

C. tertiary dentins
D. intertubular dentins

Q.93 The collagen fibres in the pulp exhibit typical cross striations at:
A. $64\ nm$
B. $63\ nm$
C. $60\ nm$
D. $54\ nm$

Q.94 Which cells are seen during inflammation of the pulp?
A. Dendritic cells
B. Plasma cells
C. Defence cells
D. Mast cells

Q.95 Which of the following occur(s) in the ageing pulp organ as it/they do(es) in any organ?
A. Fibrosis
B. Vascular changes
C. Pulp stones
D. Cell changes

Q.96 Which of the following is formed when there is premature loss of the reduced enamel epithelium protecting the newly formed enamel at the cervical region?
A. Cellular mixed stratified cementum
B. Cellular mixed fibre cementum
C. Acellular, afibrillar cementum
D. Cementoblasts

Q.97 _________ has effects on endothelial cell replication and neovascularisation.
A. Basic fibroblast growth factor
B. Acidic fibroblast growth factor
C. Transformation growth factor
D. Platelet derived growth factor

Q.98 Which are the cells that resorb bone and tend to be large and multinucleated?
A. Osteoclasts
B. Osteoblasts
C. Fibroblasts
D. Cementoblasts

Q.99

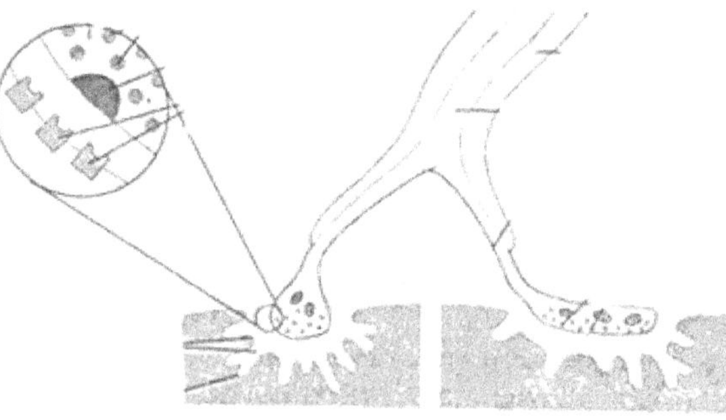

What does the diagram represent?
A. Synapses in the cerebral cortex
B. Structure of the neuromuscular junction
C. Neuro-modulators
D. Spinal cord neuron

Q.100 Which of the following is a chemical synapse?
A. Gap junction
B. Neuromuscular junction
C. Postsynaptic cell
D. Neuro-modulator junction

Part B

Q.101 Which of the following are located in the deeper layer of the epithelium and harbour nerve endings, and are connected to adjacent cells by desmosomes?

A. Langerhans cells

B. Odland bodies

C. Merkel cells

D. Melanophores

Q.102 In the surface texture of gingiva, which of the following is a form of adaptive specialization or reinforcement for function?

A. Stippling

B. Calcification

C. Enlargement

D. Non- Keratinization

Q.103 The terminal portion of the principal fibres that are inserted into cementum and bone are termed as _________.

A. neoplasm fibre

B. sharpey's fibres

C. lingual fibre

D. microvilli

Q.104

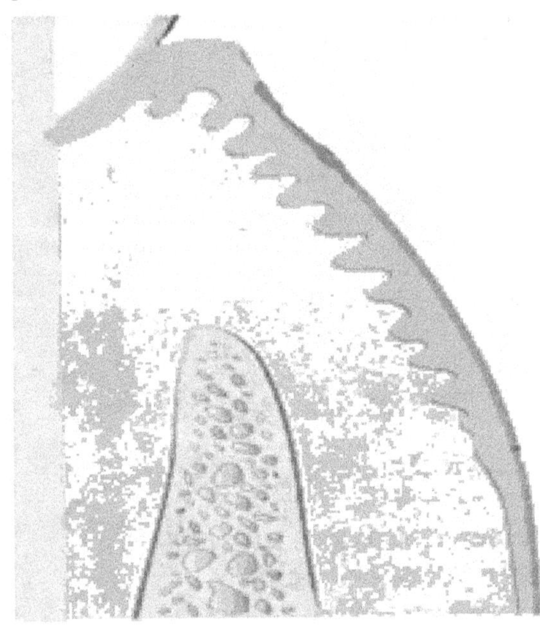

Which of the following is shown by this diagram?

A. Gingiva

B. Dentine

C. Enamel

D. Dental pulp

Q.105 Which is formed after the tooth reaches the occlusal plane, is more irregular and contains cells in individual spaces that communicate with each other through a system of anastomosing canaliculi?

A. Cellular cementum

B. Enamel cementum junction

C. Dentine cementum junction

D. Aceullar afibrillar cementum

Q.106

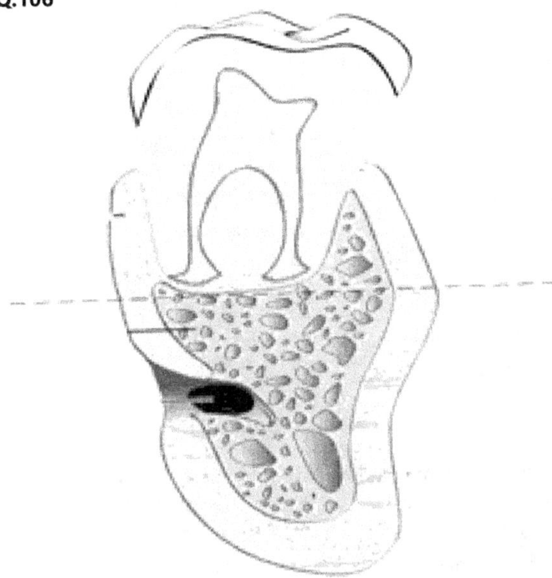

This is the section through the human jaw with tooth in situ. What does the dotted line represent?

A. Separation between the spongy bone and basal bone

B. Separation between the spongy bone and alveolar bone

C. Separation between the alveolar bone and basal bone

D. Separation between the spongy bone and cortical bone

Q.107 Which is the term given to the bone adjacent to the periodontal ligament that contains a great number of sharpey's fibres?

A. Alveolar bone

B. Bundle bone

C. Interdental septum

D. Periosteum

Q.108 When the denuded areas extend through the marginal bone, the defect is called a _________.

A. fenestration

B. dehiscence

C. remodelling

D. stippling

Q.109 The __________ of the periodontal ligament accompanies the arterial supply.

A. lymphatics

B. venous drainage

C. cribiform plate

D. bone marrow

Q.110 For the impact of gingival inflammation, several studies clearly indicate that early in _____, the formation is more rapid on tooth surfaces facing inflamed gingival margins than on those adjacent to healthy gingivae.

A. Dental plaque

B. Dental caries

C. Vivo plaque

D. Vivo caries

Q.111 Which are acute lesions that may result in very rapid destruction of the periodontal tissues?

A. Necrotizing periodontal diseases

B. Abscesses of the periodontium

C. Periodontitis as maintenance of systemic diseases

D. Microbial specificity in periodontitis

Q.112 Which is a gram negative cigar shaped bacillus with pointed ends?

- **A.** S.oralis
- **B.** F.nucleatum
- **C.** Campylobacter rectus
- **D.** Eubacterium species

Q.113 ________ in the sub-gingival area is considered to be a major contribution factor to plaque build-up and subsequent gingival inflammation.

- **A.** Mucosae
- **B.** Roughness
- **C.** Toughness
- **D.** Inflammation

Q.114 In radiotherapy, ________ helps to minimize the adverse effects of the radiation, while maximizing the death rate for the tumor cells.

- **A.** X-rays
- **B.** fractionation
- **C.** filtering
- **D.** stippling

Q.115 In treatment planning, which phase includes step by step planning of all the restorative, endodontic, surgical, orthodontic, and prosthetic rehabilitation procedures?

- **A.** Systemic phase
- **B.** Corrective phase
- **C.** Preparatory phase
- **D.** Immediate phase

Q.116 In maxillary first primary molar, the entire lingual surface is generally made up of one definite _____, which is rounded.

- **A.** mesiolingual clasp
- **B.** mesiolingual cusp
- **C.** distolingual clasp
- **D.** distolingual cusp

Q.117 In which growth assessment methods, the positional changes can be studied in a three-dimensional system?

- **A.** Superimposition
- **B.** Stereo-pairs images
- **C.** Electromyography
- **D.** Vital staining

Q.118 In enamel, ______ occurs as in amelogenesis imperfecta type III.

- **A.** hyper-calcification
- **B.** hypocalcification
- **C.** demineralisation
- **D.** mineralisation

Q.119 Which of the following developmental stage of freud indicates that it extends through late childhood to puberty?

- **A.** Oral stage
- **B.** Anal stage
- **C.** Phallic stage
- **D.** Latency stage

Q.120 In the observational learning process, which of the following represents the statement that one must store a mental representation of what has been witnessed or observed in their memory?

- **A.** Attention process
- **B.** Retention process
- **C.** Psychological process
- **D.** Motivational process

Q.121 Which is one of the primary emotions acquired soon after birth?

- **A.** Fear
- **B.** Anxiety
- **C.** Depression
- **D.** Stress

Q.122 The FAO was formed in the year ___.

- **A.** 1946
- **B.** 1945
- **C.** 1944
- **D.** 1942

Q.123 Which of the following represents about the science of compiling, classifying and tabulating numerical data and expressing the results in a mathematical or graphical form?

- **A.** Epidemiology
- **B.** Statistics
- **C.** Social sciences
- **D.** Principles of administration

Q.124 Which of the following antibacterial enzymes is a small, highly positive enzyme that catalyzes the degradation of the negatively charged peptidoglycan matrix of microbial cell walls?

- **A.** Lacto-peroxidase
- **B.** Lysozyme
- **C.** Lacto-ferrin
- **D.** IgA

Q.125 Which of the following is necessary for the normal growth of teeth?

- **A.** Calcium
- **B.** Vitamin B complex
- **C.** Vitamin D
- **D.** Phosphorous

Q.126 Which bacterium is the most intimately associated with initiation and development of carious lesion?

- **A.** Streptococcus mutans
- **B.** Lactobacillus
- **C.** Bacillus anthracis
- **D.** Pox virus

Q.127 Which of the following test measures the number of S. mutans colony forming units (CFU), unit volume of saliva by culturing the plaque from discrete sites for detecting and quantitating S. mutans colonized on teeth?

- **A.** The swab test
- **B.** S. mutans level in saliva
- **C.** Dip slide method for S. mutans count
- **D.** Salivary buffer capacity

Q.128 Which of the following is that bone of the jaws which contains the sockets for the teeth?

- **A.** Maxillary arch
- **B.** Mandibular arch
- **C.** Alveolar process
- **D.** Palate

Q.129

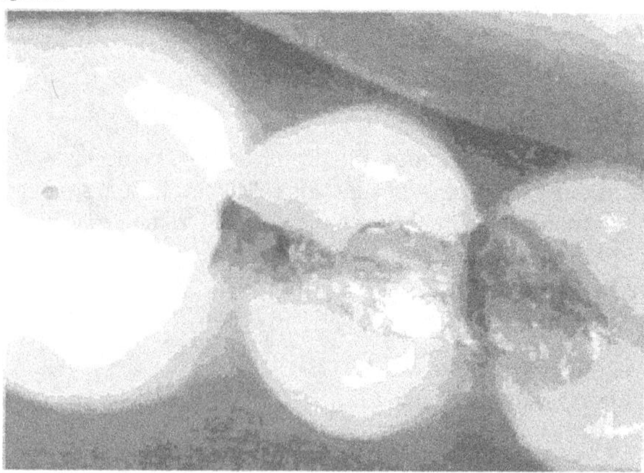

Which of the following defects in tooth structure, indicated in operative dentistry, is shown by the above diagram?

- **A.** Dental caries

B. Developmental defects

C. Repair and replacement of existing defective restorations

D. Silver Amalgam renewed

Q.130 Which of the following specialized structures in enamel represents the changes in the direction of enamel rods that minimize cleavage in the axial direction and produce an optical appearance?

A. Gnarled enamel

B. Enamel tufts

C. Hunter Schreger bands

D. Prism less enamel

Q.131 Which of the following is the vital connective tissue of the tooth?

A. Enamel   **B.** Dentine

C. Alveolar bone   **D.** Pulp

Q.132 In mechanics of mandible motion, which of the following is often described with respect to only one side of the mandible for the purpose of defining the relative motion of the mandibular to the maxillary teeth?

A. Complex motion   **B.** Lateral movements

C. Rotation   **D.** Translation

Q.133 Which of the following zones of enamel is relatively unaffected by caries attack?

A. Surface zone   **B.** Body of the lesion

C. Dark zone   **D.** Translucent zone

Q.134 Small amounts of fluoride can increase the resistance of tooth structure to __________.

A. mineralisation   **B.** demineralization

C. calcification   **D.** oxidation

Q.135 Which of the following is used as a liner in deep cavity preparations?

A. Calcium hydroxide

B. Glass Ionomer cement

C. Zinc phosphate

D. Silicate cement

Q.136 Which is released while removing old amalgams while monomers are released during polishing or removal of composite restorations?

A. Aerosol   **B.** Arsenic vapours

C. Mercury vapours   **D.** Nitric oxide

Q.137 Which of the following is the loose connective tissue that surrounds blood and lymphatic vessels, nerves and the fibre bundles?

A. Periodontal ligament

B. Interstitial tissue

C. Cementum

D. Periodontal fibers

Q.138 The most common pulpal injury is __________.

A. bacterial   **B.** viral

C. fungal   **D.** oral non-hygienic

Q.139 Which is a localized collection of pus in the alveolar bone at the root apex of a tooth following death of the pulp with extension of the infection through the apical foramen into the periradicular tissues?

A. Acute alveolar abscess

B. Acute apical periodontitis

C. Acute exacerbation of a chronic lesion

D. Chronic alveolar abscess

Q.140 Which of the following is the response to a low grade, chronic inflammation of the periradicular area as a result of a mild irritation through the root canal?

A. Condensing osteitis

B. Radicular cyst

C. External root resorption

D. Granuloma

Q.141 Which of the following is indicated in pulpally involved children's permanent teeth in which the root apex is not completely formed?

A. Gingivectomy   **B.** Pulpotomy

C. Alveolectomy   **D.** Pulpectomy

Q.142

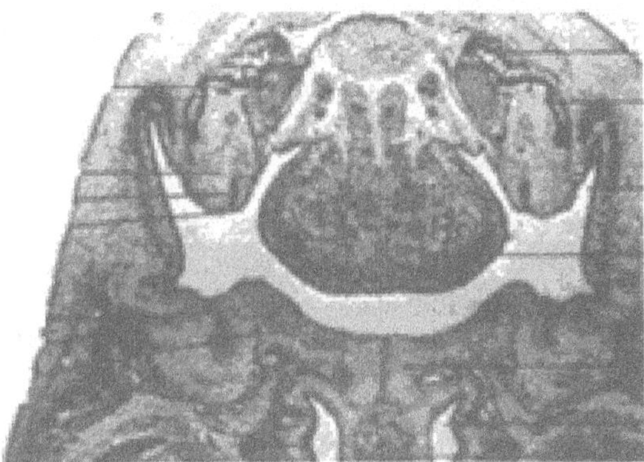

What does this figure represent?

A. Development dental pulp

B. Development of face

C. Development of skull

D. Development of the cranium

Q.143 Which of the following craniofacial anomalies represents a birthmark or a growth present at birth which is composed of blood vessels that can cause functional or aesthetic problems?

A. Hemifacial microsomia

B. Vascular malformation

C. Hemangioma

D. Deformational plagiocephaly

Q.144 Which of the following is a frequent tumour of the skin analogous to the oral papilloma?

A. Verruca vulgaris

B. Verruciform xanthoma

C. Papillary hyperplasia

D. Squamous acanthoma

Q.145 Which of the following is a malignancy of the fat cells?

A. Liposarcoma

B. Hemangioendothelioma

C. Hemangiopericytoma

D. Kaposi sarcoma

Q.146 Which of the following is a sarcoma of the bone, classically described under small round cell tumours?

A. Liposarcoma

B. Ewing's sarcoma

C. Chondrosarcoma

D. Osteosarcoma

Q.147 Which of the following is a neoplasm of a uniform population of basaloid epithelial cells arranged in solid, trabecular, tubular, or membranous patterns?

A. Myoepithelioma

B. Basal cell adenoma

C. Warthin's tumour

D. Oncocytoma

Q.148 Which of the following is a malignant epithelial tumour that is essentially limited in occurrence to minor salivary glands sites and characterized by bland, uniform nuclear features?

A. Polymorphous low grade adenocarcinoma

B. Epithelial myo-epithelial carcinoma

C. Basal cell adenocarcinoma

D. Sebaceous carcinoma

Q.149 Which of the following is the undifferentiated counterpart part of the anaplastic small cell carcinoma?

A. Small cell undifferentiated carcinoma

B. Large cell undifferentiated carcinoma

C. Lympho-epithelial carcinoma

D. Small cell carcinoma

Q.150 Which is defined as an oncogenic cyst with the histologic features of a dentigerous cyst that surrounds a tooth crown that has erupted through bone but soft tissue and is clinically visible as a soft fluctuant mass on the alveolar ridges?

A. Eruption cyst

B. Kerato-cysts

C. Dental lamina cyst

D. Periapical cyst

Q.151 Which of the following is the true neoplasm of enamel organ type issue that does not undergo differentiation to the point of enamel formation?

A. Ameloblastoma

B. Calcifying epithelial odontogenic tumour

C. Periapical cyst

D. Residual cyst

Q.152 Which of the following is ghost cell carcinoma?

A. Ameloblastic fibroma

B. Ameloblastic carcinoma

C. Ameloblastoma

D. Periapical cyst

Q.153 Which of the following is a granulomatous disease that was found to affect horses?

A. Actinomycosis

B. Botryomycosis

C. Tularemia

D. Melioidosis

Q.154 Which of the following is a relatively uncommon disease in which the newborn infant acquires the infection during passage through the birth canal of a mother who is suffering from herpetic vulvo-vaginitis?

A. Herpetic eczema

B. Herpetic conjunctivitis

C. Disseminated herpes simplex of the newborn

D. Herpetic whitlow

Q.155 Which of the following diseases can be characterised by white plaques that cannot be removed by scraping?

A. Angular cheilitis

B. Hyperplastic candidiasis

C. Erythematous candidiasis

D. Pseudomembranous candidiasis

Q.156

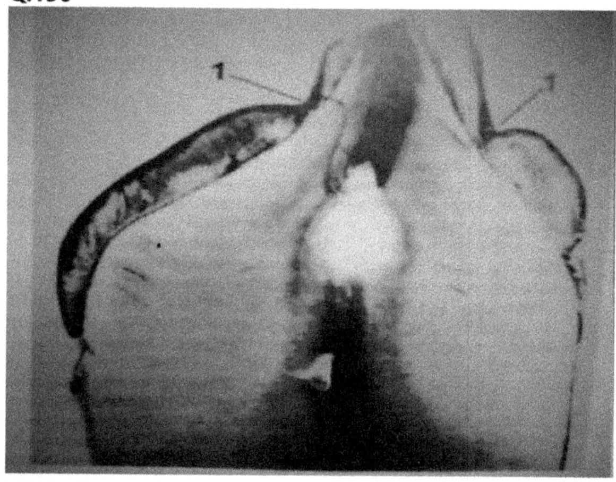

This is the ground section of a tooth, showing a pit-like defect on both the labial and lingual surfaces.

Which of the following defects is due to that pit?

A. Environmental enamel hypoplasia

B. Enamel hypomineralisation

C. Enamel defect

D. Enamel pitting

Q.157

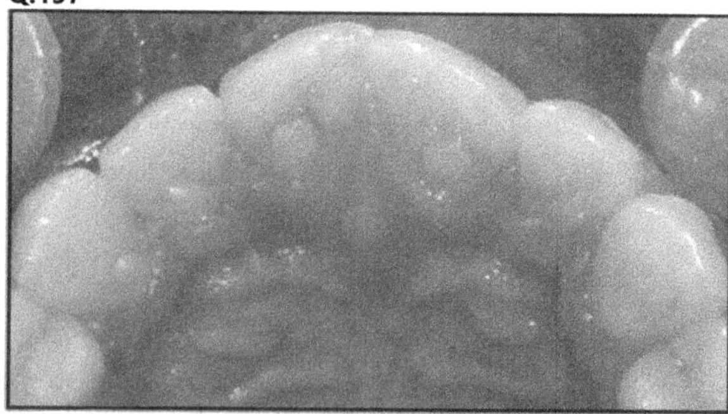

This is the picture of a patient showing an anomalous structure that projects lingually from the cingulum areas of the maxillary or mandibular permanent incisor. What is it called?

A. Enamel cusp

B. Talon cusp

C. Dens in dente

D. Concrescence

Q.158

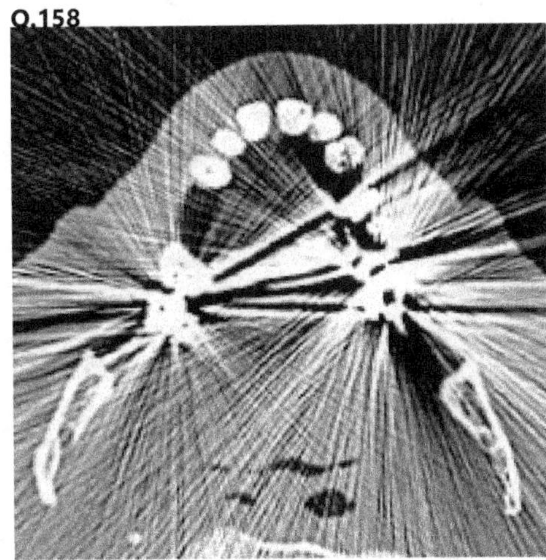

What does this radiograph represent?

A. MRI

B. Computed tomography

C. Ultrasonography

D. Sialography

Q.159

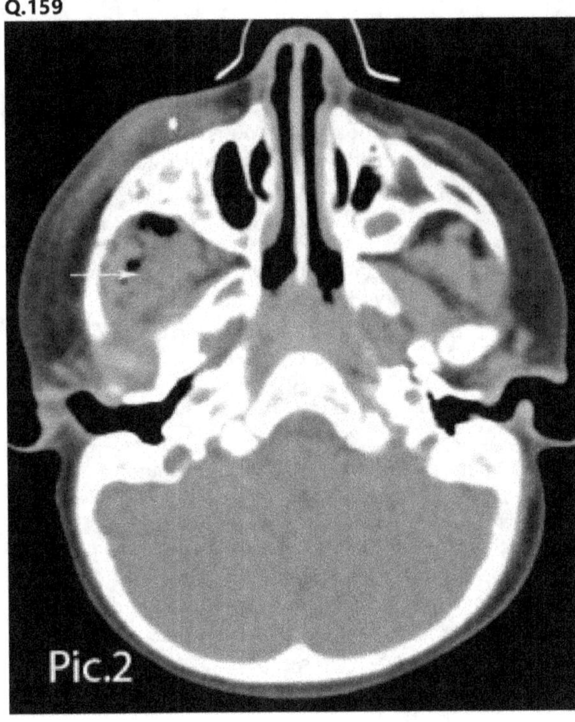

Which of the following is represented by this image?

A. Lateral view of the soft tissue window

B. Axial view of the soft tissue window

C. Anterior view of the soft tissue

D. Posterior view of the soft tissue

Q.160 Which is the most common subepithelial blistering disease which occurs chiefly in adults over the age of 60 years?

A. Pemphigoid vegetans

B. Pemphigoid vulgaris

C. Bullous pemphigoid

D. Linear IgA disease

Q.161 The most common cause of single ulcers on the oral mucosa is:

A. oral lesions

B. trauma

C. carcinoma

D. caries

Q.162 Which of the following is caused by an infection with a saprophytic fungus that normally occurs in soil or as a mold on decaying food?

A. Mucormycosis

B. Blastomycosis

C. Histoplasmosis

D. Pemphigoid vulgaris

Q.163 Which of the following is a rare X-linked disorder characterised by a series of oral changes that lead eventually to an atrophic leukoplakic oral mucosa, with the tongue and cheek being most severely affected?

A. White sponge nevus

B. Dyskeratosis congenita

C. Frictional keratosis

D. Linea Alba

Q.164 Which of the following is commonly used as a root canal irrigant and may cause serious ulcerations due to accidental contact with oral soft tissues?

A. Sodium hypochlorite

B. Hydrogen peroxide

C. Silver nitrate

D. Aspirin burn

Q.165 Which of the following may alter the oral mucous membranes, predisposing them to colonization and invasion?

A. Xerostomia and chronic local irritants

B. Acute atrophic candidiasis

C. Denture stomatitis

D. Chronic atrophic candidiasis

Q.166 The consumption of _______ two or three times per week and improved oral hygiene can also help to treat oral lesions.

A. milk

B. yogurt

C. cheese

D. green vegetables

Q.167 Which of the following diseases occurs on the male and female genital mucosae and in the oral mucosa as an erythroplakic, leukoplakic or papillomatous lesion?

A. Oral lichen planus

B. Bowen's disease

C. Lichenoid reactions

D. Graft versus host disease

Q.168 Which is the tumor of putative vascular origin?

A. Angiosarcoma

B. Kaposi's sarcoma

C. Varix

D. Brown melanotic lesions

Q.169 Which of the following diseases is the most common among white populations that live in sunbelt regions of the world?

A. Brown melanotic lesions
B. Cutaneous melanoma
C. Nevo-cellular nevus and blue nevus
D. Drug-induced melanosis

Q.170 Which of the following is a common lesion that develops on the hard palate in response to chronic denture irritation in approximately 3 to 4% of denture wearers?

A. Palatal papillary hyperplasia
B. Pyogenic granuloma
C. Epulis fissuratum
D. Inflammatory hyperplasias

Q.171 Which of the following is a non-neoplasmic connective tissue proliferation usually occurring on the trunk or extremities of young adults?

A. Giant cell granuloma
B. Pseudo-sarcomatous fasciitis
C. Pseudo-epitheliomatous hyperplasia
D. Benign lymphoid hyperplasia

Q.172 Which of the following is an inherited disorder that is characterized by seizures and mental retardation associated with hamartomatous glial proliferations and neuronal deformity in the central nervous system?

A. Acanthosis nigricans
B. Tuberous sclerosis
C. Albright's syndrome
D. Paget's disease

Q.173

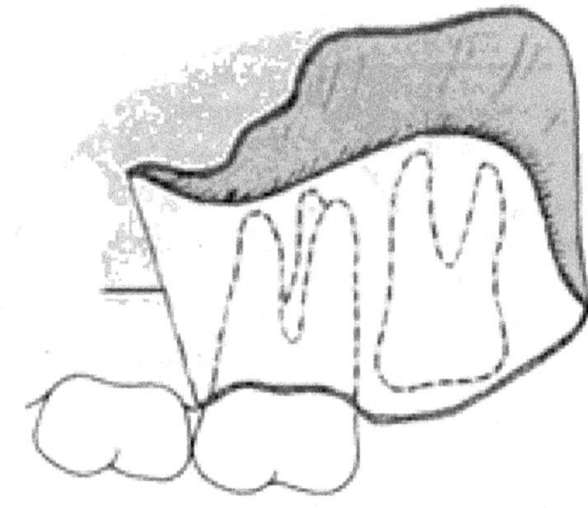

There are three types soft of designed oral soft tissues flaps. Which type does the above diagram indicate?

A. Horizontal and single vertical incisions
B. Horizontal and two vertical incisions
C. Single horizontal incision
D. Vertical Incision

Q.174

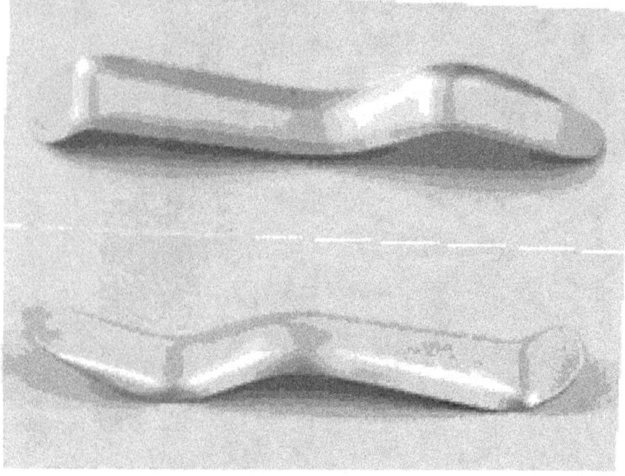

Identify the given instrument.

A. Minnesota retractor
B. Henahan and seldin retractors
C. Weider retractor
D. Austin retractor

Q.175 Which hepatitis virus is spread primarily by contact with the feces of the infected individuals?

A. Hepatitis A
B. Hepatitis B
C. Hepatitis C
D. Hepatitis D

Q.176 In incision, the blade of which number is sharp and pointed and is used primarily for making small stab incisions, such as incising an abscess?

A. No. 11
B. No. 12
C. No. 15
D. No. 10

Q.177 The single rooted maxillary teeth are usually removed with __________ maxillary universal forceps.

A. 65
B. 88 L
C. 150 S
D. 150

Q.178 The topical anesthesia is short lived and therefore, the surgical procedure should be the one that can be accomplished within ______.

A. 10 to 20 minutes
B. 15 to 30 minutes
C. 10 to 30 minutes
D. 15 to 45 minutes

Q.179 Which of the indications for removal of teeth indicates that it may be a result of a patient declining endodontic treatment or of a root canal that is tortuous, calcified and untreatable by standard endodontic techniques?

A. Caries
B. Pulpal necrosis
C. Periodontal disease
D. Orthodontic disease

Q.180 Which of the following results from the inflammation involving the muscle of mastication?

A. Edema
B. Trismus
C. Ecchymosis
D. Esthetics

Q.181 In soft tissue injuries, which is the most common soft tissue injury during oral surgery and surgical extraction of the tooth?

A. Tear of the mucosal flap
B. Puncture wound
C. Stretch or abrasion

D. Root fracture

Q.182 Which of the following is important for the construction of a stable retentive maxillary denture?

A. Mandibular tuberosity
B. Maxillary tuberosity
C. Maxillary arch
D. Mandibular arch

Q.183 In wound dehiscence, a common area of exposed bone after tooth extraction is the ___________.

A. mandibular ridge
B. maxillary ridge
C. internal oblique ridge
D. external oblique ridge

Q.184 Which of the following Acts was enacted to prevent hospitals from refusing to treat patients who were unable to pay or from transferring such patients to other health care facilitates before the emergency condition was identified and stabilized?

A. Americans With Disabilities Act
B. Title VI, Limited English Proficiency
C. HIPAA Privacy And Security
D. EMTALA

Q.185 Mandibular tori are bony protuberances on the _____ aspect of the mandible that usually occur in the premolar area.

A. lingual   **B.** labial   **C.** mesial   **D.** distal

Q.186 Which of the following is known as epulis fissurata or denture fibrosis?

A. Lingual frenectomy
B. Labial frenectomy
C. Inflammatory fibrous hyperplasia
D. Mandibular retro-molar pad reduction

Q.187 Health is a state of complete physical, mental and social well–being and not merely the absence of disease or _____.

A. Illness   **B.** Deformity
C. Infirmity   **D.** Sickness

Q.188 In principle of primary health care, the first key principle in the primary health care strategy is ______ of health services.

A. community participation
B. equitable distribution
C. inter-sectoral coordination
D. appropriate technology

Q.189 Which of the following mortality rates indicates an aggregation of industry, over crowded and inferior housing, poverty and large families and an increased risk of infection and accidents?

A. Birth rate
B. Density of population
C. Geographical
D. Secular variation

Q.190 Among the given types of controlled trials, which of the following have been concerned with evaluating therapeutic agents?

A. Clinical trials
B. Preventive trials
C. Risk factor trials
D. Cessation experiments

Q.191 In uses of epidemiology, which of the following indicates that the modern analytical epidemiology enables us to predict an individual's chances or risks for developing a disease or health related event even in the absence of obvious etiological hypothesis?

A. Community diagnosis
B. Rise and fall of disease
C. Planning and evaluation
D. Evaluation of individuals risk

Q.192 Where do the Clostridium perfringens occur?

A. Algae   **B.** Water   **C.** Faeces   **D.** Humus

Q.193 Which of the following incineration is used for health care waste?

A. Pyrolytic incinerations
B. Single chamber incineration
C. Rotary kiln
D. Dry air incineration

Q.194 In the principles of health education, which of the following can be defined as the fundamental desire for learning in an individual?

A. Credibility   **B.** Interest
C. Participation   **D.** Motivation

Q.195 According to educational aids used in health education, on which of the following principles are the visual aids based?

A. Principle of Sound
B. Principle of Electricity
C. Principle of Projection
D. Principle of Magnetism

Q.196 Good clinical practice is observed in all phases of clinical practice EXCEPT:

A. Phase V   **B.** Preclinical
C. Phase II   **D.** Phase I

Q.197 Which of the following substance indicates that it must be obtained by dietary means because of a lack of capacity in the human body to synthesize it?

A. Amino acids   **B.** Vitamins
C. Iron   **D.** Proteins

Q.198 Which of the following factors is an obligate factor in collagen metabolism?

A. Protein   **B.** Vitamins
C. Amino-acids   **D.** Iron

Q.199 Which of the following functional aspects of society govern the expectations of social behaviour according to the

contemporary conventional norm within a society, social class or group?

A. Social norms
B. Customs and habits
C. Etiquettes and conventions
D. Social values

Q.200 Which of the five year plans were to develop the basic infrastructures and manpower visualized by the Bhore committee?

A. First five year plan
B. Second five year plan
C. Third five year plan
D. Fourth five year plan

Q.201 Reciprocal clasp and retentive clasp are the two metal fingers of

A. extra coronal retainers
B. intra coronal retainers
C. Both A and B
D. only intra coronal retainers

Q.202 Fovea palatine are situated in:

A. Hard palate
B. Soft palate
C. At the junction of hard and soft palate
D. Their position is not fixed

Q.203

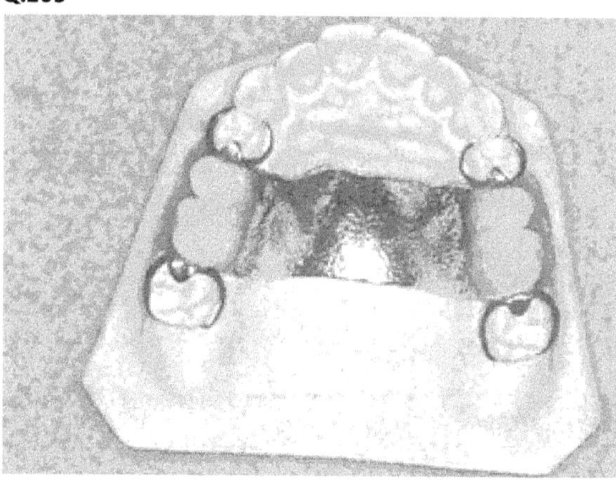

What is this denture called?

A. Tooth-tissue supported removable partial denture
B. Tooth supported removable partial denture
C. Tooth-bone supported removable partial denture
D. Bone-tissue supported removable partial denture

Q.204

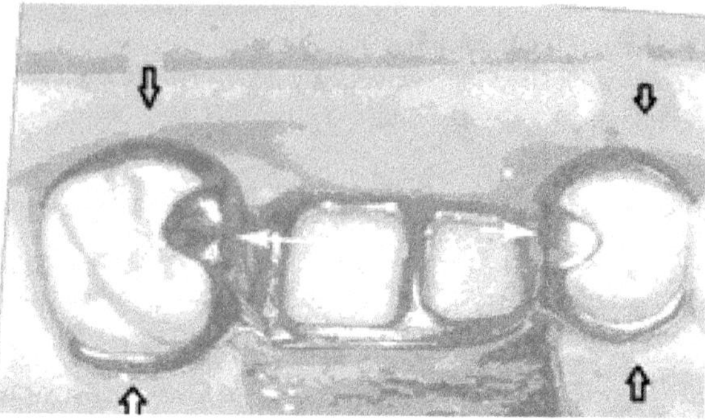

Each component of a removable partial denture has a name that is descriptive of its function. What do the arrows in the diagram indicate?

A. Major connector
B. Minor connectors
C. Clasp assemblies
D. Denture base

Q.205 Like their intra-coronal counterparts, extra-coronal attachments derive their retention from closely fitted components termed as __________.

A. matrices and patrices
B. extra-coronal attachments
C. retentive clasp assemblies
D. semi-precision attachments

Q.206 Many of the extra-coronal attachments permit vertical movement of prostheses during occlusal-loading. This mechanical accommodation is intended to minimize the transfer of potentially damaging forces to the abutments. This led to _____ theories of removable partial denture design.

A. stress breaking or stress directing
B. stress compression
C. attachments breaking
D. None of these

Q.207 Composite forces can be broken down into _______.

A. force vectors
B. force scalars
C. magnitude
D. torque

Q.208 During the design process, the practitioner must consider the ability of the individual teeth to withstand _______.

A. pain
B. forces
C. stress
D. pressure

Q.209 In organising the diagnostic examination during the first appointment, a thorough _______ should be completed and reviewed.

A. treatment
B. diagnostic
C. health history
D. oral history

Q.210 In organising the diagnostic examination during first appointment, final and accurate _____ should be made and diagnostic casts should be generated.

A. maxillary and mandibular impressions
B. casting
C. oral examinations
D. All of the above

Q.211 In diagnostic mounting procedure, verification of these relationships by means of additional ______ and comparison of occlusal contacts on the articulator with those in the mouth are carried out.

A. articular
B. dental arch
C. dental implant
D. centric relation

Q.212 The three-dimensional relationship between the patient's maxillary arch and ______ must be simulated in the diagnostic mounting.

A. mandibular arch
B. mandibular condyles
C. maxillary condyles
D. All of the above

Q.213 Which of the following surveying tools is used to determine the parallelism of surfaces on a dental cast?

A. Carbon marker
B. Undercut gauges
C. Wax knife
D. Analysing rod

Q.214 The primary cause of Bennet movement is due to contraction of:

A. Lateral pterygoid
B. Medial pterygoid
C. Masseter
D. Temporalis

Q.215

This is the schematic diagram of the skull of a 12 week old embryo. What does the dotted white and shaded part represent?

A. Chondrocranium
B. Desmocranium
C. Philtrum
D. Primordium

Q.216 The pharynx develops early from the lateral wall of ______ and from the underlying mesenchyme.

A. epithelial tissue
B. endodermal tissue
C. stem cells
D. ectodermal tissue

Q.217 ______ growth occurs during the accomplishment of the full morphogenetic pattern of the mandible.

A. Endochondral
B. Endodermic
C. Epithelial
D. Ectodermal

Q.218 In neuromuscular trophism, moss indicates that skeletal muscle ontogenesis normally requires ______ innervation to proceed past the stage of myo-tubes.

A. sensory nerves
B. moto-neurons
C. stimulatory nerves
D. motor nerves

Q.219 Carpel radiograph is used for assessment of:

A. Bone condition
B. Chronological age
C. Treatment plan
D. Skeletal maturation

Q.220 What is the increase in inter-canine arch width during the period of permanent incisor eruption?

A. 3 to 4 mm
B. 3 to 6 mm
C. 1 to 3 mm
D. 2 to 4 mm

Q.221 The term centric relation has been widely used by the ____ for some time.

A. endodontist
B. prosthetist
C. prosthodontist
D. periodontist

Q.222 It is vitally important that the dentist makes sure that the ______ and centric occlusal position are the same and are in harmony with centric relation and the postural resting position of the mandible.

A. habitual occlusion position
B. postural occlusal position
C. granular position
D. differing occlusal position

Q.223 Salzmann aptly defines occlusion in dentistry as the changing interrelationship of the opposing surfaces of the maxillary and mandibular teeth, which occurs during the movements of the mandible and full terminal contact of the ______ .

A. maxillary and mandibular dental arches
B. lingual palate
C. maxillary arch only
D. alveolar bones

Q.224 Which of the following arch forms is based on the trifocal ellipse?

A. MacConnaill and Scher
B. Brader arch form
C. Catenary curve
D. Currier arch form

Q.225 Which of the following terms is applied to the distance which the maxillary incisal margin closes vertically past the mandibular incisal margin, when the teeth are brought into habitual or centric occlusion?

A. Over bite
B. Over jet
C. Open bite
D. Close bite

Q.226 The super-numerary teeth may grow from prior to birth or as late as ______ years of age.

A. 11 to 15 years
B. 10 to 12 years
C. 9 to 11 years
D. 8 to 13 years

Q.227 In case of missing teeth, the supernumerary teeth are usually found in ______ as missing teeth are frequent in both jaws.

A. mandible
C. both jaws
B. maxilla
D. mandible only

Q.228 In case of missing teeth, the term __________ refers to congenital absence of many teeth.

A. hypodontia
C. anodontia
B. oligodontia
D. endodontia

Q.229 Which of the following is a short-lived paracrine mediator?

A. Sulphur oxide
C. Hydrogen oxide
B. Nitric oxide
D. Carbon-dioxide

Q.230 Which of the following is a cellular property that enables neurons to perform their functions?

A. Synaptic
C. Axonal transport
B. Excitability
D. Active transmission

Q.231 Which of the following involves the recognition of skin indentation by Merkel cell endings and Ruffini's corpuscles?

A. Flutter vibration
B. Touch-pressure sensation
C. Proprioception
D. Diffusion

Q.232 Many neurons in the raphe nuclei release ___ as a neurotransmitter.

A. serotonin
C. acetylcholine
B. creatinine
D. auxin

Q.233 Electromagnetic radiation of wavelength between 400 nm and 700 nm make up the:

A. UV light
C. visible light
B. IR light
D. radio waves

Q.234 From which of the following is creatinine formed?

A. Arginine
C. Leucine
B. Lysine
D. Histamine

Q.235 Which of the following would not act as a source of glycine by transamination?

A. Alanine
C. Glutamate
B. Aspartate
D. Glyoxylate

Q.236 Glutamate dehydrogenase in mitochondria is activated by:

A. ATP
B. GTP
C. NADH
D. ADP

Q.237 Which among the following options is a true statement about glycine?

A. It is an essential amino acid.
B. It contains sulphur-containing amino acid at 4th position.
C. It has a guanidine group.
D. It is an optically inactive amino acid.

Q.238 Which enzyme is deficient in albinism?

A. Tyrosinase
B. Tyrosine hydroxylase
C. Phenylalanine hydroxylase
D. Homo-gentisate oxidase

Q.239 The main aim of the first line therapy in Phenylketonuria is:

A. replacement of the defective enzyme
B. replacement of the deficient product
C. to reduce phenylalanine levels in the plasma and brain
D. giving the missing amino acid by diet

Q.240 A 40-year-old woman presents with progressive palmoplantar pigmentation. X-ray spine shows calcification of IV disk. On adding Benedict's reagent to urine, it gives greenish-brown precipitate and blue-black supernatant fluid. What will be the diagnosis in this case?

A. Phenylketonuria
B. Alkaptonuria
C. Tyrosinemia type 2
D. Argininosuccinic aciduria

// Smart Answer Sheet //

Correct Indicates percentage of students who answered questions correctly.

Skipped Indicates percentage of students who skipped questions.

Q.	Ans.	Correct / Skipped	Q.	Ans.	Correct / Skipped	Q.	Ans.	Correct / Skipped	Q.	Ans.	Correct / Skipped	Q.	Ans.	Correct / Skipped
1	B	14.81 % / 3.71 %	17	C	9.26 % / 66.67 %	33	A	22.22 % / 66.67 %	49	B	14.81 % / 68.52 %	65	B	24.07 % / 68.52 %
2	A	27.78 % / 66.66 %	18	B	11.11 % / 68.52 %	34	B	1.85 % / 64.82 %	50	B	14.81 % / 68.52 %	66	A	5.56 % / 70.37 %
3	A	11.11 % / 68.52 %	19	B	24.07 % / 68.52 %	35	D	5.56 % / 68.51 %	51	A	9.26 % / 68.52 %	67	C	3.7 % / 68.52 %
4	D	22.22 % / 66.67 %	20	A	7.41 % / 64.81 %	36	D	5.56 % / 66.66 %	52	D	5.56 % / 66.66 %	68	B	9.26 % / 68.52 %
5	B	24.07 % / 68.52 %	21	B	20.37 % / 66.67 %	37	C	9.26 % / 66.67 %	53	C	14.81 % / 66.67 %	69	B	16.67 % / 68.52 %
6	B	16.67 % / 68.52 %	22	C	3.7 % / 66.67 %	38	C	5.56 % / 68.51 %	54	B	22.22 % / 68.52 %	70	A	14.81 % / 68.52 %
7	B	11.11 % / 66.67 %	23	C	14.81 % / 68.52 %	39	A	7.41 % / 68.52 %	55	A	11.11 % / 68.52 %	71	A	25.93 % / 68.51 %
8	A	7.41 % / 68.52 %	24	B	7.41 % / 64.81 %	40	A	9.26 % / 68.52 %	56	B	18.52 % / 66.67 %	72	A	31.48 % / 66.67 %
9	C	18.52 % / 68.52 %	25	C	3.7 % / 68.52 %	41	D	1.85 % / 68.52 %	57	B	11.11 % / 68.52 %	73	A	16.67 % / 66.66 %
10	B	3.7 % / 68.52 %	26	B	5.56 % / 68.51 %	42	B	18.52 % / 66.67 %	58	B	12.96 % / 68.52 %	74	A	22.22 % / 68.52 %
11	A	29.63 % / 68.52 %	27	D	12.96 % / 68.52 %	43	A	25.93 % / 68.51 %	59	C	16.67 % / 68.52 %	75	A	18.52 % / 68.52 %
12	B	7.41 % / 66.66 %	28	B	12.96 % / 66.67 %	44	B	14.81 % / 66.67 %	60	B	14.81 % / 66.67 %	76	B	12.96 % / 68.52 %
13	A	20.37 % / 68.52 %	29	D	9.26 % / 68.52 %	45	B	16.67 % / 68.52 %	61	C	18.52 % / 66.67 %	77	C	29.63 % / 66.67 %
14	B	11.11 % / 66.67 %	30	C	5.56 % / 66.66 %	46	C	16.67 % / 66.66 %	62	B	7.41 % / 68.52 %	78	B	16.67 % / 68.52 %
15	B	20.37 % / 68.52 %	31	B	7.41 % / 66.66 %	47	D	27.78 % / 68.52 %	63	A	12.96 % / 68.52 %	79	D	11.11 % / 68.52 %
16	D	18.52 % / 66.67 %	32	A	9.26 % / 66.67 %	48	B	9.26 % / 66.67 %	64	D	11.11 % / 66.67 %	80	B	3.7 % / 66.67 %

Q.	Ans.	Correct	Skipped
81	B	3.7 %	66.67 %
82	B	12.96 %	66.67 %
83	A	12.96 %	68.52 %
84	B	3.7 %	68.52 %
85	A	18.52 %	66.67 %
86	B	22.22 %	68.52 %
87	D	14.81 %	68.52 %
88	B	24.07 %	68.52 %
89	B	11.11 %	68.52 %
90	A	16.67 %	68.52 %
91	B	22.22 %	68.52 %
92	B	20.37 %	68.52 %
93	A	12.96 %	68.52 %
94	B	9.26 %	66.67 %
95	B	7.41 %	68.52 %
96	C	16.67 %	66.66 %

Q.	Ans.	Correct	Skipped
97	A	9.26 %	66.67 %
98	A	24.07 %	68.52 %
99	B	18.52 %	68.52 %
100	B	20.37 %	66.67 %
101	C	7.41 %	66.66 %
102	A	29.63 %	66.67 %
103	B	29.63 %	68.52 %
104	A	29.63 %	66.67 %
105	A	12.96 %	68.52 %
106	C	11.11 %	68.52 %
107	B	20.37 %	68.52 %
108	B	16.67 %	68.52 %
109	B	12.96 %	68.52 %
110	C	3.7 %	68.52 %
111	B	3.7 %	68.52 %
112	B	9.26 %	68.52 %

Q.	Ans.	Correct	Skipped
113	B	20.37 %	68.52 %
114	B	7.41 %	66.66 %
115	B	12.96 %	68.52 %
116	B	16.67 %	68.52 %
117	B	12.96 %	68.52 %
118	B	18.52 %	68.52 %
119	D	14.81 %	68.52 %
120	B	20.37 %	62.96 %
121	A	29.63 %	66.67 %
122	B	5.56 %	66.66 %
123	B	25.93 %	68.51 %
124	B	16.67 %	62.96 %
125	A	16.67 %	68.52 %
126	A	29.63 %	68.52 %
127	B	11.11 %	68.52 %
128	C	29.63 %	66.67 %

Q.	Ans.	Correct	Skipped
129	C	18.52 %	68.52 %
130	C	16.67 %	66.66 %
131	D	27.78 %	68.52 %
132	B	25.93 %	68.51 %
133	A	12.96 %	68.52 %
134	B	27.78 %	62.96 %
135	A	24.07 %	68.52 %
136	C	16.67 %	68.52 %
137	B	9.26 %	68.52 %
138	A	29.63 %	68.52 %
139	A	11.11 %	68.52 %
140	A	14.81 %	68.52 %
141	B	24.07 %	68.52 %
142	A	7.41 %	66.66 %
143	B	7.41 %	68.52 %
144	A	12.96 %	66.67 %

Q.	Ans.	Correct	Skipped
145	A	27.78 %	68.52 %
146	B	18.52 %	66.67 %
147	B	14.81 %	68.52 %
148	A	11.11 %	68.52 %
149	A	18.52 %	68.52 %
150	A	22.22 %	68.52 %
151	A	16.67 %	68.52 %
152	B	16.67 %	66.66 %
153	B	16.67 %	66.66 %
154	C	16.67 %	68.52 %
155	B	16.67 %	68.52 %
156	A	16.67 %	68.52 %
157	B	25.93 %	68.51 %
158	B	16.67 %	68.52 %
159	B	22.22 %	68.52 %
160	C	16.67 %	68.52 %

Q.	Ans.	Correct / Skipped	Q.	Ans.	Correct / Skipped	Q.	Ans.	Correct / Skipped	Q.	Ans.	Correct / Skipped	Q.	Ans.	Correct / Skipped
161	B	24.07 % / 66.67 %	177	D	7.41 % / 68.52 %	193	A	12.96 % / 68.52 %	209	C	18.52 % / 68.52 %	225	A	25.93 % / 68.51 %
162	A	18.52 % / 68.52 %	178	B	12.96 % / 68.52 %	194	D	7.41 % / 66.66 %	210	A	16.67 % / 66.66 %	226	B	11.11 % / 68.52 %
163	B	12.96 % / 68.52 %	179	B	20.37 % / 68.52 %	195	C	16.67 % / 68.52 %	211	D	16.67 % / 68.52 %	227	B	20.37 % / 68.52 %
164	A	29.63 % / 68.52 %	180	B	27.78 % / 66.66 %	196	B	16.67 % / 68.52 %	212	A	20.37 % / 68.52 %	228	B	16.67 % / 66.66 %
165	A	20.37 % / 68.52 %	181	A	31.48 % / 66.67 %	197	B	20.37 % / 68.52 %	213	D	12.96 % / 68.52 %	229	B	11.11 % / 68.52 %
166	B	7.41 % / 68.52 %	182	C	11.11 % / 66.67 %	198	D	3.7 % / 68.52 %	214	A	25.93 % / 66.66 %	230	B	16.67 % / 68.52 %
167	B	14.81 % / 68.52 %	183	C	7.41 % / 68.52 %	199	C	7.41 % / 68.52 %	215	A	12.96 % / 68.52 %	231	B	20.37 % / 68.52 %
168	B	7.41 % / 68.52 %	184	D	5.56 % / 68.51 %	200	B	7.41 % / 68.52 %	216	B	16.67 % / 68.52 %	232	A	12.96 % / 66.67 %
169	B	7.41 % / 68.52 %	185	A	29.63 % / 68.52 %	201	A	14.81 % / 68.52 %	217	A	25.93 % / 68.51 %	233	C	18.52 % / 68.52 %
170	A	14.81 % / 68.52 %	186	C	20.37 % / 68.52 %	202	C	14.81 % / 68.52 %	218	B	9.26 % / 66.67 %	234	A	22.22 % / 68.52 %
171	B	9.26 % / 68.52 %	187	C	9.26 % / 68.52 %	203	B	7.41 % / 68.52 %	219	D	20.37 % / 68.52 %	235	B	7.41 % / 68.52 %
172	B	12.96 % / 66.67 %	188	B	14.81 % / 68.52 %	204	C	20.37 % / 68.52 %	220	A	18.52 % / 66.67 %	236	D	9.26 % / 68.52 %
173	B	11.11 % / 66.67 %	189	B	22.22 % / 68.52 %	205	A	11.11 % / 68.52 %	221	C	29.63 % / 66.67 %	237	D	7.41 % / 68.52 %
174	A	14.81 % / 68.52 %	190	A	18.52 % / 68.52 %	206	A	25.93 % / 68.51 %	222	A	24.07 % / 66.67 %	238	A	16.67 % / 68.52 %
175	A	22.22 % / 68.52 %	191	D	16.67 % / 68.52 %	207	A	14.81 % / 68.52 %	223	A	20.37 % / 68.52 %	239	C	12.96 % / 68.52 %
176	A	14.81 % / 68.52 %	192	C	14.81 % / 68.52 %	208	B	22.22 % / 66.67 %	224	B	5.56 % / 66.66 %	240	B	11.11 % / 68.52 %

Performance Analysis

Avg. Score (%)	17.29%
Toppers Score (%)	99.17%
Your Score	

Part A

Q.1 In neutrophils, oxidative killing is also known as the _____ and is mediated by the NADPH oxidase enzyme complex, which converts oxygen into reactive oxygen species such as hydrogen peroxide and superoxide that are lethal to microorganisms.

A. Circulatory burst   **B.** Respiratory burst
C. Pumping burst   **D.** Antibodies burst

Q.2 Which are small soluble proteins that act as multi- purpose chemical messengers?

A. Pinocytes   **B.** Cytokines
C. Collagen   **D.** Inoblasts

Q.3 Troponin T is elevated in

A. Thyrotoxicosis
B. Viral hepatitis
C. Myxoedema
D. Myocardial infarction

Q.4 In the classification of autoimmune diseases, which type of hypersensitivity indicates that activated T cells and macrophages mediate phagocytosis and NK cell recruitment?

A. Type I hypersensitivity
B. Type II hypersensitivity
C. Type III hypersensitivity
D. Type IV hypersensitivity

Q.5 Which of the following regulates pro-inflammatory cytokine production?

A. Sodium cromoglycate
B. Corticosteroids
C. Antigen-specific immunotherapy
D. Omalizumab

Q.6 Fever, clubbing, and Osler's nodes occur in:

A. Leptospirosis
B. Typhoid fever
C. Infective endocarditis
D. Rheumatic fever

Q.7 Sexually-transmitted infections are acquired

A. By direct contact between oral membranes
B. Through inhalation
C. By direct contact between mucous membranes
D. Through blood transfer

Q.8 Which of the following antiparasitic agents inhibits neurotransmitter function, causing Helminth muscle paralysis?

A. Ivermectin   **B.** Niclosamide
C. Piperazine   **D.** Praziquantel

Q.9 Which of the following drugs, commonly causing toxicity in overdose, includes the sulphonyl-ureas (e.g., chlorpropamide, glibenclamide, gliclazide and glipizide and tolbutamide), biguanides (metformin and phenformin) and insulins?

A. Antipsychotic drugs   **B.** Antidiabetic agents
C. Antimalarials   **D.** β-blockers

Q.10 Which of the following toxins cause a variety of effects, depending on the type of toxin and produce specific features that can help in diagnosis?

A. Haemostasis system toxins
B. Cardiotoxins
C. Myotoxins
D. Excitatory neurotoxins

Q.11 Most rapid relief of symptoms of angina pectoris is found with the administration of:

A. Barbiturate   **B.** Ibuprofen
C. Oxygen   **D.** Nitrates

Q.12 Which of the following, are a disparate group of drugs that cause prominent sensory disturbances?

A. Stimulants   **B.** Sedatives
C. Hallucinogens   **D.** Organic solvents

Q.13

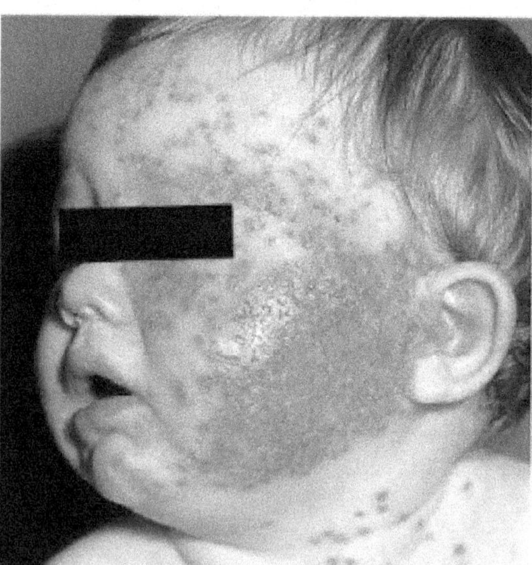

This is the picture of a child having an infection by HSV. Which of the following diseases is indicated by the picture?

A. Herpetic stomatitis   **B.** Herpetic whitlow
C. Eczema herpeticum   **D.** Varicella zoster

Q.14

This is a diagram of the anatomy of the lymph node. What does 'X' indicate?

A. Para-cortex
B. Cortex
C. Medulla
D. Afferent lymph

Q.15 All are malignant tumors, except:

A. Chloroma
B. Fibromatosis
C. Askin's tumor
D. Liposarcoma

Q.16 Interleukin secreted by macrophages, stimulating lymphocytes is:

A. INF alpha
B. TNF alpha
C. IL-1
D. IL-6

Q.17 Which of the following is not true regarding super-antigens?

A. Bind T cells irrespective of antigen specificity of TCR
B. Bind directly to both MHC II and T cell receptor causing T cell activation
C. Bind to cleft or antigen binding groove in the MHC II molecule
D. Bind directly to lateral aspect of T cell receptor

Q.18 What is nitro-blue tetra-zolium test used for?

A. Phagocytes
B. Complement
C. T cell
D. B cell

Q.19 Which of the following interleukin is characteristically produced in a Th1 response?

A. IL-1
B. IL-4
C. IL-5
D. IL-10

Q.20 Epithelial granuloma caused by _________________.

A. neutrophil
B. cyto-toxic T cells
C. helper T cells
D. NK cells

Q.21 In which of the following options is the arthritis erosion not seen?

A. Rheumatoid arthritis
B. Systemic lupus erythematosus (SLE)
C. Psoriasis
D. Gout

Q.22 A child has a white patch over the tonsils. Diagnosis is made by culture in:

A. loeffler medium
B. LJ medium
C. blood agar
D. tellurite medium

Q.23 All are true about Corynebacterium diphtheriae, except that:

A. Iron is required for toxin production
B. Toxin production is responsible for local reaction
C. Non-sporing, non-capsular and non motile
D. Toxin production is by lysogenic conversion

Q.24 Metachromatic granules are found in:

A. Diphtheria bacilli
B. Mycoplasma
C. Gardnerella vaginalis
D. Chlamydia
E. Staphylococcus

Q.25 All are true about Corynebacterium diphtheria, except that:

A. Deep invasion is not seen
B. Elek's test is done for toxigenicity
C. Metachromatic granules are seen
D. Toxigenicity is mediated by chromosomal change

Q.26 In a completely and adequately immunized child against diphtheria, the throat swab was collected. It showed the presence of C. diphtheriae organisms on Albert staining. These organisms can have which one of the following properties on further processing?

A. It can grow on potassium tellurite media.
B. It would show a +ve elek's gel precipitation test.
C. It can be pathogenic to experimental guinea pig.
D. It can produce cytotoxicity in tissue culture.

Q.27 Which of the following investigations should not be done on a child with fever and pharyngitis?

A. Widal test
B. ASO
C. Throat swab and culture
D. Chest X-ray

Q.28 Which of the following is true about diphtheria?

A. Faucial diphtheria is more dangerous than laryngeal diphtheria and palatal paralysis is irreversible.
B. Laryngeal diphtheria mandates tracheostomy.
C. Child is infectious with faucial diphtheria.
D. Myocarditis may be a complication.
E. Palatal paralysis is reversible.

Q.29 Which of the following is a half-cylinder of muscle and fascia attached above to the base of the skull and below to the margins of the esophagus?

A. Pharynx
B. Larynx
C. Trachea
D. Vocal cord

Q.30 Sounds produced by the __________ are modified in the pharynx and oral cavity to produce speech.

A. trachea
B. vocal cord
C. larynx
D. alveolar bones

Q.31 The hyoid bone is posteriorly attached to the _____________.

A. larynx
B. pharynx
C. trachea
D. oesophagus

Q.32 There are ___________pairs of cranial nerves.
A. 10
B. 12
C. 15
D. 8

Q.33 Cranial X nerve is known as ____________.
A. occulomotor nerve
B. vagus nerve
C. ocular nerve
D. olfactory nerve

Q.34 Cervical nerves C8 emerges between _________.
A. CVI and TI
B. CVII and TI
C. CVIII and TII
D. CXI and TI

Q.35 The anterior rami of C5 to C8, together with large components of the anterior ramus of TI form the _______, which innervate(s) the upper limb.
A. parasympathetic fibers
B. sympathetic fibers
C. sensory nerves
D. branchial plexus

Q.36 The skull has _________ bones.
A. 21
B. 12
C. 20
D. 22

Q.37 Which process of the frontal bone projects inferiorly forms the upper lateral rim of the orbit?
A. Zygomatic process
B. Frontal process
C. Alveolar process
D. Nasal process

Q.38 Which is the large opening in the nasal region and the anterior opening of the nasal cavity?
A. Piriform aperture
B. Cribiform aperture
C. Ramus of mandible
D. Lower jaw

Q.39 Most of the anterior part of the middle of the base of the skull consists of the _________.
A. hyoid bone
B. sphenoid bone
C. occipital bone
D. temporal bone

Q.40 Which of the following is placed between the greater wing of the sphenoid anteriorly and the basilar part of the occipital bone posteriorly?
A. Articular tubercle
B. Occipital condyles
C. Petrous part of the temporal bone
D. Mandibular fossa

Q.41

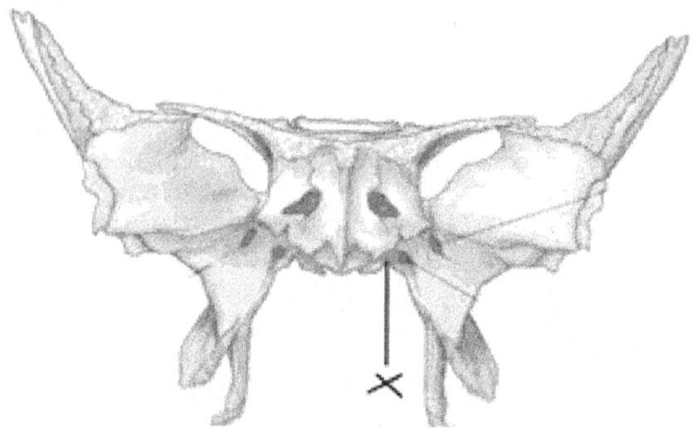

This is the picture of the postero-superior view of the sphenoid bone. What does 'X' indicate?
A. Foramen rotundum
B. Palato-vaginal groove
C. Pterygo-palatine canal
D. Pterygo-palatine fossa

Q.42

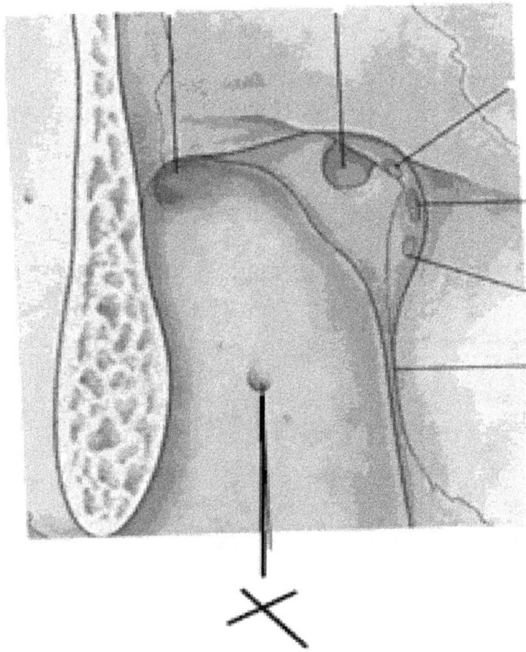

This diagram is the lateral view of the pterygopalatine fossa. What does 'X' indicate?
A. Palatine canal
B. Foramen rotundum
C. Alveolar foramen
D. Spheno-palatine foramen

Q.43 Which of following is a subcategory of restorative material and includes products used for dental restorations and appliances that are not intended for moderate term or long term applications?
A. Direct restorative materials
B. Indirect restorative materials
C. Temporary restorative materials

D. Preventive dental materials

Q.44 Water molecules is an example of which of the following bonding?

A. Hydrogen bonding
B. Covalent bonding
C. Metallic bonding
D. Ionic bonding

Q.45 At what temperature do the atoms (or molecules) of a solid possess some kinetic energy?

A. At absolute zero temperature
B. Above absolute zero temperature
C. Isotropic temperature
D. 273 °K

Q.46 Which is the process by which a metal surface is discolored when a reaction with a sulfide, oxide, chloride or other chemical causes a thin film to form?

A. Rheology
B. Tarnish
C. Waxing
D. Electrolytic polishing

Q.47 Which is defined as relative inability of a material to deform plastically?

A. Brittleness
B. Ductility
C. Malleability
D. Hardness

Q.48 Which of the following represents the relative amount of elastic energy per unit volume released on unloading of a test specimen?

A. Resilience
B. Shear stress
C. Yield strength
D. Shear strength

Q.49 Which is an example of an alloy for which the component metals have limited solid solubility?

A. Eutectic system
B. Electronic system
C. Silver copper system
D. Gold copper system

Q.50 Which is a polymer made of two or more monomer species and identical monomer units occurring in relatively long sequences along the main polymer chain?

A. Block polymer
B. Random polymer
C. Graft or branched copolymer
D. Polymerisation by-product

Q.51 Which is the ability of a polymer to behave as an elastic solid (spring) and as a viscous liquid (dashpot)?

A. Viscoelastic
B. Stretch
C. Stress
D. Elasticity

Q.52 Melting point of methacrylate is

A. -48 °C
B. -49 °C
C. -50 °C
D. -47 °C

Q.53 Which of the following is used in Ni-Cr alloys in concentrations of 1wt% to 2 wt% to increase the cast ability of these alloys and lower their melting range?

A. Nickel
B. Beryllium

C. Mercury
D. Germanium

Q.54 Which of the following is defined as the expressions of fluid onto the surface of gel structures, given that this process allows hydrocolloid impressions to achieve equilibrium through stress relaxation?

A. Hysteresis
B. Syneresis
C. Autolysis
D. Rheology

Q.55 Which of the following impression pastes and impression plasters are called as mucostatic impression materials?

A. Sodium hypochlorite
B. Zinc oxide eugenol
C. Agar hydrocolloid
D. Hydrogen chloride

Q.56 Which of the following is defined as the change in strain per unit time during the loading of a structure?

A. Stress
B. Strain rate
C. Pressure
D. Force

Q.57 Which of the following results in a dramatic increase in conduction velocity?

A. Autolysis
B. Myelination
C. Proliferation
D. Diffusion

Q.58 In chemical synapse, the time that elapses between an action potential in the presynaptic nerve terminal and the postsynaptic potential, typically about $0.5\ msec$, is called a __________.

A. synaptic elapses
B. synaptic delay
C. synaptic elevation
D. synaptic depression

Q.59 Acetylcholine is released in small packets called __________.

A. quarks
B. quanta
C. quintal
D. quantum

Q.60 Which of the following is/are responsible for phosphorylating particular proteins in the cell?

A. G proteins
B. Collagen
C. Protein kinases
D. Protein phosphatases

Q.61 Which of the following serine threonine protein phosphates is called as calcineurin?

A. PP-1
B. PP-2B
C. PP-2C
D. PP-2

Q.62 Which of the following is released by endothelial cells and certain neurons?

A. Sulphur oxide
B. Nitric oxide
C. Nitrous oxide
D. Carbon dioxide

Q.63

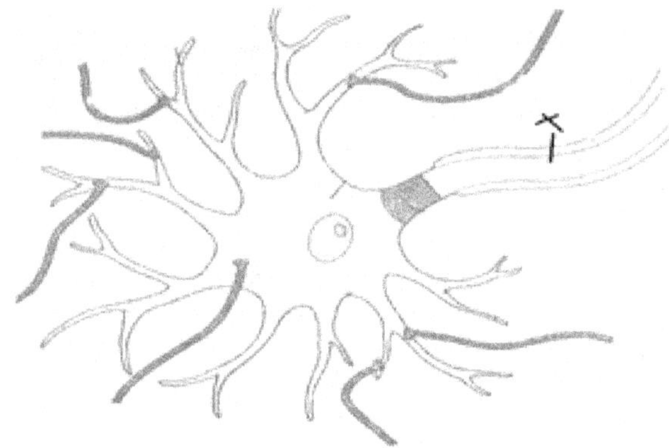

This is a diagram of the spinal motor neuron with multiple synapses on both soma and dendrites. What does the 'X' indicate?

A. Myelin sheath

B. Axon

C. Soma

D. Axon hillock

Q.64 All are true about glutathione, except that:

A. It is a tripeptide

B. It converts hemoglobin to methemoglobin

C. It conjugates xenobiotics

D. It is co-factor of various enzymes

Q.65 Nitric oxide is synthesised from:

A. Arginine

B. Citrulline

C. Alanine

D. Cysteine

Q.66 Histidine load test is used for:

A. Folate deficiency

B. Histidine deficiency

C. Histamine deficiency

D. None of these

Q.67 All are true about nitric oxide, except that:

A. It is produced from arginine

B. Nitric oxide synthase has three iso-forms

C. It is otherwise called endothelium derived relaxing factor

D. It acts through cAMP

Q.68 MSUD type IA is due to mutation of:

A. BCKA decarboxylase E1 α

B. BCKA decarboxylase E1 β

C. BCKA decarboxylase E2

D. Dihydrolipoyl transacylase E2 subunit

Q.69 Which of the following is not formed from branched chain amino acid?

A. Xanthurenate

B. Tiglyl CoA

C. Aceto-acetyl CoA and Acetyl CoA

D. Acetyl CoA and Succinyl CoA

Q.70 Branched-chain keto-acid decarboxylation is defective in:

A. Maple syrup urine disease

B. Hartnup disease

C. Alkaptonuria

D. GMI gangliosidosis

Q.71 Which of the following indicates the passage of drugs through aqueous pores in the membrane or through para-cellular spaces?

A. Passive diffusion

B. Filtration

C. Specialised transport

D. Absorption

Q.72 Which of the following refers to the rate and extent of absorption of a drug from a dosage form?

A. Bioavailability

B. Distribution

C. Redistribution

D. Biotransformation

Q.73 Which of the following CYP iso-enzymes are important in the biotransformation of > 15 commonly used drugs including phenytoin, warfarin as well as ibuprofen and tolbutamide which are narrow safety margin drugs?

A. CYP3A4/5

B. CYP2D6

C. CYP2C8/9

D. CYP2C19

Q.74 Which is the active transfer of organic acids and bases by two separate classes of relatively non-specific transporters which operate in the proximal tubules?

A. Tubular reabsorption

B. Tubular secretion

C. Glomerular filtration

D. Travel level strategy

Q.75 Which of the following principles of drug actions connotes a non-selective, often noxious effect and is particularly applied to less specialised cells?

A. Stimulation

B. Depression

C. Irritation

D. Replacement

Q.76 Which of the following represents any molecule which selectively attaches to particular receptors or sites?

A. Ligand

B. Partial agonist

C. Antagonist

D. Inverse agonist

Q.77 When one drug decreases or abolishes the action of another, they are said to be

A. antagonists

B. inhibitors

C. receptors

D. synergies

Q.78 Which of the following severity of adverse drug reactions directly or indirectly contributes to death of the patient?

A. Minor

B. Moderate

C. Severe

D. Lethal

Q.79 Which of the following drugs or its metabolite induces a cell mediated immune response which on exposure to light of longer wave lengths produces a papular or eczematous contact dermatitis like picture?

A. Phototoxic

B. Photo-allergic

C. Photosensitivity

D. Physical dependence

Q.80 In which of the following nervous systems is the motor limb anatomically divided into sympathetic and parasympathetic?

A. Somatic cells
B. Autonomic afferents
C. Autonomic efferents
D. Autonomic nervous system

Q.81 Which is the major neuro-humoral transmitter at autonomic, somatic as well as central sites?

A. Acetylcholine
B. Hemi-cholinium
C. Scopolamine
D. Atropine

Q.82 Which has an overall CNS stimulant action?

A. Atropine
B. Acetylcholine
C. Epinephrine
D. Hemi cholinium

Q.83 Which of the following substances acts as the transmitter at postganglionic sympathetic sites (except sweat glands, hair follicle, and some vasodilator fibres) in certain areas of the brain?

A. Noradrenaline
B. Adrenaline
C. Dopamine
D. Atropine

Q.84 Which of the following substances stimulates respiratory centre, specially if it has been depressed?

A. Ephedrine
B. Amphetamine
C. Phenylephrine
D. Dobutamine

Q.85 Which of the following cells are developed from the ectoderm along the lateral margins of the neural plate?

A. Mast cells
B. Stem cells
C. Neural crest cells
D. Ectodermal cells

Q.86 Which are condensed masses of cells derived from mesoderm located adjacent to the neural tube?

A. Primary palate
B. Callus
C. Somites
D. Morula

Q.87 Which of the following cysts are situated in the mid-line of the maxillary alveolar prominence?

A. Branchial cleft cysts
B. Globulomaxillary cysts
C. Anterior palatine cysts
D. Nasolabial cysts

Q.88 In tooth development surrounding the combined enamel organ and dental papilla, the third part of the tooth bud formed is called _____________.

A. alveolar sac
B. dental papilla
C. dental follicle
D. dental pulp

Q.89 In which of the following nutrient deficiencies do the ameloblasts fail to differentiate properly?

A. Vitamin A
B. Vitamin B
C. Vitamin C
D. Vitamin D

Q.90 Which is the hardest calcified tissue in the human body?

A. Dentine
B. Enamel
C. Bone
D. Plasma

Q.91 The temperature resistance of enamel measured by AC impedance spectroscopy is in the frequency range from _______.

A. 3 to 30 Hz
B. 5 to 13 Hz
C. 5 to 20 Hz
D. 7 to 120 Hz

Q.92 The average concentrations of calcium in dry weight % of human tooth enamel is __________.

A. 43.4%
B. 36.6%
C. 17.7%
D. 2.3%

Q.93 Larger enamel elevations are termed as __________.

A. enamel cord
B. enamel brochs
C. enamels rods
D. enamel lamellae

Q.94 Which of the following arise at the dentinoenamel junction and reach into the enamel to about one fifth to one third of its thickness?

A. Enamel lamellae
B. Enamel tufts
C. Enamel cuticle
D. Enamel brochs

Q.95 __________ is the principal type of collagen found in the dentin.

A. Type I collagen
B. Type II collagen
C. Type III collagen
D. Type IV collagen

Q.96 Which is the first formed dentin in the crown underlying the dentinoenamel junction?

A. Mantle dentin
B. Circum-pulpal dentin
C. Reactive dentin
D. Secondary dentin

Q.97 Which of the following occupies the center of each tooth and consists of soft connective tissue?

A. Enamel
B. Dental pulp
C. Dental lamellae
D. Dentine

Q.98 Which is an inherited disorder that results from the action of a dominant gene and may be almost as common as hemifacial microsomia?

A. Goldenhar syndrome
B. Treacher collins' syndrome
C. Labial pits
D. Lingual anomalies

Q.99 Which of the following is called the universal tumor?

A. Lipoma
B. Dermoid
C. Sarcoma
D. Carcinoma

Q.100 Which of the following occur due to the accumulation of secretions of a gland caused by obstruction of the duct?

A. Retention cysts
B. Distension cysts
C. Exudation cysts
D. Cystic tumors

Part B

Q.101 Which of the following joins the mesial surface at an acute angle and the distal surface at an obtuse angle?

A. Labial edge
B. Lingual edge
C. Lateral edge
D. Incisal edge

Q.102 In the Universal System of Teeth Identification, number 17 indicates the
- **A.** Mandibular left third molar
- **B.** Mandibular left second molar
- **C.** Mandibular left first molar
- **D.** Maxillary left second molar

Q.103 In the embryonic period, the palatal fusion normally gets completed by the
- **A.** 4th week   **B.** 5th week   **C.** 6th week   **D.** 8th week

Q.104 Foetal period is characterized by
- **A.** Occipital development
- **B.** Osseous development
- **C.** Septum development
- **D.** Cranium development

Q.105 Which of the following individuals are tall, thin and fragile with long and slender extremities having minimal subcutaneous fat and muscle tissue?
- **A.** Ectomorph
- **B.** Mesomorph
- **C.** Endomorph
- **D.** Isomorph

Q.106 Which of the following growth assessment methods depict(s) the pattern of the postnatal bone deposition over an extended time period?
- **A.** Electromyography
- **B.** Vital staining
- **C.** Radioisotopes
- **D.** Natural markers

Q.107 Which of the following indicates the anomalies of size like microdontia and macrodontia?
- **A.** Initiation or bud stage
- **B.** Proliferation or cap stage
- **C.** Morpho-differentiation stage
- **D.** Histo-differentiation or bell stage

Q.108 Fear is:
- **A.** A primary emotion acquired soon after birth
- **B.** A primary emotion acquired in utero
- **C.** A primary emotion acquired several years after birth
- **D.** Not a primary emotion

Q.109 Which of the following is defined as the statistical procedure by which the participants are allocated into groups usually called study and control groups to receive or not to receive an experimental preventive or therapeutic procedure or intervention?
- **A.** Biostatistics
- **B.** Randomisation
- **C.** Manipulation
- **D.** Blinding

Q.110 Which of the following preventive trials occur most frequently?
- **A.** Trials of vaccine and chemo-prophylactic drugs
- **B.** Trials of antibiotics and chemo-prophylactic drugs
- **C.** Trials of antiseptic and antibiotics drugs
- **D.** Trials of analgesics and chemo-prophylactic drugs

Q.111 The provisional guideline value for arsenic in drinking water is
- **A.** 0.1 mg/litre
- **B.** 0.01 mg/litre
- **C.** 0.10 mg/litre
- **D.** 0.001 mg/litre

Q.112 Bleaching powder or chlorinated lime is a white amorphous powder. How much percent of available chlorine does it contain?
- **A.** 32%
- **B.** 33%
- **C.** 34%
- **D.** 35%

Q.113 Which of the following chemical disinfectants has an inactivating effect against all micro-organisms including bacteria, viruses, and bacterial spores?
- **A.** Formaldehyde
- **B.** Ethylene oxide
- **C.** Glutaraldehyde
- **D.** Sodium hypochlorite

Q.114 Which of the following is also known as ascorbic acid?
- **A.** Vitamin C
- **B.** Folic acid
- **C.** Iron
- **D.** Vitamin B2

Q.115 Which of the following is defined as the overall rate adjusted for the effects of differences in population composition?
- **A.** Case fatality rate
- **B.** Mortality rate
- **C.** Standardised rate
- **D.** Infant mortality rate

Q.116 Which of the following phases of trials is performed on larger groups and is designed to assess the effectiveness of a drug or device, to determine the appropriate dosage and to investigate its safety?
- **A.** Phase I
- **B.** Phase II
- **C.** Phase III
- **D.** Phase IV

Q.117 Which of the following independent variables (other than the hypothesized causal variable) can have an effect on the dependent variable but the distribution of which is systematically correlated with that of the hypothesized causal variable?
- **A.** Independent and dependent variables
- **B.** Confounding variables
- **C.** Control variables
- **D.** Intermediate or intervening variables

Q.118 Sea water contains _____ salts in solution.
- **A.** 2%
- **B.** 3.5%
- **C.** 21%
- **D.** 0.2%

Q.119 Which of the following removes both permanent and temporary hardness of water?
- **A.** Lime
- **B.** Sodium carbonate
- **C.** Caustic soda
- **D.** Charcoal

Q.120 Which of the following methods is used in controlled tipping where the terrain is moderately sloping?
- **A.** Trench method
- **B.** Ramp method
- **C.** Area method
- **D.** Seasonal method

Q.121 Which of the following chemical disinfectants is a reddish-yellow gas at ambient temperature?
- **A.** Formaldehyde
- **B.** Ethylene oxide
- **C.** Chlorine dioxide
- **D.** Sodium hypochlorite

Q.122 Which of the following health promotions generate(s) living and working conditions that are safe, stimulating, satisfying and enjoyable?

A. Building healthy public policy

B. Creating supportive environments for health

C. Strengthening community action for health

D. Developing personal skills

Q.123 Which of the following vitamins is fat soluble?

A. Vitamin A   **B.** Vitamin B

C. Vitamin C   **D.** Vitamin B1

Q.124 The requirement of vitamin E is _____ per gram of essential fatty acids.

A. 0.13 mg   **B.** 0.8 mg

C. 0.4 mg   **D.** 0.002 mg

Q.125 The intake of which of the following should be at least equal to the intake of calcium?

A. Iodine   **B.** Vitamin D

C. Phosphorous   **D.** Proteins

Q.126 The deficiency of which of the following nutrients causes neurological deficits, dermatitis and immunological changes while its excess improves cell mediated immune response?

A. Vitamin A   **B.** Protein

C. Omega 3-fatty acid   **D.** Iron

Q.127 Which of the following is not an anti-oxidant?

A. β-carotene   **B.** Vitamin C

C. Vitamin E   **D.** Vitamin B

Q.128 Which of the following indicates the comparative study of cultures?

A. Ethnology   **B.** Archaeology

C. Linguistics   **D.** Social anthropology

Q.129 Which of the following is a clinical diagnosis that refers to an uncommon and poorly-understood inflammatory disorder of the lip?

A. Van der Woude Syndrome

B. Cheilitis syndrome

C. Focal epithelial hyperplasia

D. Fibromatosis gingivae

Q.130 The clinical features of which of the following diseases include soft well-circumscribed, sessile, mucosal nodule, commonly bilateral, located lingual to the mandibular cuspid, between the free gingival margin and the mucogingival junction?

A. Fibromatosis gingivae

B. Retro-cuspid papilla

C. Aglossia and macroglossia syndrome

D. Macroglossia

Q.131 Which of the following is also seen in Melkersson–Rosenthal syndrome?

A. Cleft tongue   **B.** Fissured tongue

C. Tongue tie   **D.** Macroglossia

Q.132 Which of the following is not a disease but can be a symptom of a certain disease?

A. Aplasia

B. Hemifacial microsomia

C. Xerostomia

D. Sialoadenitis

Q.133 Which of the following is a developmental variation which is thought to arise as a result of an invagination in the surface of the tooth crown before calcification has occurred?

A. Dilaceration   **B.** Talon cusp

C. Dens in dente   **D.** Den Evaginatus

Q.134 Which type of patients does not have stigmata of osteogenesis imperfecta?

A. Brandywine type

B. Dentin dysplasia

C. Dentinogenesis imperfecta

D. Regional odonto-dysplasia

Q.135 Which of the following premature eruptions may be associated with certain systemic conditions, including rickets, cretinism and cleidocranial dysplasia?

A. Delayed eruption

B. Multiple unerupted teeth

C. Embedded and impacted teeth

D. Eruption sequestrum

Q.136 Which of the following impactions represents that the third molar is in a horizontal position with respect to the body of the mandible and the crown may or may not be in contact with the distal surface of the second molar crown or roots?

A. Mesio-angular impaction

B. Disto-angular impaction

C. Vertical impaction

D. Horizontal impaction

Q.137 The histological features of which of the following cysts shows that its lining usually consists of stratified squamous epithelium overlying a relatively dense fibrous connective tissue band that may show chronic inflammatory cell infiltration?

A. Nasopalatine duct cyst

B. Median palatal cyst

C. Globulomaxillary cyst

D. Median mandibular cyst

Q.138 Which of the following lesions occur among smokers, especially bidi smokers?

A. Leukokeratosis nicotina palati

B. Palatal erythema

C. Central palatal atrophy of the tongue

D. Lesions associated with betel quid chewing

Q.139 Which of the following tumors may arise from ducts of minor salivary glands or from the overlying surface epithelium?

A. Basaloid squamous cell carcinoma

B. Adenosquamous carcinoma

C. Undifferentiated carcinoma

D. Adenoid squamous cell carcinoma

Q.140 Which of the following is/are discrete, solitary mass of neoplastic monoclonal plasma cells in either bone marrow or a soft tissue site?

A. Plasmacytoma

B. Hemocytoma

C. Fibroblasts

D. Pinocytes

Q.141 Which of the following nerve tissue origins shows degeneration of distal portion of the nerve after severance of nerve fibres begins with swelling, fragmentation and disintegration of the axis cylinders and myelin sheath?

A. Traumatic neuroma

B. Multiple endocrine neoplasia syndrome

C. Neurofibroma

D. Neuro-lemmoma

Q.142

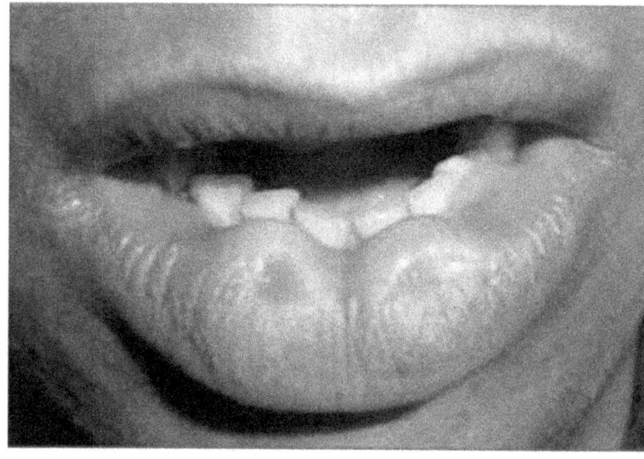

This is the picture of the boy's mouth with Van der Woude syndrome. What does the picture indicate?

A. Bilateral lip pits

B. Congenital lip pits

C. Congenital commissural pits

D. Bilateral commissural lip pits

Q.143

What does this picture represent?

A. Bifidness of the tip of the tongue

B. Large fissured tongue

C. Cleft tongue

D. Benign migratory glossitis

Q.144 Which of the following studies of orthodontics implies that an abnormal situation exists?

A. Preventive orthodontics

B. Interceptive orthodontics

C. Corrective orthodontics

D. Surgical orthodontics

Q.145 Which of the following is defined as the "sense of well-being" that arises from satisfaction or dissatisfaction with the areas of life that are important to that person?

A. Quality of life of a person

B. Health of a person

C. Mental health of a person

D. Wealth of a person

Q.146 When in embryonic period (after conception) is the human embryo little more than 3 mm in length and the head begins to take shape?

A. 2 weeks **B.** 7 weeks **C.** 9 weeks **D.** 1 week

Q.147 The fusion of the maxillary processes occurs in the _____ embryo during the seventh week.

A. 14.5 mm **B.** 15.5 mm **C.** 13.5 mm **D.** 12.5 mm

Q.148 The point at which the first and second branchial arches merge is marked by the foramen caecum. It is

A. just behind the sulcus terminalis

B. in front of the sulcus terminalis

C. away from the sulcus terminalis

D. towards the sulcus terminalis

Q.149 In endochondral bone formation, which of the following differentiate(s) from the original mesenchymal cells and form a rough model, enclosed by peri-chondral cells of the future bone?

A. Osteocytes **B.** Chondrocytes

C. Coenocytes **D.** Polygonal bone

Q.150 The gum pad is divided into how many segments by transverse grooves?

A. 10 segments **B.** 11 segments

C. 12 segments **D.** 13 segments

Q.151 How long does it take to complete deciduous dentition and its full function?

A. One and a half year **B.** Two and a half year

C. Three and half-year **D.** Four and half-year

Q.152 In _______, mandibular incisors are flared more labially by tongue action and freedom from incisal contact.

A. class I malocclusion

B. class II malocclusion

C. class III malocclusion

D. class IV malocclusion

Q.153 Stomato-gnathics deal with

A. Functional anatomy

B. Functional physiology

C. Functional enzymes

D. Functional hormones

Q.154 Benninghoff made an exhaustive study of the architecture of the cranial and facial skeleton and of the so-called

A. Law transformation of bone

B. Stress trajectories

C. Ugly duckling pattern

D. Late mesial shift of molars

Q.155 In Andrews's six keys to normal occlusion, which of the following keys refers to tight contacts?

A. Key III   **B.** Key IV   **C.** Key V   **D.** Key VI

Q.156 Which of the following is the best when the plane of occlusion is relatively flat?

A. Malocclusion   **B.** Inter-cuspation

C. Dynamic occlusion   **D.** Inter occlusion

Q.157

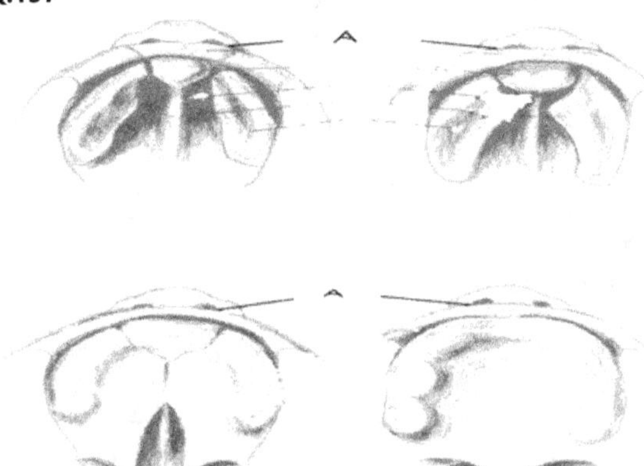

In the diagram of four stages of palatal development, A represents

A. External nares

B. Median nasal process

C. Median palatal process

D. Nasal cavity

Q.158 In which of the following epithelia does the stratum corneum retain pyknotic nuclei and disperse the keratohyalin granules not giving rise to a stratum granulosum?

A. Keratinized   **B.** Ortho-keratinized

C. Para-keratinized   **D.** Non-keratinized

Q.159 In blood supply sources of the gingiva, which of the following emerge from the crest of the interdental septa and extend parallel to the crest of the bone to anastomose with vessels of the periodontal ligament?

A. Supra-periosteal arterioles

B. Vessels of the periodontal ligament

C. Arterioles

D. Carotid nerves

Q.160 Which of the following principle fiber groups of the periodontal ligament fan out from the cementum to the tooth in the furcation areas of multi-rooted teeth?

A. Apical group

B. Inter-radicular group

C. Oblique group

D. Horizontal group

Q.161 Which of the following is composed almost entirely of densely packed bundles of Sharpey's fibers and lack of cells?

A. Acellular a fibrillar cementum

B. Acellular extrinsic fiber cementum

C. Cellular mixed stratified cementum

D. Cellular intrinsic fibre cementum

Q.162 Which of the following gingival diseases are relatively uncommon in immune-competent individuals but occur more frequently in immune-compromised individuals and those with normal oral flora distributed by the long term use of broad-spectrum antibiotics?

A. Gingival diseases of specific bacterial origin

B. Gingival diseases of fungal origin

C. Gingival diseases of viral origin

D. Gingival diseases of genetic origin

Q.163 Which of the following types of plaque is found at or above the gingival margin and when in direct contact with the gingival margin and is referred to as marginal plaque?

A. Dental plaque

B. Vivo plaque

C. Supra-gingival plaque

D. Sub-gingival plaque

Q.164 Which of the following perio-pathogens are a non-motile, pleomorphic rod and Gram-negative obligate anaerobe?

A. Tannerella forsythia

B. Porphyromonas gingivalis

C. Prevotella intermedia

D. Prevotella nigrescens

Q.165 Plaque has the ability to concentrate calcium at how many times its level in saliva?

A. 10 to 20 times   **B.** 2 to 20 times

C. 3 to 30 times   **D.** 4 to 40 times

Q.166 Which of the following cells recognise diverse antigens using a low-affinity trans-membranous complex?

A. B-cells

B. T-cells

C. Lymphocytes

D. Neutrophils and monocytes

Q.167 Which of the following are arachidonic acid metabolites generated by cyclooxygenases (COX-1, COX-2)?

A. Proteinases   **B.** Cytokines

C. Prostaglandins   **D.** Keratinocytes

Q.168 Which of the following are highly efficient resident antigen-presenting cells derived from peripheral blood monocytes?

A. Epithelial cells   **B.** Macrophages

C. Dendritic cells   **D.** Fibroblasts

Q.169 Which of the following can be used to reduce excessive levels of enzymes, cytokines and prostanoids as well as to modulate osteoclast and osteoblast function?

A. HMT

B. Anti-inflammatory mediators

C. Radiotherapy

D. Chemotherapy

Q.170

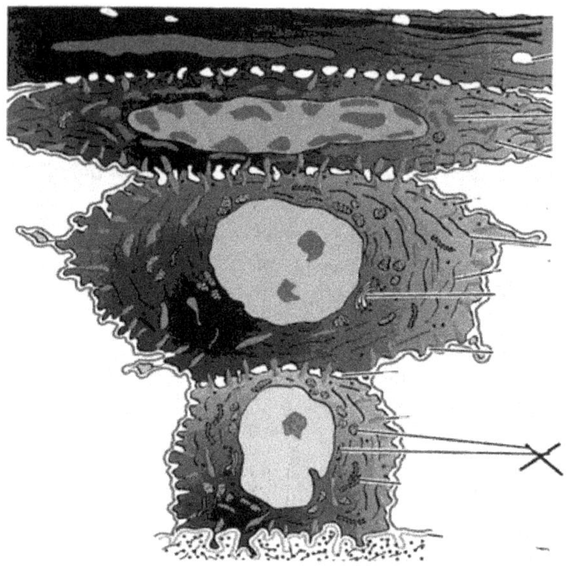

This is the picture of the cells from various layers of stratified squamous epithelium as seen by electron microscopy. What does 'X' indicate?

A. Granular endoplasmic reticulum

B. Mitochondria

C. Basement membrane

D. Golgi complex

Q.171

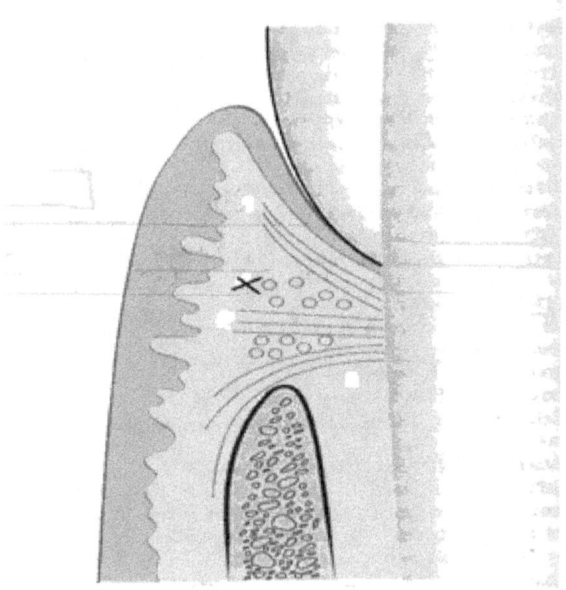

What does 'X' represent?

A. Crest of the gingiva

B. Outer surface

C. Periosteum of the labial plate

D. Circular fibres

Q.172

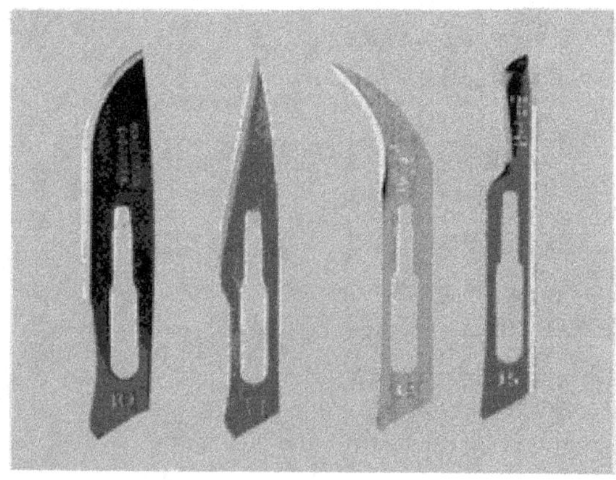

Which of the following scalpel blades are included in oral surgery?

A. Blade numbers 10, 11, 12 and 15

B. Blade numbers 11, 17, 12 and 15

C. Blade numbers 10, 15, 12 and 11

D. Blade numbers 10, 12, 15 and 17

Q.173

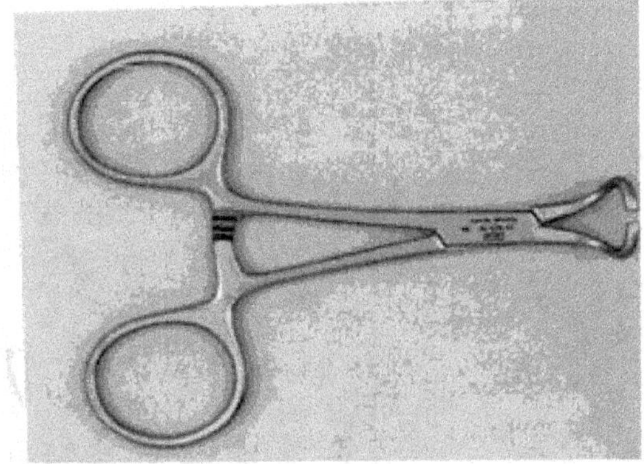

What is this instrument called?

A. Towel clip
B. Artery forceps
C. Needle holder
D. Tissue goggle

Q.174 Which of the following is the breakdown of the living tissue by the action of micro-organisms and is usually accompanied by inflammation?

A. Sterility   **B.** Sepsis   **C.** Lysis   **D.** Grafting

Q.175 Which of the following principles of incisions through epithelial surfaces suggests that the surgeon plan to re-approximate should be made with the blade held perpendicular to the epithelial surface?

A. First principle
B. Second principle
C. Fourth principle
D. Fifth principle

Q.176 Which of the following is the most severe type of nerve injury and involves a complete loss of nerve continuity?

A. Neurapraxia
B. Axonotmesis
C. Neurotmesis
D. Hyper-natraemia

Q.177 Which of the following instruments is used most commonly for removing bone in dentoalveolar surgery?

A. Rongeurs
B. Bur and handpiece
C. Mallet and chisel
D. Bone file

Q.178 The forceps most commonly used for single-rooted teeth are

A. Number 151
B. Number 15
C. Number 150
D. Number 17

Q.179 Pains caused by which of the following cannot be relieved even by endodontic and complex restorative procedures?

A. Periodontal disease
B. Cracked teeth
C. Impacted teeth
D. Jaw fractures

Q.180 Which of the following teeth are usually extracted with forceps no. 17?

A. Mandibular molars
B. Maxillary molars
C. Incisors
D. Premolars

Q.181 In the technique of open extraction of multi-rooted teeth, if the crown of the __________ is missing or fractured, the roots should be divided into two buccal roots and a palatal root.

A. mandibular molar
B. maxillary molar
C. maxillary premolar
D. canines

Q.182 When a tooth is partially impacted with a large amount of soft tissue over the axial and occlusal surfaces, the patient frequently has one or more episodes of

A. Dental caries
B. Periodontal disease
C. Pericoronitis
D. Root resorption

Q.183 Which of the following has three large and strong roots?

A. Maxillary first molar
B. Maxillary second pre-molar
C. Maxillary third molar
D. Mandibular first pre-molar

Q.184 In muco-periosteal flaps, if the patient is edentulous, the envelope incision is usually made along the scar at the

A. Posterior end of the envelope incision
B. Crest of the ridge
C. Envelope component of the incision
D. Crestal bone

Q.185 Which of the following fails to erupt into the dental arch within the expected time?

A. Cracked tooth
B. Impacted tooth
C. Dental caries affected tooth
D. Abutment tooth

Q.186 Which of the following diseases is caused by coxsackievirus A10?

A. Acute lympho-nodular pharyngitis
B. Chicken pox
C. Erythema multi-forme
D. Contact allergic stomatitis

Q.187 Which of the following is an immune mediated disease that may be initiated either by deposition of immune complexes in the superficial microvasculature of skin and mucosa or cell mediated immunity?

A. Erythema multiforme
B. Contact allergic stomatitis
C. Oral ulcers secondary to cancer chemotherapy
D. Acute necrotising ulcerative gingivitis

Q.188 Which of the following was classically described as the triad of symptoms including recurring oral ulcers, recurring genital ulcers and eye lesions?

A. RAS
B. SAS
C. Behcet's syndrome
D. Recurrent herpes simplex virus infection

Q.189 Which of the following blistering disorders chiefly affects children below the age of 5 years?

A. Mucous membrane pemphigoid
B. Linear IGA disease

C. Chronic bullous disease

D. Erosive lichen planus

Q.190 Which of the following is a rare autosomal dominant disorder characterised by oral lesions and bilateral limbal conjunctival plaques?

A. Leuko-edema

B. White sponge nevus

C. Hereditary benign intraepithelial dyskeratosis

D. Dyskeratosis congenita

Q.191 Which of the following lesions of oral tissues may result from chronic irritation due to repeated sucking, nibbling or chewing?

A. Linea alba

B. Dyskeratosis congenita

C. Actinic keratosis

D. Induced keratosis

Q.192 Which of the following is commonly used by health care practitioners as a chemical cautery agent for the treatment of aphthous ulcers?

A. Aspirin burn

B. Silver nitrate

C. Hydrogen peroxide

D. Sodium hypochlorite

Q.193 Smokeless tobacco contains which of the following known carcinogens proven to cause mucosal alterations?

A. N-nitronicotine

B. N-nitro-sonor-nicotine

C. N-nicotine acetylcholine receptor

D. N-neo-nicotinoids

Q.194 Which of the following diseases includes a variety of clinically recognised conditions in which mycelial invasion of the deeper layers of the mucosa and skin occurs, causing a proliferative response of host tissue?

A. Median rhomboid glossitis

B. Chronic hyperplastic candidiasis

C. Chronic multifocal candidiasis

D. Chronic muco-cutaneous candidiasis

Q.195 Which of the following is a common chronic immunologic inflammatory muco-cutaneous disorder that varies in appearance from keratotic to erythematous and ulcerative?

A. Erythroplakia

B. Oral lichen planus

C. Lichenoid reactions

D. Bowen's disease

Q.196 Melanin is derived from which of the following?

A. Cytosine

B. Albumin

C. Collagen

D. Tyrosine

Q.197 Which of the following is/are called the focal dilation of a vein or group of venules?

A. Patrix

B. Divergence

C. Varix

D. Dilacerations

Q.198 Which of the following are present as rapidly proliferative nodular tumours?

A. Angio-sarcoma

B. Kaposi's sarcoma

C. Hereditary haemorrhagic telangiectasia

D. Blue nevus

Q.199

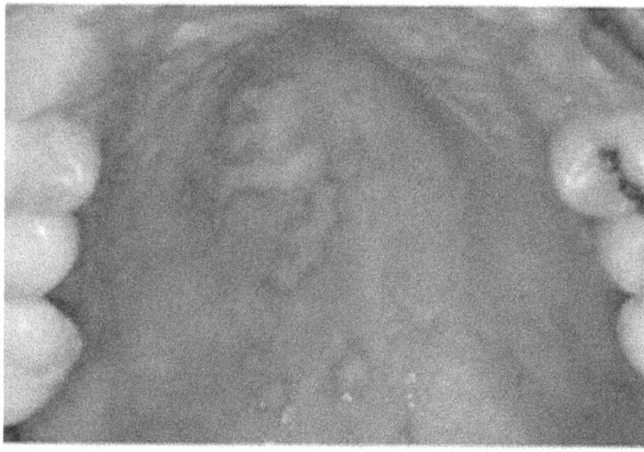

This is the picture of a 17 year old girl having unerupted palatal vesicles and intense marginal gingiva. These characteristics mean which of the following infections?

A. Acute periodontitis abscess

B. Herpangina

C. Primary herpes

D. Varicella zoster infection

Q.200

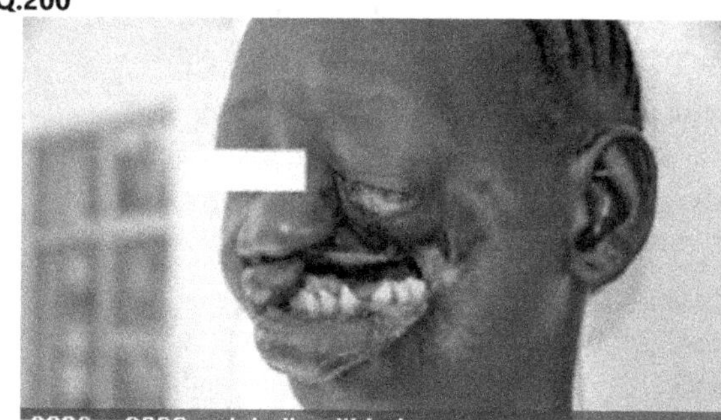

Which of the following diseases is represented by this picture?

A. Palatal ulceration

B. Cancrum oris or noma

C. Aphthous stomatitis

D. Behcet's syndrome

Q.201 Which of the following is a surface loss of dental hard tissues other than by caries or trauma?

A. Dental caries

B. Tooth wear

C. Traumatic injury

D. Developmental defect

Q.202 Which of the following is the mechanical wear of opposing teeth seen on contacting occlusal surfaces, incisal edges and proximal surfaces?

A. Attrition

B. Abrasion

C. Erosion

D. Abfraction

Q.203 Which of the following tooth numbering systems is called the Angular or Grid system?

A. Zsigmondy Palmer system

B. American Dental Association (ADA) system

C. Federation Dentaire International (FDI) system

D. Universal system

Q.204 Which of the following refers to caries that is leftover in completed tooth preparation, either by the operator's neglect or intentionally?

A. Forward caries **B.** Backward caries

C. Residual caries **D.** Chronic caries

Q.205 Which of the following is a membrane secreted by the ameloblast cell finally after enamel formation is completed?

A. Pellicle

B. Primary enamel cuticle

C. Dentinoenamel junction

D. Enamel spindle

Q.206

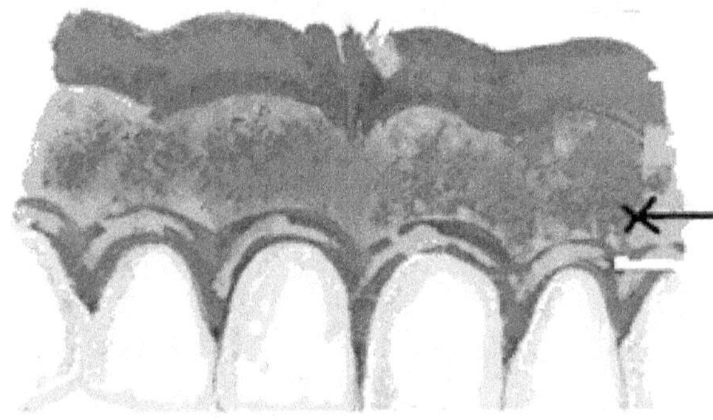

This is the picture of normal gingiva. What does 'X' represent?

A. Frenulum

B. Alveolar mucosa

C. Attached gingiva

D. Free gingival groove

Q.207

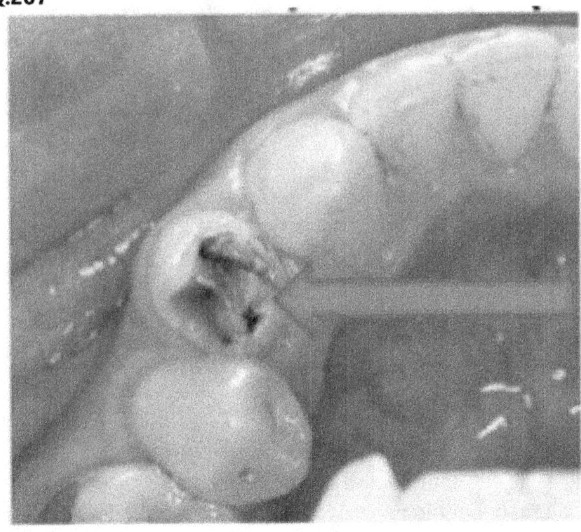

Which of the following types of caries does this diagram represent?

A. Residual caries **B.** Arrested caries

C. Chronic caries **D.** Rampant caries

Q.208 Which of the following defects indicates abnormal loss of tooth surface because of direct frictional forces between the teeth and external objects or from frictional forces between contacting teeth in the presence of an abrasive medium?

A. Attrition **B.** Abrasion

C. Erosion **D.** Abfraction

Q.209 Which of the following is/are used for prophylactic coverage of a medically compromised patient and in special circumstances, an adjunctive treatment of acute periapical or periodontal infection?

A. Antiseptics **B.** Antibiotics

C. Analgesics **D.** Aspirin

Q.210 The primary function of which of the following throughout the life of the pulp is to produce and deposit dentin?

A. Ameloblasts **B.** Odontoblasts

C. Cementoblasts **D.** Endoblasts

Q.211 The pattern of calcification around the odontoblastic processes forms the dentinal tubules. The dentin between these tubules is called

A. Predentin layer **B.** Intertubular dentin

C. Dentinal tubules **D.** Incremental lines

Q.212 Which of the following is the main constituent of pulp and is a part of the matrix that surrounds and supports the cellular and vascular elements of pulp?

A. Cell free zone **B.** Cell rich zone

C. Ground substance **D.** Central zone.

Q.213 Which of the following is a bone-like calcified tissue that covers the roots of the teeth?

A. Alveolar bone **B.** Gingiva

C. Cementum **D.** Dentin

Q.214 Which of the following are believed to be immature elastic fibres and transverse the periodontal ligament in an axial direction?

A. Collagen fibres **B.** Oxytalan fibres

C. Vascular fibres **D.** Interstitial tissues

Q.215 Retentive clasp is located in an undercut area of the clinical crown and resists displacement of the prosthesis _______ the underlying hard and soft tissues.

A. Away from **B.** Towards

C. On **D.** In between

Q.216 In extra coronal, the retentive and reciprocal components lie ____ the external surfaces of the abutment.

A. On **B.** Over

C. Beneath **D.** Away from

Q.217 Which of the following statements is correct?

A. A flexible major connector may cause severe damage to

the hard and soft tissues of the oral cavity.

B. A flexible major connector never causes severe damage to the hard and soft tissues of the oral cavity.

C. A rigid major connector may cause severe damage to the hard and soft tissues of the oral cavity.

D. A rigid major connector may cause mild damage to the hard and soft tissues of the oral cavity.

Q.218 Which of the following allows forces to be concentrated on individual teeth and segments of the residual ridges?

A. Rigidity
B. Flexibility
C. Brutality
D. None of the above

Q.219 The point of greatest tooth convexity allows each retentive clasp arm to return to its

A. Strained or passive state
B. Strained or active state
C. Unstrained or passive state
D. Unstrained or active state

Q.220 According to Prothero's explanation, the contours of a clinical crown resemble two cones sharing a common base. The line formed at the junction of these cones represents the greatest diameter of the tooth. This diameter is commonly referred to as the

A. Diameter of the contour
B. Base of the contour
C. Horizontal length of the contour
D. Height of the contour

Q.221 Which of the following periodontal ligaments is/are arranged to absorb axial forces?

A. Soft tissues
B. Fibres
C. Teeth
D. Abutment

Q.222 Which of the following forces of smaller magnitude can be extremely destructive to the supporting structures of a tooth and should be avoided whenever possible?

A. Axial forces
B. Non-axial forces
C. Sagital forces
D. Frontal forces

Q.223 Which of the following systolic pressures should be considered to have a potentially serious medical condition for which medical consultation is indicated?

A. Systolic Pressure exceeding 120 mm Hg or diastolic pressure exceeding 80 mm Hg

B. Systolic Pressure exceeding 140 mm Hg or diastolic pressure exceeding 100 mm Hg

C. Systolic Pressure exceeding 150 mm Hg or diastolic pressure exceeding 110 mm Hg

D. Systolic Pressure exceeding 130 mm Hg or diastolic pressure exceeding 90 mm Hg

Q.224 During the patient interview phase of the diagnostic process, the practitioner should establish rapport with the patient, gain insight into the _________ make-up of the patient, explore physical problems that may affect the treatment and determine the patient's expectations for restorative therapy.

A. Physiologic
B. Psychologic
C. Mechanical
D. All of the above

Q.225 It is necessary to select a facebow that is compatible with the _________ that is to be used.

A. Articular
B. Dental arch
C. Dental implant
D. Centric relation

Q.226 The most accurate method for making a facebow transfer is to determine the patient's ______ and to use this axis for positioning the facebow.

A. Articular
B. True hinge axis
C. Arbitrary hinge axis
D. Centric relation

Q.227

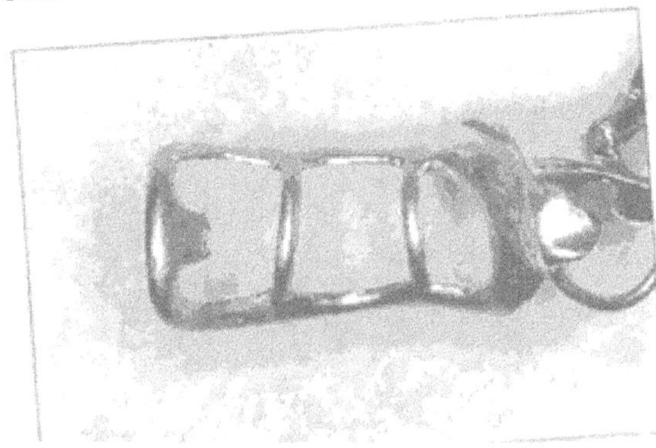

This is a minor connector. Which of the following types of construction does it represent?

A. Mesh construction
B. Ladder-like network
C. Open construction
D. It extends two thirds of the edentulous ridge

Q.228

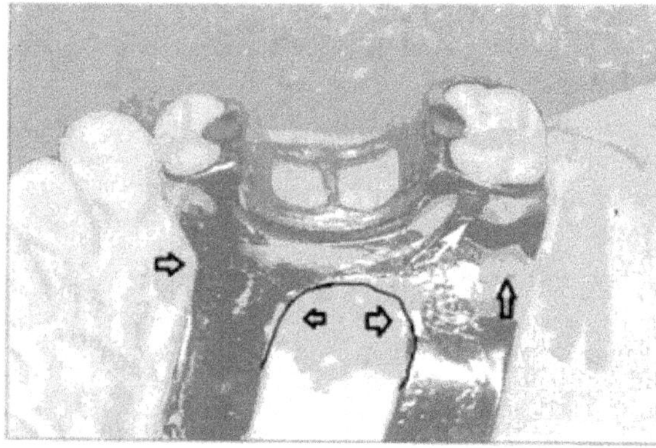

This is a picture of major connectors. Which of the following contours should all major connectors exhibit?

A. Sharp angles
B. Rounded contours
C. Rough contours
D. Slanting contours

Q.229 Which of the following is a capsulated tumour?

A. Papilloma
B. Fibroma
C. Bursae
D. Infective papilloma

Q.230 Which of the following is a congenital localised cluster of dilated lymph sacs in the skin and subcutaneous tissue that has failed to join the normal lymph system during development period?

A. Lymph cyst   **B.** Lymphangioma

C. Calcinosis cutis   **D.** True neuroma

Q.231 Isotonic volume depletion is corrected by _______ normal saline.

A. 0.8%   **B.** 0.9%   **C.** 1.0%   **D.** 2.0%

Q.232 Which of the following hypernatremia is seen in more salt intake, excess steroids, sodium bicarbonate/hypertonic saline infusion (salt again)?

A. Euvolemic   **B.** Hypo-volaemic

C. Hyper-volaemic   **D.** Pseudo volaemic

Q.233 Which of the following was the first mal-absorptive procedure done for obesity?

A. Laparoscopic adjustable gastric banding

B. Jejunoileal bypass

C. Roux-en-Y Gastric bypass

D. Laparoscopic RYGB

Q.234 Which of the following shocks can occur due to injury to the liver, spleen, bone fractures, haemo-thorax, vascular injury, severe bleeding on table during surgeries of thyroid, liver, portal vein or major vessels?

A. Vasovagal shock

B. Neurogenic shock

C. Hypo-volemic shock

D. Cardiogenic shock

Q.235 Which of the following is the spontaneous arrest of bleeding?

A. Hemostasis   **B.** Hemolysis

C. Hematoma   **D.** Haemophilia

Q.236 Which of the following contains growth factor derived from cultured fibroblasts which promotes wound healing?

A. Biobrane   **B.** Opsite

C. Transcyte   **D.** Integra

Q.237 Which of the following investigations is useful in suspected cases of renal arterial injury and intimal tears, traumatic aneurysm and aortic occlusion?

A. Abdominal diagnostic paracentesis

B. Diagnostic laparoscopy

C. Arteriography

D. Doppler assessment of major vessels

Q.238 Which of the following is a contagious pustular dermatitis of the hand due to a para-pox virus infection?

A. Orf

B. Milker's Nodes

C. Compound palmar ganglion

D. Acute suppurative tenosynovitis

Q.239

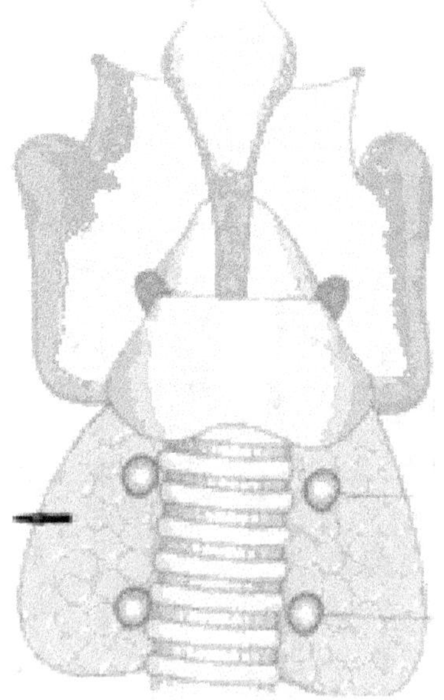

This is the picture of anatomical location of parathyroids. Which of the following is represented by the arrow mark?

A. Thyroid glands

B. Parathyroid (IV) glands

C. Lingual thyroid

D. Thymus glands

Q.240

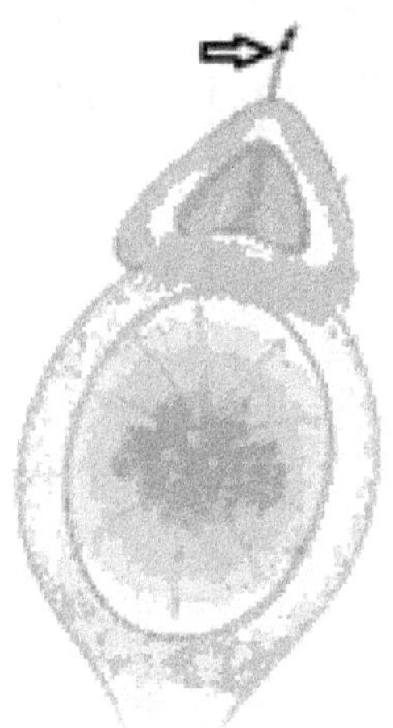

This is the picture of a cut-section of adrenal glands. What does the arrow indicate?

A. Adrenal gland

B. Renal fascia

C. Septum

D. Diaphragmatic attachment

// Smart Answer Sheet //

Correct   Indicates percentage of students who answered questions correctly.

Skipped   Indicates percentage of students who skipped questions.

Q.	Ans.	Correct / Skipped	Q.	Ans.	Correct / Skipped	Q.	Ans.	Correct / Skipped	Q.	Ans.	Correct / Skipped	Q.	Ans.	Correct / Skipped
1	B	41.94 % / 12.9 %	17	C	3.23 % / 41.93 %	33	B	48.39 % / 41.93 %	49	A	35.48 % / 41.94 %	65	A	48.39 % / 41.93 %
2	B	38.71 % / 35.48 %	18	A	12.9 % / 41.94 %	34	B	25.81 % / 38.71 %	50	A	22.58 % / 38.71 %	66	A	38.71 % / 41.94 %
3	D	41.94 % / 41.93 %	19	D	12.9 % / 41.94 %	35	D	12.9 % / 41.94 %	51	A	41.94 % / 41.93 %	67	D	9.68 % / 41.93 %
4	D	16.13 % / 41.93 %	20	C	12.9 % / 38.71 %	36	D	45.16 % / 38.71 %	52	A	25.81 % / 41.93 %	68	A	6.45 % / 41.94 %
5	B	12.9 % / 41.94 %	21	B	12.9 % / 41.94 %	37	A	35.48 % / 41.94 %	53	B	38.71 % / 41.94 %	69	A	9.68 % / 41.93 %
6	C	32.26 % / 41.93 %	22	C	9.68 % / 38.71 %	38	A	35.48 % / 41.94 %	54	B	32.26 % / 41.93 %	70	A	35.48 % / 38.71 %
7	C	32.26 % / 41.93 %	23	B	9.68 % / 41.93 %	39	B	45.16 % / 41.94 %	55	B	25.81 % / 41.93 %	71	B	19.35 % / 41.94 %
8	C	9.68 % / 41.93 %	24	A	38.71 % / 38.71 %	40	C	29.03 % / 41.94 %	56	B	32.26 % / 41.93 %	72	A	51.61 % / 35.49 %
9	B	48.39 % / 41.93 %	25	D	9.68 % / 41.93 %	41	B	25.81 % / 41.93 %	57	B	35.48 % / 41.94 %	73	C	6.45 % / 41.94 %
10	A	16.13 % / 38.71 %	26	A	6.45 % / 41.94 %	42	D	22.58 % / 35.48 %	58	B	32.26 % / 38.71 %	74	B	6.45 % / 41.94 %
11	D	45.16 % / 41.94 %	27	A	19.35 % / 41.94 %	43	C	48.39 % / 41.93 %	59	B	22.58 % / 41.94 %	75	C	12.9 % / 41.94 %
12	C	22.58 % / 41.94 %	28	A	32.26 % / 38.71 %	44	B	12.9 % / 41.94 %	60	C	12.9 % / 41.94 %	76	A	32.26 % / 41.93 %
13	C	29.03 % / 41.94 %	29	A	25.81 % / 41.93 %	45	B	16.13 % / 41.93 %	61	B	12.9 % / 41.94 %	77	A	51.61 % / 41.94 %
14	B	22.58 % / 38.71 %	30	C	16.13 % / 38.71 %	46	B	54.84 % / 38.71 %	62	B	32.26 % / 41.93 %	78	D	48.39 % / 41.93 %
15	B	25.81 % / 41.93 %	31	B	16.13 % / 41.93 %	47	A	41.94 % / 41.93 %	63	B	41.94 % / 41.93 %	79	B	22.58 % / 41.94 %
16	C	22.58 % / 41.94 %	32	B	51.61 % / 41.94 %	48	A	41.94 % / 41.93 %	64	B	16.13 % / 41.93 %	80	D	41.94 % / 38.71 %

Q.	Ans.	Correct / Skipped	Q.	Ans.	Correct / Skipped	Q.	Ans.	Correct / Skipped	Q.	Ans.	Correct / Skipped	Q.	Ans.	Correct / Skipped
81	A	48.39 % / 41.93 %	97	B	54.84 % / 41.93 %	113	A	12.9 % / 38.71 %	129	B	19.35 % / 38.71 %	145	A	25.81 % / 38.71 %
82	A	25.81 % / 41.93 %	98	A	25.81 % / 41.93 %	114	A	58.06 % / 38.71 %	130	B	25.81 % / 38.71 %	146	B	32.26 % / 38.71 %
83	A	22.58 % / 41.94 %	99	A	41.94 % / 41.93 %	115	C	22.58 % / 38.71 %	131	B	38.71 % / 38.71 %	147	A	19.35 % / 38.71 %
84	B	22.58 % / 41.94 %	100	A	48.39 % / 38.71 %	116	B	9.68 % / 38.71 %	132	C	45.16 % / 38.71 %	148	A	29.03 % / 38.71 %
85	C	48.39 % / 41.93 %	101	D	25.81 % / 38.71 %	117	B	29.03 % / 38.71 %	133	C	41.94 % / 38.71 %	149	B	35.48 % / 38.71 %
86	C	32.26 % / 41.93 %	102	A	19.35 % / 38.71 %	118	B	12.9 % / 38.71 %	134	A	35.48 % / 35.49 %	150	A	51.61 % / 38.71 %
87	C	16.13 % / 41.93 %	103	D	19.35 % / 38.71 %	119	B	29.03 % / 38.71 %	135	A	22.58 % / 38.71 %	151	B	16.13 % / 38.71 %
88	C	41.94 % / 41.93 %	104	D	25.81 % / 38.71 %	120	B	25.81 % / 35.48 %	136	D	32.26 % / 38.71 %	152	B	22.58 % / 38.71 %
89	A	38.71 % / 41.94 %	105	A	45.16 % / 38.71 %	121	C	3.23 % / 38.71 %	137	B	6.45 % / 38.71 %	153	A	45.16 % / 38.71 %
90	B	51.61 % / 41.94 %	106	B	12.9 % / 38.71 %	122	B	19.35 % / 38.71 %	138	A	35.48 % / 38.71 %	154	B	25.81 % / 38.71 %
91	B	19.35 % / 41.94 %	107	C	51.61 % / 38.71 %	123	A	45.16 % / 38.71 %	139	B	6.45 % / 38.71 %	155	C	22.58 % / 38.71 %
92	B	12.9 % / 41.94 %	108	A	41.94 % / 38.71 %	124	B	22.58 % / 35.48 %	140	A	41.94 % / 38.71 %	156	B	32.26 % / 38.71 %
93	B	22.58 % / 41.94 %	109	B	19.35 % / 38.71 %	125	C	12.9 % / 38.71 %	141	A	16.13 % / 38.71 %	157	A	22.58 % / 38.71 %
94	B	41.94 % / 41.93 %	110	A	38.71 % / 38.71 %	126	C	29.03 % / 38.71 %	142	A	22.58 % / 38.71 %	158	C	32.26 % / 38.71 %
95	A	45.16 % / 41.94 %	111	B	19.35 % / 38.71 %	127	D	35.48 % / 38.71 %	143	B	58.06 % / 38.71 %	159	C	3.23 % / 38.71 %
96	A	51.61 % / 41.94 %	112	B	16.13 % / 38.71 %	128	A	32.26 % / 38.71 %	144	B	22.58 % / 38.71 %	160	B	48.39 % / 38.71 %

Q.	Ans.	Correct / Skipped	Q.	Ans.	Correct / Skipped	Q.	Ans.	Correct / Skipped	Q.	Ans.	Correct / Skipped	Q.	Ans.	Correct / Skipped
161	B	35.48 % / 38.71 %	177	A	32.26 % / 38.71 %	193	B	6.45 % / 38.71 %	209	B	48.39 % / 38.71 %	225	A	35.48 % / 38.71 %
162	B	29.03 % / 38.71 %	178	A	25.81 % / 38.71 %	194	B	19.35 % / 38.71 %	210	B	48.39 % / 38.71 %	226	B	22.58 % / 38.71 %
163	C	58.06 % / 38.71 %	179	B	22.58 % / 38.71 %	195	B	25.81 % / 38.71 %	211	B	51.61 % / 38.71 %	227	B	41.94 % / 38.71 %
164	B	16.13 % / 38.71 %	180	A	19.35 % / 35.49 %	196	D	38.71 % / 38.71 %	212	C	19.35 % / 35.49 %	228	B	38.71 % / 38.71 %
165	B	6.45 % / 38.71 %	181	B	45.16 % / 38.71 %	197	C	29.03 % / 38.71 %	213	C	48.39 % / 38.71 %	229	A	25.81 % / 38.71 %
166	B	3.23 % / 38.71 %	182	C	54.84 % / 38.71 %	198	A	16.13 % / 38.71 %	214	B	38.71 % / 38.71 %	230	B	25.81 % / 38.71 %
167	C	51.61 % / 38.71 %	183	A	54.84 % / 38.71 %	199	C	12.9 % / 38.71 %	215	A	38.71 % / 38.71 %	231	B	32.26 % / 38.71 %
168	B	25.81 % / 38.71 %	184	B	38.71 % / 38.71 %	200	B	48.39 % / 38.71 %	216	A	32.26 % / 38.71 %	232	C	35.48 % / 38.71 %
169	A	16.13 % / 38.71 %	185	B	54.84 % / 38.71 %	201	B	51.61 % / 38.71 %	217	A	29.03 % / 38.71 %	233	B	19.35 % / 38.71 %
170	B	12.9 % / 38.71 %	186	A	29.03 % / 38.71 %	202	A	58.06 % / 38.71 %	218	B	22.58 % / 35.48 %	234	C	41.94 % / 38.71 %
171	D	48.39 % / 38.71 %	187	A	38.71 % / 38.71 %	203	A	35.48 % / 38.71 %	219	C	19.35 % / 38.71 %	235	A	58.06 % / 38.71 %
172	A	61.29 % / 35.48 %	188	C	45.16 % / 38.71 %	204	C	51.61 % / 38.71 %	220	D	32.26 % / 35.48 %	236	C	12.9 % / 38.71 %
173	A	45.16 % / 38.71 %	189	C	12.9 % / 38.71 %	205	B	45.16 % / 38.71 %	221	B	41.94 % / 38.71 %	237	C	12.9 % / 38.71 %
174	B	35.48 % / 38.71 %	190	C	22.58 % / 38.71 %	206	C	54.84 % / 38.71 %	222	B	16.13 % / 38.71 %	238	A	19.35 % / 38.71 %
175	C	6.45 % / 38.71 %	191	A	22.58 % / 38.71 %	207	C	12.9 % / 38.71 %	223	D	3.23 % / 38.71 %	239	A	38.71 % / 38.71 %
176	C	35.48 % / 38.71 %	192	B	19.35 % / 38.71 %	208	B	32.26 % / 38.71 %	224	B	41.94 % / 38.71 %	240	D	19.35 % / 38.71 %

Performance Analysis

Avg. Score (%)	22.92%
Toppers Score (%)	58.23%
Your Score	

Mock Test 08

Part A

Q.1 Which of the following drugs should be removed by dialysis?

A. Digoxin

B. Salicylates

C. Benzodiazepines

D. Organophosphates

Q.2 Which of the following is true?

A. As the concentration of the drug increases over the therapeutic range, only the bound form of the drug increases.

B. The bound form is not available for metabolism, but is available for excretion.

C. Acidic drugs bind to beta globulin and basic drugs bind to albumin.

D. Binding sites are non-specific and one drug can displace the other.

Q.3 In a patient with nephrotic syndrome and hypoalbuminemia, protein binding of which of the following drugs will not be affected?

A. Tolbutamide

B. Morphine

C. Diazepam

D. Valproate

Q.4 Drug transport mechanisms include:

A. Active transport and Passive transport

B. Lipid solubility

C. Bioavailability

D. Distribution

Q.5 Duration of action of IV administered drug depends on

A. protein binding

B. opacity

C. distribution density

D. lipid insolubility

Q.6 Causes for reduced bioavailability include:

A. High first pass metabolism

B. Increased absorption

C. IV drug administration

D. High lipid solubility

Q.7 CYP 3A4 enzymes are affected by

A. Fexofenadine

B. Phenytoin

C. Carbamazapine

D. Azithromycin

Q.8 Which of the following statements is true?

A. If a drug is administered rectally, it follows 1st order kinetics.

B. If a drug is administered IM, it follows zero order kinetics.

C. If a drug is administered IV, it follows 1st order kinetics.

D. Bioavailability is usually lower after oral administration than IV administration.

Q.9 CYP-450 inducer is:

A. Cimetidine

B. Ketoconazole

C. Phenobarbitone

D. DDT

Q.10 Drug distribution is influenced by

A. plasma protein binding

B. lipid insolubility

C. stress

D. gender

Q.11 Which of the following statements is true about route of drug administration?

A. 80% bioavailability is by IV injection.

B. IM administration needs sterile technique.

C. ID injection do not produce local tissue necrosis and irritation.

D. Inhalation produces delayed systemic bioavailability.

Q.12 Volume of distribution of drugs is altered in:

A. Obesity

B. Old age

C. Neonate

D. All of the above

Q.13 Which of the following is not a prodrug?

A. Mercaptopurine

B. Dipivefrine

C. Enalapril

D. Phenytoin

Q.14 High hepatic extraction ratio is not seen in

A. propanolol

B. lidocaine

C. ampicillin

D. imipramine

Q.15 In acute inflammation, which of the following results due to the contraction of endothelial cell cytoskeleton?

A. Delayed transient increase in permeability

B. Early transient increase in permeability

C. Delayed permanent increase in permeability

D. Early permanent increase in permeability

Q.16 Delayed prolonged bleeding is caused by:

A. histamine

B. leukocyte dependent injury

C. IL-I

D. direct injury to endothelial cells

Q.17 Earliest transient change following tissue injury will be:

A. Neutropenia

B. Neutrophilia

C. Monocytosis

D. Lymphocytosis

Q.18 The complement is fixed best by which of the following immunoglobulins?

A. IgG

B. IgM

C. IgA

D. IgD

Q.19 Multinucleated giant cells are formed due to the fusion of:

A. Basophils

B. Eosinophils

C. Epithelioid cells

D. Monocytes

Q.20 Major basic protein is formed by:

A. Lymphocyte

B. Basophil

C. Neutrophil

D. Eosinophils

Q.21 Epithelioid granuloma may be seen in all of the following conditions, except:

A. Sarcoidosis
B. Tuberculosis
C. Pneumocystic carinii pneumonia
D. Hodgkin's syndrome

Q.22 Virus mediated transfer of host DNA from one cell to another is known as:

A. Transduction
B. Transformation
C. Transcription
D. Integration

Q.23 Methicillin resistance in Staphylococcus aureus is due to:

A. β-lactamase
B. mecA gene
C. AMPC gene
D. porin develop

Q.24 Which of the following is true about Lambda phage?

A. It causes mad cow disease.
B. Lytic and lysogenic interconversion can't occur.
C. Lytic form incorporates within host DNA and multiplies causing rupture of cell membrane.
D. Lysogenic form incorporates with host DNA and remains dormant.

Q.25 The following phenomenon is responsible for anti-biotic resistance in bacteria due to slime production:

A. Co-aggregation
B. Biofilm formation
C. Mutation evolving in altered target site for antibiotics
D. Mutation evolving a target bypass mechanism

Q.26 Pyomyositis is caused by:

A. Clostridium
B. Staphylococcus aureus
C. Streptococcus
D. E. coli

Q.27 Property encoded by plasmid is:

A. Involved in multi-drug resistance transfer
B. Not involved in conjugation
C. Imparts capsule deformation
D. Imparts pili deformation

Q.28 Which of the following is true about bacteriophage?

A. Can transmit toxin to bacteria
B. Bacteria which transmits DNA to another bacteria
C. Causes transformation of bacteria
D. A virus which invades bacteria

Q.29 Which of the following is a special entity, common in leg, forearm, thigh, and arm?

A. Compartment syndrome
B. Crush syndrome
C. Hypertrophic scar
D. De-gloving injury

Q.30 Which of the following is a break in the continuity of the covering epithelium, either skin or mucous membrane due to molecular death?

A. Ulcer
B. Inflammation
C. Cancer
D. Burst

Q.31 Which of the following is due to the failure of fusion of the two palatine processes?

A. Cleft palate
B. Maxillofacial injury
C. Cleft lip
D. None of these

Q.32 Smoking cessation- Not a first-line drug option?

A. Clonidine
B. Nicotine replacement (patches)
C. Varenicline
D. Bupropion

Q.33 Which of the following is caused due to fungal infection?

A. Traumatic stomatitis
B. Aphthous stomatitis
C. Candida stomatitis
D. Vincent's ulcerative stomatitis

Q.34 Which of the following is a destructive ulceration with gangrene seen in cancrumn oris and chancroid?

A. Melanotic ulcer
B. Bazin's disease
C. Rodent ulcer
D. Phagedena

Q.35 Which of the following is a J-shaped salivary gland?

A. Parotid gland
B. Submandibular salivary gland
C. Minor salivary gland
D. Ectopic salivary gland

Q.36 Lingual lipase is secreted from:

A. tongue glands
B. salivary gland
C. parotid gland
D. submandibular salivary gland

Q.37 Which of the following is a protrusion of mucosa through Killian's dehiscence?

A. Pharyngeal pouch
B. Laryngocele
C. Ludwig's angina
D. Cystic hygroma

Q.38 Which of the following occurs in professional trumpet players, glass blowers, and in people with chronic cough?

A. Branchial fistula
B. Laryngocele
C. Ludwig's angina
D. Branchial cyst

Q.39 Where does the thyroid gland develop from?

A. Cells from the peripheral floor between the first and second peripheral pouches
B. Cells from the superior floor between the first and second peripheral pouches
C. Cells from the pharyngeal floor between the first and second pharyngeal pouches
D. Cells from the inferior floor between the first and second peripheral pouches

Q.40

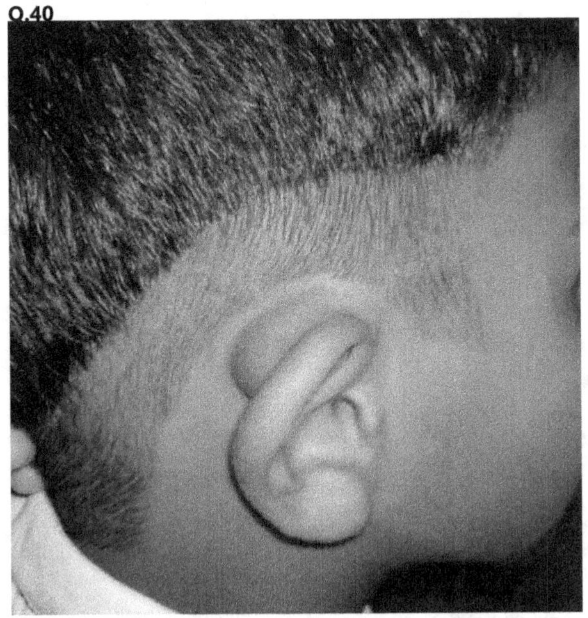

Which tumour is indicated through this picture?

A. Lipoma
B. Dermoid cyst
C. Sebaceous cyst
D. Papilloma

Q.41

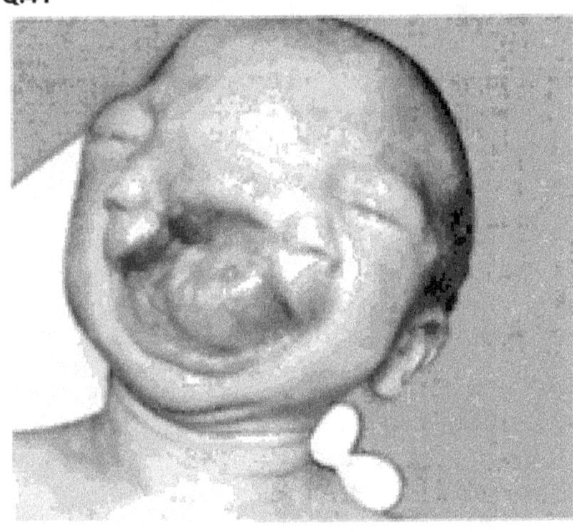

Which of the following diseases is depicted by this diagram?

A. Chordoma
B. Epignathus
C. Ganglion
D. Neuroma

Q.42

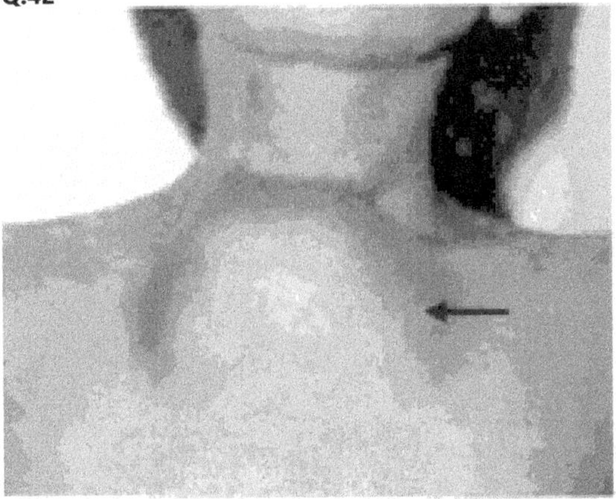

Which of the following diseases is illustrated though this picture?

A. Mycotic aneurysm
B. Thoracic aortic aneurysm
C. Fat embolism
D. Saddle embolus

Q.43 Which of the following is the standard reference position of the body used to describe the location of structures?

A. Anatomical position
B. Frankfurt position
C. Sagittal position
D. Dorsal position

Q.44 What are X-rays comprised of?

A. Protons
B. Photons
C. Leptons
D. Neutrons

Q.45 Which muscles of the back move the upper limbs and the ribs?

A. Extrinsic muscles
B. Intrinsic muscles
C. Primary muscles
D. Secondary muscles

Q.46 Which of the following form the peripheral nervous system (PNS)?

A. Canial nerves and spinal nerves
B. Brain and spinal cord
C. Spinal cord and cranial nerves
D. Brain and spinal nerves

Q.47 Which of the following is a thick, flexible, soft tissue partition oriented longitudinally in a median sagittal position?

A. Mediastinum
B. Diaphragm
C. Pleural cavity
D. Thoracic cavity

Q.48

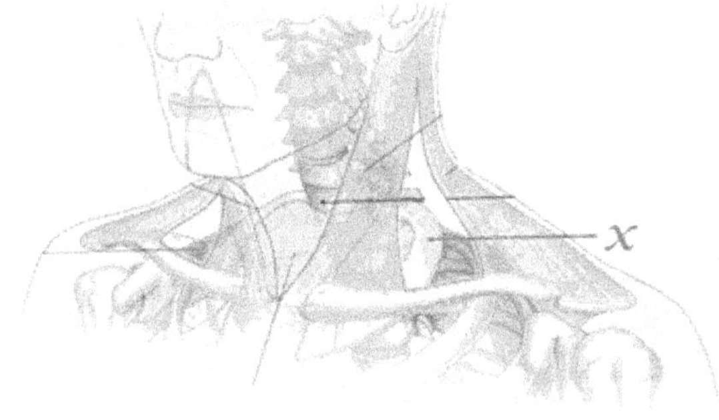

This picture shows the anterior and posterior triangles of the neck. What does 'X' indicate?

A. Anterior triangle   **B.** Posterior triangle
C. Trapezius   **D.** Axillary inlet

Q.49 Which of the following houses major elements of the gastrointestinal system?

A. Stomach   **B.** Abdomen   **C.** Kidneys   **D.** Bladder

Q.50 Where is the gut tube suspended from?

A. Posterior abdominal wall and partly from the anterior abdominal wall

B. Anterior abdominal wall and partly from the posterior abdominal wall

C. Thoracic wall and cavity

D. Musculotendinous diaphragm

Q.51

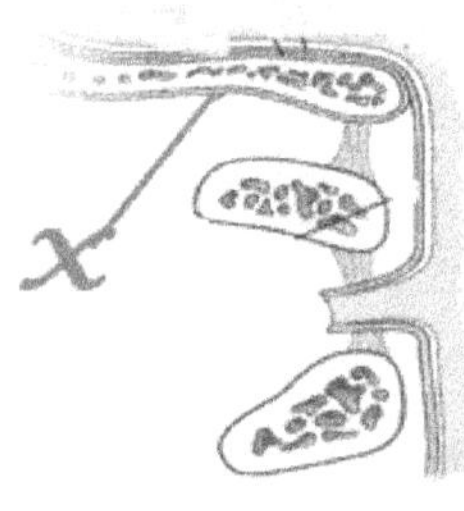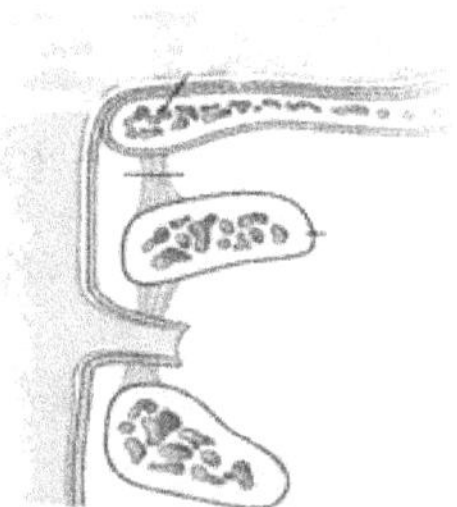

This picture shows cranial meninges. What does 'X' indicate?

A. Foramen magnum   **B.** Vertebral Column
C. Periosteum   **D.** Spinal dura mater

Q.52

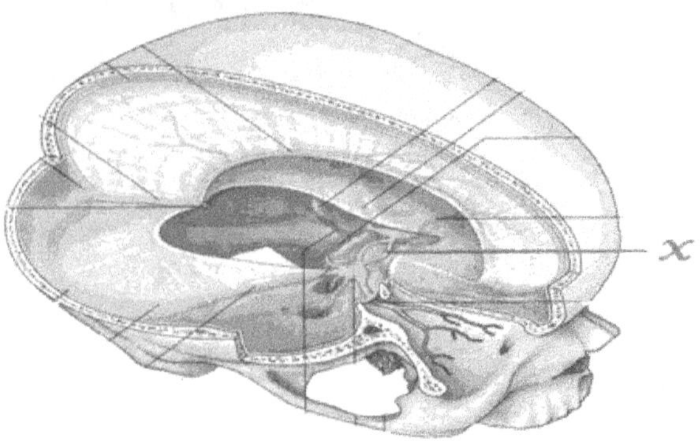

This picture shows the veins, meninges and dural venous sinuses. What does 'X' indicate?

A. Intercavernous sinus   **B.** Sphenoparietal sinus
C. Basilar sinus   **D.** Sigmoid sinus

Q.53 Which of the following is formed by the proximal regions of the thigh and by the inguinal ligament?

A. Popliteal fossa   **B.** Femoral triangle
C. Posteromedial side   **D.** None of these

Q.54 Which tissue is considered as most primitive both ontogenetically as well as phylogenetically?

A. Parenchyma   **B.** Collenchyma
C. Sclerenchyma   **D.** Aerenchyma

Q.55 Which of the following is/are associated with the lateral aspect of the lower portion of the neck?

A. Lower limbs   **B.** Upper limbs
C. Abdomen   **D.** Thorax

Q.56 Which of the following is changed by sliding and rotating the scapula on the thoracic wall?

A. Wrist joint   **B.** Elbow joint
C. Glenohumeral joint   **D.** Saddle joint

Q.57 Which is an acute phase reactant synthesized by the liver, which opsonizes invading pathogens?

A. Collagen   **B.** Cryoglobulins
C. C-reactive protein   **D.** T-lymphocytes

Q.58 Which of the following anti-depressant drugs is/are less cardiotoxic, less sedative, and has/have fewer anticholinergic effects than tricyclics?

A. Selective serotonin re-uptake inhibitors

B. Newer anti-depressants

C. Monoamine oxidase inhibitors

D. Moclobemide

Q.59 _________ bind metal ions and are used to treat, for example, iron and copper overload syndrome.

A. Chelating agents   **B.** Oxidizing agents
C. General anesthetics **D.** Enzymes

Q.60 In _______, asymmetry occurs all the centres of potential asymmetry (chiral centres).

A. Diastereomers   **B.** Enantiomers

C. Polymers   **D.** Non-polymers

Q.61 Some drugs are inactivated in the gut and need to be given parenterally, whereas others are removed by metabolism during absorption, or by enzymes in the gut and liver. This is called:

A. second-pass metabolism
B. first-pass metabolism
C. assimilation
D. absorption

Q.62 The main route drug excretion is by the kidney, where drugs are filtered at the _______ and reabsorbed or secreted by the renal tubules.

A. glomerulus   **B.** Bowman's capsule
C. nephron   **D.** bladder

Q.63 Abbreviation of EBM is:
A. Evidence-Based Medicine
B. Ethics Based Medicine
C. Electronic Based Medicine
D. Effect Based Medicine

Q.64 Benefit to drug therapy is often expressed as the so called _________, which is the number of patients who need to be treated in order to produce benefit.
A. evidence based medicine (EBM)
B. number needed to treat (NNT or NNT_B)
C. balance of benefit
D. pharmacokinetics

Q.65 NNT_H for one venous thromboembolism is:
A. 130   **B.** 143   **C.** 29   **D.** 17

Q.66 Which is directly involved in DNA and RNA synthesis and its requirements increase during embryonic development?
A. Niacin   **B.** Pyridoxine
C. Folate   **D.** Riboflavin

Q.67 All human cells are derived from the zygote (the fertilized) ovum, a single _______ stem cell capable of producing all cell types.
A. Totipotent   **B.** Multipotent
C. Solar potent   **D.** Energy potent

Q.68 The immune system has evolved to protect the _________ from pathogens while minimizing damage to the self tissue.
A. host   **B.** recipients
C. donors   **D.** antibodies

Q.69 The tightly packed highly _________ cells of the skin constantly undergo renewal and replacement which physically limits colonisation by microorganisms.
A. non-keratinised   **B.** keratinised
C. para keratinised   **D.** plasmolysed

Q.70

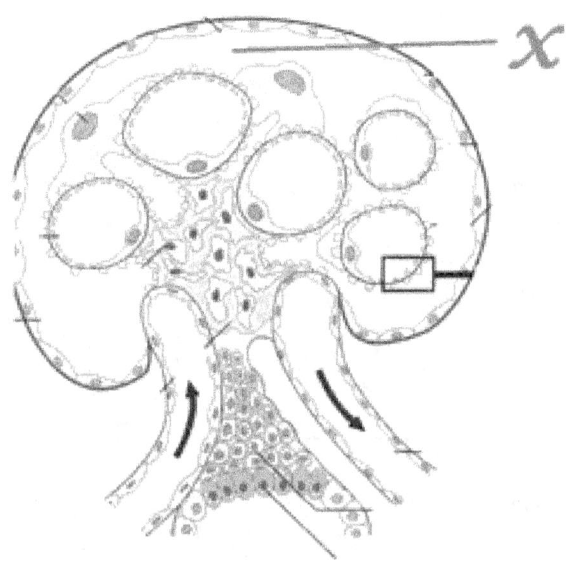

This is the schematic cross-section of a glomerulus. What does 'X' indicate?
A. Epithelial cell   **B.** Mesangial matrix
C. Urinary space   **D.** Macula densa

Q.71 Which vitamin is related to a cofactor in glycine metabolism?
A. Vit E   **B.** Thiamine
C. Folic acid   **D.** Cyanocobalamine

Q.72 Most of the vitamin B12 in the body is stored as:
A. Methyl B12   **B.** Hydroxy B12
C. Cyanocobalamine   **D.** None of the above

Q.73 Which vitamin is synthesized by intestinal Bacteria?
A. Vitamin B   **B.** Vitamin D
C. Vitamin E   **D.** Vitamin K

Q.74 Tryptophan load tests help in the evaluation of the deficiency of the vitamin:
A. Folic acid   **B.** Niacin
C. Pyridoxine   **D.** Cyanacobalamine

Q.75 The action of Vitamin K in the formatting of clotting factor is through:
A. Post transcription
B. Post translation
C. Golgi complex
D. Endoplasmic reticulum

Q.76 What disease is caused by Vitamin B1 deficiency?
A. Pellagra
B. Angular cheilitis
C. Megaloblastic anemia
D. Beriberi

Q.77 Vitamin C is present in largest amount in the body in:
A. Eye   **B.** Kidneys

C. Testes **D.** Adrenal Cortex

Q.78 Which of the following is the poorest source of Vitamin C?

A. Milk **B.** Guava **C.** Cabbage **D.** Radish

Q.79 The 3D's, Dermatitis, Diarrhea, Dementia are seen in the deficiency of:

A. Thiamine **B.** Riboflavin
C. Niacin **D.** Pyridoxine

Q.80 The maximum content of Vitamin E is present in:

A. Cod liver oil **B.** Fish liver oil
C. Wheat germ oil **D.** Liver

Q.81 Vitamin K deficiency is indicated by:

A. Low platelet count
B. Increased prothrombin time
C. Decreased prothrombin time
D. None of the above

Q.82 Collagen formation is affected in the deficiency of:

A. Vitamin B **B.** Vitamin C
C. Vitamin D **D.** Vitamin E

Q.83 Which vitamin is related to avidin?

A. Biotin **B.** Niacin
C. Thiamine **D.** Phylloquinone

Q.84 Coenzyme A contains which of the following Vitamins?

A. Biotin **B.** Pyridoxine
C. Pantothenic acid **D.** Niacin

Q.85 The cell membrane is also called ________.

A. epidermis **B.** plasma membrane
C. endoderm **D.** transmembrane

Q.86 Which of the following protect(s) the cell?

A. Glycocalyx **B.** Glycolipids
C. Golgi apparatus **D.** Phospholipids

Q.87 The process of ingestion of fluid or other small molecules is called ________.

A. phagocytosis **B.** pinocytosis
C. exocytosis **D.** endocytosis

Q.88 Which of the following contain(s) various structural elements like organelles, inclusions and cytoskeleton?

A. Cells **B.** Cytoplasm
C. Nucleus **D.** Golgi apparatus

Q.89 Which of the following is/are made up of microtubules and microfilaments?

A. Nuclei **B.** Cytoskeleton
C. Mitochondria **D.** Golgi bodies

Q.90 What is RER?

A. Rough Endoplasmic Reticulum
B. Rich Endoplasmic Reticulum
C. Reverse Endoplasmic Reticulum
D. Rejecting Endoplasmic Reticulum

Q.91 The convex surface of ______ is called forming face.

A. cytoplasm **B.** Golgi complex
C. nucleus **D.** mitochondria

Q.92 In mitochondria, the inner membrane is arranged in a series of folds called

A. matrix granules
B. cristae
C. ribonucleoprotein particles
D. elementary particles

Q.93 The process of digesting the old organelles of cytosol and returning the digested components again to the cytosol is called:

A. Heterophagy **B.** Autophagy
C. Autolysis **D.** Catalase

Q.94 Which of the following is the basic tissue of the body?

A. Basement membrane
B. Epithelium
C. Intercellular contact
D. Glandular epithelia

Q.95 Which of the following tissues lines serous membrane?

A. Stratified epithelium **B.** Endothelium
C. Mesothelium **D.** Urothelium

Q.96 In which process of secretion is the whole cell shed along with secretory product?

A. Apocrine **B.** Holocrine
C. Merocrine **D.** Connexons

Q.97

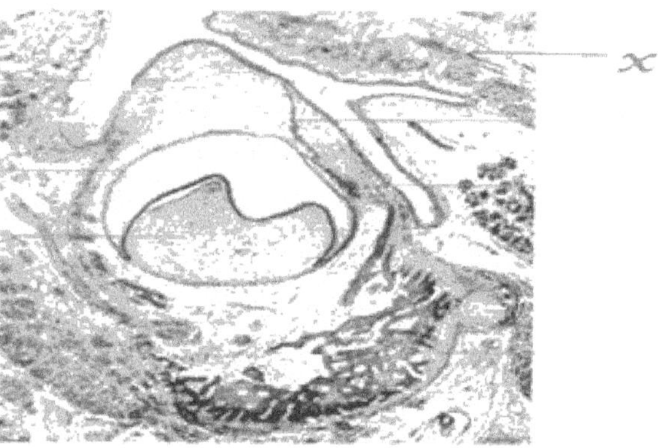

This is the diagram of the advanced bell stage of tooth development of human embryo. What does 'X' indicate?

A. Dental lamina **B.** Dental papilla
C. Tongue **D.** Dental ridge

Q.98

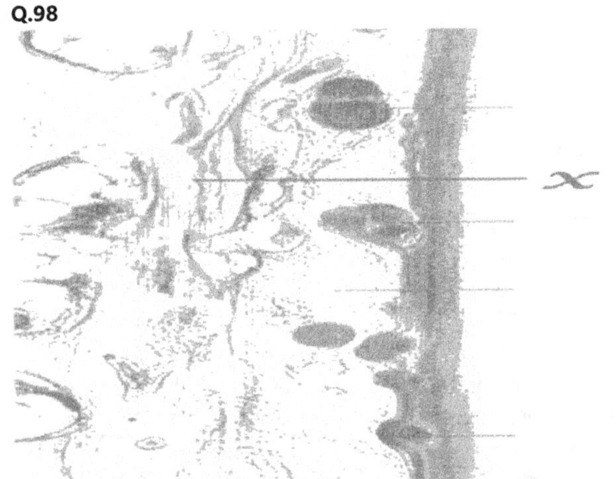

This is the cementicles in the periodontal ligament. What does 'X' indicate?

A. Free cementicle
B. Alveolar bone
C. Attached cementicle
D. Periodontal ligament

Q.99 The cytosol of a cell at rest is _____ relative to the extracellular fluid.

A. electro-positive
B. electro-negative
C. neutral
D. None of the above

Q.100 The steady-state properties of the mixture of permeant and im-permeant ions are described by which of the following?

A. Nernst equation
B. Electrochemical equilibrium
C. Gibbs-Donnan equilibrium
D. Maxwell equations

Part B

Q.101 Which of the following postulated that health prevailed when the four humors - phlegm, yellow bile, blood and black bile - were in equilibrium?

A. Indian medicine
B. Chinese medicine
C. Greek medicine
D. Egyptian medicine

Q.102 Which of the following is termed as any loss or abnormality of physiological, psychological, or anatomical structure or function?

A. Impairment
B. Disability
C. Handicap
D. Rehabilitation

Q.103 Screening for oral cancer comes under which level of prevention?

A. Secondary level
B. Tertiary level
C. Primary level
D. None of these

Q.104 The ratio of the number of new cases of a specific disease during a specified time interval in a population to the total population at risk during the same time interval and the whole is multiplied by 100 is known as:

A. Incidence
B. Attack rate
C. Prevalence
D. Point prevalence

Q.105 Which of the following represents the ratio of $\dfrac{\text{The incidence of disease (or deaths) among exposed}}{\text{Incidence of disease (or death) among non-exposed}}$?

A. Attributable risk
B. Population risk
C. Relative risk
D. Bias

Q.106 DDT concentration in water should **not** exceed

A. 2 mg/litre
B. 3 mg/litre
C. 4 mg/litre
D. 5 mg/litre

Q.107 Which of the following is the surface of each unit of filter bed?

A. 80 to 90 m^2
B. 90 to 100 m^2
C. 70 to 80 m^2
D. 60 to 80 m^2

Q.108 Which of the following is a supplement and **not** a substitute to sand filtration?

A. Sulphonation
B. Chlorination
C. Oxidation
D. De-oxidation

Q.109 Which of the following is called high test hypochlorite?

A. Chloramine
B. Chlorine gas
C. Perchloron
D. Chloride

Q.110 Which of the following is a powerful oxidizing agent?

A. Chlorine
B. Ozone
C. Graphite
D. Deuterium

Q.111 Which of the following is correct about sullage?

A. It is waste water which also contains human excreta.
B. It is waste water which does not contain human excreta.
C. It is waste water which contains liquid excreta from houses.
D. It is waste water that contains animal excreta.

Q.112 Which of the following is an easy method for disposal of dry refuse and is also suitable for reclamation of land?

A. Dumping
B. Incineration
C. Composting
D. Burial

Q.113 Which of the following is a high temperature dry oxidation process in waste handling?

A. Transportation of waste
B. Incineration
C. Storage
D. Burial

Q.114 Which of the following chemical disinfectants inactivates microorganisms?

A. Ethylene oxide
B. Sodium hypochlorite
C. Glutaraldehyde
D. Formaldehyde

Q.115 Where are mamelons present?

A. Occlusal edges
B. Incisal edges
C. Lingual edges
D. Canine corners

Q.116 Which of the following growths terminates when adult maturity is attained and/or growth ceases?

A. Postnatal growth
B. Prenatal growth
C. Embryonal period
D. Foetal period

Q.117 Which of the following disappears by 24th week of intrauterine life?

A. Prenatal growth of mandible
B. Meckel's cartilage
C. Postnatal growth of mandible
D. Craniofacial growth

Q.118 Which of the following methods is used to study soft tissues?

A. Craniometry
B. Cephalometry
C. X-ray cephalometry
D. Metal indicator

Q.119 In which of the following is a cap formed due to uneven growth in different parts of the bud?

A. Initiation stage
B. Proliferation stage
C. Apposition stage
D. Calcification and maturation

Q.120 Cycas and Adiantum resemble each other in:

A. Seeds
B. Motile sperms
C. Cambium
D. Vessels

Q.121 Which of the following includes emergence of permanent canines, premolars and second permanent molars and establishment of permanent occlusion?

A. Inter-transitional stage
B. Late transitional stage
C. Permanent dentition stage
D. Pre-eruptive stage

Q.122 Which of the following procedures involves filling containers made of high density polyethylene or metal drums with waste?

A. Encapsulation
B. Safe burying
C. Inertisation
D. Microwave irradiation

Q.123 Which of the following is the degree to which the message is perceived as trustworthy by the receiver?

A. Interest
B. Participation
C. Motivation
D. Credibility

Q.124 Which of the following principles refers to repetition needed in health education?

A. Reinforcement
B. Comprehension
C. Motivation
D. Participation

Q.125 Which of the following is the stage in which an individual decides to put a new idea or method into practice?

A. Stage of evaluation
B. Stage of trial
C. Stage of unawareness
D. Stage of adoption

Q.126 Which of the following refers to the flow of information from the audience to the sender?

A. Message
B. Receiver
C. Feedback
D. Sender

Q.127 Which of the following is the principle that dictates that health care professionals respect a patient's right to make decisions concerning the treatment plan?

A. Ethical principle
B. Autonomy
C. Justice
D. Truthfulness

Q.128 What is jurisprudence?

A. Study and theory of law
B. Study and theory of medicine
C. Study and theory of physics
D. Study and theory of dentistry

Q.129 Some clinicians advise giving no more than 4 ml of a local anaesthetic solution with a __________ concentration of epinephrine for a total adult dose of 0.04 mg in any 30 minute period.

A. 1 : 10
B. 1 : 1000
C. 1 : 100,000
D. 1 : 100

Q.130 If the _______ has been successful (based on cardiac stress testing), oral surgery can proceed soon thereafter, with the same precautions as those used for patients with angina.

A. angiogram
B. angioplasty
C. orthopnea
D. percussion

Q.131 Which of the following patients should be treated by a non-pharmacologic anxiety-reduction protocol and have vital signs carefully monitored during surgery?

A. Patients who have had a myocardium
B. Patients who have had a cerebrovascular accident (stroke)
C. Patients who have angina
D. Patients who have a coronary heart disease

Q.132 Pacemakers pose _________ to local surgery and no evidence exists that shows the need for antibiotic prophylaxis in patients with pacemakers.

A. contraindications
B. no contraindications
C. acceptance
D. rejection

Q.133 _________ is a respiratory disorder that exhibits shortness of breath when the patient is in supine position.

A. Angina
B. Paroxysmal nocturnal dyspnea
C. Orthopnea
D. Ankle edema

Q.134 Removal of tissue from a living individual for diagnostic purposes is called:

A. Autopsy
B. Biopsy
C. Cytology
D. Aspiration

Q.135 In renal failure, which of the following is best undertaken the day after a dialysis treatment has been performed?

A. Corticosteroid therapy
B. Radio therapy
C. Chemotherapy
D. Elective oral surgery

Q.136 Chronically elevated blood pressure for which the cause is unknown is called:

A. Mild hypertension
B. Essential hypertension
C. Acute hypertension
D. Chronic hypertension

Q.137 Elective oral surgery for patients with severe hypertension, that is ____ should be postponed until the pressure is better controlled.

A. systolic pressure of 180 mm Hg or more or diastolic pressure of 110 mm Hg or more

B. systolic pressure of 100 mm Hg or more or diastolic pressure of 180 mm Hg or more

C. systolic pressure of 200 mm Hg or more or diastolic pressure of 110 mm Hg or more

D. systolic pressure of 160 mm Hg or more or diastolic pressure of 100 mm Hg or more

Q.138 The production of which of the following vitamins dependent on coagulation factors (II, VII, IX, X) may be depressed in severe liver disease?

A. Vitamin A   B. Vitamin B_{12}

C. Vitamin K   D. Vitamin C

Q.139 Insulin-dependent diabetes, is associated with

A. Hypotension   B. Headache

C. Hyperglycemia   D. None of these

Q.140

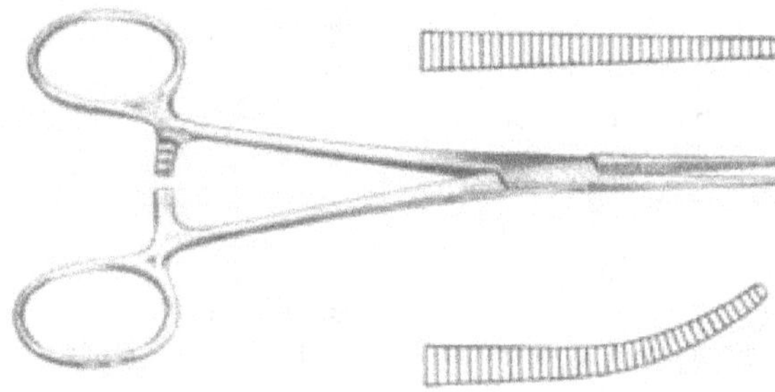

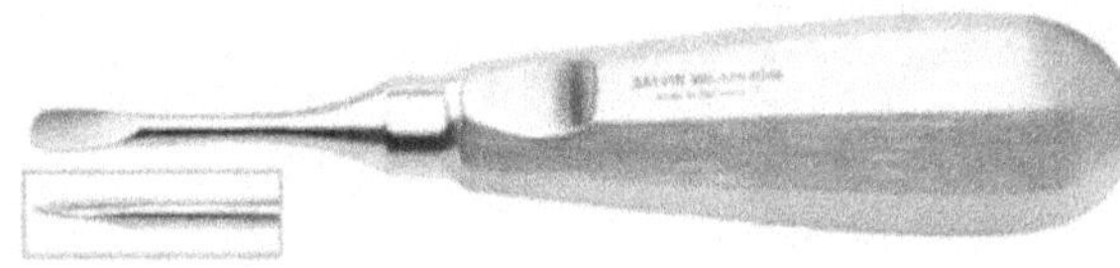

Which of the following surgical tools is illustrated in this picture?

A. Needle holder   B. Hemostat

C. Mallet   D. Rongeurs

Q.141

What is the name of this tool?

A. Straight elevator

B. Straight handle

C. Extraction forceps

D. English style of forceps

Q.142

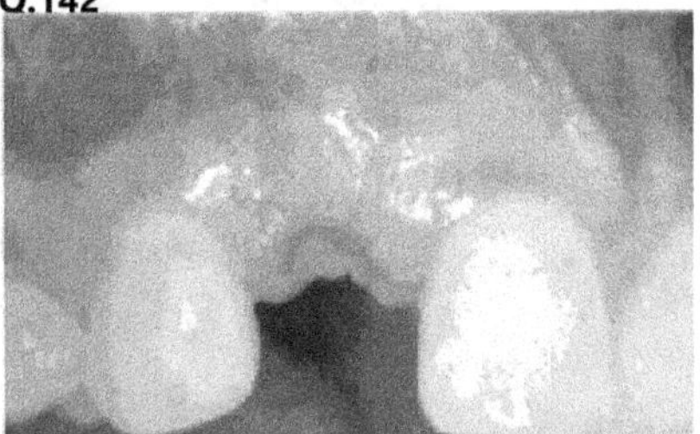

Which of the following treatments is recommended for this patient?

A. Soft tissue incision

B. Interim prosthesis

C. Atraumatic extraction

D. Prosthetics

Q.143 Which of the following carry the odontoblast process?

A. Dentinal tubules

B. Enamel tufts

C. Collagen fibres

D. Undifferentiated mesenchymal cells

Q.144 Which of the following are important guides in occlusion?

A. Incisors   B. Canines

C. Premolars   D. Molars

Q.145 Which of the following result(s) in irritation and trauma to the attachment apparatus?

A. Overcontoured restorations

B. Un-contoured restorations

C. Proximal contact area

D. Proximal contours of the teeth adjacent to the contact area

Q.146 Which of the following represents the gelatinous mass of bacteria adhering to the tooth surface?

A. Dental plaque   B. Dental caries

C. Time   D. Diet

Q.147 Which enamel lesion zone lies deeper to the body of the lesion?

A. Surface zone   B. Body of the lesion

C. Dark zone   D. Translucent zone

Q.148

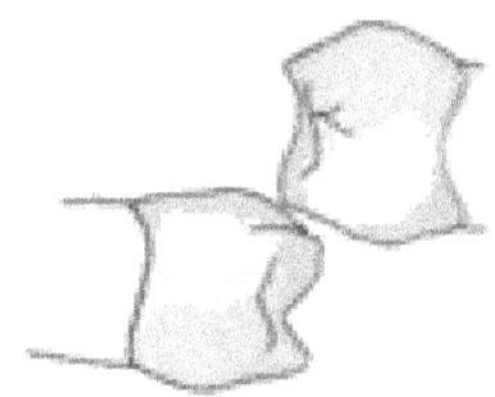

Which of the following represents this crossbite?

A. Normal   **B.** Facial crossbite
C. Lingual crossbite   **D.** Edge to edge bite

Q.149

Which of the following is depicted through this picture?

A. Contra angle micromotor handpiece
B. Contra angle airotor handpiece
C. Straight handpiece
D. Dental bur

Q.150 Which treatment is used to treat both types of acute irreversible pulpitis?

A. Palliative procedures
B. Pulpectomy
C. Endodontic treatment
D. Palpation

Q.151 To complete the emergency treatment of an acute alveolar abscess, which number of the blade is used?

A. 10   **B.** 12   **C.** 25   **D.** 16

Q.152 Which endodontic emergency procedure is often mistaken for an acute alveolar abscess?

A. Acute reversible pulpitis
B. Acute irreversible pulpitis
C. Acute alveolar abscess
D. Acute periodontal abscess

Q.153 The result of trauma to an anterior tooth of a child or young adult causes:

A. edentulous space   **B.** tooth avulsion
C. fractured root   **D.** caries

Q.154 Which of the following are the pain relievers?

A. Antibiotics   **B.** Antipyretics
C. Analgesics   **D.** Astringents

Q.155 Which of the following is used to increase cellular density?

A. Palatal shelf   **B.** Vestibule
C. Ectomesenchyme   **D.** Endo-mesenchyme

Q.156

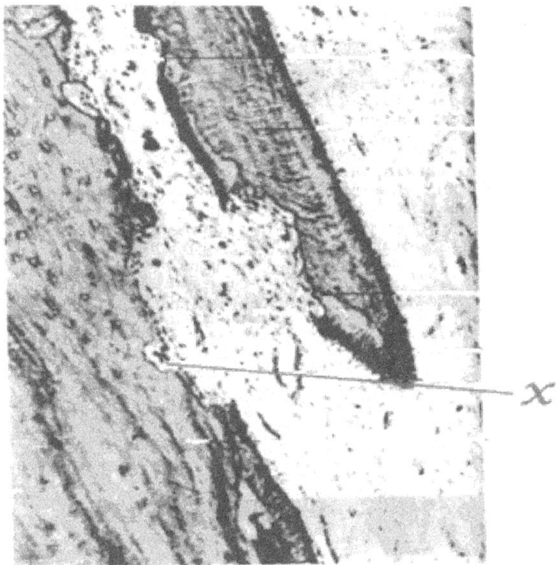

This is the picture of the periodontal ligament. What does 'X' indicate?

A. New bone apposition
B. Howship's lacunae
C. Cementum
D. Reversal line

Q.157 Which of the following gingivae is a shallow crevice or space around the tooth and is bounded by the surface of tooth on one side?

A. Marginal gingiva   **B.** Gingival sulcus
C. Attached gingiva   **D.** Interdental gingiva

Q.158 Which of the following processes involves keratinisation?

A. Proliferation   **B.** Differentiation
C. Accommodation   **D.** Protrusion

Q.159 Which of the following gingival epithelia is formed by the confluence of the oral epithelium and the reduced enamel epithelium during tooth eruption?

A. Sulcular epithelium
B. Junctional epithelium
C. Marginal epithelium
D. Interdental epithelium

Q.160 Which of the following is the preponderant cellular element in the gingival connective tissue?

A. Ameloblast   **B.** Fibroblast
C. Odontoblast   **D.** Pre-odontoblast

Q.161 Which of the following is the principle fibre?

A. Periodontal ligament
B. Odontoblast
C. Ameloblast
D. Pre-odontoblast

Q.162 Which of the following principal fibre groups radiate in a rather irregular region of the socket?

A. Interradicular group **B.** Apical group
C. Oblique group **D.** Horizontal group

Q.163 Which of the following are called cementicles?

A. Calcified masses **B.** Calcified stones
C. Calcified fibres **D.** Calcified fluids

Q.164 Which of the following is the most common gingival disease?

A. Gingivitis that is associated with dental plaque
B. Gingivitis that is associated with dental caries
C. Gingivitis that is associated with dental cavity
D. Gingivitis that is associated with dental occlusion trauma

Q.165 What is acquired pellicle?

A. Saliva-derived layer after polishing
B. Saliva dried layer
C. Dry mouth
D. Most wetted layer of saliva

Q.166 Which of the following perio-pathogens indicate/s a non-motile, spindle-shaped, highly pleomorphic rod and Gram-negative obligate anaerobe?

A. Actinobacillus actinomycetem-comitans
B. Tannerella forsythia
C. Porphyromonas gingivalis
D. Prevotella intermedia and prevotella nigrescens

Q.167 Which of the following rare motile organisms is involved in periodontitis?

A. Campylobacter rectus
B. Fusobacterium nucleatum
C. Eubacterium species
D. Peptostreptococcus micros

Q.168 Which of the following types of trauma results in gingival recession with denudation of the root surface?

A. Acute tooth brush trauma
B. Chronic tooth brush trauma
C. Occlusion trauma
D. None of these

Q.169

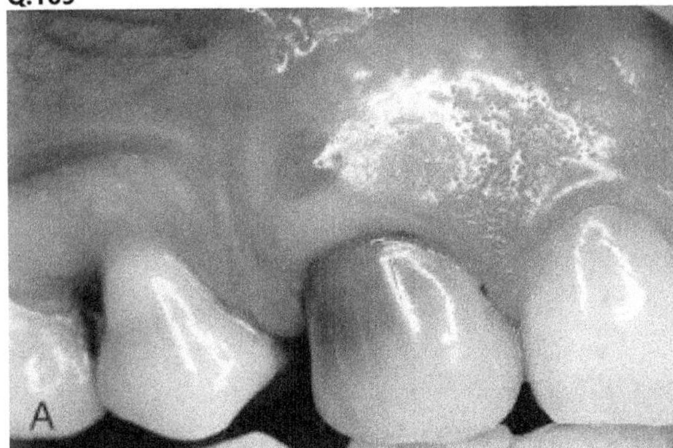

Which of the following is indicated through this picture?

A. Fistula **B.** Lesions
C. Plaque **D.** Acute abscess

Q.170

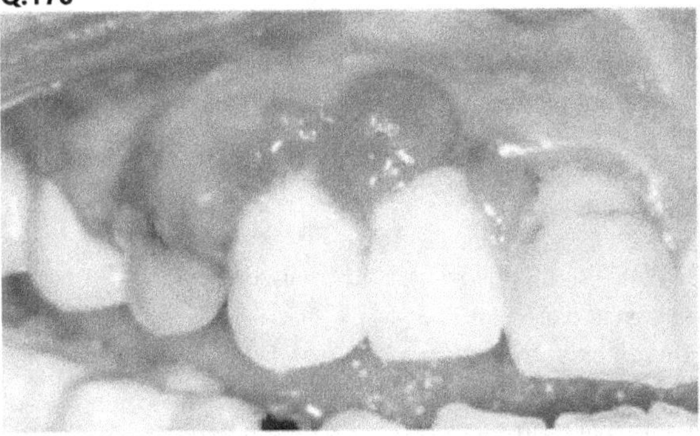

This is a picture of pyogenic granulomas. It will mostly affect:

A. Pregnant women
B. Elderly men
C. Non-pregnant women
D. Children

Q.171 Which of the following is a folic acid?

A. Vitamin B **B.** Vitamin C
C. Vitamin D **D.** Vitamin K

Q.172 Which of the following is an autosomal dominant syndrome?

A. Van der woude syndrome
B. Sjogren's syndrome
C. Beckwith Wiedemann syndrome
D. Behcet's syndrome

Q.173 Which gland develops in the embryo from the ventral floor of the pharynx by means of an endodermal invagination or diverticulum?

A. Thymus **B.** Thyroid **C.** Adrenal **D.** Pituitary

Q.174 Which of the following is an uncommon idiopathic condition that presents with isolated or grouped plaques in the skin of the head and neck?

A. Lymphoid hamartoma
B. Angio-lymphoid hyperplasia with eosinophilia
C. Lingual varices
D. Lympho-epithelial cyst

Q.175 Which of the following terms refers to angulation or a sharp bend or curve in the root or crown of a formed tooth?

A. Dilaceration **B.** Concrescence
C. Gemination **D.** Talon cusp

Q.176 Which of the following develop from the third tooth bud arising from the dental lamina near the permanent tooth bud?

A. Turner's teeth
B. Supernumerary teeth
C. Abutments
D. Wisdom teeth

Q.177 Which of the following is a sensitive type of cell and easily damaged?

A. Cytoblast

C. Ameloblast

B. Endoblast

D. Odontoblast

Q.178 In the impacted mandibular third molars, which impaction position shows that the crown is in contact with the distal surface of the root or crown of the second molar?

A. Mesio-angular impaction

B. Disto-angular impaction

C. Vertical impaction

D. Horizontal impaction

Q.179 Which of the following is a rare fissural cyst?

A. Palatal and alveolar cyst

B. Thyroglossal tract cyst

C. Nasoalveolar cyst

D. Epidermal inclusion cyst

Q.180 Heterotopic islands of gastric mucosa have been found in the:

A. esophagus

C. urinary bladder

B. large intestine

D. spleen

Q.181 Which of the following represents a reactive phenomenon of the epithelium rather than true neoplasm?

A. Keratoacanthoma

B. Squamous acanthoma

C. Squamous papilloma

D. Oral nevi

Q.182 Mottled enamel is produced by:

A. Syphilis

C. Fluorine

B. Febrile diseases

D. Acids

Q.183 Which of the following is an abnormality of the buccal mucosa that clinically resembles early leukoplakia?

A. Leukoplakia

C. Leukoedema

B. Palatal erythema

D. Erythroplakia

Q.184 Which of the following is a chronic, progressive, scarring disease, that predominantly affects people of South East Asia Origin?

A. Oral lichen planus

B. Oral submucous fibrosis

C. Basal cell carcinoma

D. Epidermoid carcinoma

Q.185 The rate of expression of macroglossia in phenotypes of Beckwith-Wiedemann syndrome is:

A. 0.07 per 1000 live births

B. 0.08 per 1000 live births

C. 0.01 per 1000 live births

D. 0.05 per 1000 live births

Q.186 Dr. Angle described his edge-wise appliance as which of the following?

A. Latest and best in orthodontics

B. Bone growing appliance

C. Both of the above

D. None of the above

Q.187 Who cemented a band on teeth for the first time?

A. Magill   **B.** Case   **C.** Angle   **D.** Bourand

Q.188 Which of the following statements is correct regarding the size of the face at birth and adulthood?

A. The face forms 2/3rd the bulk of head whereas in an adult, it forms 1/3rd of the bulk.

B. The face forms 1/2 the bulk of the head throughout the life.

C. The face forms 1/3rd the bulk of the head whereas in an adult, it forms 1/8th of the bulk.

D. The face forms only 1/8th of bulk of head whereas in an adult, it forms 1/3rd to 1/2 of the bulk.

Q.189 Hard palate begins to develop:

A. 4th week in utero

C. 8th week in utero

B. 6th week in utero

D. 10th week in utero

Q.190 A child at 7 and $\frac{1}{2}$ years of age receives an extended course of tetracycline. Clinical crowns of which of the following teeth are likely to show discolouration?

A. Only premolars are affected

B. Only incisors and first molars

C. No teeth will be discoloured to an aesthetically objection degree

D. All permanent teeth will be discoloured

Q.191 Which of the following positions will the permanent mandibular incisor buds be relative to primary incisors?

A. Inferior and lingual

C. Superior and lingual

B. Inferior and buccal

D. Superior and facial

Q.192 Roux and others have proposed which of the following?

A. Law of transformation of bone

B. Law of bone loading

C. Law of orthogonality

D. Trajectorial theory

Q.193 Which of the following portal reflexes are of greatest significance to orthodontics?

A. Sucking and rooting reflex

B. Rooting, swallowing, and swallowing reflex

C. Sucking and pharyngeal space maintenance

D. Swallowing and pharyngeal space maintenance

Q.194 Dental arch form is ultimately determined by:

A. facial type

B. angle classification

C. facial growth pattern

D. balance between facial and intra-oral muscles

Q.195 Functional pseudo-overbite is caused by the supra-eruption of which of the following?

A. Incisors

C. Canines

B. Molars

D. Premolars

Q.196 The majority of malocclusion seems to be:

A. class II with deep bite

B. class II with proclined incisors

C. class III with anterior open bite

D. class I with crowding

Q.197 Which of the following is represented by the outer envelope in Ackerman and Proffit's classification?

A. Profile
B. Alignment
C. Vertical relation
D. Transverse relation

Q.198 Which of the following appliances is used to treat thumb sucking?

A. Bionator
B. Crib appliance
C. Activator
D. Frankel appliance

Q.199 Observational theory was put forward by:

A. Skinner   **B.** Bandura   **C.** Maslow   **D.** Mahler

Q.200 Which of the following salivary glands alter the facial contour and may lift the ear lobe?

A. Parotid glands
B. Submandibular glands
C. Sublingual glands
D. Minor salivary glands

Q.201 Which of the following instruments is used to examine the ocular fundus directly for lesions?

A. Statoscope
B. Sphygmomanometer
C. Ophthalmoscope
D. Glucometer

Q.202 Which of the following cranial nerves functions includes both cochlear and vestibular components?

A. Cranial II
B. Cranial VI
C. Cranial VII
D. Cranial VIII

Q.203 The _______ transmits sensory information to your brain regarding smells that you encounter.

A. optic nerve
B. ocular nerve
C. olfactory nerve
D. facial nerve

Q.204 Which of the following herpes viruses cause oral mucosa disease?

A. HSV1 and HSV2
B. HHV-8 and HHV-7
C. HHV6A and HHV6B
D. HHV6 and HHV7

Q.205 Which of the following is an excellent topical anesthetic for oral mucosa?

A. Aspirin
B. Acetaminophen
C. Dyclonine hydrochloride
D. Cetrizine

Q.206 Delayed hypersensitivity causes which of the following?

A. Acute necrotising ulcerative gingivitis
B. Oral ulcers
C. Contact allergic stomatitis
D. Recurrent aphthous stomatitis

Q.207 Which of the following is a muco-cutaneous autoimmune blistering disease?

A. Sub-epithelial bullous dermatoses
B. Mucous membrane pemphigoid
C. Pemphigus vegetans
D. Pemphigus vulgaris

Q.208 In which of the following imaging modalities techniques is energy added to the system in the form of RF pulses and equilibrium is destabilised?

A. Computed tomography
B. Magnetic resonance imaging
C. Ultrasonography
D. Conventional tomography

Q.209 Which of the following is contraindicated for patients, including those with demand type cardiac pacemakers, due to interference by electrical and magnetic fields?

A. Computed tomography
B. Magnetic resonance imaging
C. Ultrasonography
D. Conventional tomography

Q.210 Arthrography and sialography are used in dentistry under

A. nuclear medicine
B. ultrasonography
C. contrast enhanced radiography
D. computed radiography

Q.211 Which of the following imaging techniques do/does **not** carry some types of radio-biologic risk?

A. US and MRI
B. Conventional tomography
C. Computed tomography
D. Contrast enhanced radiography

Q.212 Single-photon emission computed tomography is used to localize and qualify.

A. disk position
B. bone
C. ligament tear
D. dentinal tear

Q.213 Which of the following are used to evaluate disc position with respect to the head of condyle?

A. Frontal images
B. Sagittal images
C. Transverse images
D. Axial images

Q.214 How much does an MRI cost (per examination)?

A. $100   **B.** $1000   **C.** $1500   **D.** $2000

Q.215 Which of the following is the branch of dental art and science that deals with the replacement of missing teeth and oral tissues to restore and maintain oral form, function, appearance and health?

A. Prosthodontics
B. Prosthesis
C. Prosthetics
D. Prosthetikos

Q.216 Three major divisions of prosthodontics are:

A. fixed prosthodontics, removable prosthodontics and maxillofacial prosthodontics
B. fixed prosthodontics, removable prosthodontics and implant prosthodontics
C. removable complete prosthodontics, removable partial prosthodontics and fixed prosthodontics
D. complete denture prosthetics, removable prosthetics and fixed prosthetics

Q.217 A rest contacts the surface of the _____ to prevent movement of the removable partial denture towards the underlying tissues.

A. minor connector **B.** major connector

C. clasp **D.** abutment tooth

Q.218 Which of the following joins the components on one side of the arch with those on the opposite side?

A. Minor connector **B.** Major connector

C. Clasp **D.** Abutment tooth

Q.219 Which of the following statements is true?

A. Patrix is the first component and matrix is the second component of the intracoronal direct retainers

B. Matrix is the first component and patrix is the second component of the intracoronal direct retainers.

C. Matrix is the first component and patrix is the second component of the intracoronal indirect retainers.

D. Patrix is the first component and matrix is the second component of the intracoronal indirect retainers.

Q.220 If components are fabricated in metal using high-precision manufacturing techniques, then the intracoronal retainers are considered:

A. precision attachment

B. protrusion attachment

C. lingual attachment

D. All of these

Q.221 The intersection of any two planes forms a:

A. Vertical axis **B.** Linear axis

C. Frontal axis **D.** Horizontal axis

Q.222 Which of the following are the three types of axes corresponding to the three planes?

A. Transverse, vertical and sagittal axes

B. Transverse, horizontal and sagittal axes

C. Frontal, vertical and sagittal axes

D. Transverse, vertical and frontal axes

Q.223 Information must be obtained from patient interviews, radiographic evaluation, __________ and appropriate consultations with medical and dental specialists.

A. Oral examination

B. Diagnostic mounting of casts

C. Preliminary survey and design procedures

D. All of the above

Q.224 Too often, the design of a removable partial denture is determined after all other phases of patient treatment have been:

A. cured **B.** completed

C. diagnosed **D.** None of the above

Q.225 The primary objective of a diagnostic mounting procedure is to properly position the diagnostic casts on a:

A. dental arch **B.** dental articulator

C. dental implant **D.** cast stop

Q.226 Diagnostic mounting procedure is divided into how many phases?

A. Two phases **B.** Three phases

C. Four phases **D.** None of the above

Q.227

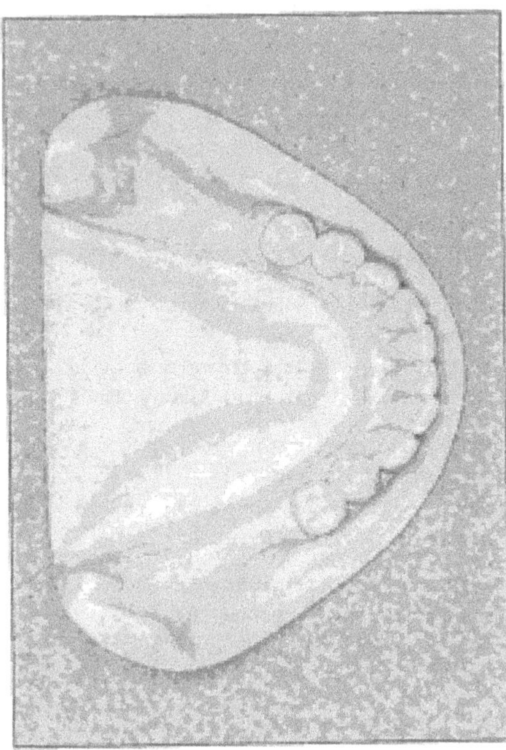

Which of the following Kennedy class arches is indicated through this diagram?

A. Mandibular Kennedy class I arch

B. Mandibular Kennedy class II arch

C. Mandibular Kennedy class III arch

D. Mandibular Kennedy class IV arch

Q.228

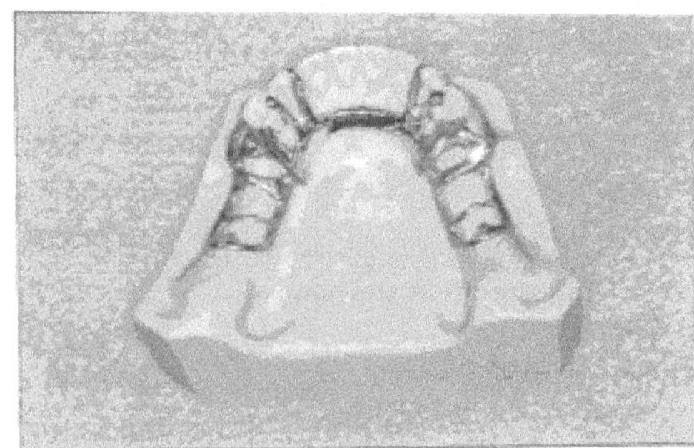

Which of the following is illustrated through this diagram?

A. Labial bar major connector

B. Lingual bar major connector

C. Palatal bar major connector

D. Lingual plate major connector

Q.229 The term "trituration means":

A. Lysing amalgam alloy
B. Mixing of amalgam alloy and mercury
C. Removal of the excess mercury
D. None of the above

Q.230 Dynamic creep is the:
A. Continuing alloying between Silver-T in alloy and mercury
B. Deformation of set amalgam during the function
C. Process whereby alloy is wetted by mercury
D. Spread of amalgam during packing

Q.231 The highest concentration in amalgam filling is found:
A. At the margin of the restoration
B. In the centre of the restoration
C. In the deepest part of the restoration
D. None of the above

Q.232 The dental amalgam is most resistant to:
A. Compressive stress
B. Impact stress
C. Shear stress
D. Tensile stress

Q.233 The proportional limit is defined as:
A. The maximum stress in a structure
B. The minimum force required to cause a structure to break
C. The maximum stress that can be induced without permanent deformation
D. The maximum elongation under tension that can be measured before failure

Q.234 The modulus of elasticity is defined as:
A. The stress at the proportional limit
B. The strain at the proportional limit
C. The stress/strain ratio within proportional limit
D. None of the above

Q.235 The point at which stress of a material exhibits a specific limited deviation P is called:
A. Proportional limit
B. Tensile strength
C. Ultimate strength
D. Yield strength

Q.236 Hardness number which does not depend upon the ductility of metal is:
A. Knoop Hardness Number (KHN)
B. Vicker's Hardness Number (VHN)
C. Rockwell Hardness Number (RHN)
D. Brinells Hardness Number (BHN)

Q.237 Ability of an orthodontic wire to spring back to its original shape is evaluated by:
A. Brittleness
B. Resilience
C. Tensile strength
D. Toughness

Q.238 Ultimate tensile strength refers to:
A. Stress before rupture
B. Shear strain
C. Longitudinal compressive strength
D. Horizontal compressive strength

Q.239 When solid gets wet completely, contact angle is:
A. 90 degrees
B. 0 degree
C. 0 - 90 degrees
D. Greater than 90 degrees

Q.240 Property of the material which describes the resistance to abrasion is:
A. Hardness
B. Yield strength
C. Modulus of elasticity
D. None of the above

// Smart Answer Sheet //

Correct — Indicates percentage of students who answered questions correctly.

Skipped — Indicates percentage of students who skipped questions.

Q.	Ans.	Correct / Skipped
1	B	17.27 % / 22.33 %
2	D	14.08 % / 18.04 %
3	B	11.55 % / 30.8 %
4	A	37.4 % / 24.21 %
5	A	22.77 % / 35.65 %
6	A	31.13 % / 37.08 %
7	B	15.18 % / 29.48 %
8	D	32.78 % / 36.64 %
9	C	11.66 % / 33.0 %
10	A	38.83 % / 36.86 %
11	B	23.43 % / 31.25 %
12	D	58.42 % / 26.07 %
13	D	17.16 % / 33.34 %
14	C	14.52 % / 22.11 %
15	B	18.26 % / 33.56 %
16	D	19.25 % / 25.85 %

Q.	Ans.	Correct / Skipped
17	B	35.09 % / 25.42 %
18	B	17.6 % / 37.41 %
19	C	22.77 % / 33.89 %
20	D	16.83 % / 5.06 %
21	C	20.24 % / 22.33 %
22	A	39.71 % / 19.48 %
23	B	7.59 % / 34.1 %
24	D	13.64 % / 10.89 %
25	B	15.29 % / 35.43 %
26	B	17.49 % / 37.08 %
27	A	24.75 % / 34.0 %
28	D	38.5 % / 17.39 %
29	A	18.04 % / 37.41 %
30	A	61.39 % / 20.35 %
31	A	62.6 % / 29.81 %
32	A	14.74 % / 26.29 %

Q.	Ans.	Correct / Skipped
33	C	64.58 % / 24.86 %
34	D	11.22 % / 13.75 %
35	B	38.83 % / 34.0 %
36	A	18.15 % / 26.51 %
37	A	32.23 % / 25.86 %
38	B	30.03 % / 37.08 %
39	C	33.77 % / 31.47 %
40	B	30.36 % / 36.97 %
41	B	29.59 % / 33.78 %
42	B	49.17 % / 20.91 %
43	A	38.06 % / 33.89 %
44	B	58.53 % / 24.31 %
45	A	23.54 % / 35.98 %
46	A	35.86 % / 21.9 %
47	A	23.54 % / 34.33 %
48	B	33.99 % / 27.07 %

Q.	Ans.	Correct / Skipped
49	B	32.45 % / 35.76 %
50	A	8.14 % / 37.51 %
51	C	22.55 % / 31.47 %
52	A	33.22 % / 24.43 %
53	B	30.25 % / 22.78 %
54	A	24.2 % / 37.19 %
55	B	30.69 % / 30.26 %
56	C	23.87 % / 27.29 %
57	C	29.48 % / 36.2 %
58	A	13.75 % / 37.08 %
59	A	42.13 % / 30.37 %
60	B	17.27 % / 27.83 %
61	B	37.4 % / 23.33 %
62	A	28.05 % / 37.41 %
63	A	48.07 % / 31.58 %
64	B	16.61 % / 28.05 %

Q.	Ans.	Correct / Skipped
65	A	6.49 % / 36.74 %
66	C	25.63 % / 37.3 %
67	A	46.31 % / 30.81 %
68	A	43.89 % / 36.75 %
69	B	30.91 % / 36.64 %
70	C	10.45 % / 37.18 %
71	C	13.2 % / 35.2 %
72	A	16.94 % / 15.95 %
73	D	31.68 % / 23.88 %
74	C	12.65 % / 37.52 %
75	B	14.96 % / 32.01 %
76	D	27.61 % / 37.52 %
77	D	28.71 % / 33.56 %
78	A	40.15 % / 37.85 %
79	C	30.36 % / 35.76 %
80	C	14.41 % / 26.84 %

Q.	Ans.	Correct	Skipped	Q.	Ans.	Correct	Skipped	Q.	Ans.	Correct	Skipped	Q.	Ans.	Correct	Skipped	Q.	Ans.	Correct	Skipped
81	B	38.72 %	31.36 %	97	A	28.6 %	33.34 %	113	B	36.19 %	43.46 %	129	C	26.95 %	45.44 %	145	B	9.02 %	44.78 %
82	B	43.89 %	28.94 %	98	B	13.75 %	36.97 %	114	A	5.94 %	38.72 %	130	B	24.31 %	38.73 %	146	A	51.6 %	39.05 %
83	A	21.78 %	34.66 %	99	B	15.51 %	35.76 %	115	B	45.87 %	43.79 %	131	B	18.59 %	42.03 %	147	C	26.84 %	44.23 %
84	C	16.94 %	37.74 %	100	C	9.46 %	33.22 %	116	A	32.45 %	40.82 %	132	B	23.21 %	41.15 %	148	C	20.13 %	41.26 %
85	B	43.67 %	33.67 %	101	C	16.94 %	40.27 %	117	B	37.62 %	40.38 %	133	C	17.93 %	40.6 %	149	B	45.21 %	44.89 %
86	A	10.12 %	37.84 %	102	A	20.46 %	37.63 %	118	B	27.5 %	45.22 %	134	B	49.06 %	35.54 %	150	C	33.22 %	45.33 %
87	B	24.53 %	35.87 %	103	A	14.3 %	43.02 %	119	B	22.99 %	43.79 %	135	D	17.82 %	44.23 %	151	A	10.56 %	42.8 %
88	B	26.84 %	37.96 %	104	A	24.31 %	39.72 %	120	B	11.66 %	27.5 %	136	B	18.26 %	41.04 %	152	D	25.41 %	39.94 %
89	B	29.04 %	37.08 %	105	C	23.32 %	44.78 %	121	B	22.44 %	39.17 %	137	A	15.07 %	40.6 %	153	B	42.24 %	39.06 %
90	A	51.49 %	37.84 %	106	A	15.18 %	45.0 %	122	A	18.48 %	38.07 %	138	C	35.31 %	44.89 %	154	C	47.63 %	45.0 %
91	B	24.75 %	37.3 %	107	A	7.7 %	42.02 %	123	D	25.19 %	43.79 %	139	C	39.49 %	43.02 %	155	C	12.21 %	42.25 %
92	B	43.45 %	37.96 %	108	B	22.11 %	44.67 %	124	A	33.11 %	33.78 %	140	B	27.94 %	44.78 %	156	B	30.91 %	41.26 %
93	B	25.52 %	37.52 %	109	C	15.29 %	43.13 %	125	B	23.76 %	44.67 %	141	A	46.53 %	44.23 %	157	B	27.5 %	44.67 %
94	B	45.54 %	29.49 %	110	B	20.68 %	45.22 %	126	C	34.98 %	45.11 %	142	B	23.65 %	38.62 %	158	B	18.81 %	44.78 %
95	C	7.48 %	37.18 %	111	B	11.77 %	43.13 %	127	B	22.0 %	44.01 %	143	A	34.32 %	44.23 %	159	B	28.6 %	42.47 %
96	B	21.78 %	33.23 %	112	A	13.31 %	40.6 %	128	A	34.98 %	37.74 %	144	B	17.93 %	39.94 %	160	B	31.79 %	40.82 %

Q.	Ans.	Correct / Skipped
161	A	48.62 % / 39.17 %
162	B	6.6 % / 45.0 %
163	A	24.53 % / 42.91 %
164	A	46.86 % / 41.48 %
165	A	25.19 % / 44.89 %
166	B	5.17 % / 45.33 %
167	A	6.93 % / 42.9 %
168	B	31.79 % / 44.56 %
169	A	20.57 % / 44.67 %
170	A	43.45 % / 44.78 %
171	A	36.08 % / 44.45 %
172	A	16.61 % / 35.98 %
173	B	25.52 % / 39.06 %
174	B	11.77 % / 45.11 %
175	A	45.65 % / 43.35 %
176	B	27.61 % / 44.78 %

Q.	Ans.	Correct / Skipped
177	C	17.82 % / 41.7 %
178	A	32.56 % / 45.22 %
179	C	11.99 % / 43.35 %
180	A	19.58 % / 37.08 %
181	B	8.36 % / 40.15 %
182	C	36.19 % / 40.71 %
183	C	31.24 % / 44.23 %
184	B	19.69 % / 45.11 %
185	A	6.49 % / 43.01 %
186	C	18.59 % / 45.33 %
187	A	8.36 % / 44.45 %
188	D	5.5 % / 45.22 %
189	B	19.14 % / 45.0 %
190	C	13.31 % / 45.11 %
191	A	28.27 % / 45.0 %
192	A	7.26 % / 45.33 %

Q.	Ans.	Correct / Skipped
193	D	5.39 % / 45.11 %
194	D	22.77 % / 40.71 %
195	A	28.05 % / 44.89 %
196	D	26.73 % / 43.24 %
197	B	13.42 % / 43.35 %
198	B	39.82 % / 45.33 %
199	B	13.42 % / 44.34 %
200	A	45.54 % / 43.24 %
201	C	35.31 % / 42.58 %
202	D	23.98 % / 45.11 %
203	C	35.53 % / 45.0 %
204	A	33.66 % / 45.33 %
205	C	31.13 % / 43.46 %
206	C	17.6 % / 45.44 %
207	A	7.37 % / 45.11 %
208	B	17.16 % / 41.7 %

Q.	Ans.	Correct / Skipped
209	B	34.65 % / 45.22 %
210	C	33.33 % / 40.93 %
211	A	20.02 % / 44.45 %
212	B	11.99 % / 39.83 %
213	B	14.19 % / 45.22 %
214	B	10.89 % / 40.05 %
215	A	44.44 % / 45.11 %
216	A	14.08 % / 43.13 %
217	D	22.88 % / 45.0 %
218	B	43.45 % / 39.83 %
219	B	10.34 % / 44.45 %
220	A	23.1 % / 40.05 %
221	B	20.24 % / 41.15 %
222	C	4.73 % / 40.92 %
223	D	28.93 % / 45.0 %
224	B	23.43 % / 41.92 %

Q.	Ans.	Correct / Skipped
225	B	42.02 % / 45.33 %
226	B	10.56 % / 45.22 %
227	A	29.7 % / 44.56 %
228	B	40.37 % / 40.05 %
229	B	41.36 % / 45.44 %
230	B	27.17 % / 45.44 %
231	A	21.56 % / 44.67 %
232	A	32.34 % / 44.34 %
233	C	30.58 % / 45.33 %
234	C	38.06 % / 45.44 %
235	D	12.54 % / 45.33 %
236	A	20.46 % / 45.33 %
237	B	34.21 % / 45.33 %
238	A	20.24 % / 45.44 %
239	B	26.73 % / 45.22 %
240	A	27.83 % / 45.33 %

Performance Analysis

Avg. Score (%)	20.52%
Toppers Score (%)	100.0%
Your Score	

Q.1 Which of the following is the deepest layer of the scalp and is the periosteum on the outer surface of the calvaria?

A. Connective tissue

B. Aponeurotic layer

C. Loose connective tissue

D. Pericranium

Q.2

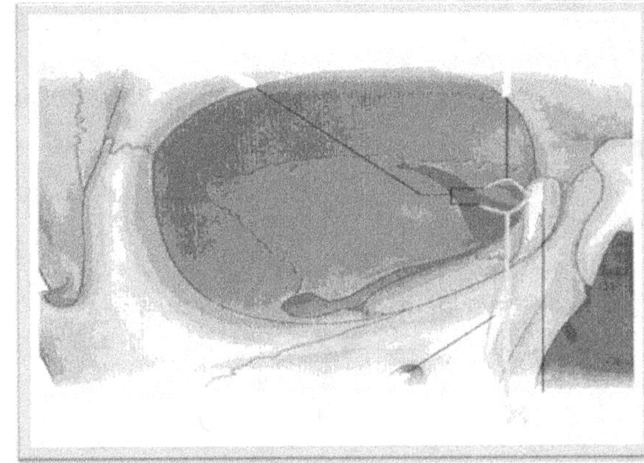

What does 'X' in this picture indicate?

A. Lacrimal sac

B. Puncta

C. Nasolacrimal duct

D. Lacrimal canaliculi

Q.3

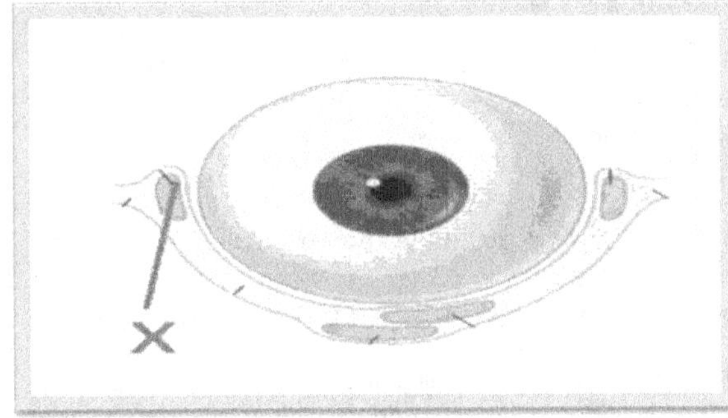

This is the anterior view of check ligament of the eye. What does 'X' indicate?

A. Lateral rectus muscle

B. Medial rectus muscle

C. Inferior oblique muscle

D. Inferior rectus muscle

Q.4

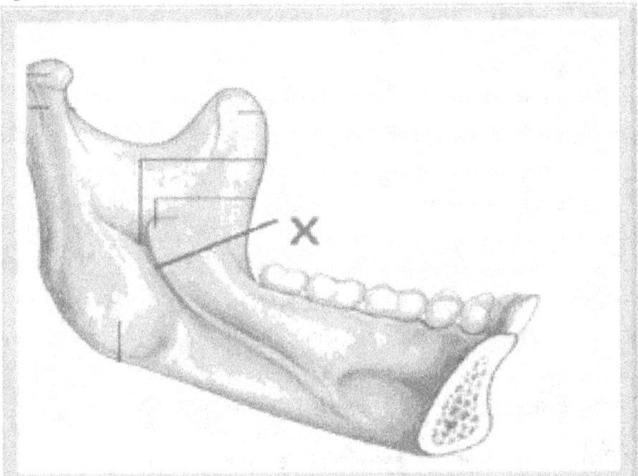

This is the lateral view of the left side of the mandible. What does 'X' indicate?

A. Pterygoid fovea

B. Mylohyoid groove

C. Lingula

D. Mandibular foramen

Q.5 Which of the following is/are a major constituent of plasma membranes?

A. Proteins

B. Cholesterol

C. Carbohydrates

D. Vitamins

Q.6 Which of the following is responsible for the release of secretory proteins by many cells?

A. Endocytosis

B. Exocytosis

C. Autolysis

D. Photolysis

Q.7 Which of the following is defined as the flow of water across a semipermeable membrane from a compartment where the solute concentration is lower to one where the solute concentration is greater?

A. Osmosis

B. Autolysis

C. Spherocytosis

D. Hydrolysis

Q.8 Which of the following is the simplest amino acid which is an inhibitory neurotransmitter released by certain interneurons in the spinal cord and brainstem?

A. Glycine   B. Lysine   C. Cysteine   D. Arginine

Q.9 Which of the following affects only cells in the immediate vicinity of the cell that produces it?

A. Sulphide

B. Nitrous oxide

C. Nitric oxide

D. Nitrate

Q.10 Which of the following is a pigment formed from incompletely degraded membrane components and accumulates in some neurons?

A. Lipofuscin

B. Melanin

C. Neuromycin

D. Neurofuscin

Q.11

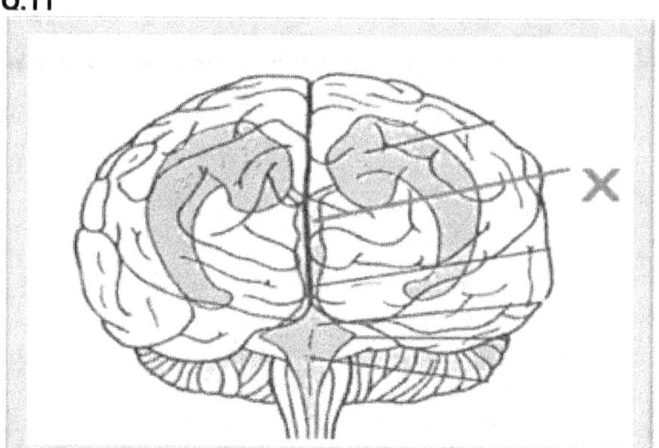

This is the picture of the ventricular system in situ from the front. What does 'X' indicate?

A. Lateral ventricle   **B.** Third ventricle
C. Cerebral aqueduct   **D.** Fourth ventricle

Q.12 Protein separation based on size (mass or molecular weight) is done in all of the following, except:

A. Ultrafiltration
B. Native gel electrophoresis
C. 2D gel electrophoresis
D. Gel filtration chromatography

Q.13 In SDS-PAGE, proteins are separated on the basis of:

A. Mass   **B.** Charge
C. Density   **D.** Solubility

Q.14 Molecules up to size 4KD is identified by:

A. Gene array chip
B. Electron spray ionization
C. Quadrupole mass spectrometry
D. Matrix-assisted laser desorption ionization

Q.15 Collagen of which type is found in hyaline cartilage?

A. Type I   **B.** Type II   **C.** Type III   **D.** Type IV

Q.16 The structural proteins are involved in maintaining the shape of a cell or in the formation of matrices in the body. The shape of these protein is:

A. Globular   **B.** Fibrous
C. Stretch of beads   **D.** Planar

Q.17 Quarter staggered arrangement is seen in-

A. Immunoglobulin   **B.** Haemoglobin
C. Collagen   **D.** Keratin

Q.18 All of the following are required for hydroxylation of proline in collagen synthesis, except:

A. O_2
B. Vitamin
C. Mono-oxygenases
D. Pyridoxal phosphate

Q.19 Which of the following is the first hard tissue of the tooth to form?

A. Dentin   **B.** Enamel

C. Cementum   **D.** Alveolar bone

Q.20 Which of the following cells are located at the center of epithelial enamel organ, between the outer and inner enamel epithelia?

A. Cementoblasts   **B.** Ameloblasts
C. Polygonal cells   **D.** Mesenchymal cells

Q.21 Peg-shaped teeth with the permanent upper central incisor showing a notched incisal edge may be seen in individuals born with congenital syphilis. This condition is known as

A. Enamel hypoplasia
B. Hutchinson's incisor
C. Peg incisor
D. Morpho-differentiation

Q.22 The genes coding for _______ is present in X and Y chromosomes.

A. Odontoblasts   **B.** Fibrinogen
C. Amelogenin   **D.** Cementoblasts

Q.23 The changes occurring in the ameloblasts after the secretory stage and prior to the onset of the maturation process are called the _______ stage.

A. Modulation   **B.** Re-modulation
C. Transition   **D.** Transformation

Q.24 Which of the following forms the walls of the tubules in all but dentin near the pulp?

A. Peritubular dentin
B. Intertubular dentin
C. Predentin
D. Odontoblasts process

Q.25 Apatite crystals of dentin resemble those found in bone cementum and they are _______ times smaller than those found in enamel.

A. 200   **B.** 300   **C.** 400   **D.** 500

Q.26 When 1 mm² of dentin is exposed, about _______ living cells are damaged.

A. 20,000   **B.** 30,000   **C.** 40,000   **D.** 50,000

Q.27 The permeability of radicular dentin near the pulp is only about _______ that of coronal dentin.

A. 10%   **B.** 20%   **C.** 30%   **D.** 40%

Q.28 A patient of acute lymphocytic leukemia with fever and neutropenia develops diarrhea after administration of amoxicillin therapy. Which of the following organisms is most likely to be the causative agent?

A. Salmonella typhi
B. Clostridium difficile
C. Clostridium perfringens
D. Shigella flexneri

Q.29 The average size of the apical foramen of the maxillary teeth in the adult is-

A. 0.3 mm   **B.** 0.4 mm   **C.** 0.5 mm   **D.** 0.6 mm

Q.30 Which of the following release inflammatory chemokine interleukin-8, which is chemotactic for neutrophils?

A. Odontoblasts

B. Ameloblasts

C. Cementoblasts

D. Fibroblasts

Q.31 Most of the lymphocytes present in the pulp are

A. T lymphocytes

B. B lymphocytes

C. neutrophils

D. basophils

Q.32

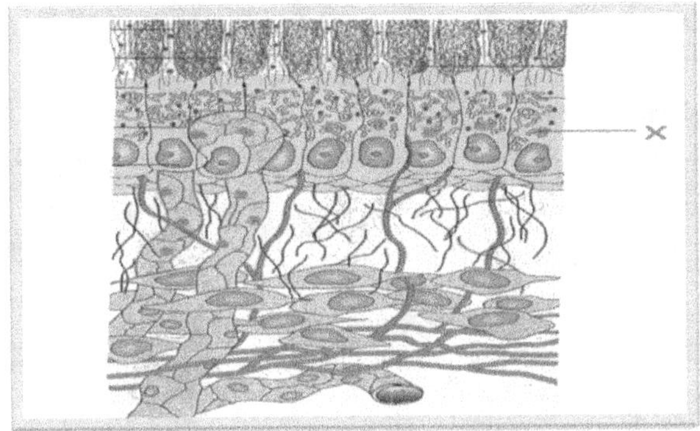

This is the diagram of the odontogenic zone. What does the 'X' indicate?

A. Nerve ending

B. Odontogenic zone

C. Golgi apparatus

D. Mitochondria

Q.33

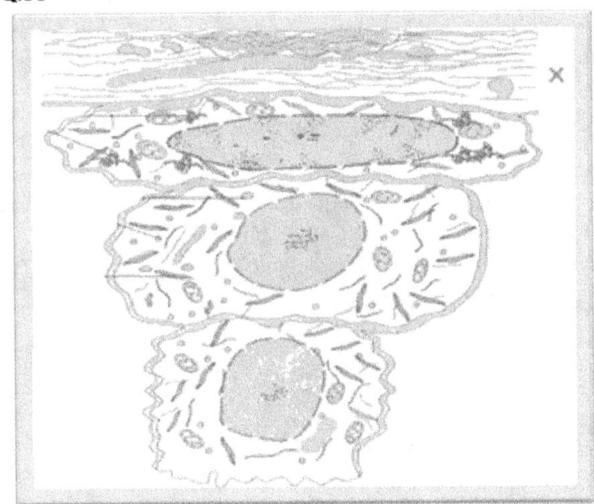

This is the diagram showing details of the different cell layers of the ortho-keratinised epithelium. What does the 'X' indicate?

A. Keratinised surface layer

B. Granular intermediate layer

C. Prickle cell layer

D. Basal layer

Q.34 On biopsy, characteristic finding of malignant mesothelioma is

A. Myelin

B. Desmosin

C. Weibel-Palade bodies

D. Branching microvilli

Q.35 Hyper-coagulation in nephrotic syndrome is caused by

A. Loss of antithrombin III

B. Decreased fibrinogen

C. Decreased metabolism of vitamin K

D. An increase in protein C

Q.36 A 7-year-old boy presented with generalized edema. Urine examination revealed marked albuminuria. Serum biochemical examinations showed hypo-albuminemia with hyper-lipidaemia. A Kidney biopsy was undertaken. On light microscopic examination, the kidney appeared normal. Electron microscopic examination is most likely to reveal

A. Fusion of foot processes of the glomerular epithelial cells

B. Rare-fraction of glomerular basement membrane

C. Deposition of electron-dense material in the basement membrane

D. Thin basement membrane

Q.37 In glomerular disease, which of the following is mainly excreted in urine.

A. Albumin

B. Globulin

C. Light chain

D. Heavy chain

Q.38 Peptic ulceration occurs at all of the following sites except

A. Lesser curvature

B. First part of duodenum

C. Lower end of esophagus

D. Stoma of gastric portion of gastrojejunostomy

Q.39 Which of the following is true about Hypertrophic gastropathy?

A. It is seen in Menetrier disease and ZES.

B. It is seen in Menetrier disease and ZES.

C. It shows cerebriform fugacity on liver.

D. It is less in fundus and body.

Q.40 From which of the following does gastrointestinal stromal malignancy arise?

A. Smooth muscles

B. Nerve cells

C. Interstitial cells of Cajal

D. Vascular endothelium

Q.41 An 18-year-old male presented with acute onset descending paralysis of 3 days duration. There is also a history of blurring of vision for the same duration. On examination, the patient has quadriparesis with areflexia. Both the pupils are non-reactive. The most probable diagnosis is-

A. Poliomyelitis

B. Botulism

C. Diphtheria

D. Porphyria

Q.42 Which of the following statements is not true regarding botulism?

A. Infant botulism is caused by ingestion of preformed toxin.

B. Clostridium toxins A, B, E and F cause human disease.

C. The gene for botulism toxin is coded by bacteriophage.

D. Cl. bratii may cause botulism.

Q.43 Which of the following is not true about Botulism toxin?

A. Short lifespan

B. Increased acetyl-choline release

C. Used for treatment in Blepharospasm, static and dynamic wrinkles

D. Irreversibly decreases ACh NM junction

Q.44 The most important and potential agent that can be used for bioterrorism is:

A. Yersinia pestis

B. Variola virus

C. Mycobacterium tuberculosis

D. Clostridium botulinum

Q.45 Clinical diphtheria is caused by:

A. C. Diphtheria

B. C. pyogens

C. C. ulcerans

D. Streptococcus pyogens

Q.46 A malignant pustule is a term used for-

A. An infected malignant melanoma

B. A carbuncle

C. A rapidly spreading rodent ulcer

D. Anthrax of skin

Q.47 Which of the following systemic routes of drug administration has the chief advantage that the liver is bypassed and drugs with high first-pass metabolism can be absorbed directly into systemic circulation?

A. Oral

B. Sublingual

C. Rectal

D. Cutaneous

Q.48 In non-synthetic reactions, which of the following is the converse of oxidation and involves cytochrome P-450 enzymes working in the opposite direction?

A. Oxidation

B. Reduction

C. Hydrolysis

D. Cyclization

Q.49 Which of the following muscarinic receptors is primarily a neuronal receptor located on ganglion cells and central neurons, especially in the cortex, hippocampus and corpus striatum?

A. M_1

B. M_2

C. M_3

D. M_4

Q.50 Which of the following is a natural alkaloid inhibitor of cerebral AChE, having in addition weak agonistic action on nicotinic receptors?

A. Riva-stigmine

B. Donepezil

C. Galantamine

D. Neostigmine

Q.51 Which of the following are membrane-bound G- protein-coupled receptors which function primarily by increasing or decreasing the intercellular production of second messengers cAMP, or IP_3/DAG?

A. Adrenergic receptors

B. Non-adrenergic receptors

C. Dopamine receptors

D. Catalytic receptors

Q.52 Which of the following β blockers is the prototype of cardio-selective (β₁) blockers; nearly 50 times higher dose is needed to block isoprenaline induced vasodilation?

A. Sotalol

B. Timolol

C. Pindolol

D. Metaprolol

Q.53 Which of the following causes changes in shape of platelets and is a weak aggregator through 5-HT₂A receptors?

A. 5-HT

B. 5-HT_1

C. 5-HT_2

D. 5-HT_{2B}

Q.54 Topical PGFs analogues like latanoprost and isopropyl unoprostone are one of the first choice drugs in:

A. Cataract

B. Glaucoma

C. Peptic ulcer

D. Abortion

Q.55 Which of the following displaces warfarin, naproxen, sulfonyl-ureas, phenytoin, and methotrexate from binding sites on plasma proteins?

A. Analgesic

B. Aspirin

C. Paracetamol

D. Antipyretic

Q.56 Which of the following immunomodulators inhibit(s) proliferation of activated lymphocytes in patients with active rheumatic arthritis?

A. Immunosuppressants

B. Sulfasalazine

C. Chloroquine and hydroxyl-chloroquine

D. Leflunomide

Q.57 Which of the following is the first long-acting selective 2 agonist with a slow onset of action used by inhalation on a twice daily schedule for maintenance therapy and for nocturnal asthma, but not for acute symptoms?

A. Bambuterol

B. Salmeterol

C. Terbutaline

D. Formoterol

Q.58 Which of the following is an antihistaminic (H₁) with some cromoglycate like action; stimulation of immunogenic and inflammatory cells (mast cells, macrophages, eosinophils, lymphocytes, neutrophils) and mediator release are inhibited?

A. Sodium cromoglycate

B. Ketotifen

C. Theophylline

D. Ephedrine

Q.59 Which of the following is a newer D_2 agonist; more potent; more D_2 selective and longer acting (T1/2 > 60 days) than bromocriptine; needs to be given only twice weekly?

A. Cabergoline

B. Bromocriptine

C. Gonadotropin

D. Octreotide

Q.60 In reactions to insulin, which of the following is the most frequent and potentially the most serious reaction?

A. Hypoglycemia

B. Local reaction

C. Allergy

D. Edema

Q.61 Which of the following consists of all synthetic components that can be used to repair or replace tooth structure, including primers, bonding agents, liners, cement bases, amalgams, resin-based composites, compomers, hybrid ionomers, cast metals. etc?

A. Direct restorative material
B. Indirect restorative material
C. Restorative dental material
D. Temporary restorative material

Q.62 When water boils, energy is needed to transform the liquid to vapour. This quantity of energy is known as:
A. Heat of fusion
B. Heat of solidification
C. Heat of vaporization
D. None of these

Q.63 Which of the following is the tenacious deposit of microscopic debris that covers enamel and dentin surfaces that have been prepared for a restoration?
A. Enamel-dentin interstitial layer
B. Smear layer
C. Cuticle
D. Periodontal sediments

Q.64 Which of the following mechanisms has been commonly used in dentistry because of the absence of truly adhesive cements or restorative materials?
A. Micromechanical bonding
B. Acid-etching technique
C. Mechanical bonding
D. Adhesion

Q.65 Which of the following alone may be inappropriate for evaluating either the wear resistance or abrasiveness of different classes of materials, such as a metallic material compared with a synthetic resin?
A. Hardness
B. Ductility
C. Galvanic shock
D. Creep

Q.66 The wavelengths between 300 and 400 nm are referred to as:
A. Far-ultraviolet radiation
B. Middle ultraviolet radiation
C. Near-ultraviolet radiation
D. Very near-ultraviolet radiation

Q.67 The materials of low thermal conductivity are called:
A. Conductors
B. Insulators
C. Dielectrics
D. Super conductors

Q.68 Which of the following can be generated when structures are flexed?
A. Compressive stress
B. Tensile stress
C. Shear stress
D. Flexural stress

Q.69 The elastic modulus of enamel is about ___ times greater than that of dentin.
A. Two
B. Three
C. Four
D. Five

Q.70 Which of the following is generally determined by subjecting a rod, wire or dumbbell shaped specimen to tensile loading?
A. Permanent deformation
B. Cold working
C. Tensile strength
D. Flexure strength

Q.71 The ability of a material to sustain considerable permanent deformation without rupture under compression, as in hammering or rolling into a sheet, is termed ______.
A. Ductility
B. Malleability
C. Brittleness
D. Hardness

Q.72 Which of the following is/are the stable cluster of atoms of a new phase that forms within a parent phase, such as during the solidification of a metal?
A. Valence electrons
B. Nucleus
C. Conduction electrons
D. Protons

Q.73 Which of the following is the chemical reaction in which low molecular weight monomers or small polymers are converted into higher molecular weight materials to attain desired properties?
A. Chain transfer
B. Curing
C. Induction
D. Termination

Q.74 Polymers that have only one type of repeating units are called:
A. Monomers
B. Homopolymers
C. Copolymers
D. Block polymers

Q.75 Which of the following is a special form of cell division that only occurs in the post-pubertal testis and the foetal and adult ovary?
A. Meiosis
B. Mitosis
C. Binary fission
D. Cellular division

Q.76 Which of the following is the term given to the phenomenon whereby several different mutations cause the same phenotype?
A. Polymorphism
B. Allelic heterogeneity
C. Locus heterogeneity
D. De novo mutations

Q.77 Which of the following express a unique immunoglobulin receptor on their cell surface which binds to soluble antigen?
A. B lymphocytes
B. T lymphocytes
C. Neutrophils
D. Basophils

Q.78 Which of the following is the gold standard of allergy testing?
A. Skin prick
B. Ige test
C. Supervised exposure to allergen
D. Mast cell tryptase

Q.79 Which of the following also occurs in healthy individuals whose thermoregulatory mechanisms are intact but insufficient to cope with the intensity of the thermal stress?
A. Hypothermia
B. Hyperthermia
C. Heat stroke
D. Heat cramps

Q.80 Which of the following is/are necessary for normal growth, foetal development, fertility, haematopoiesis and immune function?

A. Carotene
B. Retinoids
C. Thiamine
D. Riboflavin

Q.81 Which of the following results from an inherited increase in iron absorption?

A. Anemia
B. Osteoporosis
C. Haemochromatosis
D. Acrodermatitis Enteropathica

Q.82 Which of the following antibody detection tests involves the antibodies and antigen migrating through gels, with or without the assistance of electrophoresis and forming insoluble complexes where they meet?

A. Direct agglutination
B. Indirect agglutination
C. Immunodiffusion
D. Immuno-chromatography

Q.83 Which of the following are very effective anti-gram-negative antibiotics?

A. Ketolides
B. Aminoglycosides
C. Lincosamides
D. Macrolides

Q.84 Which of the following is used to treat fluke infections with Fasciola hepatica?

A. Bithionol
B. Diethylcarbamazine
C. Ivermectin
D. Niclosamide

Q.85 Which of the following is available as a water–soluble hydrochloride salt suitable for nasal inhalation?

A. Amphetamine
B. Cocaine
C. Cannabis
D. Quinine

Q.86 Which of the following is the converse of depression and is characteristic of mania?

A. Elation
B. Delusion
C. Agitation
D. Ego

Q.87 Which of the following refers to a severe chronic form of factitious disorder?

A. Gnarled syndrome
B. Munchausen syndrome
C. Sjogren syndrome
D. Bulimia nervosa

Q.88

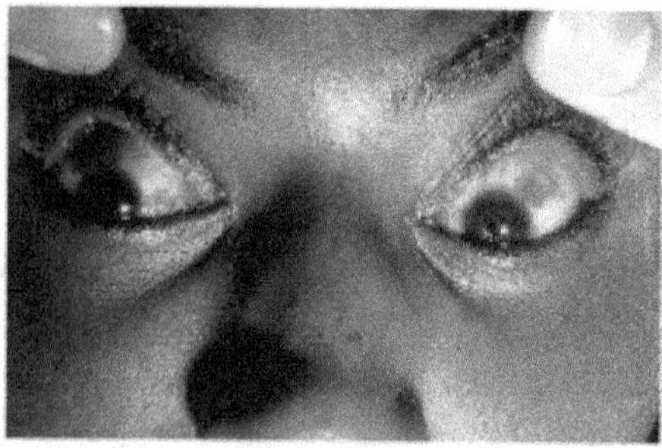

Which disease's clinical feature is depicted by this picture-injected conjunctiva?

A. Louse-borne relapsing fever
B. Leptospirosis
C. Glaucoma
D. Rat fever

Q.89 Which of the following is a chronic, irregular, undetermined ulcer due to Mycobacterium ulcerans infection?

A. Arterial ulcer
B. Bairnsdale ulcer
C. Martorell's ulcer
D. Marjolin's ulcer

Q.90 Which of the following is infection and suppuration with destruction of the skeletal muscle, commonly due to Staphylococcus aureus and Streptococcus pyogens, occasionally due to gram-negative organisms?

A. Acute pyomyositis
B. Necrotising fasciitis
C. Anthrax
D. Nosocomial infection

Q.91 Which of the following cysts are due to minor pricks or trauma, epidermis gets buried into the deeper subcutaneous tissue which causes reaction and cyst formation?

A. Sequestration dermoids
B. Tubulo-dermoids
C. Implantation dermoids
D. Angular dermoids

Q.92 Which of the following is a sac-like cavity containing fluid within, which in normal location prevents friction between tendon and bone?

A. Fibroma
B. Bursa
C. Wart
D. Neuroma

Q.93 Which of the following is a common chamber for the digestive and respiratory tracts?

A. Larynx
B. Pharynx
C. Trachea
D. Oesophagus

Q.94 Which of the following is neither a part of the cranium nor of the facial skeleton?

A. Maxilla
B. Mandible
C. Pharynx
D. Larynx

Q.95 Which of the following is the major bony element of the posterior part of the base of the skull?

A. Temporal bone
B. Occipital bone
C. Sphenoid bone
D. Parietal bone

Q.96 The posterior boundary of the middle cranial fossa is formed by the anterior surface of the petrous part of the petromastoid part of the-

A. Temporal bone
B. Sphenoid bone
C. Hyoid bone
D. Occipital bone

Q.97 Which of the following arteries is usually a small branch of the maxillary artery that enters the middle cranial fossa through the foramen ovale and supplies areas medial to this foramen?

A. Accessory meningeal artery

B. Posterior meningeal artery

C. Anterior meningeal artery

D. Ascending pharyngeal artery

Q.98 Which of the following is a thin, delicate membrane that closely invests the surface of the brain?

A. Arachnoid mater

B. Pia mater

C. Dura mater

D. Falx cerebri

Q.99 Which of the following sinuses receive blood not only from cerebral veins, but also from the ophthalmic veins and emissary veins?

A. Inferior petrosal sinuses

B. Cavernous sinuses

C. Superior sagittal sinuses

D. Dural venous sinuses

Q.100 Which of the following nerves leaves the anterior surface of the brainstem between the midbrain and the pons?

A. Oculomotor nerve

B. Optic nerve

C. Vagus nerve

D. Trochlear nerve

// Smart Answer Sheet //

Correct   Indicates percentage of students who answered questions correctly.

Skipped   Indicates percentage of students who skipped questions.

Q.	Ans.	Correct / Skipped	Q.	Ans.	Correct / Skipped	Q.	Ans.	Correct / Skipped	Q.	Ans.	Correct / Skipped	Q.	Ans.	Correct / Skipped
1	D	39.13 % / 4.35 %	17	C	26.09 % / 26.08 %	33	A	56.52 % / 26.09 %	49	A	30.43 % / 26.09 %	65	A	43.48 % / 26.09 %
2	D	39.13 % / 21.74 %	18	D	13.04 % / 26.09 %	34	D	21.74 % / 21.74 %	50	C	17.39 % / 26.09 %	66	C	39.13 % / 26.09 %
3	A	56.52 % / 26.09 %	19	A	43.48 % / 26.09 %	35	A	17.39 % / 26.09 %	51	A	39.13 % / 26.09 %	67	B	60.87 % / 26.09 %
4	B	47.83 % / 26.08 %	20	C	34.78 % / 21.74 %	36	A	39.13 % / 26.09 %	52	D	30.43 % / 26.09 %	68	B	30.43 % / 26.09 %
5	B	21.74 % / 26.09 %	21	B	65.22 % / 21.74 %	37	A	60.87 % / 26.09 %	53	A	30.43 % / 21.74 %	69	B	47.83 % / 26.08 %
6	B	34.78 % / 26.09 %	22	C	39.13 % / 21.74 %	38	D	39.13 % / 26.09 %	54	B	26.09 % / 26.08 %	70	C	30.43 % / 26.09 %
7	A	60.87 % / 26.09 %	23	C	30.43 % / 26.09 %	39	A	30.43 % / 26.09 %	55	B	52.17 % / 26.09 %	71	B	47.83 % / 26.08 %
8	A	43.48 % / 26.09 %	24	A	47.83 % / 21.74 %	40	C	47.83 % / 26.08 %	56	D	8.7 % / 26.08 %	72	B	21.74 % / 21.74 %
9	C	39.13 % / 26.09 %	25	B	39.13 % / 26.09 %	41	B	26.09 % / 26.08 %	57	B	34.78 % / 26.09 %	73	B	34.78 % / 26.09 %
10	A	30.43 % / 26.09 %	26	B	21.74 % / 26.09 %	42	A	26.09 % / 21.74 %	58	B	26.09 % / 26.08 %	74	B	39.13 % / 26.09 %
11	B	34.78 % / 26.09 %	27	B	39.13 % / 26.09 %	43	B	30.43 % / 26.09 %	59	A	21.74 % / 26.09 %	75	A	47.83 % / 26.08 %
12	B	21.74 % / 26.09 %	28	B	30.43 % / 21.74 %	44	D	30.43 % / 26.09 %	60	A	65.22 % / 26.08 %	76	B	39.13 % / 26.09 %
13	A	21.74 % / 26.09 %	29	B	43.48 % / 26.09 %	45	A	65.22 % / 26.08 %	61	C	34.78 % / 26.09 %	77	A	39.13 % / 26.09 %
14	C	26.09 % / 21.74 %	30	A	30.43 % / 21.74 %	46	D	52.17 % / 21.74 %	62	C	65.22 % / 26.08 %	78	A	47.83 % / 26.08 %
15	B	34.78 % / 26.09 %	31	A	47.83 % / 26.08 %	47	B	34.78 % / 26.09 %	63	B	52.17 % / 26.09 %	79	A	56.52 % / 26.09 %
16	B	17.39 % / 26.09 %	32	C	39.13 % / 26.09 %	48	B	39.13 % / 26.09 %	64	A	39.13 % / 26.09 %	80	B	43.48 % / 21.74 %

Q.	Ans.	Correct		Q.	Ans.	Correct		Q.	Ans.	Correct		Q.	Ans.	Correct		Q.	Ans.	Correct
		Skipped				Skipped				Skipped				Skipped				Skipped
81	C	52.17 % 26.09 %		85	B	39.13 % 26.09 %		89	B	30.43 % 26.09 %		93	B	43.48 % 26.09 %		97	A	52.17 % 26.09 %
82	C	30.43 % 21.74 %		86	A	26.09 % 26.08 %		90	A	30.43 % 26.09 %		94	B	39.13 % 21.74 %		98	B	43.48 % 26.09 %
83	B	47.83 % 26.08 %		87	B	39.13 % 26.09 %		91	C	43.48 % 26.09 %		95	B	60.87 % 26.09 %		99	B	52.17 % 26.09 %
84	A	21.74 % 26.09 %		88	A	43.48 % 26.09 %		92	B	47.83 % 26.08 %		96	A	43.48 % 26.09 %		100	A	34.78 % 26.09 %

Performance Analysis

Avg. Score (%)	26.0%
Toppers Score (%)	96.25%
Your Score	

Q.1 Which of the following is a large muscle that completely surrounds each orbital orifice and extends into each eyelid?

A. Orbicularis oculi

B. Corrugator supercilii

C. Nasalis

D. Buccinator

Q.2 Which of the following is a large, thin sheet of muscle in the superficial fascia of the neck?

A. Platysma

B. Auricular muscle

C. Occipitofrontalis

D. Orbicularis oris

Q.3 Which of the following is the part of head that extends from the superciliary arches anteriorly to the external occipital protuberance and superior nuchal lines posteriorly?

A. Scalp

B. Transverse facial vein

C. Pericranium

D. Lymphatic

Q.4

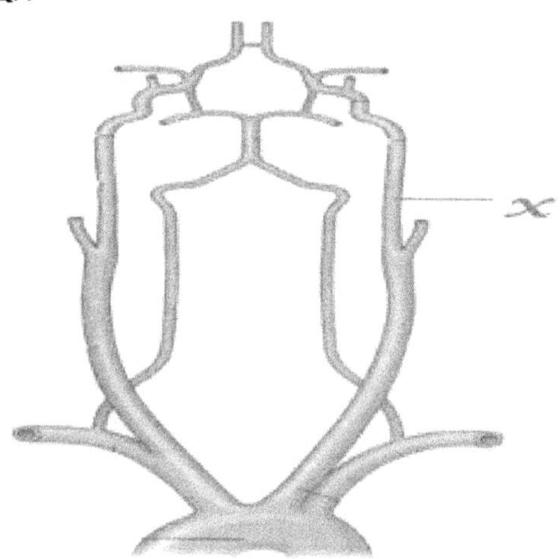

This is the schematic diagram of the arterial supply to the brain. What does 'X' indicate?

A. Basilar artery

B. Left internal carotid artery

C. Left vertebral artery

D. Brachiocephalic artery

Q.5

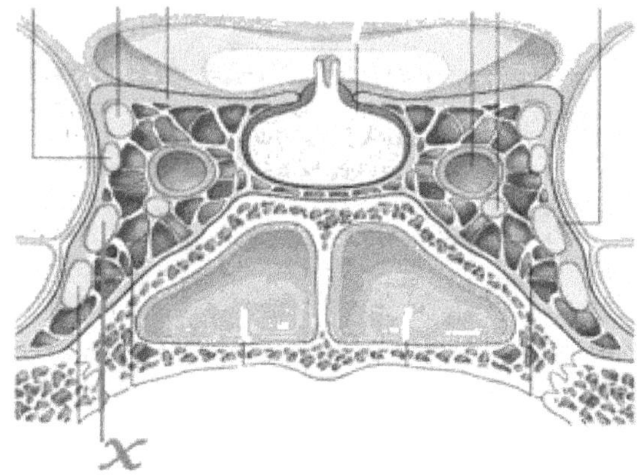

This is the picture of cavernous sinus. What does "X" indicate?

A. Sphenoid sinus

B. Ophthalmic division of trigeminal nerve

C. Maxillary division of trigeminal nerve

D. Mandibular division

Q.6

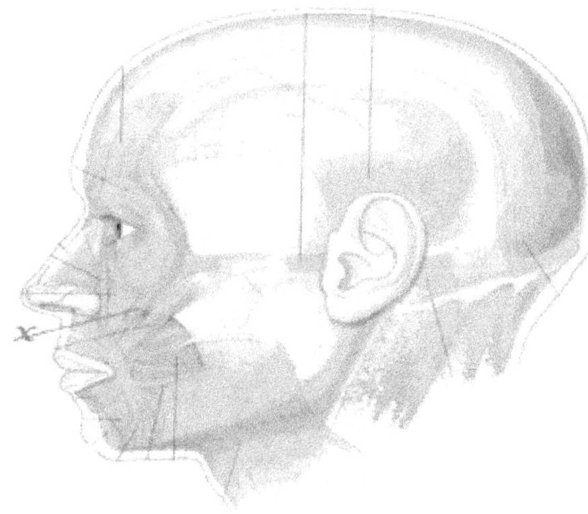

This is the schematic diagram of facial muscles. What is indicated by 'X'?

A. Zygomaticus minor

B. Zygomaticus major

C. Levator labii superiors

D. Nasalis

Q.7 Which of the following is transported into muscle and fat cells by facilitated transporters?

A. Glucose

B. Amino acids

C. Epithelial cells

D. Protein

Q.8 An ion in equilibrium across a membrane satisfies the-

A. Nernst equation
B. Gibbs-donnan equation
C. Maxwell equation
D. Van der waals equation

Q.9 Ion transport processes are required for the regulation of cell:

A. Volume
B. Density
C. Membrane
D. Oxidation

Q.10 When a nerve or muscle cell is depolarised slowly, the normal threshold may be passed without an action potential being fired; this is called:

A. Accommodation
B. Transportation
C. Recession
D. Resorption

Q.11 Which of the following receptors are ligand–gated channels that conduct both Na^+ and K^+?

A. Aspirin
B. Acetylcholine
C. Collagen
D. Glucose

Q.12 Which of the following is a transmitter in the pain pathways and gastrointestinal tract?

A. Substance P
B. Ach
C. Polypeptide
D. Glucagon

Q.13 Where is the organ of Corti located?

A. Scala vestibuli
B. Basilar membrane
C. Spiral laminae
D. Reissner's membrane

Q.14 The following is the major type of collagen in basement membrane:

A. Type I   B. Type II   C. Type III   D. Type IV

Q.15 Proteins are sorted by:

A. Golgi bodies
B. Mitochondria
C. Ribosomes
D. Nuclear membrane

Q.16 Endoplasmic reticulum signal transduction is through-

A. Translocon
B. Chaperone
C. Ubiquitin
D. Mannose 6 Phosphate

Q.17 The following is not a function of Endoplasmic Reticulum:

A. Protein synthesis
B. Muscle contraction
C. Protein sorting
D. Protein glycosylation

Q.18 Name the targeting sequence that directs Endoplasmic Reticulum (ER) resident protein in retrograde flow to ER in COPI vesicle.

A. KDEL   B. KDAL   C. DALK   D. KDUL

Q.19 Which of the following is not a protein-misfolding disease?

A. Prion disease
B. Alzheimer's disease

C. Beta thalassemia
D. Ehlers danlos syndrome

Q.20 All of the following are true about chaperons except:

A. They belong to the heat shock proteins.
B. The have a wide range of expression.
C. They are present from bacteria to human.
D. Ubiquitin is the most important chaperone.

Q.21 The pulp organ cells produce the _______ that surrounds and protects the pulp.

A. Enamel
B. Dentin
C. Cementum
D. Gingiva

Q.22 Which of the following are nodular, calcified masses appearing in either or both the coronal and root portions of the pulp organ?

A. Denticles
B. Fibrosis
C. Vascular changes
D. Caries

Q.23 Which of the following contain(s) the cytoplasmic process of the odontoblasts?

A. Dentinal tubules
B. Enamel
C. Periodontal ligament
D. Alveolar process

Q.24 Which of the following cells of the extrinsic ocular muscles originate from the prechordal plate?

A. Ameloblasts
B. Myoblasts
C. Cementoblasts
D. Odontoblasts

Q.25 Which of the following cysts or fistulas may arise from the rests of epithelium in the visceral arch area?

A. Branchial cleft cysts
B. Globulomaxillary cysts
C. Palatine cysts
D. Nasolabial cysts

Q.26 Which of the following mutants arrest tooth development at the bud stage?

A. Msx-1   B. Msx-2   C. Msx-3   D. Msx-4

Q.27 Which of the following forms a protective covering of variable thickness over the entire surface of the crown?

A. Enamel
B. Dentin
C. Cementum
D. Pulp

Q.28 Which of the following are thin, leaf-like structures that extend from the enamel surface toward the dentinoenamel junction?

A. Enamel lamellae
B. Enamel papillae
C. Dentinal tubules
D. Pulp

Q.29 The cells of the inner enamel epithelium are derived from the _______ layer of the oral epithelium.

A. Ameloblast
B. Odontoblast
C. Basal cell
D. Neoplasm

Q.30 Which of the following secrete proteases of different types, of which metallo-proteases and serine proteases are important?

A. Ameloblasts   **B.** Cementoblasts
C. Odontoblasts   **D.** Basal cells

Q.31 Which of the following provides the bulk and general form of the tooth and is characterised as a hard tissue with tubules throughout its thickness?

A. Dentin

B. Enamel

C. Cementum

D. Periodontal ligament

Q.32 The odontoblast process is composed of microtubules of _______ in diameter.

A. 20 μm   **B.** 30 μm   **C.** 40 μm   **D.** 50 μm

Q.33

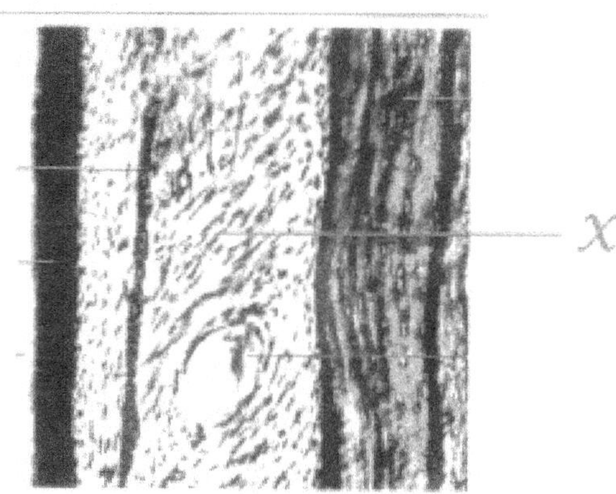

This is the diagram of a long strand of epithelium in periodontal ligament. What does 'X' indicate?

A. Alveolar bone

B. Periodontal ligament

C. Blood vessel

D. Dentin

Q.34

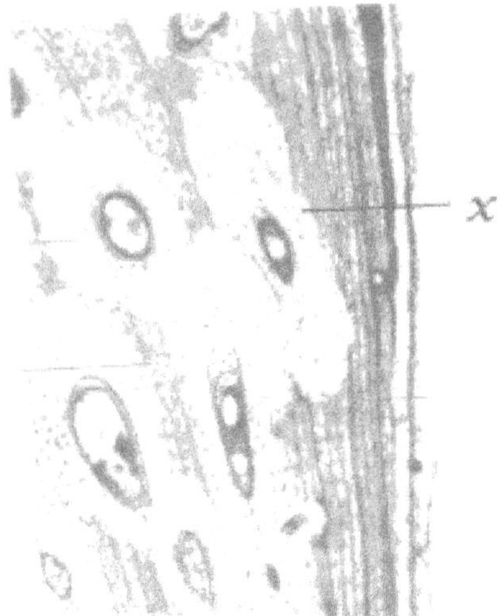

This is the picture of the appositional growth of the mandible by formation of circumferential lamellae. What does 'X' indicate?

A. Circumferential lamellae

B. Reversal line

C. Resting line

D. Interstitial lamellae

Q.35 Albuminocytologic dissociation occurs in cases of

A. Guillain Barre Syndrome

B. TB Meningitis

C. Motor Neuron Disease

D. Demyelinating Disorder

Q.36 Which of the following is not a Prion disease?

A. Creutzfeldt-Jakob disease

B. Fatal Familial insomnia

C. Gerstmann-Straussler-Scheinker syndrome

D. Parkinson's disease

Q.37 Which of the following is the best described etiology for Berry aneurysm?

A. Degeneration of internal elastic lamina

B. Degeneration of tunica media

C. Defect in muscular layer

D. Low grade inflammation in the vessel wall

Q.38 The most common site for medulloblastoma is:

A. Medulla   **B.** Cerebellum
C. Cerebrum   **D.** Pineal gland

Q.39 Commonest type of intracranial tumor is:

A. Astrocytoma   **B.** Medulloblastoma
C. Meningioma   **D.** Secondaries

Q.40 Which of the following is the receptor on neuronal membrane that induces development of glioma?

A. CD 45   **B.** CD 133   **C.** CD 33   **D.** CD 24

Q.41 Patients with Hashimoto's thyroiditis are at increased risk of developing:

A.   Papillary Carcinoma
B.   Follicular Carcinoma
C.   T-Cell Lymphoma
D.   B-Cell Lymphoma

Q.42 The following is the characteristic of Bacillus cereus food poisoning:

A.   Presence of fever
B.   Presence of abdominal pain
C.   Absence of vomiting
D.   Absence of diarrhoea

Q.43 Which of the following is true regarding anthrax?

A.   M'Fadyean reaction shows capsule.
B.   Humans are not usually resistant to infection.
C.   Less than 100 spores can cause pulmonary infection.
D.   Gram stain shows organism with bulging spores.

Q.44 Non-invasive diarrhoea can be caused by:

A. Shigella
B. Bacillus cereus
C. Salmonella
D. Y. enterocolitica

Q.45 A patient presents with vomiting who ate rice 6 hours before. The most probable cause is:

A. Bacillus cereus
B. Staph aureus
C. Cl. diffcile
D. All of the above

Q.46 A farmer presents with multiple discharging sinuses in the leg not responding to antibiotics. The most likely organism involved in the diagnosis is-

A.   Madurella mycetomatis
B.   Actinomycete
C.   Nocardia
D.   Sporothrix

Q.47 Actinomycotic mycetoma is caused by:

A.   Actinomyces
B.   Candida
C.   Madurella mycetomi
D.   Staphylococcus

Q.48 Which of the following is/are the most predominant constituent of sulphur granules of actinomycosis?

A.   Organism
B.   Neutrophils and monocytes
C.   Monocytes and lymphocytes
D.   Eosinophils

Q.49 Which of the following drug administration routes can be used when the patient is having recurrent vomiting or is unconscious?

A. Oral
B. Sublingual
C. Rectal
D. Cutaneous

Q.50 Oxidative reactions are mostly carried out by a group of mono-oxygenases in the ______, which in the final step involve a Cytochrome P-450 hemoprotein, NADPH, Cytochrome P-450 reductase and molecular O_2.

A. Spleen
B. Liver
C. Heart
D. Lung

Q.51 Which of the following has prominent muscarinic actions and also stimulates ganglia mainly through ganglionic muscarinic receptors?

A. Pilocarpine
B. Bethanechol
C. Phalloidin
D. Carbamate

Q.52 Which of the following decreases secretion of acid, pepsin and mucus in the stomach, but the primary action is on volume of secretion so that pH of gastric contents may not be elevated unless diluted by food?

A. Atropine
B. Adrenaline
C. Ach
D. Muscarinic

Q.53 Which of the following is the most effective drug for motion sickness?

A. Ach
B. Carbachol
C. Pilocarpine
D. Hyoscine

Q.54 Which of the following adrenergic drugs crosses to brain and causes stimulation?

A. Ephedrine
B. Amphetamine
C. Dobutamine
D. Phenylephrine

Q.55 Which of the following is the first of the highly selective α_1 blockers having $\alpha_1 : \alpha_2$ selectivity ratio 1000 : 1?

A. Phentolamine
B. Prazosin
C. Terazosin
D. Doxazosin

Q.56 Which of the following is the first adrenergic antagonist capable of blocking both α and β receptors?

A. Carvedilol
B. Labetalol
C. Timolol
D. Betaxolol

Q.57 Which of the following is [2(4-imidazolyl)-ethylamine]?

A. Adrenaline
B. Histamine
C. Ach
D. Atropine

Q.58 Which of the following is atypical antipsychotic and is a combined $5\text{-}HT_{2A}$ + dopamine D_2 antagonist similar to clozapine?

A. Cyproheptadine
B. Clozapine
C. Risperidone
D. Ondansetron

Q.59 Which of the following drugs indicates that it is not useful in fever due to heat stroke and only external cooling lowers the body temperature?

A. Analgesic
B. Antipyretic
C. Aspirin
D. Anti-inflammatory

Q.60 Which of the following is/are antimalarial drug(s) found to induce remission in up to 50% patients of RA but take(s) 3-6 months?

A.   Immunosuppressants
B.   Sulfasalazine
C.   Chloroquine and hydroxychloroquine
D.   Azathioprine

Q.61 Which of the following is a metabolic disorder characterised by hyper-uricaemia?

A. Gout　　　　　　　　**B.** Arthritis
C. Antigout　　　　　　**D.** Glaucoma

Q.62 In drugs for cough, which of the following sooth the throat and reduce afferent impulses from the inflamed/irritated pharyngeal mucosa, thus provide symptomatic relief in dry cough arising from throat?
A. Pharyngeal demulcents
B. Expectorants
C. Antitussives
D. Adjunct antitussives

Q.63 Which of the following is the cement, coating or restorative material that either seals pits and fissures or that releases a therapeutic agent such as fluoride or chlorhexidine to prevent or arrest the demineralisation of tooth structure?
A. Direct restorative material
B. Indirect restorative material
C. Preventive restorative material
D. Dental restorative material

Q.64 Which of the following may be either elastic or plastic or elastic and plastic?
A. Strain　　**B.** Stress　　**C.** Pressure　　**D.** Force

Q.65 The simplest alloy is a ______ in which atoms of two metals are located in the same crystal structure, such as face-centred cubic, body-centred cubic and hexagonal close packed.
A. Solid solution　　　　**B.** Semi-solid solution
C. Pure solution　　　　**D.** Solid

Q.66 If the sizes of two metallic atoms differ by less than approximately ______, they posses a favourable size factor for solid solubility.
A. 12%　　**B.** 13%　　**C.** 14%　　**D.** 15%

Q.67 A ______ copper alloy, sometimes used to inlay purposes in deciduous teeth, is known as sterling silver.
A. 92.5% Ag and 7.5% Cu
B. 91.5% Ag and 8.5% Cu
C. 99.5% Ag and 0.5% Cu
D. 93.5% Ag and 6.5% Cu

Q.68 Cross-linking of a low molecular weight polymer increases the softening temperature, known as the:
A. Gradient temperature
B. Glass transition temperature
C. Transition temperature
D. Absolute temperature

Q.69 Which of the following is determined not only by a material's composition but also by the biological environment in contact with the material?
A. Hardness　　　　　　**B.** Corrosion
C. Abrasion　　　　　　**D.** Tensile strength

Q.70 Which of the following components of the tooth is a connective tissue containing normal elements such as fibroblasts, collagen, capillaries and nerves?
A. Dentin　　**B.** Pulp　　**C.** Root　　**D.** Enamel

Q.71 Which of the following is the most allergenic metal known, with an incidence of somewhere between 10% and 20%, depending on the study?
A. Copper　　　　　　**B.** Nickel
C. Beryllium　　　　　**D.** Mercury

Q.72 Which of the following has the lowest viscosity and ranks as one of the least stiff of the elastomeric impression materials of similar consistency?
A. Polysulphide
B. ZOE
C. Polyether
D. Sodium hypochlorite

Q.73 The typical sol-gel reaction can be described as a reaction of soluble alginate with ______ and the formation of an insoluble calcium alginate gel.
A. Calcium sulphate
B. Sodium hypochlorite
C. Sodium chloride
D. Polysulphide

Q.74 The hemihydrate is ______ more soluble in water than is the dihydrate near room temperature (20°C).
A. 3 times　　**B.** 4 times　　**C.** 5 times　　**D.** 6 times

Q.75 Which of the following is the most commonly used accelerator in dental materials?
A. Polysulphide　　　　**B.** Chloride
C. Potassium sulphate　　**D.** Hydrogen sulphate

Q.76 Which of the following is used as a border at the perimeter of an impression to provide an enclosed boundary for the base of the cast, to be made from a poured material such as gypsum or resin?
A. Baseplate wax　　　　**B.** Boxing wax
C. Corrective wax　　　　**D.** Dental wax

Q.77 Which of the following is the main site of energy production within the cell?
A. Mitochondria
B. Ribosomes
C. Cytoplasm
D. Endoplasmic reticulum

Q.78 Which of the following diseases can be present with a movement disorder, weight loss or psychiatric symptoms or with a combination of all three?
A. Epilepsy
B. Huntington disease
C. Dysmorphic syndrome
D. Retinoblastoma

Q.79 Which of the following cells are short-lived cells with a half life of 6 hours, and are produced at the rate of 10^{11} cells daily?
A. Lymphocytes　　　　**B.** RBC
C. Neutrophils　　　　　**D.** Basophils

Q.80 Which of the following is/are highly effective at filtering blood and is/are an important site of phagocytosis of senescent erythrocytes, bacteria, immune complexes and other debris?

A. Thymus
B. Spleen
C. Lymph nodes
D. Bone marrow

Q.81 Which of the following nutrients prevents oxidation of polyunsaturated fatty acids in cell membranes by free radicals?

A. Vitamin A
B. Vitamin B
C. Vitamin C
D. Vitamin E

Q.82 Absorption of which of the following nutrients may be impaired in malabsorption secondary to small intestinal disease?

A. Calcium
B. Phosphorus
C. Iodine
D. Zinc

Q.83 Which of the following are only effective against gram-positive organisms and are used against MRSA and ampicillin-resistant enterococci?

A. Aminoglycosides
B. Ketolides
C. Glycopeptides
D. Folate antagonists

Q.84 Which of the following is/are used topically for skin infections and orally for onychomycosis?

A. 5- fluorocytosine
B. Griseofulvin
C. Terbinafine
D. Echinocandins

Q.85 Which of the following inhibits oxidative phosphorylation, causing paralysis of helminths?

A. Ivermectin
B. Niclosamide
C. Piperazine
D. Praziquantel

Q.86 Which of the following is associated with vasodilation and myocardial depression?

A. Hypertension
B. Hypotension
C. Sensitivity
D. Stress

Q.87 Which of the following may be the presenting feature of an underlying malignancy and presents with rapid onset of cerebellar ataxia?

A. Peripheral neuropathy
B. Encephalomyelitis
C. Cerebellar degeneration
D. Retinopathy

Q.88 Which of the following is most commonly due to over production of PTHrP, which binds to the PTH receptor and elevates serum calcium by stimulating osteoclastic bone resorption and increasing renal tubular reabsorption of calcium?

A. Hypernatremia
B. Hypercalcaemia
C. Hyperkalaemia
D. Hypocalcaemia

Q.89 Which of the following diseases is caused by the Coxsackie viruses, and primarily affects the children and teenagers in the summer months?

A. Herpangina
B. Monkey pox
C. Small pox
D. Cow pox

Q.90

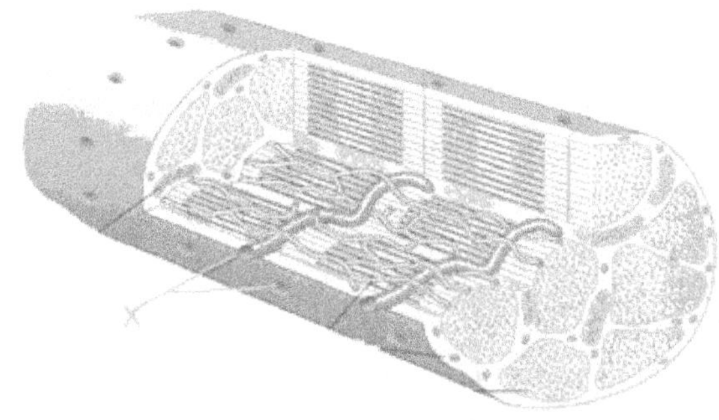

This is the schematic diagram of myocytes and a muscle fibre. What does "X" indicate?

A. Mitochondria
B. Transverse tubules
C. Sarcoplasmic reticulum
D. Ribosomes

Q.91 Which of the following ulcers is common in toes, feet or legs and often can occur in upper limb digits?

A. Ischaemic ulcer
B. Martorell's ulcer
C. Bairnsdale ulcer
D. Rodent ulcer

Q.92 Which of the following is an acute non-suppurative infection and spreading inflammation of lymphatics of skin and subcutaneous tissues due to beta haemolytic streptococci, staphylococci, and clostridial organisms?

A. Lymphangitis
B. Erysipelas
C. Abscess
D. Septicaemia

Q.93 Which of the following is a benign tumor with localized overgrowth of all the layers of the skin?

A. True papilloma
B. Infective papilloma
C. Fibroma
D. Wart

Q.94 Which of the following is a cystic swelling occurring in relation to tendon sheath or synovial sheath or joint capsule?

A. Ganglion
B. Chordoma
C. Epignathus
D. Neurilemmoma

Q.95 Which of the following is usually due to water deficit?

A. Hyper-natraemia
B. Hypo-kalemia
C. Hypo-natraemia
D. Hyper-kalemia

Q.96 Which of the following is/are obtained by organic liquid fractionation of plasma and is/are stored in dried form?

A. Fibrinogen
B. Platelet
C. Packed cells
D. Prothrombin

Q.97 Which of the following is a charred, denaturated, full thickness, deep burn with contracted dermis?

A. Eschar
B. Contracture in burn wound
C. Electrical burn
D. Inhalation injury

Q.98 Which of the following may be beneficial especially for IVC, aorta, iliac vessels and portal system, but with hemoperitoneum visualisation window may be poor and vessels can be better identified by contrast CT scan?

A. Abdominal diagnostic paracentesis
B. Diagnostic laparoscopy
C. Arteriography
D. Doppler assessment of major vessels

Q.99 Which of the following is commonly due to fungal infection or Candida infection?

A. Acute paronychia
B. Chronic paronychia
C. Apical subungual infection
D. Acute suppurative tenosynovitis

Q.100 Most of the bones of the head are interconnected by _______, which are immovable fibrous joints.

A. Sutures
C. Muscular joints
B. Tiny bones
D. Nerves

Q.101 The larynx and the trachea are _______ to the digestive tract in the neck.

A. Superior **B.** Anterior **C.** Posterior **D.** Inferior

Q.102 The junction of the sagittal and coronal sutures is the-

A. Bregma **B.** Lambda **C.** Dipole **D.** Calva

Q.103 In the posterior half of the middle part of the base of the skull are the occipital bone and the paired-

A. Sphenoid bones
C. Frontal bones
B. Hyoid bones
D. Temporal bones

Q.104 Which of the following sutures is between the paired parietal bones?

A. Coronal suture
C. Lambdoid suture
B. Sagittal suture
D. Frontal suture

Q.105 Which of the following include(s) the falx cerebri, tentorium cerebelli, falx cerebelli and the diaphragma sellae?

A. Dural partitions
B. Dural venous sinuses
C. Spinal extra dural space
D. Sub arachnoid space

Q.106 Cerebrospinal fluid is produced by the _______, primarily in the ventricles of the brain.

A. Choroid plexus
C. Pia mater
B. Dural partitions
D. Ethmoid arteries

Q.107 Which of the following is the acute development of a focal neurological deficit as a result of localised or diffused cerebral hypoperfusion?

A. Stroke
C. Dementia
B. Shock
D. Heart attack

Q.108 Which of the following sinuses receives blood from the inferior sagittal sinus, cerebral veins from the posterior part of the cerebral hemispheres, the great cerebral vein draining deep areas of the cerebral hemispheres, superior cerebellar veins and veins from the falxcerebri?

A. Sagittal sinus
B. Straight sinus
C. Superior sagittal sinus
D. Sigmoid sinus

Q.109 The 12 pairs of _______ are part of the peripheral nervous system and pass through foramina or fissures in the cranial cavity.

A. Cranial nerves
C. Facial nerves
B. Cervix nerves
D. Renal nerves

Q.110 The final muscle in the nasal group is the-

A. Procerus
C. Alar part
B. Depressor septinasi
D. Transverse part

Q.111

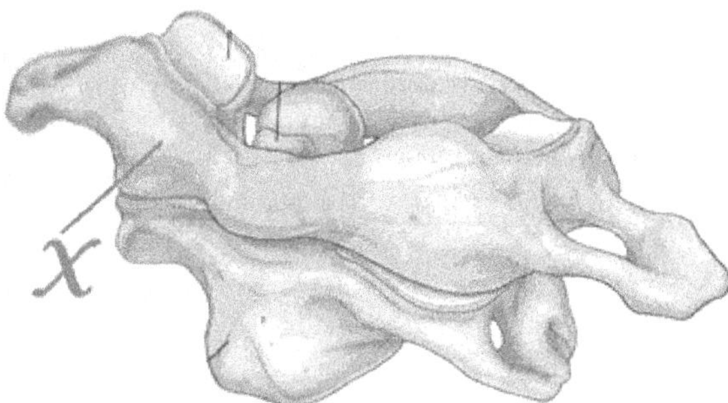

This is the diagram of the atlas and axis. What does 'X' indicate?

A. Atlas C1
B. Axis
C. Articular facet for dens
D. Superior articular surface

Q.112

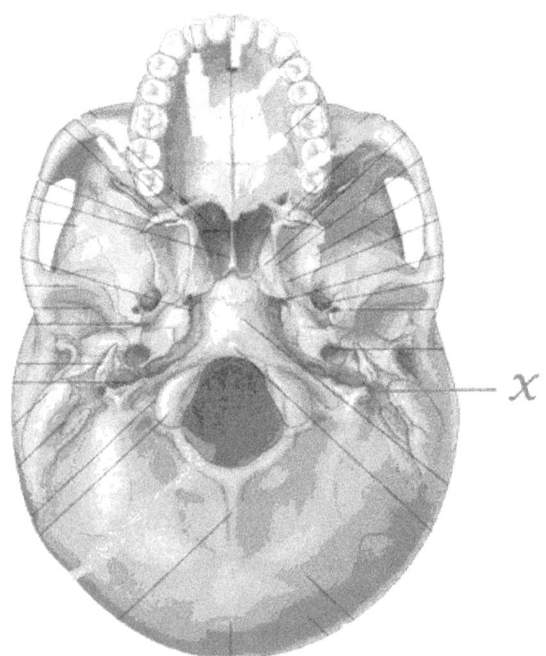

This is the inferior view of the skull. What does 'X' indicate?

A. Carotid canal   **B.** Hypoglossal canal
C. Pterygoid canal   **D.** Foramen spinosum

Q.113

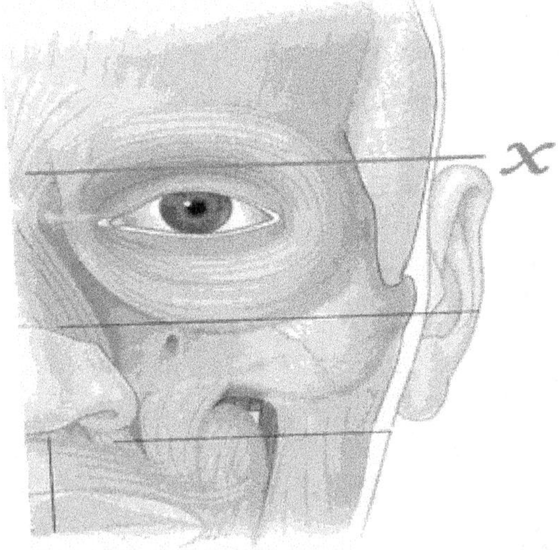

This is the picture of the nasal group of facial muscles. What does 'X' indicate?

A. Nasalis   **B.** Alar part
C. Transverse part   **D.** Procerus

Q.114 Which of the following is/are found mostly in plasma membranes, where their carbohydrates moieties protrude from the external surface of the membrane?

A. Glycolipids   **B.** Cholesterol
C. Glucose   **D.** Amino acids

Q.115 Which of the following is an important neurotransmitter and neuromodulator?

A. Nitric oxide   **B.** Sulphur oxide
C. Amino acid   **D.** Glucagon

Q.116 Which of the following is a common painful condition caused by inflammation of one or more joints?

A. Arthritis   **B.** Paralysis
C. Fracture   **D.** Osteoporosis

Q.117 Which of the following greatly alters the electrical properties of the axon?

A. Myelination   **B.** Stimulation
C. Neutralisation   **D.** Autolysis

Q.118 Skeletal muscle cells can be as long as

A. 1 to 2 cm   **B.** 2 to 3 cm
C. 3 to 4 cm   **D.** 4 to 5 cm

Q.119 Membrane _____ are enzymes, transporters and receptors.

A. Proteins   **B.** Glycoproteins
C. Glycolipids   **D.** Cholesterol esters

Q.120

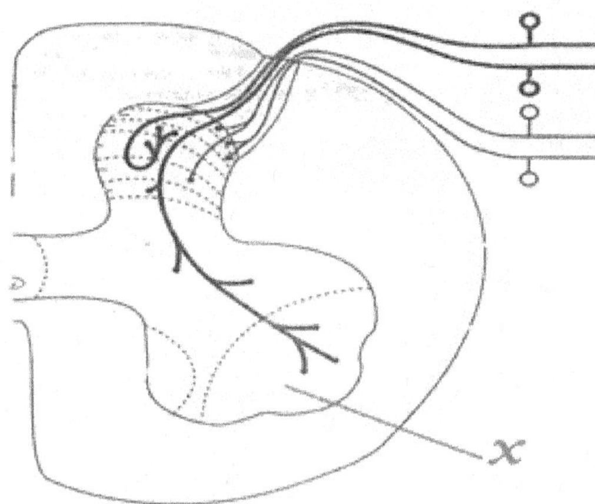

This is the diagram of distribution of the large and small primary afferent fibres in the spinal cord. What does 'X' indicate?

A. Gray matter   **B.** White matter
C. Lateral funiculus   **D.** Ventral funiculus

Q.121 Which of the following amino acids can have O-glycosylation linkage in oligosaccharide molecule?

A. Asparagine   **B.** Glutamine
C. Serine   **D.** Cysteine

Q.122 Which of the following is a suicide enzyme?

A. Lipoxygenase
B. Cyclo-oxygenase
C. Thromboxane synthase
D. 5' Nucleotidase

Q.123 All of the following enzymes are involved in oxidation and reduction, except:

A. Dehydrogenases   **B.** Hydrolases
C. Oxygenases   **D.** Peroxidases

Q.124 Which of the following is a coenzyme in a decarboxylation reaction?

A. Niacin   **B.** Biotin
C. Pyridoxine   **D.** Riboflavin

Q.125 Non-competitive enzyme inhibition leads to

A. V_{max} decrease   **B.** V_{max} increase
C. V_{max} unchanged   **D.** Km increase

Q.126 Km changes and V_{max} remains the same. What is the type of enzyme inhibition?

A. Competitive inhibition
B. Non-competitive inhibition
C. Uncompetitive inhibition
D. Suicide inhibition

Q.127 What is true about isoenzymes?

A. Catalyse the same reaction
B. Same quaternary structure
C. Same distribution in different organs
D. Same enzyme classification with same number and name

Q.128 Cell marking studies in chick and mouse embryos have shown that only the _____ forms the embryo.

A. epiblast
B. hypoblast
C. endoblast
D. cytoblast

Q.129 Which of the following has the formative cells of bone and cementum?

A. Periodontal ligament
B. Dentin
C. Cementum
D. Alveolar bone

Q.130 Nerve fibres from the _______ cranial nerves extend into the mesoderm of the first four visceral arches.

A. 5th, 8th, 9th, 10th
B. 6th, 7th, 8th, 9th
C. 5th, 7th, 9th, 10th
D. 5th, 6th, 7th, 8th

Q.131 Which of the following is enclosed in the invaginated portion of the enamel organ?

A. Dental papilla
B. Dental lamella
C. Enamel papilla
D. Enamel lamella

Q.132 During the advanced bell stage, the boundary between inner _____ and odontoblasts outlines the future dentinoenamel junction.

A. Enamel epithelium
B. Dentinal epithelium
C. Cementum epithelium
D. Pulpal epithelium

Q.133 Which of the following has always been observed as a non-electrical conductive material?

A. Enamel
B. Dentin
C. Root
D. Pulp

Q.134 The _____ material of enamel is hydroxyapatite.

A. Organic
B. Inorganic
C. Hydrophilic
D. Hydroxyl

Q.135 Which of the following is believed to play a role in production of the enamel itself, either through control of fluid diffusion into and out of the ameloblasts or by the actual contribution of necessary formative elements or enzymes?

A. Stratum intermedium
B. Inner enamel epithelium
C. Cervical loop
D. Stellate reticulum

Q.136 Which of the following exist within tubules in dentin?

A. Alveolar processes
B. Odontoblasts processes
C. Periodontal processes
D. Attached gingivae

Q.137 Which of the following is an extending from the cervical region of the crown to the root apex?

A. Radicular or root pulp
B. Dental pulp
C. Apical foramen
D. Coronal pulp

Q.138 Blood capillaries, which appear as endothelium lined tubes are _____ in diameter.

A. 8 to 10 micrometres
B. 10 to 12 micrometres
C. 14 to 16 micrometres
D. 17 to 19 micrometres

Q.139 The tooth pulp is initially called the:

A. Dental lamella
B. Dental papilla
C. Enamel papilla
D. Dental pulp

Q.140

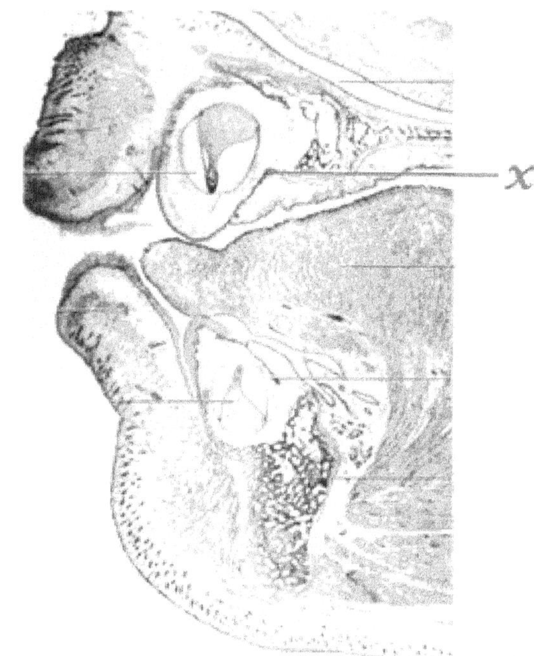

This is the sagittal section through head of a human fetus, 200 mm in length and about 18 weeks, in region of central incisors. What does 'X' indicate?

A. Nasal cavity
B. Hard palate
C. Bud of permanent tooth
D. Tongue

// Smart Answer Sheet //

Correct — Indicates percentage of students who answered questions correctly.

Skipped — Indicates percentage of students who skipped questions.

Q.	Ans.	Correct / Skipped
1	A	53.33 % / 10.0 %
2	A	60.0 % / 40.0 %
3	A	43.33 % / 43.34 %
4	B	36.67 % / 40.0 %
5	B	13.33 % / 43.34 %
6	A	26.67 % / 43.33 %
7	A	50.0 % / 43.33 %
8	A	40.0 % / 43.33 %
9	A	33.33 % / 43.34 %
10	A	26.67 % / 43.33 %
11	B	43.33 % / 43.34 %
12	A	33.33 % / 43.34 %
13	B	26.67 % / 43.33 %
14	D	26.67 % / 40.0 %
15	A	30.0 % / 43.33 %
16	A	20.0 % / 43.33 %

Q.	Ans.	Correct / Skipped
17	B	40.0 % / 40.0 %
18	A	23.33 % / 43.34 %
19	D	23.33 % / 43.34 %
20	D	23.33 % / 30.0 %
21	B	50.0 % / 40.0 %
22	A	50.0 % / 40.0 %
23	A	46.67 % / 43.33 %
24	B	33.33 % / 33.34 %
25	A	30.0 % / 43.33 %
26	A	30.0 % / 43.33 %
27	A	56.67 % / 43.33 %
28	A	56.67 % / 40.0 %
29	C	10.0 % / 43.33 %
30	A	26.67 % / 40.0 %
31	A	53.33 % / 43.34 %
32	A	23.33 % / 43.34 %

Q.	Ans.	Correct / Skipped
33	B	16.67 % / 40.0 %
34	B	23.33 % / 36.67 %
35	A	30.0 % / 40.0 %
36	D	16.67 % / 43.33 %
37	B	16.67 % / 40.0 %
38	B	16.67 % / 43.33 %
39	D	16.67 % / 43.33 %
40	B	13.33 % / 43.34 %
41	D	13.33 % / 43.34 %
42	B	40.0 % / 40.0 %
43	A	20.0 % / 43.33 %
44	B	36.67 % / 40.0 %
45	A	36.67 % / 43.33 %
46	A	33.33 % / 40.0 %
47	A	46.67 % / 43.33 %
48	A	16.67 % / 43.33 %

Q.	Ans.	Correct / Skipped
49	C	40.0 % / 43.33 %
50	B	30.0 % / 43.33 %
51	A	30.0 % / 43.33 %
52	A	30.0 % / 40.0 %
53	D	26.67 % / 40.0 %
54	A	20.0 % / 43.33 %
55	B	20.0 % / 43.33 %
56	B	16.67 % / 43.33 %
57	B	26.67 % / 43.33 %
58	C	16.67 % / 43.33 %
59	B	20.0 % / 43.33 %
60	C	36.67 % / 43.33 %
61	A	43.33 % / 40.0 %
62	A	30.0 % / 43.33 %
63	C	40.0 % / 43.33 %
64	A	40.0 % / 43.33 %

Q.	Ans.	Correct / Skipped
65	A	43.33 % / 43.34 %
66	D	10.0 % / 43.33 %
67	A	33.33 % / 43.34 %
68	B	33.33 % / 43.34 %
69	B	43.33 % / 43.34 %
70	B	46.67 % / 43.33 %
71	B	26.67 % / 43.33 %
72	A	36.67 % / 36.66 %
73	A	50.0 % / 40.0 %
74	B	30.0 % / 43.33 %
75	C	43.33 % / 43.34 %
76	B	30.0 % / 43.33 %
77	A	56.67 % / 43.33 %
78	B	23.33 % / 43.34 %
79	C	16.67 % / 43.33 %
80	B	43.33 % / 40.0 %

Q.	Ans.	Correct	Skipped
81	D	40.0 %	40.0 %
82	A	33.33 %	40.0 %
83	C	6.67 %	43.33 %
84	C	23.33 %	43.34 %
85	B	3.33 %	43.34 %
86	B	36.67 %	43.33 %
87	C	20.0 %	43.33 %
88	B	30.0 %	43.33 %
89	A	36.67 %	43.33 %
90	B	33.33 %	43.34 %
91	A	30.0 %	43.33 %
92	A	23.33 %	43.34 %

Q.	Ans.	Correct	Skipped
93	A	33.33 %	43.34 %
94	A	26.67 %	40.0 %
95	A	20.0 %	43.33 %
96	A	26.67 %	43.33 %
97	A	20.0 %	43.33 %
98	D	23.33 %	43.34 %
99	B	13.33 %	43.34 %
100	A	56.67 %	43.33 %
101	B	26.67 %	43.33 %
102	A	46.67 %	43.33 %
103	D	33.33 %	43.34 %
104	B	36.67 %	43.33 %

Q.	Ans.	Correct	Skipped
105	A	33.33 %	43.34 %
106	A	30.0 %	43.33 %
107	A	30.0 %	43.33 %
108	B	13.33 %	40.0 %
109	A	56.67 %	43.33 %
110	B	16.67 %	40.0 %
111	A	30.0 %	43.33 %
112	A	23.33 %	40.0 %
113	D	40.0 %	43.33 %
114	A	40.0 %	40.0 %
115	A	36.67 %	43.33 %
116	A	53.33 %	43.34 %

Q.	Ans.	Correct	Skipped
117	A	33.33 %	43.34 %
118	A	20.0 %	40.0 %
119	A	26.67 %	43.33 %
120	A	30.0 %	40.0 %
121	C	13.33 %	40.0 %
122	B	16.67 %	40.0 %
123	B	23.33 %	43.34 %
124	C	26.67 %	40.0 %
125	A	30.0 %	43.33 %
126	A	23.33 %	43.34 %
127	A	23.33 %	43.34 %
128	A	20.0 %	40.0 %

Q.	Ans.	Correct	Skipped
129	A	40.0 %	43.33 %
130	C	36.67 %	40.0 %
131	A	40.0 %	43.33 %
132	A	56.67 %	40.0 %
133	A	43.33 %	40.0 %
134	B	40.0 %	43.33 %
135	A	10.0 %	43.33 %
136	B	50.0 %	40.0 %
137	A	40.0 %	43.33 %
138	A	30.0 %	40.0 %
139	B	33.33 %	43.34 %
140	C	30.0 %	43.33 %

Performance Analysis	
Avg. Score (%)	28.39%
Toppers Score (%)	97.32%
Your Score	

// Notes //

// Notes //